CLINICIANS IN COURT

CLINICIANS
in COURT

A Guide to Subpoenas, Depositions,
Testifying, and Everything Else
You Need to Know

SECOND EDITION

Allan E. Barsky

THE GUILFORD PRESS
New York   London

© 2012 The Guilford Press
A Division of Guilford Publications, Inc.
72 Spring Street, New York, NY 10012
www.guilford.com

Paperback edition 2014

Printed in the United States of America

This book is printed on acid-free paper.

Last digit is print number: 9 8 7 6 5 4 3

The author has checked with sources believed to be reliable in his efforts to provide
information that is complete and generally in accord with the standards of practice
that are accepted at the time of publication. However, in view of the possibility of
human error or changes in behavioral, mental health, or medical sciences, neither the
authors, nor the editor and publisher, nor any other party who has been involved in
the preparation or publication of this work warrants that the information contained
herein is in every respect accurate or complete, and they are not responsible for any
errors or omissions or the results obtained from the use of such information. Readers are
encouraged to confirm the information contained in this book with other sources.

Library of Congress Cataloging-in-Publication Data

Barsky, Allan Edward.
  Clinicians in court : a guide to subpoenas, depositions, testifying, and everything else you
need to know / Allan E. Barsky. — 2nd ed.
    p. cm.
  Includes bibliographical references and index.
  ISBN 978-1-4625-0355-1 (hardcover : alk. paper)
  ISBN 978-1-4625-1310-9 (paperback : alk. paper)
  1. Evidence, Expert—United States.   2. Witnesses—United States.   3. Medical records—
Law and legislation—United States.   4. Clinics—Employees—Legal status, laws, etc.—
United States.   I. Title.
  KF8961.B37 2012
  347.73′67—dc23
                                                                        2011050061

To the memory of my beloved mother,
Edith Barsky, 1927–2012

ABOUT THE AUTHOR

Allan E. Barsky, JD, MSW, PhD, is Professor of Social Work at Florida Atlantic University, where he teaches graduate courses on professional ethics, conflict resolution, social work practice skills, and substance abuse. Dr. Barsky received his JD from the University of Toronto, his MSW from Yeshiva University, and his PhD from the University of Toronto. He has practiced social work and mediation in legal settings that include the criminal court in New York and the family courts in New York, Toronto, and Fort Lauderdale. He is chair of the National Ethics Committee of the National Association of Social Workers, and is a past president of the Ontario Association for Family Mediation. Dr. Barsky's book credits include *Ethics and Values in Social Work*, *Conflict Resolution for the Helping Professions*, and *Alcohol, Other Drugs, and Addictions*. His research has been published in *Negotiation Journal*, *Family and Conciliation Courts Quarterly*, *Child Welfare*, *Conflict Resolution Quarterly*, and *Child and Youth Services Review*. His research has also been presented at international conferences in London, Helsinki, Jerusalem, and Amsterdam.

PREFACE

CAVEAT EMPTOR: The contents of this book are for information purposes only and should not be construed as providing legal advice. Laws vary widely among the states, and the only certainty is that laws will change. Although the strategies in this book may assist you in handling a specific situation, your only true protection may lie in obtaining independent legal advice from a properly licensed attorney who specializes in the areas of law that are pertinent to your case. I disclaim all legal liability for reliance on any and all material in this volume.

"Arrgh! What's with all this legalese—and in fine print and with Latin, no less! Can't I ever get a straight answer out of an attorney? They make everything so complicated. And why do they always have to cover their backsides with these silly disclaimers?"

I confess: Law is complicated. Easy answers are possible. However, easy answers are possibly misleading. I do not want to expose myself to a lawsuit, but I also don't want to mislead or expose you to legal liability. With all these disclaimers, what good is this book? The "aforementioned disclaimer notwithstanding," I have tried to write this book with plain language descriptions of the law, legal processes, and your potential roles within these processes. My hope is that you can use this book:

- To gain general professional knowledge.
- To learn how to inform clients about the legal implications of their

relationship with you (either as a treating clinician or as a professional who evaluates clients from psychological or social perspectives).

- To prepare for or avoid situations in which you may be called to testify as an expert or non-expert witness.
- To prepare for a particular court action or adjudicative proceeding in which you have been called to testify.
- To devise strategies to deal with emotional and stressful situations that may arise in the course of the legal proceeding.
- To develop agency policies on confidentiality, privileged information, record keeping, and responding to subpoenas.
- To assist other clinicians who may be called to give evidence in a proceeding.

This book is designed not only to increase your comfort with legal processes and terminology, but to help you ask informed questions when seeking legal advice. The practical tips can help you present your evidence more effectively. Since this is not a cookbook, do not follow the tips by rote. Reflect on your role and context, as well as whether a particular suggestion fits with your circumstances.

The law and our involvement in legal processes are dynamic. The rules and case law governing testimony and witnesses change over time and across jurisdictions. Yet, while the law is dynamic, any book offering advice on how to address a dynamic system is static. I cannot anticipate how statutes, case law, or codes of ethics will change. I can only discuss what exists today. Many details have been omitted so as not to overwhelm, but also so as not to misinform. Given that laws vary across states and over time, this book focuses on legal principles. As a witness, you do not need to be an attorney with a 3-year law degree. You may need to hire an attorney to help you understand complicated and changing laws, as well as the specifics of a particular case.[1] Rather than taking the information in this book as absolute, use it to guide questions. For example, you can take recommendations for preparing reports to your attorney and ask whether she[2] believes these apply to your situation.

In my attempt to provide interesting, realistic, and thought-provoking examples, some questions and illustrations ask you to ponder choices that

---

[1] Another benefit of retaining properly licensed legal counsel is that the attorney will have liability insurance to cover damages you may incur as a result of negligent errors or omissions by the attorney.

[2] For ease of reading, I will alternate the use of male and female pronouns for various paragraphs and topics rather than use s/he or other language to cover both genders for each situation.

verge on the unethical, or are, in fact, unethical. In practice, there may be occasions when you feel pressure to act in a manner that is not completely honest, legal, or ethical. By working through these examples I hope you will gain the insight and moral fortitude to do the right thing when such dilemmas arise.

I have tried to make this book readable for nonattorneys. Still, I have used some legal jargon to help you become more conversant with communication in legal arenas. The Glossary at the end of this volume provides definitions of these legal terms, and the Index can be used to locate further uses of these terms. The Resources section includes websites for professional associations and legal databases that you can use to do further research (especially access to state and federal laws).

Each attorney may have his own suggestions and advice. If his advice seems inconsistent with something you have understood from this book, ask questions to clarify and work toward a mutual understanding of the issues. You will be in a better position to heed your attorney's advice if you are better informed. Your attorney may also have her own suggestions for further reading. For example, some attorneys provide witnesses with a memorandum of how to prepare for a hearing. In the Appendices of this volume, I provide sample documents that you may find useful for your own practice. Your attorney may be able to comment on these documents or provide you with additional samples that meet the specific needs of your case and jurisdiction.

Those who have read the first edition of this book will notice a number of changes. First, although Jonathan Gould, my coauthor on the first edition, is not an author on this edition, I sincerely thank Jon for all of his contributions, many of which continue to be expressed in this second edition. Jon has incredible experience and knowledge in forensic practice, particularly in the field of family law. Among the other changes in this book are the updates in research, case law, statutes, and practice. For instance, research on mock juries and interviews with actual jurors has shed light on strategies that witnesses can use to ensure their testimony comes across as credible and persuasive. In addition, the role of clinicians as trial consultants has developed as an area of specialized practice. Traditionally, attorneys decided whom to call as witnesses, how to present evidence, and how to prepare witnesses. With the growth in research and interest in forensic practice among mental health professionals, clinicians now provide attorneys with greater assistance in these matters.

This edition pays greater attention to ethical issues, including the distinctions between a treating clinician and a professional who has been hired specifically to conduct a forensic evaluation. In response to comments and feedback from readers of the first edition, I have added "Appendix G: For

Further Reflection." This appendix provides additional case scenarios and questions designed to stimulate further thought and apply key concepts in additional contexts of practice. These questions challenge readers to understand different aspects of the law, become familiar with local laws in their own states, and think through potential areas of conflict between their roles as treating clinicians, fact witnesses, and expert witnesses. Readers may reflect individually, or consult with supervisors or peers. Instructors and workshop leaders may use these topics to spark discussion, insight, and debate. (For those interested in using the book as the basis for a course, I have made an instructor's manual available on my website, *www.barsky. org/clinicians.*)

To signify the maturing of this book, you may also note that the child in the primary case study, Debra, has grown up (see Chapter 1). She is now an adolescent rather than an infant, allowing her to play a more active role with the clinicians involved in this case study.

In terms of the order of topics presented, some reviewers of the first edition asked why the materials on expert witnesses, pretrial processes, and forensic reports are provided toward the end of the book. This book is designed for clinicians who are new to participating in court proceedings, particularly clinicians whose primary role is to provide help or treatment to clients, rather than to provide expert evaluations and testimony about them. Accordingly, the first five chapters introduce readers to the legal system and discuss how to prepare for court proceedings as a fact witness. Fact witnesses do not need to know about the qualifications of expert witnesses or how to write forensic reports. Moreover, fact witnesses generally do not participate directly in depositions or other pretrial processes unless they are a direct party in the court proceedings (e.g., plaintiff or defendant). For clinicians who may be called as expert witnesses, the latter chapters of this volume focus on these topics. These chapters provide a good foundation regarding the role of an expert witness. If you plan to specialize in a particular field of forensic practice—for instance, family law, mental health, or criminology—you can build on this foundation with additional education and training that concentrates on your field.

Regardless of the expertise and other resources you bring to bear, participating effectively in legal processes requires significant informational and emotional preparation. However, serving as a witness does not have to be a harrowing experience. I hope this book provides you with useful insights and strategies, helping you not only to cope, but also to prosper in your work with courts or in other legal processes.

ACKNOWLEDGMENTS

In researching, writing, and editing this book, I owe a debt of gratitude to many people. Among those who have provided constructive feedback, I thank Diane Green, Lisa Estrin, Deena Mandell, Marvin Bernstein, Julio Arboleda-Florez, Jennifer Becker, Steve Eichler, Jessica Ponn, and various students who have provided me with insightful suggestions. I am grateful to Dr. Michele Hawkins (Director) and the Florida Atlantic University School of Social Work for their ongoing support of my teaching and research. I am also indebted to Jim Nageotte, Anna Nelson, Jennifer DePrima, and The Guilford Press for their encouragement and assistance in conceptualizing, focusing, reviewing, editing, and marketing this project through the first two editions.

A lot has happened to me in the years since publishing the first edition of this book. In 2000 I had just moved to the United States, and my coauthor, Jon Gould, was extremely generous in helping me rewrite a Canadian version (*Counselors as Witnesses*, published by Canada Law Book) for an American audience. I am now American, not only by virtue of gaining citizenship, but also by being immersed in local culture and having the opportunity to work with various American attorneys, mediators, forensic experts, professional associations, and systems.

My partner, Greg (or legally married husband, as I am now permitted to call him in some states), and I have added a beautiful daughter, Adelle, to our family. Greg continues to be my favorite research assistant, on call day and night (at least until 8 P.M.). Adelle is a constant source of inquiry, asking what I am working on and making me look at my work from a fresh perspective. Not only have I learned how to explain confidentiality and ethics to an 8-year-old, but I have an 8-year-old who comes to my classes to help teach confidentiality, ethics, and interviewing children.

CONTENTS

CLINICIANS IN COURT

PROLOGUE

In a precursor to the modern court system, trial by ordeal was used in medieval times to facilitate justice (Ho, 2003/2004). For example, trial by hot water required that an accused claiming innocence place one hand in boiling hot water; if, after 3 days, the hand remained unscathed, the accused was declared innocent. Similarly, there were trials by fire, by poison, and by being submerged in cold water to see whether "divine intervention" would intercede, thereby indicating the accused's innocence. Unfortunately, even today's comparatively "civilized" trials are still an ordeal for all too many witnesses. Consider the following examples, each of which references the most relevant chapter in this volume in terms of information that would have been useful to the imperiled clinician:

> Anders is a counselor who works with refugees. One of his clients was turned down in her initial application for refugee status. Anders was called to provide information at the appeal hearing. As he was speaking, everyone looked at him in amazement, as if they did not understand what he was saying. Anders suddenly realized he was mixing up facts from his own family—also immigrants—with facts from his client's family. (Chapter 2)

> Melanie recently graduated with a master's degree in psychology and is ready to take on the world. In one of her first cases, an attorney asks Melanie to testify at a public court hearing. The attorney tells her, "You don't need to prepare. Just show up and answer the questions as honestly as possible." During the actual testimony, Melanie realizes that the attorney is trying to blame her for the client's predicament. Melanie feels duped and badgered by the attorney. The judge chastises

her for going off on tangents and not answering the questions directly. She wonders, "Did I miss the class when they told us about going to court?" (Chapter 3)

Danielle was a parent–youth mediator who worked with a court-affiliated diversion program. In her personal life, she was going through separation from a man who mistreated her during their marriage. One day, when she was waiting to be called into court for a child visitation hearing, her estranged husband approached her with a gun. (Chapter 4)

Dr. Jalal has been subpoenaed to court to testify about the impact of sexual abuse on a young client named Honi. During his testimony, Dr. Jalal realizes that his testimony may have a retraumatizing effect on Honi, who is in the courtroom. Honi is already in tears. To protect Honi from further harm, Dr. Jalal tells the attorney that it is not appropriate for him to discuss the details of Honi's abuse. The attorney tells Dr. Jalal that his job is to answer the questions, not to be Honi's psychotherapist or protector. The attorney notes that it might actually be good for the jury to see Honi's emotional reactions. (Chapter 4)

Edna provides therapy for people with AIDS. One of her clients was involved in civil rights litigation, having been fired from his job because of his condition. In preparing her records for the hearing, Edna whited out certain sections of her notes and rewrote them. She submitted a photocopy of the notes so that the whited-out sections could not be seen. One of the attorneys asked for the original copy of her notes, whereupon Edna started to ramble incessantly. The judge asked the attorney, "Can't you control your witness?" (Chapters 4, 5, and 6)

Harrison provides counseling and support services to elderly clients who are mourning the loss of a loved one. He keeps very detailed clinical records. He also assures his clients that the records are confidential. He is horrified one day when his treatment records are subpoenaed because one of his clients is accused of "conspiring to commit terror." (Chapter 6)

Rebecca is a psychiatrist who reviews the status of patients who have been committed involuntarily to a mental health facility. In preparation for one case, Rebecca was too busy to see the patient personally and relied on reports from the psychologists who had been working with the patient on an ongoing basis. Although the psychologists had recommended that the patient remain in the facility, Rebecca had no firsthand knowledge of the reasons for this recommendation. The court ordered that the patient be released, given the lack of firsthand evidence to indicate whether the client posed a threat to herself or others. (Chapter 7)

Erica is a newly hired probation officer. Recently she was responsible for writing a presentence report for a man convicted of gross sexual indecency. Her report included graphic details of his alleged activities. Given her lack of training, she thought the report was only for the judge and attorneys, not realizing that it would become public when entered into the court records. When embarrassing details were released through the media, the man became despondent and attempted suicide. Erica felt responsible for his despair. (Chapter 8)

Bert has been asked to submit a report to court in a case involving Maggie, a woman who claims to have suffered traumatic brain injury as a result of a violent mugging. When Bert met Maggie, he was convinced that her brain injury was real. When reviewing the results of a test called the *Computerized Assessment of Response Bias* (CARB; CogniSyst, 2008), he notes that Maggie exhibited a strong tendency to exaggerate symptoms. The results of the CARB test seem strange because they do not fit with the impression he received from interviewing Maggie. Bert ponders whether he should report the results of the CARB test or simply provide his clinical impressions. (Chapter 8)

Joel is a social worker who works with autistic children. The parents of one of Joel's clients believed the child was not improving, and was actually regressing. The parents filed a complaint against Joel with the state social work licensing board. (Chapter 9)

Each of these scenarios is based on a true story. In doing research for this volume, I asked clinicians, "What was your worst experience in relation to court or similar legal proceedings?" Virtually everyone had at least one memorable story. Often these memories recounted embarrassing experiences. Some experiences revealed a lack of understanding of the legal system. Others underscored the tension between clinicians safeguarding their client's confidential material and attorneys trying to determine the facts of a case. As a result, these experiences led some clinicians to avoid courts and attorneys at all cost. Others said that they have learned from their experiences and now feel more comfortable when they are involved in "legal situations." All colleagues who shared their war stories concurred that they would have preferred not to have learned their lessons solely through *trial and error.*

This book is my attempt to provide a better understanding of the potential challenges posed to you when interacting with the legal system. There are war stories. There are suggestions. There are warnings. Above all else, I provide a framework of practical information and suggestions for thinking about the tensions between the legal system and clinical practice in psychology, social work, and related professions. This book is neither a final nor a definitive work. It will guide and challenge you. It will teach you to think about the tensions between these two dynamic fields of endeavor. Ultimately, it will ask you to consider who you are and what values you hold dear, while also conforming to the legal demands posed by your participating in legal processes. Enjoy your journey of learning and self-exploration.

Chapter 1

INTRODUCTION

Clinicians may be called as witnesses in a range of circumstances, from court hearings to private arbitrations to government tribunals (i.e., boards or panels that have quasi-judicial functions). While attorneys have access to a wealth of books and training on how to gather evidence and prepare and examine witnesses, far fewer resources exist for mental health or human service professionals who do not specialize in forensic practice. Clinicians are frequently drawn into judicial and quasi-judicial processes with little information about the legal system or their roles as potential witnesses (Bartol & Bartol, 2008; Madden, 2003). This predicament can be scary and risky. Clinicians' interests may be very different from those of the attorneys who contact them. Further, many clinicians fear that their credibility, competence, and honesty may be attacked, making them subject to professional and personal embarrassment on the witness stand (Brodsky, 2004). This book is intended to provide you, the treating therapist or clinician, with an understanding of the legal system, the different roles you might be asked to play as a potential witness, and how to prepare for these varied roles, including how to prepare written reports and other records.

We begin with three basic questions: Who is a clinician? What is a witness? When and why might you be called as a witness?

1. *Who is a clinician?* Clinicians come from varied backgrounds, including psychology, psychiatry, social work, education, criminal justice, child welfare, nursing, and pastoral counseling. This book focuses on "treating clinicians," as opposed to "forensic mental health professionals." The primary role of a treating clinician is to help a client by providing one or more of the following services: psychotherapy, counseling, case management, treatment planning, mediation, education, emotional and social

support, or problem-solving assistance. In contrast, the primary role of a forensic clinician is to provide assistance to one or more parties involved in a legal process (e.g., the plaintiff, defendant, judge, and/or jury). Forensic clinicians have specialized training in gathering, analyzing, and presenting evidence in court or other legal proceedings. Although some treating clinicians have forensic training, most treating clinicians do not. Accordingly, this book is geared toward treating clinicians. This book can also provide foundational knowledge for novice forensic mental health professionals. However, they will need more advanced and specialized knowledge pertaining to their particular fields of forensic practice (e.g., fitness to stand trial, probation and parole risk assessment, child custody, child abuse and neglect, jury selection, eyewitness memory, psychological damages in civil lawsuits, and involuntary hospitalization due to mental illness).

2. *What is a witness?* In common parlance, a witness is someone who has observed or experienced an event. Within the legal sphere, a witness is someone who can provide proof of or attest to a fact or event. Sometimes (as I describe in Chapter 7 on the use of experts), witnesses are asked to provide opinions rather than just facts. Witnesses present information in court and other adjudicative proceedings (i.e., legal processes in which information is presented to an individual or tribunal that has certain decision-making authority, such as a workers' compensation board). Many examples in this book use the court as the chief prototype of the adjudicative process. The reason for focusing on court processes is that the court trial is one of the most formal types of hearing processes. While full court trials are not the most common type of hearing, other hearings tend to be based on the procedural principles of a trial. If a clinician is prepared for the rigors of a court hearing, she will generally be equipped for less formal processes as well. However, I also discuss other types of adjudicative processes and identify the different concerns for clinicians involved in these processes. Adjudicative processes can involve multiple parties with overlapping and conflicting interests. To simplify matters, examples used in this book focus on disputes between two parties with adversarial interests.

3. *When and why might you be called as a witness?* Different types of clinicians are more or less likely to find themselves in the position of being called upon as a witness. At one extreme, forensic evaluators are professionals who gather information using specialized forensic methodology for the express purpose of presenting a forensic interpretation of this information to a court or another legal dispute resolution process (Bartol & Bartol, 2008; Maschi & Killian, 2011). Forensic psychiatrists, for example, may work within the criminal justice system to help the police or state prosecution gather evidence to identify the person who committed a crime.

Inquests into the cause of death in a suspected suicide case may require the use of psychological autopsies. Sexual abuse cases may engage forensic psychologists to conduct forensic psychological assessments, assisting the police, the court, or an attorney representing the alleged perpetrator. Traditionally, legal processes relied on psychiatrists as forensic experts for two reasons. The first is that many state and federal laws required a medical professional to conduct the evaluations. The second is that courts believed that psychiatrists possess a dependable level of expertise because, as medical professionals, they are subject to a high level of science education, professional training, role status, and professional regulation.

Since the 1960s, clinicians from other disciplines have gained acceptance as forensic specialists in certain fields of knowledge within their expertise (Bartol & Bartol, 2008; *Jenkins v. United States*, 1962). To economize on resources, some systems have divested responsibilities from traditional doctoral-level trained experts and transferred them to practitioners from disciplines with less advanced degrees who garner lower fees. In addition, psychology, social work, and other mental health professions have moved toward higher standards of evidence-based practice and competence-based educational qualifications in order to be recognized as professions on equal footing with psychiatry and medicine.

Clinicians who work in forensic settings (including psychiatric wards, child protection agencies, and probation and parole offices) can also expect to be called as witnesses as part of their work (Bernstein & Hartsell, 2005; Munson, 2009). Whereas a *forensic expert* is hired specifically to investigate a case and prepare evidence for court, a *clinician working in a forensic setting* provides clinical services in addition to gathering and preparing evidence that may be presented in court. Thus forensic clinicians sometimes incur a dual role, raising ethical challenges that are the subject of passionate debate in the literature (Bush, Connell, & Denney, 2006; Gould & Martindale, 2009; Zur, n.d.). Professional codes of ethics generally suggest that practitioners avoid dual relationships (American Psychiatric Association [APA], 2010, s.3.05; National Association of Social Workers [NASW], 2008, s.1.06; note that throughout this textbook, references to APA and NASW will refer to specific standards in the codes of ethics of the American Psychological Association and the National Association of Social Workers[1]). Sometimes, dual relationships are difficult to avoid. In a

---

[1]If you are a member of a different professional association, there may be similar standards in your code of ethics. I have chosen to limit references to two codes of ethics due to the limitations of space and complexity. The choice of social work and psychology was based on the relatively large numbers of these professionals.

psychiatric facility, for example, forensic clinicians play the role of treating therapist, working with involuntarily committed patients to help them regain their competence or mental health. On the other hand, these same clinicians may be asked to testify about the progress of their patients. Their testimony may take the form of clinical testimony detailing the patient's progress during therapy, or it may entail describing the results of a more formal assessment. The ethical challenge lies in balancing the information needs of the court about the patient's progress with the ethical guidelines about maintaining appropriate boundaries between the role of treating clinician and forensic evaluator. Probation officers, parole officers, hospital-based clinicians, juvenile court clinicians, and child protection workers are the most common types of clinicians with this dual role. A child protection worker, for example, has an obligation to ensure that a child is safe from abuse or neglect. Ideally, the worker fulfills this mandate by engaging the family on a voluntary basis while taking on the roles of clinician, support worker, and case manager. To protect the child, however, the worker must also conduct investigations, present information to the court, and monitor the enforcement of court orders. In some cases, after a treating professional provides testimony, the clinician may not be able to continue to play the treating role: the client may feel hurt by the testimony, sense betrayal, or lose trust in the clinician as a helping agent. In other cases, the treating professional may be able to re-engage the client, discuss the "impact of testifying" on their relationship, and move forward in the helping process.

Clinicians who work outside the legal system may be less likely to be called as witnesses but should be aware of the types of circumstances in which they may be called. Clinical practice with different segments of the population incurs different possibilities of being called as a witness. Clinicians who work with the elderly may be called as witnesses about mental competence for the purposes of appointing a power of attorney to take responsibility for decisions related to the elder person's property and health care. Clinicians who work with perpetrators or victims of crime may be called for criminal proceedings. Mediators or arbitrators with separating couples may be called as witnesses in child custody and visitation disputes.[2] Clinicians who work with clients with psychiatric disorders may be called for involuntary hospitalization cases. Vocational rehabilitation counselors may be called to provide information in workers' compensation cases. Youth care workers who deal with aggressive clients in residential settings

---

[2]Mediators and arbitrators often ask clients to agree from the outset that they will not call the mediator or arbitrator to court to testify. Generally, courts will respect such agreements in order to encourage people to resolve their conflicts outside of court, in a confidential dispute resolution process.

may be subjected to assaults and be called to testify as victims. The list of examples could go on and on. Unfortunately, some clinicians are afraid to work with psychiatric patients or others where a significant risk of legal involvement may be required. In accordance with the ethical principles of justice and access to services (APA, 2010, Principle D; NASW, 2008, Values), clinicians should not discriminate against these groups. Equipped with sufficient legal knowledge and professional competence, clinicians often find that they need not fear this type of work.

In addition to participating in court proceedings, clinicians may be called as witnesses in various forums. Examples of administrative courts and quasi-judicial hearings include social assistance appeals, human rights and discrimination boards, immigration proceedings, public housing appeals, special commissions of inquiry, legislative committees, and criminal injuries compensation boards. Powers vary among administrative court and quasi-judicial forums according to statutes enacted by state legislatures. These powers also vary from state to state. Some tribunals have the power to make nonbinding recommendations, while others have the power to make enforceable rulings.

A clinician can become involved in a legal proceeding as a party to an action, as a witness for the court, or as a witness for an attorney. What defines "a party" to a legal proceeding? A party is either the person initiating a complaint (called a complainant or plaintiff) or the recipient of the complaint (called a respondent or defendant). A party has a direct stake in the outcome of the case. In a case where the client is suing a clinician for malpractice or professional negligence, the client is the plaintiff and the clinician is the defendant. To defend herself and on the advice of counsel, the clinician may act as a witness in court or before a professional disciplinary tribunal. There is an old saying that an attorney who defends himself has a fool as a client. An analogue exists for clinicians. When clinicians attempt to defend themselves before a licensing board or in any legal arena, they operate outside of their professional area of competence. The result may be a less-than-competent defense. Further, there is always concern that when clinicians engage in behavior normally associated with attorneys, the clinician needs to be very careful not to overstep his professional boundaries and engage in functions restricted to those authorized to practice law.

Besides having to defend yourself against charges lodged against you in your role as a clinician, there may be times when you are in the role of plaintiff. In other words, you may file a suit against another party. For example, a clinician may find occasion to sue a client to recover unpaid fees for services. Clinicians who work in residential facilities with children may be involved in cases as guardians or act in the place of a parent (called *in loco parentis*). Thus, the clinician and her agency may need to initiate proceedings to protect the interests of the child to obtain a specialized education placement or to sue a person who has injured the child. In some situations, a party may elect not to be a witness in her own case. However, clinicians need to be aware of situations where they may be both a party and a witness. Knowing the ethical issues involved in such dual roles is important. It is often useful to talk with colleagues and request their advice. Communicating immediately with your state licensing board, ethics committee chairperson, and other persons knowledgeable about the ethics of clinical practice is also recommended. You could also talk with your attorney to shed light on the ethical and legal liability risks related to engaging in dual roles.

Clinicians who have assumed the role of advocate for a client or social cause may also wish to present themselves as witnesses. Advocates, however, may not make effective witnesses, as they may appear biased to one party. Clinicians need to be aware of the potential conflicts between these roles and the possible ethical dilemmas posed by such advocacy.

Being called as a witness may be unrelated to your work as a clinician. For example, you may witness a crime on the street as a passerby or be personally involved in a landlord–tenant dispute. Although information in this volume may help you prepare as a witness, in such circumstances you are really a lay witness rather than a witness in your professional capacity. You may actually be a more effective witness if you deemphasize your professional training when you testify in these circumstances.

Ideally, preparation for being a witness in your professional capacity begins before you initiate services. If you have given the matter no thought— simply waiting until an incident occurs and then an attorney calls—you will be at a real disadvantage. To begin preparing for the prospect of being a witness, you should consider a broad range of factors (see Figure 1.1).

As you read through this volume, highlight the sections that are relevant to the situations you are most likely to face and identify areas where you need more information. If you work in an agency, join with your coworkers and supervisors to develop policies and establish standards of practice. If you are in private practice, consult with legal advisors and colleagues from your profession to establish policies and procedures for your own practice. By taking these steps, you will be better equipped to be an effective witness, and perhaps even to avoid situations where you might otherwise be called as a witness.

Being a witness is not a situation that you should fear or avoid at all costs. A formal hearing may be a constructive or necessary way to deal with certain types of conflict. Further, you may not be able to avoid being called as a witness one day. You may find that you actually enjoy forensic work and want to specialize in the area. You might even find it exhilarating

- What laws, if any, regulate my profession?
- What professional codes of ethics or standards of professional conduct do I need to follow?
- What are the professional practice guidelines to which I aspire?
- What is the legal mandate, if any, of my agency and my role within that agency?
- What contractual obligations does my agency have with the government or other funding sources?
- What agency policies need to be considered?
- Who is my client?
- How does my client view my role? What expectations have I raised about the services I offer, including confidentiality and professional competence? In terms of informed consent, what does my client understand regarding the limits of confidentiality should I be called into court or subpoenaed to testify?
- What types of conflicts may arise between my clients and myself? How likely are these conflicts to escalate beyond informal dispute resolution processes? What can be done to reduce this risk?
- What types of conflicts may arise between my clients and significant people in their lives? How likely are these conflicts to escalate beyond informal dispute resolution processes? How likely am I to be brought into these proceedings? What can be done to reduce this risk?
- What is my role as a clinician? What is my role as a witness? What are the potential conflicts between these roles?
- What are my strengths as a potential witness? Which witness skills do I need to work on?

FIGURE 1.1. Role reflection questions.

to act like a detective, gathering evidence to solve mysteries such as, "Who committed the crime," "Are the plaintiff's injuries valid or feigned," and "Should the client be maintained in a psychiatric facility because he poses a serious, imminent risk to self or others?" In addition, premier forensic experts draw lucrative fees as trial consultants and expert witnesses (Brodsky, 2009). Even if you prefer to steer clear of the stresses of adversarial legal processes, you can still learn how best to tolerate and fulfill your obligations as a witness in a professional manner.

CASE SCENARIO: THE CARVEYS

The following scenario is used to illustrate issues and strategies *throughout this volume*. For ease of reference, the first initial of each person's name corresponds with the first letter of that person's role in the scenario

(P, parent; D, daughter; F, family therapist; M, mediator; A, attorney; S, social work investigator; E, evaluator).

> Paula Carvey (36 years old) and Philip Carvey (34 years old) have been married for 15 years. They are the parents of a 13-year-old daughter, Debra. Although the first 2 years of marriage fulfilled their dreams of wedded bliss, the honeymoon ended when Debra was born. Paula is African American, Baptist, and a strict disciplinarian. Philip is Irish American, Catholic, and very indulgent as a parent. Debra was baptized in Paula's church and raised primarily in the Baptist traditions. Paula and Philip have had challenges due to their differences in parenting styles, as well as conflicts over how to raise their daughter in relation to her ethnic and religious identity. They decide to see a family therapist, Frieda, to help them with their parenting styles and concerns. Frieda uses an unorthodox therapy that eventually proves to be ineffective. Paula begins to suspect that Philip is having an affair and asks him to leave the home. Philip leaves, but immediately engages the services of an attorney, Alice, to help him win custody of Debra and to move back into the family home. Alice, who believes in collaborative legal practice, refers Philip and Paula to a mediator, Michael, to help them resolve their differences on an amicable basis. When Michael first contacts Paula to participate in mediation, he suggests that Paula retain her own attorney. Paula hires Art, a family law attorney known in the community to be a very aggressive. During mediation and out of the blue, Paula accuses Philip of sexually abusing Debra. Michael says he cannot continue mediation with outstanding allegations of abuse, so he encourages Paula to call child protection services if she is truly concerned about Debra's safety. Paula calls, and Sam is assigned as a social work investigator for the case. Sam conducts an investigation and meets with Debra, but cannot substantiate abuse. He suggests that the Carveys undergo a custody evaluation, thinking this will help resolve their domestic dispute. Sam hopes the evaluator will identify and report any real concerns related to child abuse. Philip and Paula agree to hire Evelyn to perform the evaluation.

If you have worked on contentious divorce cases, the multiplicity of players involved in this scenario is familiar; for others, the case may seem like a dense mystery novel, with so many characters to track. To help view the relationships between the parties, see the ecomap and genogram in Figure 1.2 (also reproduced on the last page of this book for easy reference). Understanding each player's role, and the issues each player may present to you, will enable you to make clearer decisions about how to wind your way through a legal proceeding.

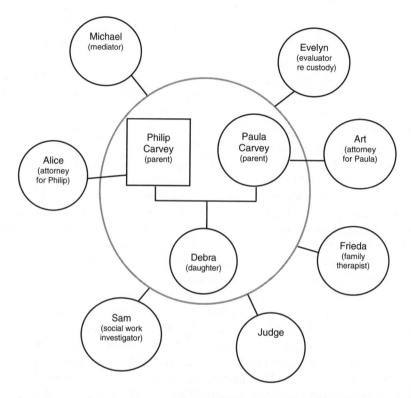

FIGURE 1.2. Genogram and ecomap for the Carvey family case scenario.

COURT AND OTHER ADJUDICATIVE HEARINGS

To provide an overview of adjudicative proceedings, the following sections offer generic descriptions of court and other adjudicative processes (i.e., legal processes in which evidence is presented to an arbitrator or tribunal to adjudicate or make decisions for the parties). To localize this information for hearings where you may be called as a witness, you will need to gather additional information specific to the courts in your jurisdiction.[3] Rules of procedure may vary depending on whether it is a state or federal court, and also depending on the type of court, for instance, a court of general jurisdiction versus a specialized court that focuses on separation and divorce, child protection, intimate partner abuse, drug charges, juvenile justice, or

---

[3]A jurisdiction is an area over which a court has power to make decisions, or a government that has power to enact and enforce laws. Courts are also divided into trial courts (including federal and state district courts) and appeal courts (including federal circuit courts of appeal, state appellate courts, state supreme courts, and the U.S. Supreme Court).

mental health (Bartol & Bartol, 2008). Administrators, clerks, attorneys, and experienced clinicians who work within these systems are often the best sources of information.

When people are faced with conflict, they can deal with it in various ways. For example, they may avoid the conflict, accommodate the other person, engage in a physical fight, seek compromise, collaborate, negotiate, argue, or problem-solve (Barsky, 2007a). In most situations, the decision to go to court or adjudication to resolve the conflict is made when parties have exhausted less formal and legalistic dispute resolution processes. In the case example, Paula and Philip have tried to deal with their marital conflict by several appropriate means. They have sought therapy. After the decision to separate and gain legal counsel, they have attempted a mediated solution. These attempts to resolve their issues outside of court did not help. Suddenly, with no historical foundation to expect an allegation, Paula accuses Philip of sexually abusing their daughter. Now the familial conflict escalates significantly. The father is not allowed to visit his child pursuant to a judge's protection order put into effect until completion of the state's child protection investigation. The mother talks with Debra about the alleged events perpetrated by her father. Debra begins to change how she views her father, becoming increasingly angry and distrusting of both parents. The attorneys fire off letters to each other, accusing the other side of playing games with the system. The investigation takes about 8 months to complete, and the result is a recommendation for a comprehensive child custody evaluation. The judge orders the evaluation and schedules a hearing for 4 months later. To protect Debra, the court directs Philip into supervised visitation with Debra for 2 hours a week. The court also suggests appointing a parenting coordinator to de-escalate the conflict between Paula and Philip, and to protect Debra from being used as a pawn in her parents' battle.

Whether you are a clinician or a party to an action, many people who become embroiled in legal battles have little information about the actual workings of legal processes. Portrayals of trials on television and in other media often convey misleading impressions. The court process can take months or even years, rather than the 2 hours we see in a movie or half an hour in a sitcom. Even live telecasts of real cases can be deceptive. You only observe what happens in the courtroom, and only a small percentage of cases—those with "juicy" issues or popular appeal—end up on television. You do not see many of the mundane elements of legal proceedings, the private negotiations, or the real impact of the process on the parties involved. As a clinician preparing to be a witness, watching courtroom dramas provides limited value beyond entertainment. If Alice were representing Philip in divorce proceedings, she would not likely have the opportunity to play to the cameras or to earn millions from the book rights.

CONCEPTS OF JUSTICE AND PROCEDURAL FAIRNESS

Conceptually, adjudicative proceedings are designed to be places where people can go to have their disputes processed in a just manner. Information is presented to an impartial judge or tribunal. In our public court system the doctrine of *stare decisis* is applied, so that "like cases are treated alike." Judges are guided by *precedents*. A precedent is a legal principle established in previous decisions made by higher courts such as state or federal appellate or supreme courts. Judges are guided also by laws passed by government. Requiring judges to follow strict legal rules ensures that people are treated equally and are not at the mercy of the unfettered whims or politics of the decision maker. Judicial discretion, however, may be required to ensure that people are treated equitably rather than equally. Judges may be able to rule differently on similar cases by distinguishing the facts of each case (Madden, 2003). Just because one family counselor using an unorthodox therapy was found liable for malpractice in one case does not mean that Frieda must be held liable for malpractice. The situation could be different, and her unorthodox intervention warranted. Legal principles are developed by courts in the process of discovering similarities and differences among cases (Brayne & Carr, 2005). Even when governments pass legislation and codify the law, judges may still exercise discretion in how they interpret and apply the law to various situations.

Procedural rules are designed to ensure that the process is fair. According to the principles of due process, each party is given notice of the issues to be raised in a case and provided an opportunity to present its information and argument. Each party can also use legal representation. The decision maker(s) must be neutral or impartial. Courts and other tribunals are based on an adversarial process in which each party has the responsibility for presenting and arguing its side of the case. The underlying premise of an adversarial process is that by having each party present its strongest case and challenge the case it opposes, truth is more likely to emerge. One aspect of procedural regulation is the law of evidence. This law defines what information may be introduced into court, how it may be introduced, and how it may be used in the decision-making process. Although attorneys have the primary responsibility for determining what evidence to call and how to call it, witnesses can be better prepared to provide effective testimony if they are familiar with some of the key laws of evidence.[4] As a forensic

---

[4]For cases in federal courts, see Federal Rules of Evidence (2010) (*www.law.cornell.edu/rules/ fre/index.html*). For state courts, locate the state's code of evidence. Evidentiary rules define what types and forms of evidence may be presented, who may act as an expert witness, what types of evidence are not allowed, and so on.

evaluator, Evelyn knows there is a good chance her custody report could be used in court and will ensure the report meets required legal standards.

Whether a court case is heard by a judge or by a judge and jury depends on the type of case:

- In criminal cases, there is constitutional right to a jury trial if the person is accused of a crime punishable by more than 6 months (U.S. Constitution, Article III). For crimes punishable by less than 6 months, each state may decide whether to require jury trials.
- In civil cases (such as a malpractice lawsuit against a clinician), one must look at the federal or state laws of civil procedure to determine whether the plaintiff has a right to a jury trial (e.g., Federal Rules of Civil Procedure, 2010). Jury trials are generally more expensive than non-jury trials, so plaintiffs may waive their right (particularly for cases involving smaller monetary disputes).
- In family law, mental health, probate,[5] and child welfare cases, trials are conducted by a judge without a jury (and often, family law and child welfare matters are handled through motions to a judge, rather than a full trial of the issues).

In jury trials, the jury has the duty of determining which facts presented by the parties are more likely to be true. The judge is responsible for determining procedural and legal issues. In a trial by judge alone, the judge is responsible for factual, legal, and procedural issues. In child custody proceedings for the Carveys, the legal issues could include how to interpret family laws regarding the best interests of the child. Whether Philip was an abusive parent would be a factual issue. How Paula's testimony about sexual abuse could be brought into court would be a procedural issue.

The *admissibility of evidence* and the *weight given to evidence* are handled as separate issues. The question of whether to allow Evelyn to testify about her report, for example, is an admissibility issue. Once the judge admits her as an expert, she is allowed to provide opinions about the family system. These opinions are drawn from the information gathered during her evaluation. The clearer the reliability, relevance, and helpfulness of the conclusions in Evelyn's report, the more weight (or value) the judge gives to her testimony (Krimsky, 2005). Because family matters are tried by a judge alone, the judge would have responsibility for all of these decisions. In cases tried by a jury, the judge determines admissibility and the jury determines what weight to give to each piece of testimony.

---

[5]Probate courts deal with matters related to wills, trusts, personal estates, competency, and protection of vulnerable adults. In some states, probate courts are separate. In others, probate matters are handled by courts of general jurisdiction.

In criminal cases, defendants have a constitutional right to be faced by the people raising allegations or charges against them. The defendants are allowed to be in the courtroom throughout the trial, so they may hear and respond to the testimony provided at trial. For victims of sexual assault or other traumatic crimes, facing the alleged perpetrator in the courtroom may be particularly difficult. In some instances, such as child witnesses, evidentiary laws may give judges discretion to allow the witness to provide testimony through a one-way video interview. Some courts also allow a child witness to give testimony from behind a one-way screen that blocks the child's view of the defendant but allows the defendant to see the child. In any case, mental health professionals may play a vital role in preparing victim-witnesses for the emotional challenges involved in testifying.

INITIATING THE COURT PROCESS

If you think about the broad range of conflicts that arise in human interaction, relatively few end up in court. Even among cases that are filed in court, fewer than 10% result in a full trial of the issues.[6] A wide variety of formal and informal processes goes on before a trial takes place (see Chapter 10). As a potential witness, how you act during the pretrial stages can increase or decrease the chance that the case will go to trial and that you will be called as a witness.

If we take the juncture at which Philip called his attorney as the point where the legal process began, there are still a number of opportunities for the case to be resolved before trial. Although some people envision attorneys as predatory hawks who are ever eager to take a case to court, attorneys have an ethical obligation to try to resolve disputes in the most constructive and cost-effective manner possible (American Bar Association [ABA], 2010, Rule 3.2). Attorneys may negotiate for settlement on behalf of their clients or engage the services of other professionals to help resolve the issues. Alice could contact Frieda to explore information Frieda gathered in family therapy.[7] This information may help Alice determine the prospects of Philip and Paula reconciling their marriage or to identify facts that would help Alice negotiate a custody arrangement that is favorable to

---

[6]In criminal cases, the defendant may plead guilty, with or without a plea bargain. Also, many cases are diverted from criminal court to community service, community mediation, problem-solving drug courts, or other diversion processes.

[7]Some states have statutory limitations on what a marital or family therapist may provide to one side in a legal dispute. There are also ethical issues involved in releasing information about therapy to one side without the express written permission of the other side. Consult an attorney for your state's statutes and your state association for the ethical responsibilities you have in such a context (APA, s.4.05; NASW, s.1.07(b)).

her client, Philip. On the facts provided, Alice contacted Michael to help mediate the case.[8] Because of their involvement with the family, both Frieda and Michael could be witnesses if the matter of child custody could not be resolved through negotiation or mediation.

If a client decides to take the case to court, the documents filed in court must identify the relevant parties and a legal cause of action. The cause of action identifies the legal grounds under which a case is brought to court. For example, if the police were to charge Philip with sexual assault on a minor, he would be identified as the defendant and the state would be identified as the prosecutor. If Paula were to sue Frieda for malpractice, Paula would be identified as the plaintiff and Frieda as the defendant.

Different documents are required to initiate different legal processes, whether it is a claim or pleadings for a civil lawsuit, a petition for divorce, involuntary psychiatric admission, or so forth.[9] These documents give the defending party notice of the allegations made and remedies sought. In Paula's malpractice lawsuit, she would indicate the amount of money she believes is necessary to compensate her for the alleged malpractice by Frieda. The party against whom the charge or claim is made is given an opportunity to submit his own documents stating his defense. This provides the initiating party notice of whether and how the defending party intends to respond to the allegations. The defendant might deny all or some of the factual allegations, or challenge the allegations based on legal, procedural, or technical considerations. For instance, Frieda might claim that Paula's malpractice lawsuit was brought after a 2-year statute of limitations period had expired. A defendant in a civil lawsuit may also issue a counterclaim against the defendant (e.g., Frieda countersues Paula for unpaid fees). As described in Chapter 8, potential witnesses may be asked to submit sworn affidavits in this exchange of documents, in support of one party's position. Witnesses are also important at this stage in helping each side know whether it has a good case and whether there is room for settlement outside of court.

PRETRIAL PROCESSES

Once a case is filed in court, parties may engage in a range of pretrial processes conducted by judges or other officers of the court. As the following

---

[8]Some jurisdictions have mandatory mediation, meaning that parties must try to mediate their dispute before they are allowed to go to trial. Typically, if parties participate in mediation, information learned in the course of mediation is inadmissible in court (unless both parties agree otherwise). Some jurisdictions have adopted the provisions of the Uniform Mediation Act (2001), but rules regarding mediation and admissibility of evidence may vary from jurisdiction to jurisdiction.

[9]Terminology for names of documents varies across states and other jurisdictions.

sections indicate, the types of pretrial processes available depend on whether the case involves criminal, civil, or other types of legal matters.

Arraignment

The first stage in a criminal case is typically an initial appearance or arraignment. A judge or grand jury must decide whether there are sufficient grounds for the criminal case to move forward with an indictment. For defendants who have been arrested and held in jail, the court also determines whether there are sufficient grounds to continue to detain the accused person (e.g., a substantial risk that the accused will flee the jurisdiction or commit further crimes). If not, the person should be released pending trial. In some cases, the person is released on bail in order to ensure the person appears for the trial. During the arraignment, the judge informs the defendant of the charges, ensures the defendant understands the charges, explains the right to legal counsel, and asks the defendant to enter a plea. The defendant may plead guilty, not guilty, not guilty by reason of insanity, or no contest (which means that the defendant admits the facts of the case but does not admit guilt). In some cases, the prosecution and defendant negotiate a plea agreement in which the defendant agrees to plead guilty, often to a lesser criminal charge, in order to receive a less severe penalty than might be incurred if the defendant pleads not guilty and was convicted of the initial charges.

If the defendant's charge and problems are related to substance abuse, mental health issues, or domestic violence, the case may diverted to a problem-solving court designed to handle such matters (see Chapter 10). Mental health professionals may be used at early stages of criminal proceedings to screen defendants for psychological risks (such as suicidal ideation), to assess a defendant's mental competency to enter a plea and to stand trial, or to assess the defendant's mental state at the time of the offence to determine whether an insanity defense could be supported (Bartol & Bartol, 2008).

Motions

In civil cases, each side may bring motions asking the court to deal with procedural or *interim* issues (i.e., issues that require a temporary decision until a final decision can be reached). Motions generally do not involve testimony from nonparty witnesses, but written evidence may be used in support of a motion (e.g., a sworn statement from Evelyn recommending interim residential custody of Debra to Philip). Some cases are decided by motions, for instance, if the defendant successfully moved to quash the plaintiff's claim because, even if the factual allegations were true, there are no legal causes of action or compensable damages incurred by the plaintiff.

An *ex parte* motion is a motion presented by one party without the other party present. Typically, due process requires that both sides of a dispute have an opportunity to respond. Courts are reluctant to entertain an *ex parte* motion unless delaying the hearing until reasonable notice could be given to the other party would cause irreparable harm; for instance, if Paula claimed Philip was physically abusing her and she was very frightened of him, the court might accept a motion for a temporary restraining order to protect Paula from harm.

Discoveries

Hollywood productions of courtroom drama are filled with surprise witnesses and testimony; however, court cases produce few courtroom surprises, since each party has an obligation to disclose its case to the other side prior to trial.[10] As a witness, you may be asked to submit to an oral deposition, to provide a written response to a list of questions in writing (interrogatories), or to provide documents such as case files, forensic evaluations, or reports (See Chapter 10 for more detailed information on pretrial discovery processes). In criminal cases, the prosecution has a duty not only to inform the defendant of its case, but also to disclose material evidence it has gathered that may be exculpatory or helpful to the defense.

Mini-Trials, Preliminary Inquiries, and Pretrial Settlement Conferences

Different jurisdictions and types of cases may offer or require different pretrial proceedings to try to resolve cases amicably or efficiently. Under Rule 16 of the Federal Rules of Civil Procedure (2010), the court is responsible for scheduling dates for filing motions, completing discovery, holding a settlement conference, and other pretrial processes. Pretrials can speed up the process by helping the parties identify whether a reasonable cause of action exists or what the likely outcome of a full trial would be. If a trial is unavoidable, pretrial conferences can narrow the issues and streamline how the trial will be conducted. Witnesses may be called for minitrials and preliminary inquiries, but generally only the parties and their attorneys attend settlement conferences. Cases often settle at this stage because one or both parties do not want to incur the expenses of a full trial. Plaintiffs, upon the advice of an attorney, may accept a smaller payment than originally sought because of the possibility they may lose outright in court.

---

[10]Some states have no pretrial discovery rules for family court cases.

Similarly, a defendant might agree to pay some compensation to avoid the chance of a larger award at trial.

The parties may also decide to resolve the case through other conflict resolution processes, such as attorney-led negotiation, mediation, or arbitration (Barsky, 2007a). Although clinicians may be asked to participate in mediation or arbitration, clinicians often work behind the scenes rather than participating directly in these processes, for instance, by providing clients with services to help with psychosocial issues, or consulting with attorneys to help them prepare and settle their cases. Formal arbitrations may require you to attend, but participation of witnesses is voluntary in most informal dispute resolution processes. Your participation in such processes could affect whether you are called to testify in a subsequent trial. You need to know the parameters of the dispute resolution process in which you are being asked to participate. Information presented in some processes is restricted from use in certain other legal proceedings. For other processes, the information is not restricted. Chapter 10 provides further information about pretrial processes and other alternatives to litigation.

Jury Selection

If the case is to be a trial by jury, then a court process called a *voir dire* is used to select jurors from a pool of citizens that have been called to the court. During the *voir dire*, the attorneys and judge may question prospective jurors to determine potential biases (in some jurisdictions, only a judge may ask questions). Attorneys may challenge a prospective juror for cause (bias or conflict of interest, such as having a personal or business relationship with one of the parties). Each attorney may also reject a certain number of prospective jurors[11] through a *peremptory challenge,* in which the attorney does not have to specify the reason for the challenge. Attorneys are not permitted to strike a juror solely on the basis of gender or race. Attorneys sometimes use mental health professionals to help them assess for bias and assist with jury selection (Cramer, Adams, & Brodsky, 2009). Historically, all juries consisted of 12 jurors, and they could not convict a defendant unless they made a unanimous decision to convict. For civil cases and less serious crimes, some states now allow fewer jurors (typically 6), or require a majority decision (e.g., 9 of 12) rather than unanimity (National Center for State Courts, n.d.). In cases that require unanimity for

---

[11]Typically, each party is allowed three peremptory strikes in federal cases, with numbers varying depending on the jurisdiction for state cases.

conviction, jurors may reach an impasse and the judge may declare a mistrial (Madden, 2003). When a mistrial occurs, a new trial is set, requiring witnesses to provide their testimony in front of a new jury.

THE TRIAL

After a case is calendared for trial,[12] the procedures still vary for different types of hearings. The following outline is intended to provide an overview. Details may vary in your jurisdiction and depending on the nature of the judicial proceeding (criminal, family, civil trial, etc.).

First, the attorneys for each party present their opening arguments, including the theory of their cases and the facts they intend to prove. In a case to appoint a guardian for a person with dementia, for instance, the attorney might state that the person's dementia has developed to the point where she can no longer manage her financial and health care decisions (i.e., the legal grounds for appointing a guardian). The attorney then provides an overview of the evidence he intends to lead in order to support this case. Following the opening arguments, each party presents various forms of evidence to try to prove its case. The party initiating the action, the plaintiff (or prosecutor in a criminal case), is first to present its case. In a child protection proceeding, for example, the attorney for the protection agency could call Sam to testify about information gathered in his investigation of abuse allegations against Philip. The plaintiff's attorney begins her questioning of Sam. This set of questioning is called a *direct examination.* Philip's attorney then has the opportunity to ask Sam questions in the *cross-examination.*[13] The agency attorney has another opportunity to ask Sam questions in the *redirect examination* (as does the defense attorney, in the recross-examination). Each type of examination has particular purposes, rules, and strategies (see Chapter 5 for more details).

In addition to oral testimony, you may be asked to provide documentary evidence (see Chapter 8). For clinicians, examples of typical documents requested are evaluations, psychosocial assessments, progress notes,

---

[12]Courts use the term "calendared" to refer to scheduling. A trial is normally calendared for a particular trial term. Trial terms typically range from 2 to 3 weeks. If your trial is calendared for the April 30 trial term and is listed on the calendar as trial number 10, this means that nine other proceedings are scheduled before your trial can begin. Whether the court will hear your case during that particular term depends on how quickly the cases scheduled before yours are resolved.

[13]There may be more than two attorneys. For instance, the court may appoint a guardian *ad litem* to act as attorney for the child.

business records, and psychological test results.[14] Documentary evidence includes electronically stored data, such as case files and statistical information. Another form of evidence is physical or "real" evidence (artifacts, video recordings, audio recordings, photographs, clothes, drug paraphernalia, or other objects). For example, photographs of scars or bruising could be used in support of allegations of abuse or assault.

After the party initiating the proceedings presents its case, the responding party may make a motion for the judge to dismiss the case on the grounds that the initiator did not provide sufficient evidence to support its claim (e.g., that the clinician committed malpractice, that the child is in need of protection, or that the defendant committed murder). If the judge issues a *direct verdict*, the case is closed and the defense does not have to present any evidence. More often, the defense will need to present evidence in order for the court to make a final determination of the issues in dispute (Madden, 2003).

As with the initiating party, the responding party examines the witnesses it calls, and the initiating party has the opportunity to cross-examine them. When both parties have finished presenting their evidence, the attorney for each party provides closing arguments. During closing arguments, attorneys typically discuss the strengths of their case as well as the weaknesses of the other party's case. Often, the closing arguments include a discussion of the credibility of key witnesses and the strength of their evidence (Maschi, Bradley, & Ward, 2009). If the trial is by jury, then the judge provides a charge (or instructions) to the jury, summarizing the evidence presented, outlining the factual questions the jury is to answer, and clarifying any legal issues. The jury meets privately to consider the questions and make its findings of fact. If the trial is by judge alone, then the judge makes these findings.

DECIDING

The decisions of a court are based on both the "burden of proof" and the "standard of proof." Burden of proof refers to which party has the

---

[14]The release of psychological test data may involve the release of *raw* data only to another mental health expert competent to interpret the test results. Consult your ethics requirements before releasing any psychological test data (See Benke, 2003, for an analysis of this issue). Even when the court orders the release of the data, it is important that you take steps to educate the court about your ethical obligations. Once you have formally made your concerns known to the court, if the court still insists on release of the test data, you are obliged to release the data. Be sure there is a signed court order directing you to do so. When uncertain, consult your state board or association, as well as a knowledgeable attorney.

primary responsibility of proving its case, whereas the standard of proof refers to the degree of certainty that the party with the burden of proof must provide. The burden and standards of proof differ for different types of cases. In most family law, malpractice, and other civil proceedings, the party bringing the action to court is responsible for proving its case "on the preponderance of the evidence." In other words, the initiating party must prove that its version of the facts is more likely to have occurred than not. In criminal proceedings, the prosecution must prove its case "beyond a reasonable doubt." In some civil cases, such as a petition to terminate parental rights due to child abuse, the petitioner must meet a higher standard of proof by providing "clear and convincing evidence."

Each criminal offense has particular legal components that must be proven, including the criminal act (*actus reas*) and the criminal state of mind (*mens rea*). Thus, in a case for murder, the prosecution must prove not only that the accused caused the death of the victim (the *actus reas*), but also that causing the death was intentional (the *mens rea*). If the accused can raise a reasonable doubt that one of these elements may not have happened, then she must be found not guilty. She does not need to prove she is innocent (Brewer & Williams, 2005). As a result, criminal prosecutions require much stronger evidence than civil proceedings. The reason for this high standard of proof is to ensure that a person is not convicted of an offense she did not commit. The downside is that some people who commit offenses will be set free because the prosecution could not meet the high standard of proof.[15]

Once the findings of fact have been reported to the court, the judge determines the legal consequences of the findings. If a person has been found guilty of a criminal offense, the judge will receive oral or written submissions, sometimes called "arguments" or "briefs," to help decide the appropriate sentence (e.g., incarceration for a specific period of time, a fine, or supervised probation). If Philip were convicted of sexual assault, then the court may consider a presentencing report prepared either by a court-affiliated worker (e.g., a probation officer) or a forensic mental health expert. Presentencing reports typically include a psychosocial assessment, psychological test results, family background, criminal history, and victim impact statement. If Frieda were found legally responsible for malpractice, then the judge would need to determine the appropriate remedy, such as monetary compensation for damages including emotional pain and

---

[15]Former NFL star O.J. Simpson was acquitted of murdering Nicole Brown Simpson and Ronald Goldman in a criminal hearing because the prosecution could not prove the elements of murder beyond a reasonable doubt. However, Goldman's family successfully sued Simpson for damages in a civil lawsuit where the standard of proof was not as high.

suffering. Once again, a report from a mental health professional could be used to assess emotional pain or other psychosocial damages. In addition to awarding damages for compensation, a judge in a civil court trial may order punitive damages. Although awarding punitive damages is much less common than compensatory damages, punitive damages may be awarded to deter people from committing wanton, willful, or malicious acts (Madden, 2003). Thus, if Frieda's malpractice were based on simple negligence (forgetting to follow up due to a highly demanding workload), the court would likely order compensatory damages but refuse to award punitive damages. If Frieda maliciously defrauded Philip and Paula for personal financial gain, the court might be more apt to award punitive damages (*Philip Morris USA v. Williams*, 2007). Plaintiffs in civil lawsuits may also claim equitable relief in which the court is asked to require certain parties to perform certain acts, for instance, for a mental health agency to change its policies or practices to protect clients in the future. An injunction is a form of equitable relief in which the court orders a person to refrain from certain acts (e.g., to stop contacting or harassing the complainant). Compensation is more common than equitable relief, which tends to be more difficult to monitor and enforce.

APPEALS

Trial court decisions are sometimes appealed to a higher court. The most common grounds for appeal are that the judge made an error of law or a procedural error during trial.[16] For example, it might be argued that the judge misinterpreted the laws on child custody or permitted irrelevant and prejudicial information to be heard. To be allowed to appeal a trial on procedural grounds, an attorney must make an objection during the trial. In some instances, an appeal is based on a "case of first impression," in which a point of law has not been dealt with previously and the judge is asked to establish a new precedent. Generally, parties cannot appeal a case on the basis that the trial judge or jury made an error in determining the facts of the case. Appellate judges defer to the judge or jury who were able to hear the testimony firsthand. To overturn a case based on a fact-related error, the appellant would need to prove that law does not permit the decision reached at trial. In criminal cases, a defendant may appeal a guilty verdict.

---

[16]A party may also appeal on the basis that the court made a finding of fact based on "no substantial evidence." Such appeals are rare because appeals courts are not authorized to question a trial judge's general findings of fact unless it is clear that there is no evidence to support a particular finding.

In contrast, the prosecution cannot appeal a verdict of not guilty, although it can appeal a sentence on the grounds that it is too lenient.

When a case is appealed, the appellate court has discretion on whether to hear the appeal. An appeal may be heard by an appellate judge or a small panel of judges. During an appeal, the facts of a case are not retried. There are no witnesses and no new evidence. The appellate court examines the record of the trial court. Appellate judges may refer to transcripts, evidence presented at trial, as well as exhibits prepared for and admitted during trial. This is one reason that it is important for clinicians to prepare thorough reports. Although oral testimony may be limited to that which is presented during direct and cross-examination, a comprehensive report may provide the appeals court with valuable information that was not presented during oral testimony at trial. As long as the trial court admitted a report into evidence, the appellate court is allowed to review it. During the appeal, the attorney for each party presents written and/or oral arguments to the court. In some cases, mental health professionals or others submit an *amicus brief*, which is a written report that provides information to the court to help it make its decision. Although the individuals or organizations submitting the brief are not parties to the original trial, they have a stake in the outcome or they possess scientific knowledge that may be useful to the court (Bartol & Bartol, 2008). In the Carvey's case, Evelyn's professional association might try to submit an amicus brief to protect the interests of other custody evaluators who would be affected by any precedents set by the appellate court's decision. If the appealing party wins, the appeals court may substitute its own order or refer the case back to the trial court to be retried. If the appeal is lost, then the trial court judgment stands.

OTHER TRIBUNALS

Noncourt tribunals vary in their levels of formality. Their processes are defined by their enabling legislation and regulations. As a prospective witness, your role may be quite different in a human rights hearing than in a professional discipline hearing. Although processes vary, most retain basic rights of procedural fairness: notice of the charges, a right to be heard, and an impartial decision maker. Some tribunals use only written submissions because oral testimony is more time-consuming and costly. Often, the most important function of a clinician as a witness is providing written reports rather than oral testimony.

Use of attorneys may be encouraged or discouraged at different types of hearings. Some processes discourage the use of attorneys to keep the process informal and to minimize costs. Informal proceedings tend to be more accessible to the public. If Paula were concerned about Frieda's conduct as a family counselor, she could sue her for malpractice in court or bring a complaint to her professional licensing body. Paula is more likely to complain to the professional body because its process is less formal and less costly.

Whereas courts have a fixed adjudicative function and process, other bodies often have overlapping functions. For example, some human rights commissions develop their own policies, giving them both law-making and adjudicative functions. Legislative committees use hearings primarily for informing their law-making functions. Other bodies have enforcement as well as adjudicative functions. Some bodies, such as an ombuds, can make recommendations but lack direct powers to make and enforce decisions. Some bodies are more investigative than adjudicative.

Investigative models are often used as a method of alternative dispute resolution, where parties agree to submit their issues to an alternative forum to the public court system. In an investigative model, the decision maker is more active than a judge in collecting information and questioning witnesses. An investigative model is a process that many clinicians who perform psychosocial assessments will be familiar with. For example, in conducting a custody assessment, Evelyn would conduct home visits, and interview and observe each family member with Debra. She would also gather information from collateral sources such as family members, pediatricians, teachers, youth clinicians, neighbors, and others who have direct observational knowledge of Debra and her relationship with each parent (Association of Family and Conciliation Courts, 2006; Gould, 2006). In contrast to a judge, an investigative decision maker is bound by the scope of her investigative powers rather than rules concerning what evidence can be heard. Your role as a witness in an investigative proceeding is vastly different from that in an adjudicative or legislative hearing.

Different tribunals have different focal points of inquiry. Criminal proceedings, compensation cases, and disciplinary proceedings tend to focus on the past. As a fact witness,[17] you may be asked about your knowledge of what happened and who did what. As an expert witness, you may be asked to hypothesize about the likelihood of certain events and their effects on another event, either an expert opinion about a past event or a prediction about a future one (Melton, Petrila, Poythress, & Slobogin, 2007). As an expert witness, you also may be asked to opine about what kind of

---

[17]Sometimes called an eyewitness, because the person can only testify about what she directly observed.

punishment or restitution is required to compensate for any wrongful acts committed. In custody, access, child protection, and legislative proceedings, the focus is on the future. Although the past may be used to inform decisions about the future, you may be asked for opinions about what needs to be done in the future for the best interests of the child, the community, and so on. Such predictions should be based on the science of your discipline, such as the research from peer-reviewed behavioral science literature. Certain forums such as legislative hearings allow for the presentation of one's political beliefs and values as well as science, while other types of hearings may limit your involvement to the presentation of "facts" or "expert opinions" based on sound scientific evidence.

OVERVIEW

Although this chapter has provided a general overview of legal processes, you probably have many questions about your role as a witness and how to respond to the challenges that may arise when you become involved in a legal process. The balance of this volume provides information and strategies on:

- How to raise awareness of your attitudes, values, and beliefs as they relate to working with courts, attorneys, judges, and legal systems. (Chapter 2)
- How to respond when you are first contacted by an attorney. (Chapter 3)
- What to discuss when meeting with an attorney. (Chapter 3)
- How to prepare for oral testimony. (Chapter 4)
- How to present oral testimony. (Chapter 5)
- How to maintain clinical records. (Chapter 6)
- How to act as an expert witness in the roles of consultant, educator of the court, and fact–opinion expert. (Chapter 7)
- How to prepare reports, affidavits, and other documentary evidence. (Chapter 8)
- How to deal with malpractice and professional complaints. (Chapter 9)
- How to participate effectively in pretrial disclosure processes and other alternatives to adjudicative hearings. (Chapter 10)

Chapters 2 through 5 are designed to prepare you for the basics of presenting factual evidence in court. The remaining chapters deal with more specialized issues, such as acting as an expert witness or participating in pretrial disclosure processes. If you are looking for information on particular topics or legal terms, check the index and glossary at the end of the book. Appendices A through F provide sample forms and legal documents. Appendix G offers interesting case scenarios and questions designed to help you reflect on various issues related to issues from each chapter. You may also use these cases and questions for discussion with colleagues in the field.

Now that we have completed the introduction, it is time for a recess. "All rise." Yes, feel free to stretch and take a break before proceeding to the next chapter.

Chapter 2

BEGINNING WITH YOURSELF

For many clinicians, the legal process is foreign, frightening, or despised. Clinicians may feel patronized and disempowered by attorneys. Part of a clinician's aversion to participating in the legal arena may be due to a lack of familiarity with the legal process. Other aspects are related to real differences between the professional identities, philosophies, and perspectives embodied in the training and experiences of clinicians and attorneys (Taylor, 2006). To be effective as a witness, you need to identify any sources of frustration or anxiety that you may have with legal processes. Awareness of these issues can help you with the same type of "conscious use of self" as a witness as your awareness of self would serve you in therapeutic interactions with your clients (Schetky & Colbach, 1982). Self-awareness can also foster a sense of self-efficacy and empowerment. If you can remain calm and poised under stress, you will be able to testify more effectively. When you feel poised and confident, you will come across as more credible and convincing (Cramer, Neal, DeCoster, & Brodsky, 2010).

Effective clinicians conduct their work by making deliberate and informed choices about how to present themselves, what to say, and how to say it. This notion of the intentional professional applies whether the clinician is diagnosing a client, performing therapy, or acting as a witness (Schön, 1990). Just as you must "begin with yourself" when working in a clinical practice role (Hunt, 2001), you must also begin with yourself when your profession takes you into the role of a witness. This reflective process starts with your asking yourself:

- "What are my *experiences* with the legal system?"
- "What *attitudes and triggers* have I developed because of these experiences?"

- "What are my professional *roles?*"
- "What *commonalties and conflicts* exist between attorneys and myself?"
- "What are my *values and ethics* as clinician who may be involved in legal proceedings?"

With this awareness and understanding, you will be better able to act and react intentionally to situations where you are in contact with the legal system.

EXPERIENCES, ATTITUDES, AND TRIGGERS

Our values and attitudes toward attorneys and the legal system are shaped by both positive and negative experiences. Such experiences can take a number of forms. A key experience could be a childhood recollection, a relationship with someone who works within the legal system, or prior interaction with the legal system in your role as a clinician. From childhood, do you remember images of attorneys as virtuous champions of justice or as self-righteous hawks and victimizers? How have movies and other media affected your views of the legal system? What horror stories and hero stories have influenced your views of attorneys? What roles have important people in your life played in relation to the legal system, whether judges, attorneys, victims, experts, offenders, policemen, or mediators? Have you ever been called to court or to a professional disciplinary hearing to testify? How did you feel you were treated?

Many clinicians are unsettled by their entry into the legal system. Attorneys are trained in the art of adversarial exchange. They appear prepared to spend days or weeks on end in the courtroom, battling with their colleagues over legal issues. They challenge, persuade, and argue. They play strategic games with the facts. In the courtroom, attorneys zealously advocate for their client's position and work hard at undermining the credibility of the other side. When the trial is over, most attorneys shake hands and leave the adversarial spirit in the courtroom.

Clinicians seem to have thinner skin. Most of us are not trained in the art of trial advocacy, nor do we spend most of our professional time in an adversarial setting. We expect empathy, honesty, concern, collaboration, and support from our colleagues. Our training compels us to be gentle, compassionate, understanding, forgiving, and constructive in our communications. Such professional expectations about communication and collegial treatment may serve us poorly when we enter the legal arena. At times, we need to adopt a Teflon veneer, allowing harsh tones and verbal confrontations to slide off rather than penetrate our sense of dignity and self-worth.

In psychological terms, *countertransference* refers to an unconscious process in which professional interactions with a client trigger feelings in the clinician related to important people or relationships in the clinician's personal life. If the clinician is aware of her countertransference and monitors potential biases, she will be in a better position to ensure that it does not hinder her effectiveness as a witness (Bush, Connell, & Denney, 2006). Consider feelings evoked by the legal process that may stem from prior experiences. For example, if Michael has had horrible experiences with authority in the past, he may feel scared, anxious, resentful, or angry when dealing with an authoritative attorney or tribunal (Vogelsang, 2001). Unchecked, these feelings may cause Michael to become unduly passive or, alternatively, argumentative with an attorney. Countertransference could also occur in relation to the substantive issues of a legal dispute. For example, Sam could have unresolved issues regarding aggression or sexual abuse from his own background. If Sam becomes involved in child protection proceedings with the Carveys, he needs to ensure that his personal feelings do not bias his ability to provide a proper assessment (Crosson-Tower, 2009).

Personal reflection is just one way to manage countertransference as a witness. Maintaining a personal log or self-check questionnaire may help to raise your awareness of how a particular case or dealing with particular legal professionals is affecting you: What feelings does this case evoke in me; where are these feelings coming from; to what extent are they related to the actual case versus events in my own life; how do they affect my behavior in the courtroom? In situations where countertransference may have a significant impact on your ability to present as a witness, further exploration with a peer, supervisor, trial consultant, or therapist may be required. Ideally, you can deal with countertransference issues prior to taking the stand. In some instances, you may need to deal with countertransference in the course of testifying, for instance, by feigning confidence and masking your nervousness or defensiveness (Cramer et al., 2010). Afterward, you may benefit from debriefing with a professional colleague or therapist.

Countertransference can also positively affect a clinician's performance as a witness. Some clinicians enjoy the attention of being asked for their opinions or advice. They may have had aspirations of becoming an attorney at one point in their lives and thrive on the opportunity to participate in legal processes. Other clinicians, consciously or unconsciously, use their emotion-tinged responses to convey genuine passion and conviction in giving their testimony. Acting as a witness may give a sense of purpose, helping ensure that truth emerges and justice is served. Clinicians can provide courts with psychological, social, and contextual information that they might not otherwise have an opportunity to consider.

If you have difficulty viewing the role of attorney in a positive light, remember the skill of empathy that treating clinicians use to engage and appreciate clients. How can you understand the attorney, from the attorney's perspective? If you question how an attorney can, in good conscience, represent a killer in a murder trial, consider the attorney's view—the attorney does not see herself as representing the "bad guy," but rather as representing a person who has a right to due process and a fair trial, including appropriate legal representation on both sides of the case (Israel, 2011).

ROLES

In a prototypical adjudicative process, the primary issue to be decided is whose version or interpretation of the facts is to be believed as the truth. From this determination, the adjudicator can decide on the appropriate disposition or remedy. An effective witness in this adjudicative process is someone who can communicate facts and opinions about those facts in a credible manner. A credible witness is one in whom the adjudicator is more likely to believe. Qualities that tend to convey credibility include candor, openness, honesty, impartiality, trustworthiness, respectfulness, likeability, knowledge, and confidence (Brodsky, Griffin, & Cramer, 2010). To be an effective witness, one must not only possess these qualities but also be perceived to possess these qualities. Credibility as a witness is akin to one of the core conditions of clinical practice, that is, genuineness (Ivey, Ivey, & Zalaquett, 2010). Professional clinicians know that, to be effective, they need to convey authenticity to their clients—otherwise, the clinician cannot develop a positive working alliance with the client. Similarly, a clinician cannot be effective as a witness unless she develops a relationship based on credibility with the decision maker(s) in the adjudicative process.

Lay witnesses are generally provided with no more than two pages of tips on how to be an effective witness. So why does a clinician need a whole book? In one sense, clinicians are already at an advantage, because honesty is a professional ethic, and clinicians are practiced in the conscious use of self. *Being credible* does not seem that hard. In the legal system, *being* credible is not enough. You must be *perceived* as credible. That is where the adversarial nature of the legal system sometimes confounds well-meaning clinicians.

The legal system presents many challenges to clinicians. On the one hand, during direct examination, the court is interested in obtaining a description of the facts as you know them. After you complete your direct examination, however, there is an opportunity for the other side to ask questions, too. This cross-examination is aimed at undermining your testimony from direct examination or making that testimony less credible. Further complicating matters are the multiple roles that clinicians play and the variety of proceedings with which clinicians may be involved. While the temptation to seek out a simple cookbook-style recipe for being an effective witness is great, your experience in legal proceedings can be much more influential and fulfilling if you take sufficient time and care to become an informed and intentional participant.

A vital first step in becoming an intentional witness is to identify your roles. Some roles may be *required*. Others may be of your choosing, based on professional and personal preferences. Consider Frieda and Sam. Frieda is a family therapist who works in private practice with people who voluntarily attend. Frieda has no ongoing relationship with legal systems. Sam is a social worker who works in a forensic setting and is directly involved with the child protection system. Although their roles as clinicians and witnesses have some similarities, significant differences also exist.

As clinicians, both Frieda and Sam are likely to view themselves as helping professionals, agents of change, and advocates for their clients. While Frieda operates in private practice and determines her own role, Sam works in the context of an agency mandated to safeguard children from abuse and neglect. Child protection laws and agency policies suggest that Sam's role is not only to provide the child and family with psychosocial services, but also to document evidence of child abuse or neglect and be prepared to present it to court should the need arise (Crosson-Tower, 2009). Accordingly, Sam must be aware of his dual role and of conflicts that arise when voluntary interventions are insufficient to ensure the welfare of a child. Given these contexts, Sam and Frieda have significantly different orientations toward the legal system. Their orientation will affect the way they keep records, their relationship with attorneys, and the way they present evidence.

As a custody evaluator, Evelyn has been appointed by the court to gather information from multiple data sources, form her opinions, and present a report. She is a forensic expert, and her role is to provide a neutral, objective assessment. Evelyn is not an advocate for Philip or Paula. She should neither provide therapy to nor mediate with Philip and Paula, since this could compromise her role as an evaluator (Association for Family and Conciliation Courts, 2006, s.8.4, APA, 2010, 3.06; NASW, 2008, s.1.06). However, the manner in which Evelyn conducts her evaluation may have therapeutic effects. For instance, the manner in which she drafts her evaluation could include conciliatory language and highlight the strengths of each parent. The lines between therapy, mediation, and evaluation are not always clear (Barsky, 2007b). Still, a reflective practitioner needs to be aware of the boundaries that her role entails as well as have an understanding of the role limitations that can affect the scope of her testimony.

COMMONALTIES, CONFLICTS, AND MOVING BEYOND

Although clinicians and attorneys often feel at odds with one another, they have a substantial set of values and methods in common. Attorneys and clinicians have common interests in client rights, advocacy, and justice (Meyer & Weaver, 2006). Although their definitions and modes of implementation may be different, their ethical commitments are similar. For example, both disciplines seek to educate others about political and human issues. Both endeavor to influence people with power to protect the interests of minorities, victims, and the disadvantaged (ABA, 2010, Preamble; APA, 2010, Principles D and E; NASW, 2008, Preamble).

Evelyn might find it personally gratifying that her assessments influence important decisions about Debra's welfare. Acting as a witness in one proceeding not only affects the welfare of an individual client but also can have much broader policy implications and affect the lives of many other people (Barsky, 2009). If Evelyn were to provide convincing information about research pertaining to identification of sexual abuse in adolescents, this research could establish a precedent that would affect how child protection authorities dealt with future cases. Clinicians may take pleasure from work in legal processes because of personal interests. Frieda may enjoy public speaking. Sam may enjoy working with Alice because of his admiration for attorneys such as those on *Law & Order* or other television shows. Evelyn may take satisfaction from responding well in a cross-examination, demonstrating that her assessment was well founded. Clinicians may even find that their experience in legal proceedings provides them with new insights to take back to their clinical work (Madden, 2003).

A clinician uses a different set of skills and orientation to function effectively in adjudicative processes. However, some traditional attributes of clinicians will be helpful in pursuing alternatives to adjudicative processes. If Michael uses his mediation skills effectively, he can help the parties resolve custody and access on a consensual, amicable basis. If Evelyn produces a sound evaluation, Alice can use this evaluation to negotiate terms of a separation agreement. A clinician's communication skills will be beneficial in all types of legal proceedings.

Unfortunately, not all clinical approaches are easily transferable to legal processes. Involvement in them is not necessarily easy or gratifying. You may feel anxious because your work is being put on trial. You may feel ridiculed or demeaned by how attorneys question you. You may become frustrated with the legal process because of a lack of control over it. If you see your role as case management or facilitation, legal proceedings can usurp that role. You may find it frustrating to operate as a mere "functionary" for the legal system (Lynch & Mitchell, 1995). As a witness, you may find that you cannot act as an advocate or helping agent for your client. Because attorneys tend to control the process, you may feel that your role is diminished to that of a passive collaborator. You may not have time for the legal requirements of documentation for day-to-day record keeping and court proceedings. Delays within the justice system and the stress of legal proceedings will affect both you and your client. You may not be properly compensated for your time. The language used by attorneys may sound obscure or convoluted. You may feel frustrated because attorneys never seem to provide straightforward advice, couching their responses with "It depends" or "I would need more information." Your participation in a controversial legal dispute can bring negative responses from colleagues or clients. You may even be followed down the street by a journalist who is researching a current case, only to be vilified on the 6 o'clock news or a YouTube video gone viral. Some of these issues can be managed once you understand them. Others have no easy solution.

The relationship between a clinician and attorney is often either a love or hate relationship, depending on each person's personal as well as professional experiences with one another. Certainly, the legal profession comprises ethical and unethical, competent and incompetent practitioners; likewise for mental health and related professions. As a potential witness, you may have the opportunity to forge successful working relationships with like-minded attorneys, but you will need to learn how to work with the full gamut of possible attorneys to effectively fulfill your roles as clinician and witness.

The following discussion outlines six conflicts between legal and clinical approaches, offering suggestions for how a clinician can deal with these conflicts.

Adversarial versus Collaborative Approaches

Clinicians work collaboratively with client systems to resolve problems in ways that foster client self-determination. While attorneys work collaboratively with their own clients, adjudication uses an adversarial process that pits one attorney's client against another's. Adjudication generally results in win–lose outcomes. Decision-making authority is placed in the hands of a judge or third-party decision maker rather than the client and/or the clinician. Incarceration for criminal activities and involuntary committals to mental health institutions exemplify the extent to which legal systems can interfere with self-determination. Whereas attorneys have traditionally had a rights orientation, clinicians tend to be more relationship oriented.

When you provide testimony that conflicts with a client's wishes, your working relationship can be hurt or even severed entirely. However, providing evidence may not be, in and of itself, the problem. A number of other factors contribute to the impact of testifying. Have you clearly identified your role to your client and the possibility that you could be called to testify? Is the agreement about your role in writing and signed by you and your client? Have you properly identified the limits of confidentiality? Are the limits of confidentiality clearly described in a written document signed by you and your client? Have you and the client already tried to resolve matters through less formal and adversarial means? Did you make real-time accurate notes about these discussions and the options proposed to avoid the litigation?

If you do have to present evidence at a hearing, the manner in which you do so is all-important (see Chapter 5). When caught up in the adversarial spirit of a proceeding, a clinician may end up presenting information in a divisive, provocative, or aggravating manner. Even though the legal process has adversarial components, a clinician is normally most effective as a witness when providing balanced, matter-of-fact information. Evelyn's written assessment will be more influential in a legal proceeding if she focuses on objective facts. "I heard Paula say that she would not allow Philip to have access to Debra; then Philip told Paula he would kidnap Debra" is a more influential statement than "Philip cannot be trusted because he plans to abduct dear, sweet Debra." Through direct and concrete statements, the clinician will seem more credible not only to the decision maker, but also to the client, both of whom may sense greater truth in the information provided.

In some situations, clinicians use the authoritative nature of legal processes to facilitate therapeutic change (Barsky, 2010; Crosson-Tower, 2009). For example, child protection workers such as Sam can use the authority of the court as part of a planned intervention to ensure that a child is protected from an abusive parent. Although clinicians prefer to work with clients on a voluntary and consensual basis, limits on self-determination exist when there is a risk of harm to the client or others. Some clinicians who work with involuntary clients feel that they, the clinicians, have too much authority; other clinicians feel they have too little authority.[1]

As a clinician, you can temper your authority and strive to work with a client on a more consensual basis by trying to work out a voluntary plan of action prior to going to court. If you cannot reach an agreement with the client, you can try to help him understand his emotional reactions to the legal consequences of his actions so that he can make an informed choice about how to respond. You can also help your client think through different options and how those options might have very different emotional consequences for him.

You cannot and should not interpret legal decisions for your client or provide legal advice. However, it is appropriate to help your client develop a better understanding of her feelings about different legal options. You may also be helpful in guiding your client to ask questions of her attorney to clarify her understanding of the legal consequences of her choices and decisions.

If you are going to be a witness in a case involving your clients, explain your role to them as early as possible.[2] To the extent that you are honest with them up front, they will be able to make better informed choices about whether and how to cooperate with you. Further, they will not be surprised if you do raise evidence against their preferences.

Clinicians representing disadvantaged groups may find the legal system particularly oppressive. They may be concerned about the negative impact of an adversarial process on their clients or find that the law contains systemic biases. For example, some domestic violence clinicians who work with abused women or children find that criminal procedure favors the rights of the accused over the rights of their clients. Accordingly, such clinicians may be reluctant to cooperate with the legal system. Conversely, some clinicians who work with men accused of perpetrating violence

---

[1]Court-mandated clients include people ordered into treatment due to concerns about child abuse, mental health (suicidal or homicidal ideation), drug use, intimate partner abuse, or other violent behavior. In some cases, clients are not formally ordered into treatment, but enter treatment under various levels of pressure from the court (e.g., agreeing to treatment in order to avoid a stiffer sentence, agreeing to treatment to be diverted from court, or agreeing to treatment as a condition of probation or parole). Clinicians need to be particularly vigilant in explaining their legal and ethical responsibilities to involuntary clients. On the one hand, clinicians are ethically obliged to honor a client's right to self-determination. If a client resists or terminates treatment, however, the clinician must also manage concerns about community safety and adhering to the court order.

[2]While this is good practice for all clinicians, it is specifically required for psychologists by the Specialty Guidelines for Forensic Psychologists (Committee on Ethical Guidelines for Forensic Psychologists, 2011). The Specialty Guidelines advise psychologists to properly inform clients about the possible use of information from the therapy relationship in a legal context as soon as it becomes clear that the information may be used in such a context.

might be reluctant to support the legal system because they believe there is bias favoring the rights of victims over the rights of alleged perpetrators.

Certainly, problems do exist. Clinicians can play a significant role in challenging injustices and advocating for change within the limits of their professional roles. However, before a clinician decides not to cooperate as a witness, she needs to be aware of the potential consequences of taking certain actions. In the extreme, refusing to cooperate can result in charges of obstructing justice or contempt of court (e.g., Crimes and Criminal Procedure, 2010). If faced with this issue, you need to weigh the risks and benefits of refusing to participate in the process against the risks and benefits of cooperating. Consult your profession's ethical standards and codes of conduct and seek the advice of colleagues. You may need to consult with not only your personal attorney but with an attorney well versed in the type of law related to your case. You may need to find associates in the community who understand the informal rules of professional conduct within the community. If appropriate, consult with your employers and seek their support for your stance.

Note that within many areas of law—particularly family law—there has been a movement within the legal profession toward collaborative law. Under this paradigm, attorneys are trained to use cooperative negotiation and problem-solving skills to help clients resolve their concerns without having to go to court (Wright, 2010). Thus clinicians may have very different experiences when working with attorneys who embrace collaborative versus adversarial approaches (see also Chapter 10).

Rules versus Fairness

Clinicians often see legal processes as rigid and formal. Attorneys view the rules and structure of these processes as necessary to ensure that the process is predictable and fair. Even when procedural justice is fulfilled in a legal sense, clinicians may see the results of certain cases as unfair and blame bad decisions on legal technicalities (e.g., "Why should a thief be acquitted just because the police did not follow the right protocol for gathering evidence?").

To some extent, the conflict between rules and fairness is illusory. Legal rules are designed to create a fair process. For example, rules about who can present what evidence and how it should be presented may seem to be unduly restrictive to someone unfamiliar with legal processes. While an attorney may seem overly compulsive about details, certainly some degree of precision is required to ensure fairness. The better a clinician can understand the reasons for the rules, the more likely he is to perceive the rules as fair. However, in some cases, legal processes do indeed seem too rigid and formal for the types of problems that need to be resolved.[3]

Once again, the clinician must decide whether to abide by the rules or challenge them. If you decide to challenge some rules in the legal system, I encourage you to challenge them in a manner consistent with the rules of law. That is, find a way to issue your challenge that does not show disrespect for the system. For example, there are ethical standards as well as professional practice guidelines about how to handle a request from the court to release raw psychological test data. One can challenge a court order to release the raw data by seeking to educate the judge about the ethical constraints placed on their release. One can also offer useful alternatives to the court's directive that may help the court to seek a path that avoids the tension between the ethical concerns of the clinician and the litigant's right to due process and a fair trial.

As a witness, you may find that you have little control over the process but that nonetheless it is more appropriate and ultimately more constructive toward achieving your long-term goals to cooperate with authorities. Making long-term systemic changes will probably require that you participate more actively in public policy and law reform processes.

Facts versus Subjective Meaning

When providing counseling or therapy, clinicians often focus on the subjective experiences of their clients. They understand psychology and social sciences are imprecise, and they learn to accept ambiguity, complex interactions, and uncertainty as fundamental to their work. The courtroom is looking for objective evidence, linear causal relationships, and predictions of behavior that can be made with a high level of certainty. When working together, attorneys and clinicians must learn how to bridge these differences.

Adjudicative processes require objective criteria to prove the existence of hard facts and to support particular assessments and recommendations. Clinicians have been accused of having difficulty in distinguishing between fact and speculation. While clinicians use objective criteria for psychological and social assessments, they also employ "soft" information and subjective opinions. *What happened* is important to attorneys, who are seeking truth in an objective sense. In contrast, *the meaning that clients attribute* is important in most clinical processes. From an attorney's perspective, this

---

[3]In family law and child welfare cases, for example, clinicians may well prefer mediation, family group conferences, or other alternative dispute resolution processes that are designed to take relationship and emotional issues fully into account.

type of orientation can make a clinician a poor investigator and witness. To avoid interprofessional misunderstandings, clinicians need to understand the differences in educational experiences, professional culture, and perspectives between attorneys and members of their own professions (Taylor, 2006).

How comfortable a clinician feels with legal processes partially depends on the theoretical framework she brings to clinical practice. Clinicians who employ behaviorism define problems and goals in observable behavioral terms. Behaviorism has a strong history of inquiry using experimental designs. This empirical approach fits well with the needs of an adjudicative process. Cognitive approaches to clinical practice also correspond well with the rational thought processes used in legal argument. In contrast, many psychoanalytic interventions are based on abstract constructs that have limited experimental research to support their validity. This makes it difficult to use psychoanalytic concepts for evidentiary proof. Similarly, clinicians who use a medical model of practice may adjust to traditional legal processes more easily than clinicians who use a more client-centered approach. Using a medical model, the clinician functions as an expert who can provide a specific diagnosis and prescription for treatment. In contrast, clinicians who use a feminist model of practice may have difficulty providing the type of concrete information needed by the courts. For example, a feminist model might encourage the clinician to view her client as an expert in her own life, which results in avoiding the use of labels, diagnosis, or prescribing for the client.[4] Any request for testimony about the client's current functioning against the standard of the DSM-5 (American Psychiatric Association, 2013) may present a dilemma for such clinicians because they do not typically use such concepts and therefore may not be expert in their application to specific client behaviors.

Some methods of research and critical thinking fit better than others with adjudicative processes. Adjudicative decision making requires parties to provide proof of particular facts (Meyer & Weaver, 2006). Accordingly, quantitative research that studies the causal relationships between

---

[4]For a more thorough discussion of theories that inform clinical practice, see Corey (2009). The following general definitions are offered for those who are unfamiliar with the theories identified in this section. According to behaviorism, people learn how to act in response to stimuli and reinforcements in their environments. For example, if a person receives positive reinforcement for behaving in a particular manner, that behavior is more likely to be repeated in the future. According to cognitive theory, people do not simply respond automatically to stimuli but rather are able to think, learn, and make conscious choices about how to act. According to psychoanalytic theory, much of human behavior depends on unconscious psychological processes, including sexual and aggressive impulses, repressed childhood memories, and irrational personal conflicts. Feminism explores the unique experiences of women and challenges male-oriented assumptions in traditional theories of psychology and social science.

phenomena fits particularly well. In quantitative research, the researcher begins with a hypothesis and designs a study to test the truth or validity of that hypothesis. Statistical analysis can help to identify the specific probability of particular events. In contrast, judges might question the reliability of findings from qualitative research since this type of methodology lacks the basics of generalizability found in experimental designs (e.g., large, random samples, pre- and posttests, control groups). For qualitative research to be accepted as persuasive evidence, a clinician may need to demonstrate methods for ensuring its reliability and relevance.[5] Interviewers who are trained to conduct qualitative interviews, for example, will know how to ask questions in a way that limits the effects of their biases on the information provided (Denzin & Lincoln, 2011). Arguably, both narrative and anecdotal evidence fit very well with the common law, which is, after all, a series of narratives or stories of what happened to real people.[6]

How a clinician operates in her clinical role need not limit her ability to be an effective witness. Frieda, for example, uses an approach to family therapy that emphasizes the clients' own subjective meanings of their experiences. If Frieda is admitted as an expert witness, she is not limited to this perspective. She can also testify about interpretations from her clinical observations and from other objective data she has gathered. Alternatively, Frieda could decide she does not want to be a "good witness." Because Frieda is not mandated to provide information to the court, she may specifically decide not to gather objective information about her clients in order to discourage anyone from calling her as a witness. If she is called, any information she possesses will be of little value to the adjudicative process.

Conflicting Roles

A clinician's legal and ethical obligations are defined by relevant laws, professional codes of conduct, and agency policies (Barsky, 2010). Thus it is crucial for clinicians to know which laws, codes of conduct, and agency policies apply to them, and in what circumstances. For instance, mental health professionals should comply with the privacy provisions of the Health Insurance Portability and Accountability Act (1996). Psychologists

---

[5]In qualitative research terms, the concept of "trustworthiness" is used to embrace the quantitative concepts of reliability and validity.

[6]Case law and qualitative research both use inductive reasoning, exploring the facts or experiences in individual cases, and moving from the specific to the general. Court decisions are made on a case-by-case basis, but attorneys and judges also look for principles that can be derived from each case and applied to similar cases. Grounded theory (a particular form of qualitative research) also explores individual experiences to inform theories that may be transferable to other situations (Denzin & Lincoln, 2011).

are expected to abide by the Ethical Principles of Psychologists and Code of Conduct (APA, 2010). Forensic psychologists are guided by the Specialty Guidelines for Forensic Psychologists (CEGFP, 2011). All of these professionals are expected to follow their agency's policies and procedures. In some instances, particularly when a professional is playing more than one role, these laws, codes of ethics, and agency policies may conflict.

Consider a situation in which a clinical social worker is compelled by a court to testify against a client. As a social work clinician her primary ethical obligation is to serve her client (NASW, 2008, s.1.01). Thus she promotes the client's right to self-determination, protects the client's confidentiality, and acts as an advocate for her client. When the social worker is compelled to testify against a client, the worker is supposed to tell the truth— the whole truth— and not just what the client would like her to say. As a witness, the social worker may not be able to honor her client's wishes and interests. Similarly, if a court asks a clinician to investigate or monitor a client, the clinician will find it difficult to maintain the trust of the client, which is necessary for an effective clinical relationship. The role boundaries involved in such work are often difficult to navigate. This is why understanding the important role-boundary issues between being both a treating clinician and a witness is critically important (Bush et al., 2006). Ordinarily, clinicians should avoid multiple forms of relationships with clients due to potential conflicts of interest (APA, 2010, s.3.05; NASW, 2008, s.1.06). In some cases, such as when as clinician is compelled to testify, multiple relationships are unavoidable. In such instances, the clinician should clarify role expectations with the client and take reasonable steps to ameliorate potential ethical conflicts, including challenges to confidentiality, informed consent, and client self-determination.

Another potential conflict arises with respect to self-disclosure. As treating practitioners, clinicians are taught to maintain professional boundaries and limit self-disclosure. As witnesses in a hearing, clinicians may be required to answer personal questions. For instance, attorneys may ask clinicians for their personal views on abortion, gun control, child rearing, sexuality, or whatever else may be pertinent to the case.

Given the potential for conflicts between the roles of clinician and witness, clinicians must decide whether to maintain both roles. When a clinician is called as a witness, she may need to discontinue service and refer the client to another clinician. For example, if Paula sues Frieda for malpractice, Frieda will likely decide that she can no longer serve the Carveys. However, Frieda still has an ethical obligation to ensure that the family has access to proper services (APA, 2010, s.3.12; NASW, 2008, s.1.16). In cases where the clinician is not being sued but is involved in the client's legal situation as a witness, the clinician may need to consult with colleagues as well as the state licensing board to determine the best course of action. Remember, even when you agree to testify for your client, you may be asked to disclose information about your client that you are not prepared to openly discuss. Despite your best intentions, once you take the stand, your full file is open to scrutiny by the attorneys and the court. It may become part of the public record. Moreover, you may be asked questions that reveal aspects of your client's behavior that were not expected to become public. The bottom line is that any time you decide to take an advocacy position for a therapy client, you may unintentionally do significant damage to your relationship with that client because of the information you may be compelled to reveal once you are on the stand.

When treating clinicians act as witnesses, one of the most difficult issues is whether to conduct themselves as advocates for the client's wishes or as objective observers. In adjudicative proceedings you will be seen as most credible if you present yourself, as well as your advocacy, in an impartial manner. This may sound paradoxical, but I believe that as a treating clinician you should ordinarily convey to the court that your understanding of the issues is drawn solely from your client's perspective[7] (Bush et al., 2006). You may also discuss how, as a result of this one-sided influence, you have formed specific beliefs about your client and his understanding of the issues. Such disclosures about your potential biases convey honesty and integrity. Further, you may indicate openness to additional information from other information sources that might shed light on aspects of your client's situation that were not presented during therapy.

How you present your advocacy is important. You can advocate and still be viewed as open to new information. Such advocacy may increase the court's view of your credibility. There are other forms of advocacy that come across as rigid and righteous. To illustrate, consider a psychiatrist who is known as an advocate for the rights of people with schizophrenia. The physician believes that, with proper medication and supervision, a particular patient will not pose a risk to self or others and should be released from a mental health institution. To make this point in a credible manner, the psychiatrist could say:

> "I have diagnosed this patient personally and I have listened to the views of the other mental health professionals who have testified at this hearing. I understand that they are concerned about his history of setting fires. During the past 2 weeks, under my medical supervision, the patient has been cooperative with his medication regimen

---

[7]Forensic evaluators may present their client's subjective perspectives, but they are also expected to use other sources of information and formulate more objective opinions to present to the court.

and his auditory hallucinations have ceased. If he continues to comply with treatment, he will not have the type of hallucinations that prompted his fire-setting conduct in the past."

Contrast this approach with the following:

> "The professionals who testified against my patient do not know what they are talking about because they haven't been working with him. This patient's right to autonomy has been violated by keeping him imprisoned against his will. He poses no threat to anyone and must be allowed to live in the community."

If the psychiatrist shows rigid and righteous bias toward a particular client with schizophrenia, her testimony will be given little weight. She may even damage her own professional reputation.

An ethically challenging issue arises when you are asked to provide testimony that the client may view as against his wishes or interests. When you are asked to provide such testimony, you may feel as though it is a betrayal of your client (APA, 2010, s.3.04; NASW, 2008, s.1.01). You and your client should discuss his feelings about your upcoming testimony. It may be useful to talk about different scenarios that may play out in court, such as a hostile cross-examination that reveals testimony that was never intended to be divulged. Explaining these possible situations with your client may help the client accept your role in court and clarify in your own mind the appropriateness of your agreement to testify.

In the Carveys' case, assume Debra's school guidance counselor has been asked to provide testimony at a custody hearing. The counselor feels sympathetic toward Debra and struggles with how he could say anything that could put Debra's wishes at risk. Debra has told the counselor that she wants to live primarily with her mother. The counselor has concerns about Paula as a parent, however, as Debra has had many unexcused absences from school on days she was in Paula's care. The counselor is concerned that Paula encourages Debra to feign illnesses or other excuses so she can spend more time with Debra. Prior to being called to testify, the counselor lets Debra know that he will put forth Debra's wishes, but he will also need to state concerns about Debra's absences. The counselor also informs Debra that it is the judge's responsibility to make the final decision about what parental arrangements are in Debra's best interests. In situations such as the one just described, your testimony may be in the client's or community's best interests, even though it is not the type of information the client wants to hear.

In contrast to purely adjudicative proceedings, in political or legislative proceedings "acting as an advocate" may be highly appropriate. In fact, acting as an advocate may even be the normal expectation in such contexts. If a group of mental health professionals was advocating for the rights of people with mental challenges, for instance, a legislator might be persuaded by their passion for social justice for their clients (Vance, 2009).

Dilemmas may arise because of conflicting legal and ethical obligations. The code of ethics for your professional association may censure what you are asked to do as a witness. Suppose, for example, a psychological association has a policy supporting a woman's right to choice regarding abortion. Would it be ethical for a psychologist to provide evidence in a case that supports a pro-life perspective? In other circumstances, a clinician may receive an unethical request from an attorney. Alice could ask Evelyn not to report certain information that hurts her client's case. Although Alice is not specifically asking Evelyn to lie, is Evelyn obliged to report full and frank information? Such dilemmas have no easy answer. They depend on the clinician's role and professional obligations. If Evelyn were hired by Philip's attorney to do an assessment, her obligations under attorney work product rules would be different than if she were appointed by the court or hired jointly by Philip and Paula. (For further discussion, see Chapter 7.) If Philip rather than Philip's attorney hired Evelyn, her obligations would also be different, as Evelyn's primary client would be Philip.

Rights versus Therapeutic Goals

Traditionally, legal education taught attorneys to focus on assessing and defending the legal rights of individuals, whereas education for mental health professionals taught clinicians to focus on therapeutic goals (e.g., improved social functioning, managing mental illness, more effective communication, and coping with stressful life events). It would be fallacious to state, however, that attorneys only focus on rights and clinicians only focus on therapeutic goals. For instance, clinicians often act as advocates for justice for individual clients and vulnerable populations (Maschi & Killian, 2011). Thus clinicians need to know about legal rights and processes. Law schools now take a broader approach to legal education, teaching students oral communication, problem solving, therapeutic jurisprudence, and other skills related to serving clients in a real-world context (American Bar Association Section on Legal Education, 2011, s.302). Still, many clinicians are concerned that attorneys focus too much on rights, taking insufficient account of the emotional effects and broader social impacts that legal cases have on individual clients and their families.

Both clinicians and attorneys believe people should take responsibility for their actions. This principle often manifests differently in the preferred methods of the two professions. The foci of the traditional criminal justice system, for example, are retribution and protection of the public. If someone commits a wrong, retributive justice demands that she be punished for her action. Punishment is also used to deter or prevent further criminal acts. Although rehabilitation plays a role in the system, clinicians frequently note that the rehabilitation aspect of the system is undervalued. If a clinician believes an individual needs therapeutic treatment or has been deprived of a supportive social environment, she may sympathize with the individual. To advance these concerns in legal processes, a clinician may need to translate them into language that fits in a legal framework. Sam might believe Philip's abusive behavior is the result of mistreatment in his own upbringing. In a traditional court trial, however, the law does not view disadvantages in one's upbringing as an excuse for behavior. If a person committed a crime, he is guilty of that crime regardless of having neglectful parents, poor education, or other challenges in life.[8]

Fortunately, the criminal justice system has expanded beyond its traditional goals of punishment and deterrence (Restorative Justice Online, n.d.). The system now includes community courts, mental health courts, victim–offender mediation, restorative circles, and other problem-solving alternatives for those who meet certain criteria (e.g., first offence). These approaches tend to fit better with the values and perspectives of the mental health professions, including compassion, respect for the dignity and worth of all people, individual and community empowerment, holistic intervention, and enhancement of human relationships.

Lack of Respect

The final type of potential conflict stems from disrespect between attorneys and clinicians. Lack of respect may result from ignorance or negative experiences with individuals in the other profession. For instance, Alice may have had difficulty with a psychiatrist as a witness in a prior case. Evelyn may view attorneys as "hired guns," determined to defend their clients and win at all costs. Resentment and disrespect may also result from differences in status and pay between the two types of professions. Disrespectful behavior is sometimes an intentional strategy, such as when an attorney uses intimidation to discredit a witness, "forgets" to provide the clinician with significant information, or sends threatening letters. Ethically, both attorneys and clinicians have a duty to show respect for other professionals

---

[8]The court may consider the person's challenges and disadvantages during the sentencing phase, as mitigating factors when determining an appropriate sentence.

and in fact, for all individuals. Despite negative clichés about attorneys, they typically behave ethically.

Extreme cases may require that you report unethical behavior to the law society. However, your customary clinical strategies can be used to defuse most situations: active listening, time-outs, identifying mutual concerns, constructive confrontation, nonjudgmental assertiveness, meeting the attorney halfway, and using "I" statements to indicate what type of treatment you prefer. This does not mean providing therapy to the attorney—regardless of whether the attorney could use it.

Consider an attorney who shows little respect for social workers. The attorney may see social workers as well-meaning and charitable but as having little training or expertise. If the social worker becomes defensive and loses his temper with the attorney, this behavior reinforces the attorney's stereotype. If the social worker tunes in to the reasons for the attorney's treatment, then the social worker may be able to confront the attorney in a constructive manner. For example, the attorney may not know the extent of the social worker's knowledge and skills, or may believe anyone can practice social work. The social worker can address these concerns by providing information about his educational background, standards of practice, specific areas of expertise, and the science behind social work. Being certified or licensed by a social work association can raise the social worker's standing with legal professionals. Having your own attorney present will also reduce the likelihood of being treated with disrespect.

Disrespect may also stem from differences in the ethics of the two professions. Attorneys have an ethical obligation to advance their clients' cause resolutely. A clinician may question how an attorney could defend people who have committed criminal acts. To see this issue from the attorney's perspective, the clinician needs to consider the "right to an attorney" and "presumption of innocence" as essential components of a fair legal process.

In some instances, clinicians perceive disrespect from attorneys even when attorneys are not intending to be disrespectful. Consider an attorney in a mental health hearing who is cross-examining a clinician about the risk of suicide. The clinician testifies that the subject of the hearing is at high risk. The attorney questions whether the clinician offers this opinion with 100% certitude. The clinician may interpret the attorney's questions as nitpicking, embarrassing, or disrespectful because nobody can predict suicidality with such precision. The attorney may not have intended to embarrass or disrespect the clinician, but rather, intended to establish doubt about her client's need for involuntary committal. As attribution theory suggests, clinicians (and all people) should be careful about attributing unsavory motives when they feel disrespected or hurt by others (Barsky, 2010).

CONCLUSION

Knowledge and experience will help to reduce anxiety and provide a feeling of greater control when you are involved in legal proceedings. In some situations, acting as a witness will be smooth and straightforward. Awareness of potentially difficult situations is the first step in preparing for worst-case scenarios. If you have had negative experiences with legal processes, take steps to ensure that they do not interfere with your ability to be effective as a witness in the future. If you view legal processes positively, then you will have an easier time working in this context. If you have taken the time to reflect on the legal system and still do not respect its processes, rules, or values, then your participation will be more difficult. While you may decide to take a stance or advocate for change, choose your battles wisely.

Chapter 3

FIRST CONTACT

Assume you are going about your clinical practice, minding your own business. A client calls and wants to talk with you about his impending legal proceeding and his expectation that you will testify for him. Perhaps an attorney calls to inform you about a complaint soon to be filed against you. Or, perhaps, an officer from the sheriff's department knocks on your door during a therapy session. Standing there, in full uniform, gun in holster, she hands you a subpoena and asks you to sign a form acknowledging service. You sign the acknowledgment and before you can ask what the subpoena is for, the officer walks out of the building. You turn around and see your client, eyes popping out of his head, wondering what you have done.

Take a deep breath and don't panic about any of these scenarios. This chapter describes how to respond to initial contacts with "legal situations" that may arise out of your clinical practice. How you react at these initial stages can dramatically affect whether and how you will be involved in any subsequent proceedings.

CONTACTED TO BE A WITNESS OR TO PROVIDE INFORMATION

When an attorney calls or writes about a legal proceeding, many clinicians feel caught off guard. Having a standard procedure in place for dealing with contacts from attorneys will help you to feel prepared and not have that "Oh my gosh, what do I do now?" feeling.

The first step is to establish a written policy. This policy should include who in your practice or agency should respond the initial legal contact, in writing or otherwise. Be sure to consider whom to consult about the policy. You may wish to involve your agency attorney as well as colleagues and staff. It is critical that the policy explain issues of confidentiality pertaining to the legal contact as well as issues concerning client–clinician privilege. In addition, you may describe how you will handle the exchange of information, anticipated affidavits, declarations, depositions, and testimony. The policy statement should also address whether clients are responsible for paying for time spent in court and in preparation for court.

When contacted by an attorney, you should gather certain information before providing any information.[1] Ask the attorney:

- "Which person or organization do you represent?"
- "How did you get my name?"
- "What is the nature of the concerns or proceedings?"
- "What information do you want?"
- "Why is this information needed?"
- "How do you want to receive this information (e.g., written report, telephone meeting, or meeting in person)?"
- "What is the time frame for the request?"

During the initial contact you do not need to give the attorney any commitments on these issues or even admit that the person referred to is your client. Instead, say something like this:

"The policy of my agency requires that I first gather information about the nature of your request. Out of respect for client confidentiality, I cannot tell you whether this person is a client of this agency. If the person is a client, I will need to speak with her and obtain a written release for confidential information. I will call you by [date] to let you know whether I have consent to speak with you. If I do not have consent, then either this person is not a client or the person is a client but refused consent to speak with you."

The attorney may express frustration if you do not immediately provide the information he is seeking. Reassure him that you need to understand the

---

[1] As a standard precaution, never speak to anyone in detail until you are sure the person is who he says he is. Law societies have registries of attorneys if you want to call to verify whether the person is a licensed attorney. At the very least, check a telephone directory or agency website for the accuracy of the telephone number and address provided. Although these precautions may sound paranoid, anyone could call you and claim to be someone entitled to your client's information. In fact, the caller could be an ex-spouse who is stalking your client, a family member, a nosy neighbor, or whomever.

request. Follow the laws and policies governing your agency before releasing any information, including whether the individual is a client. Rather than stressing that you want to cooperate, you may wish to emphasize that your responsibility is to your clients and that you will take the ethically appropriate and legally necessary steps to properly respond to the attorney's request. You could also provide the attorney with your preferred time frame, suggesting that you will provide some sort of response to his initial inquiry by a specified date. For example: "I will consider your request for information and, upon receipt of the signed release of information form you have in your possession, I will make the necessary calls and respond to you within 5 working days."

If the attorney tries to pressure you into responding immediately, resist getting into discussions before you have the proper releases and have had a chance to talk with your client about what information you intend to share with the attorney. It is common for clinicians to feel an urge to help; this is often part of why we went into a helping profession. So when an attorney or a judge asks for information that appears helpful to your client, there is a tendency to want to help by disclosing the information. However, releasing information because you wanted to help *before* you have the proper releases and a solid understanding with your client of what will be disclosed may injure the therapeutic relationship. It may result in overstepping ethical boundaries that are in place to protect your client's right to privacy. So the bottom line is *never* to disclose any client information until your client has an opportunity to provide informed consent and you have all the proper releases signed and in your file.

Do not be surprised if the attorney attempts to engage you in conversation. His job is to obtain the needed information. However, your job is to provide the information only upon proper release. You do not want to get caught off guard by the attorney's questions. Returning to our case example, Alice might ask Evelyn whether she followed her customary procedures for assessing the Carveys. If Evelyn answers "No," she may be challenged on the basis of bias, alleging that she varied from her usual procedures without any convincing reason to do so. Or, if the variations from standard procedures are changes unsupported by research or community standards, she might face a complaint to the licensing board and/or a civil suit for malpractice (which I discuss in detail in Chapter 9).

Ensure you understand the legal implications of the issues involved in the case. Also, ensure you understand the limits and boundaries of your testimonial competencies. As long as you stay within what you know and what you are professionally permitted to testify about, you will have little difficulty in the legal system. Once you step outside the boundaries of your testimonial competencies, then you are more vulnerable to ethical and legal challenges. The key is *always* to consult with colleagues and your attorney if you have any concerns about contact from a lawyer or your potential appearance as a witness in a legal proceeding. As Gutheil and Brodsky (2008) suggest, when you feel anxious about an ethical or legal situation, do not suffer alone.

It is also important to know what should and should not be discussed over the telephone. There are times when an attorney may call to ask your opinion about an issue about which you have knowledge, although you are not aware of how the information relates to any pending lawsuit. Once you provide your opinion, the attorney may present it in some form during an upcoming legal proceeding. This might result in your being called to testify even though you made the statement off the cuff, assuming it was not for public consumption. Be certain with the person on the other end of the line that you will not discuss aspects of a case without clearly understanding how the information will be used. Similarly, you may need to ask explicitly at the beginning of a conversation whether the attorney is recording the telephone call or taking contemporaneous notes. Knowing whether the attorney is taking notes or recording your conversation should help alert you to what you are able to say and how it may be used. Generally, you should not consent to recording the call, and you should not continue your participation in the call if you are concerned the call is being recorded.

If the attorney expresses urgency in her request, ask about the nature of the urgency. To the extent that you understand the urgency, you may be better able to respond. If there is an upcoming court date, there may be the possibility of a continuance (postponement of the hearing). Even if the urgency is caused by the attorney's procrastination or misuse of time in handling a case, you and your client's interests may still be best served by cooperating.

Sometimes an attorney will request information from your file. In one scenario, Philip's attorney, Alice, may request copies of Frieda's notes and assessments in her efforts to file a motion to increase Philip's times for visitation with his daughter, Debra. As the family therapist, Frieda should obtain written releases from both parents. If either parent refuses to provide a release, Frieda may be ethically and legally bound not to release the information unless a court-enforced subpoena requires her to do so (see "Confidentiality, Privilege, and Exceptions," later in this chapter). In addition to the client, you may need to consult others before providing information to an attorney. If you are working in an agency context, you may need to consult your supervisor, the director of the program, risk management department, or the agency's attorney. If you are a member of a professional organization, you may want to consult with the association.

In our ongoing example, Michael (the mediator) may have been contacted first by Art (Paula's attorney) as a potential witness. As a professional courtesy, Art should ask Alice (Philip's attorney) for permission to speak with Michael. If Art calls Michael directly, Michael should consult with Paula's attorney to decide whether he should meet with Alice and, if so, how. There is no prohibition against speaking with attorneys for both parties to a dispute, so long as issues of confidence and privilege are clearly discussed up front. These issues should be summarized in a letter or contract sent to all parties to ensure that all sides understand the rules about such conversations. During the conversation, Michael should take notes about the discussion. Upon completion of such conversations, Michael would be wise to write a summary of his notes and either file them for future reference or, if allowed, forward a letter to both attorneys summarizing his understanding of the outcome of the conversation. In this way Michael may avoid getting caught in a crossfire between attorneys who might disagree about the content and meaning of the conversation.

In some instances, the client is the one who asks for information that could be used in a legal proceeding. If the information is about the client, then the client generally has a right to those records (APA, 2010, s.4.05; NASW, 2008, s.1.07). To determine how to respond to a client's request for her file, you should also refer to any laws or regulations governing your agency (e.g., for health care providers, see the Health Insurance Portability and Accountability Act, 1996).

If you are concerned that your actions may be called into question at a legal proceeding, then you should contact your own attorney. There are two components to this scenario. The first is your legal and ethical responsibility to release records upon your client's proper written authorization. The second is the treatment issue of how the information will be released and what information will be released. It may be wise to talk with your client about the purpose of releasing the information and how best to release the information in a manner that may preserve some protection for your client–therapist relationship. It also may be useful to talk with your attorney about crafting a release statement, that is, a statement that clearly defines and limits what information will be permitted to be released from the file. There are important legal issues about confidentiality involved in your decision to release the file. There may be ways to release some information while protecting other information. Your attorney and your client's attorney may wish to talk with each other in an attempt to frame a written consent to release that limits both the information to be released and the persons to whom the information may be released.

Providing the requested information may help your client resolve a problem without going to court. In the Carveys' case, Frieda may have information that the parties could consider for the purposes of negotiating a separation agreement. Withholding this information may cause more difficulties for all concerned, and, if all releases are properly signed and executed, it could be unethical and illegal for Frieda to withhold such information.

Do Witnesses Need Legal Representation?

Ordinarily, when a person is acting as a witness, she does not need her own attorney. As a clinician with professional obligations and standards, you may want to consult an attorney for advice about confidentiality, ethical dilemmas, or how best to present evidence. Also consider participating in continuing education workshops that focus on ethics and legal issues (e.g., presentations about clinical treatment ethics, forensic treatment ethics, forensic evaluation ethics, and avoiding malpractice).

When an attorney is acting for a client and contacts you as a potential witness, that attorney does not represent you in the proceedings. The attorney calling you as a witness may be a "friendly attorney," meaning a lawyer representing interests that are generally consistent with your own. However, that attorney's responsibility is to his client and not to you. He may be unable to provide you with any advice because of the potential for a conflict of interest to emerge. That conflict would be providing legal advice to you while representing your client. No matter how "friendly" your client's attorney may be, he is not your advocate and may be unable to protect you. To illustrate, consider a request from Alice to Frieda to act as a witness in support of Philip's application for unsupervised visitation. If Frieda had information that supported this motion, then Alice may be considered a friendly attorney from Frieda's perspective. Paula's attorney would be considered an opposing attorney, since he represents Paula's interests, which are adverse to Philip's.

Although the friendly attorney does not represent you, the attorney may offer guidance and information to help you in your role as a witness to the extent that it helps his client. The information that you have to offer as evidence is information that generally supports the friendly attorney's case. Often the attorney's focus is on winning his case, not on having truth revealed. Your clinical truth may, in some ways, go against his case. The attorney may encourage you to discuss that aspect of your case. However, you have an ethical responsibility to present a fair and unbiased representation of your work, not just the aspects that favor the attorney's case. As such, aspects of your testimony may place you at odds with the attorney, who may discourage you from testifying about the full picture. This is when you must examine yourself and whom you choose to be as a witness. Are you someone who advocates for a client or someone who advocates for the truth of your experience? When they are the same, this is not a problem. When they are different, the moral and ethical challenge is to be cognizant of the dilemma and consider what would constitute professionally responsible behavior. To illustrate, consider the following example:

> Evelyn, the custody evaluator, conducts an evaluation that leads her to conclude that Paula and Philip should share parental decision-making responsibility (i.e., joint legal custody). Concerning the dispute over Debra's religious upbringing, Evelyn recommends that she continue to be raised in the Baptist tradition of her mother. Evelyn suggests that Philip was not very concerned about raising Debra as a Catholic until after the separation. Alice, Philip's lawyer, asks Evelyn to focus her testimony on Philip's ability to participate in joint parental decision making. Alice also asks Evelyn to downplay concerns about confusing Debra by introducing her to Catholic rituals and traditions. Although Evelyn does not want to show disrespect for Philip's religious beliefs, her professional obligation is to focus on what arrangements are in Debra's best interests.

Be aware of the limits of this attorney's support. Parts of your information and beliefs may go against the attorney's case. Attorneys are generally restricted from challenging or discrediting their own witnesses during a hearing. During preparation stages, however, you and the attorney may not know whether your evidence will help the attorney's case and whether you ultimately will be called as a witness. You may also be hesitant to disclose information to a "friendly attorney" that could be used against you at a subsequent hearing. If the attorney were your own attorney, you could feel free to disclose this information because your conversations with your own attorney are protected by confidentiality and attorney–client privilege; in fact, your attorney needs full disclosure in order to advise you properly. If you disclose controversial information to a friendly attorney, you do not have the same degree of control in keeping information confidential. In fact, you may have *no* control over how that information is subsequently used in litigation. It is wise to have the friendly attorney provide *in writing* an explanation of how your treatment information is to be used. By doing so, you and your client can craft a release of information that may narrowly define what information will be released and how it is to be used. Because state laws may differ on this point, it may be useful to consult both your attorney as well as an attorney for your professional association.

What If I Am Asked to Serve as a Forensic Expert?

When attorneys and courts want the services of a forensic expert, they typically contact professionals who are known for their expertise and have a proven track record in court. Thus you are not likely to receive a call to serve as a forensic expert unless you have relevant training, supervision, and experience. That said, it is possible for a court or attorney to contact a clinician whose practice has focused on treatment services and has not previously served as a forensic expert. The clinician may possess specialized knowledge or experience that is pertinent to a particular case. When deciding whether you agree to serve as a forensic expert, consider the following questions:

- "Do I possess the required expertise to serve as an expert?" For this information, you will need to know the legal issues at stake and what type of opinion evidence or other forensic services you will be asked to provide.
- "Would serving as an expert witness create any conflicts of interest?" First, ask for the names of the parties involved in the case and make sure that they are not your clients, past clients, or people who are closely related to your clients. Also, consider how serving as an expert might affect the rest of your practice: would it interfere with provision of treatment services; would clients question your commitment to them if they discovered you were providing a certain type of evidence at a public trial; and would your agency support your participation in a lawsuit? Finally, as a forensic witness, would you be seen as objective and impartial, or— given your general practice, financial interests, or public image—might you be seen as biased or predisposed toward a particular position?
- "Are there any specific credentials or qualifications required to serve as a particular type of expert (e.g., as a custody evaluator or as an administrator of certain types of psychometric testing)?" Make sure you are familiar with relevant laws that may prescribe specific qualifications for various types of forensic services.
- "How will I be paid for my services?" This question relates not only to how much you will be paid (hourly fee, retainer, etc.), but also who will pay for your services. If the court is authorizing you to act as a forensic expert, then the court order should stipulate the terms of payment. If you are being hired through an attorney, then typically the contract should be with the attorney rather than directly with the attorney's client, insurance company, or other third party (Melton et al., 2007). By contracting directly with the attorney, your work will be covered by attorney–client privilege (i.e., you are not compellable as a witness unless the attorney consents to your testifying). Further, designating the attorney as your client helps avoid any confusion by the subject of the evaluation about your role and ethical commitments; in particular, you have been hired to conduct a

forensic evaluation as part of a court case, not to provide the subject with treatment services.

In some instances, an attorney may contact you to provide expert testimony even though you were originally hired by the client as a treating clinician. In a lawsuit claiming emotional damages, for instance, you might be asked to testify about the client's cognitive and social functioning prior to an accident. As noted in Chapter 1, acting as both a treating clinician and forensic witness places the clinician in a dual relationship with the client. Generally, it is safer to avoid the dual relationship and focus on your treatment role. The attorney might argue that you have already gathered information and formulated an opinion in your case records, the client is consenting to have you testify, and you will not be asked for information that is not already reported in your records. Although you may be tempted to go along with such a request, you could point out that the opinion you provided in your case records was developed for treatment purposes and may not withstand cross-examination in court. Further, you could suggest that hiring an independent forensic expert would not only ensure that the opinions are provided by an impartial expert, but that your treatment role with the client would not be compromised by a dual relationship (Moser & Barbrack, n.d.). Finally, once you are on the witness stand, the cross-examining attorney may ask questions that go beyond what you and the hiring attorney originally intended.

The role of a forensic expert is described more fully in Chapter 7. At this point, let's refocus on situations in which you may be called to testify as a fact witness.

A CLIENT COMPLAINS

When a client complains, the clinician may feel threatened or defensive. When threatened, our natural instinct may be to fight or flee. However, aggressively confronting a client, denying an allegation, or running for cover is more likely to anger the client, resulting in an exacerbation of the problem rather than its resolution. Even if you have practiced in an ethical and competent manner, clients may issue complaints. Sometimes a complaint is the result of an angry parent in a custody battle who is seeking a target for his or her anger resulting from loss of custody.[2] Sometimes a complaint is the result of a misunderstanding. Sometimes a complaint is

---

[2]See Kirkland and Kirkland (2001) regarding child custody complaints to licensing boards and suggestions for preemptive defensive steps to protect the evaluator.

the result of sheer vengeance. Other times, a complaint is the result of poor judgment or negligence on the part of the clinician.

If a client complains directly to you, the best approach is to talk with the client about the concerns. Conflict resolution and negotiation skills are important to use in such situations (Barsky, 2007a). People often respond best when they feel they have been heard. Once you have demonstrated that you have listened to the other's concerns, that person may be more open to listening to you. The idea of "seeking first to understand and then be understood" is a useful framework in approaching a client who complains directly to you.

Many cases that end up in court could have been resolved much earlier if the parties had just tried to talk about their concerns in an informal and civilized manner. Calling an attorney at this stage is advisable if a specific action such as a formal complaint or lawsuit has been initiated. Calling an attorney is also advisable if the client has suffered serious harm. Otherwise, you may be better off inviting the client to speak with you to try to work things out. Many complaints arise out of miscommunication. Often, complaints are calls for information or listening. Use your clinical therapeutic skills: meet face to face, be supportive, explore the client's concerns, recognize the feelings of a client who believes she has been wronged, listen and demonstrate that you understand (Barsky, 2007a). If the client is asking for a remedy, find out what that is. It may be compensation or corrective action, but it may also be as simple as an explanation or an apology. She may want her complaint to be heard and acknowledged by a supervisor or person in authority.

If you have *any* doubts about how to respond, consult with a supervisor, a colleague, your insurance company, or your professional association (Barsky, 2010). Admissions or offers to remedy can incur significant legal consequences. They might even void an insurance policy. The point is not to offer any remedy before you have explored the legal consequences of your remedy.

If an attorney calls or writes regarding a complaint directed against you, do not answer the complaint until you have spoken with your supervisor, attorney, insurance adjustor, and/or professional association for advice:

> "As you can understand, I cannot speak with you about these concerns. I will have my attorney contact you."

Once you receive notice of a formal complaint against you, either in the form of a licensing board complaint or a lawsuit, immediately contact your professional liability insurance company where you or your agency hold a policy. (You *are* insured, right?)

If a client has a complaint against another practitioner, you may be asked to help your client talk with the alleged offending professional. Although you may feel a strong allegiance to help your client, you need to ask whether the support being sought is within your role as a treating therapist. It is easy to get engrossed in the client's need for support and guidance. It is also easy to get pulled into something that is outside the realm of your professional competence or role. This is a way to step into the client's conflict rather than staying within your properly defined role as a clinician.

The more you step outside your role or boundaries as treating clinician, the greater the likelihood that you will become part of the conflict (Gutheil & Brodsky, 2008). Once outside your properly defined role, you may become the target of a complaint by the other professional, who would argue that you placed yourself in a dual-role situation with the complaining client. It may be appropriate to refer the client to another professional who can help resolve the conflict. However, never choose to be that person who works at resolving the conflict while you are also the client's clinician (Barsky, 2007a).

If a client initiates formal allegations against you, then legal representation is imperative. (See Chapter 9 on malpractice.) Charges against Michael for unauthorized practice of law or a civil lawsuit against Frieda for malpractice are clear examples calling for the use of attorneys. Other situations are not as clear. For example, Sam could be involved in the inquest concerning a child's death. He may not know that his conduct is being questioned and that there might be legal consequences for his participation in the inquest. Err on the side of caution, and consult an attorney as soon as you become aware that you are involved in an aspect of another person's legal dispute.

SELECTING AN ATTORNEY

Identifying and becoming acquainted with an attorney before trouble arises is better than waiting until you are subpoenaed or sued. By developing a positive rapport, you will know that you have a trusted confidant to consult when you have the need for legal advice. Ideally your agency or private practice has an attorney who is familiar with your type of work on permanent retainer for consultation. I suggest developing a relationship with a private attorney as well. In this way you will have an attorney who is *always* your advocate and independent of any possible conflicts that might arise if you share the same attorney as your agency or practice.

If you do not already have an attorney in mind, there are several sources to consider. The board of directors of your agency might include an attorney whom you could consult. If you and your agency have conflicting interests in a legal proceeding, you may need a different attorney from the one used by the agency. You may have used an attorney to help set up your practice—to incorporate, to develop service agreements, and so on. If you are involved in a particular legal proceeding, you may want to retain the services of an attorney with special expertise (e.g., malpractice litigation, criminal law, or mental health proceedings). A colleague could provide you with a referral to an attorney she trusts, or your state professional association may know of attorneys who have practiced in your field. Finally, state or local bar associations offer attorney referral services. Professional associations may also have attorney referral information. Some referral programs offer a free half-hour consultation to help you decide whether to retain that attorney. Financial arrangements for the initial meeting should be discussed during the initial phone consultation.

There is no general right to legal counsel for witnesses involved in legal proceedings. If you are the defendant in a criminal trial, you have a right to counsel. Accordingly, a publicly funded legal aid organization will pay all or part of the attorney's fees for a person who is accused of a criminal offence and does not have the means to pay for the attorney. The rules for legal aid vary across jurisdictions in relation to what other types of cases legal aid will cover, but generally they are quite limited. If you have professional insurance, the insurance company may provide for legal representation in cases where you are a party to a legal proceeding but not where you are just a witness.[3]

Ideally, you will have lots of lead time and the freedom to select an attorney who can provide you with the services you need. Do not be shy about asking for information before retaining an attorney. Focus on information that indicates the attorney's competence: length, quality, and relevance of experience; specialized training; reputation; and skills for resolving cases in negotiation versus litigation. Consider pragmatic concerns such as time and money. An attorney with a great reputation may charge more than you can afford and may have little time for low-profile cases. You want an attorney who will pay due consideration to your case. Most attorneys work on an hourly basis. Ask what the hourly rate is, as well as an estimate of the expected time for completion of the case. Also ask the attorney if she will be handling your entire case, or whether a more junior attorney will be

---

[3]Many professional liability insurance companies provide separate coverage funds for civil litigation and for defense of licensing board complaints. These funds are typically limited and subject to certain conditions. Check your policy to ensure that you are covered for each possible occurrence, including an adequate level of coverage.

handling specific tasks. The attorney may ask for a payment up front as a retainer.[4] Let the attorney know how often you wish to be billed or inquire about the law firm's billing cycle. Let your attorney know that you want him to check with you before incurring additional legal costs. Finally, be sure the attorney does not have any conflict of interest (such as also representing your client).[5]

CONFIDENTIALITY, PRIVILEGE, AND EXCEPTIONS

Although the issues of confidentiality and privilege are straightforward in most cases, conflict and controversy do have the potential to arise. Laws, ethical codes, and agency policies are still evolving, particularly with respect to domestic violence, child maltreatment, sexual abuse, and other forms of domestic unrest. In this section, I first discuss the general principles of confidentiality and privilege. I then describe four exceptions to those principles: duties to report or warn; consent to disclose; access to information legislation; and compelling a clinician to disclose.

The obligation for clinicians to maintain confidentiality has several sources. As an ethical principle, most codes of professional conduct prescribe confidentiality and its limits. As a clinical strategy, confidentiality is offered to clients to build a safe environment in which to talk openly about personal, relationship, workplace, or family concerns, knowing that no one else will ever know what is discussed behind the closed doors of therapy. In most therapeutic models a client's trust is considered essential for effective collaborative work. As a legal obligation, the statutes and policies governing private practice as well as clinical agencies generally require the protection of a client's right to privacy (Israel, 2011).[6] As a contractual obligation, confidentiality is usually a key component of the clinician–client contract for work, whether that contract is written, oral, or implied.[7]

---

[4]If you are the plaintiff in a civil lawsuit, the attorney may agree to work on a contingency fee, basing her fees on a percentage of the judge's award or negotiated settlement for the case. If you do not win an award or negotiate a settlement, you do not pay the attorney's usual legal fees (although there may be charges for out-of-pocket expenses such as court filing fees).

[5]As a customary procedure, most law firms conduct an in-office search to ensure there is no conflict of interest prior to accepting a new case.

[6]For instance, the Health Insurance Portability and Accountability Act (1996), which governs health care providers, including mental health professionals.

[7]From a legal perspective, preferred practice suggests you should always have a signed informed-consent contract specifying the limitations of confidentiality as well as a description of privilege, if applicable.

Attorneys also value confidentiality. In fact, confidentiality of information gathered within an attorney–client relationship is well protected by law. Conflict between clinicians and attorneys arises, however, when attorneys challenge the confidentiality of the clinician–client relationship in order to further their case in legal proceedings. In some states clinician–client confidentiality is an unconditional right, while in other states the right to confidentiality can be legally challenged (Kagle & Kopels, 2008). You need to check the statutory provisions regarding confidentiality and privilege for your particular profession and your agency, as agencies such as substance abuse treatment programs and shelters for survivors of domestic violence have their own legal protections.

Legal processes may require the disclosure of information to facilitate the search for truth and justice. In addition, most cases are open to the public to ensure accountability. Clinicians may view forced disclosure and public access to information as infringements on a client's right to confidentiality as well as a serious threat to the integrity of the therapeutic relationship. Clinicians should discuss the limits of confidentiality with their clients from the outset of their work together (APA, 2010, s.4.02; NASW, 2008, s.1.07). Sometimes a clinician–client relationship can be maintained even after a clinician provides disturbing testimony against a client, particularly if the release to disclose information is properly crafted to limit what can be said and to whom. In other cases, the client will lose trust, become angry, disengage, or rebel against the clinician. More empirical research is required to explore the actual impact of forced disclosure (e.g., the impact on clinician–client relationships following disclosure and whether laws that favor disclosure increase client reluctance to seek clinical help in the future).

Disclosure in legal proceedings does not necessarily conflict with the interests of clinicians. Hearings may be viewed as a form of enforcing accountability. Accountability advances the interests of both clients and the public. In child protection proceedings, the court would review Sam's child protection work to ensure that his investigation was thorough and that he followed proper standards of practice. Sometimes clinicians are too quick to argue for confidentiality, perhaps seeing it as an absolute value or using it defensively to protect their own interests.

Privilege is a legal concept related to the principle of confidentiality. Where privilege is recognized, information gained during the course of certain professional relationships is protected from having to be disclosed in court or other legal processes. Privilege is intended to preserve communications that were not intended to be disclosed to others (NASW Legal Defense Fund, 2010). Privilege may be prescribed by legislation or recognized by common law.[8] Common law, for example, recognizes the attorney–client privilege whether or not a state specifically has legislation providing for this privilege. With few exceptions, an attorney cannot disclose communications between the attorney and her client without consent of the client. Family law legislation in most jurisdictions recognizes the privileged nature of mediation, which protects information shared in mediation from being disclosed in court unless both parties agree (cf. Association of Family and Conciliation Courts [2000], Model Standards of Practice, Standard VII). Certain medical and adoption records may also be protected by legislation. Most jurisdictions have legislation that grants privilege to communications with certain clinical professionals, including licensed psychologists, clinical social workers, and psychotherapists (Federal Psychotherapy-Patient Privilege, n.d.; *Jaffee v. Redmond*, 1996). For professional relationships not covered specifically by statutory privileges, courts may recognize a limited privilege at common law (Federal Rules of Evidence, 2010, Rule 501; Jacob & Powers, 2009). Accordingly, if there is no statutory privilege protecting confidentiality shared by a client, an attorney could advocate for recognizing privilege on the following grounds:

- The professional received information from the client in confidence that the professional would not share it with others.
- Protection of the confidence is essential to maintaining the professional relationship between the parties.
- The relationship is one that the community values and believes should be fostered.
- The injury resulting from disclosing the confidential information would be greater than the benefit to be gained from such disclosure.

Although clinicians often offer clients confidentiality, some professional relationships are not strictly confidential. For example, neither Paula nor Philip could claim privilege for information gathered by Evelyn if both parties initially agreed that Evelyn's evaluation would be used in court. In fact, if Evelyn is a court-appointed expert, Evelyn's client is the court rather than the parents. There is no legal relationship between Evelyn and the parents. The legal relationship is between Evelyn and the court, meaning that issues of privilege and confidence are between the court and the evaluator. Another context where privilege may not apply is group therapy. Some

---

[8]"Common law" refers to law derived from cases decided by judges, as opposed to statutes passed by the legislature.

courts have denied privilege to information shared during group therapy because the client has shared information with others, not just with the therapist.

Issues related to privilege can also arise when one attorney hires you to help with a case and then the attorney for the other side calls. This situation has several interesting aspects to it. For example, you may not be allowed to acknowledge to the second attorney that the first attorney has retained you. Alternatively, you may be allowed to acknowledge that you have been retained but not allowed to talk about the focus of your work. "Attorney work-product privilege" is a legal concept that protects any and all information discussed between the attorney and you as an expert who is assisting with preparation for a case (Bahadur, 2009; Miller, 2009). Until the attorney decides to reveal your participation, you may not be allowed to talk with anyone about your involvement. It is essential that you and the attorney who hired you are clear about what can and cannot be discussed with others *before* you talk with anyone else!

Police and Duties to Report

As a general rule, clinicians have no duty to report past illegal behavior to police when it is discussed within the privacy of therapy. If, during family therapy, Paula said that she used to sell cocaine because she needed the money, Frieda would not have to report Paula. There are many exceptions to this "general rule." For example, in the interests of protecting children from maltreatment, the laws in most jurisdictions require clinicians to report suspicions and actual incidents of abuse and neglect to the police or to child protection authorities.[9] Probation and parole officers are obliged to act on breaches of probation and to report certain crimes. Health professionals in some jurisdictions have a duty to trace partners of patients with certain communicable diseases such as HIV. In most jurisdictions, clinicians may also have a duty to report abuse toward vulnerable elders and people with disabilities.

Another exception arises when a clinician learns of information where there is clear and imminent danger of bodily harm (e.g., a client intends to shoot another person or plans to commit suicide). Codes of ethics generally permit breaches of confidentiality to protect an identifiable and foreseeable victim. In most states, clinicians have an affirmative duty to warn the potential victim (*Tarasoff v. Regents of University of California*, 1976) as

---

[9]Check your local state statutes, as well as the code of ethics for your professional association, for your specific reporting obligations regarding actual or suspected abuse of children, elderly adults, and people with disabilities.

well as a duty to protect.[10] If you are unsure whether the level of risk in a particular case triggers either duty, consult an attorney. Possible clinician responses include, but are not limited to:

- Counseling the client to deal with the underlying cause of the risk.
- Developing a safety plan with the client and the client's family or other support systems who can help monitor the client.
- Warning the potential victim.
- Referring the client for a second-level assessment.
- Initiating civil commitment proceedings.
- Calling the police, adult protective services, or child protective services.

Each situation will require its own response. The clinician must weigh respect for the individual's right to autonomy against the interests in preventing harm. Even if there is no legal duty to prevent harm, erring on the side of life and safety is generally preferred (Meyer & Weaver, 2006; Reamer, 2001). On the other hand, clinicians must be careful not to over-anticipate danger as a means of covering themselves against lawsuits—at the peril of completely diminishing the client's right to confidentiality.

When a clinician acts to prevent child maltreatment or other foreseeable harm, the rights to confidentiality and privilege are not completely forfeited. The clinician should release only information necessary to prevent the harm. Once authorities have gathered information from a clinician, they may try to use that information in future proceedings. The issue of what information can be used in court is separate from the issue of what information has to be reported to police or to the potential victim to prevent harm (Meyer & Weaver, 2006). For instance, if Frieda told police that Philip planned to abduct Debra, the police could act on this information in order to ensure Debra's safety (e.g., stake out Debra's school to ensure that Philip does not try to abduct Debra). If Philip showed up at the school and tried to take Debra, the police could arrest Philip and charge him with attempted abduction. At trial, if Frieda were called to testify about Philip's abduction plans, Philip's lawyer could claim privilege even though Frieda had reported the plans to the police. The court would have to determine

---

[10]In *Tarasoff*, the California Supreme Court ruled that a therapist has a duty to warn known potential victims about threats made by dangerous patients. This is commonly referred to as Tarasoff I. Tarasoff II concluded that therapists have a duty to protect (rather than just a duty to warn) innocent parties about potentially dangerous clients. Issuing a warning is included as an option under the duty to protect (see also American Psychological Association, 2010, s.4; NASW, 2008, s.1.07). In some states, including Florida, there may be no legal *duty* to warn, although the law *permits* clinicians to warn potential victims of serious, imminent harm (*Boynton v. Burglass,* 1991).

whether to breach the privilege, weighing concerns about protecting confidential therapeutic relationships against the need for evidence to ensure a just decision by the court, and applying legislation related to child abuse reporting and professional–client privilege.

In some child abuse and sexual assault investigations, police and clinicians conduct joint interviews. This approach allows police to gather evidence and clinicians to offer therapeutic help in a coordinated process.[11] The information received by police in a joint interview with a clinician would not be privileged. The police and clinical agencies should have a protocol for joint work, specifying who has access to what information held by the other organization. The protocols may even require police to use a warrant or subpoena from the court for formal production of the clinician's files.

If the police contact you during a criminal investigation, you should generally refrain from discussing confidential information unless there is a subpoena or an order from the court (discussed below). Information you share with the police may be provided to the district attorney's office (the prosecuting attorneys). The district attorney may enter this information into the court record. Information obtained by the district attorney may also be subject to disclosure to the accused so that his attorney can prepare for trial. You should cooperate with the police as necessary to prevent the occurrence of significant harm (particularly, danger to people) while also maintaining a watchful eye on your ethical responsibilities to your clients.

Finally, a duty to disclose information may arise if a clinician knows of information that could prevent a miscarriage of justice. Unless a clinician is a probation officer or other officer of the court, there is no legal obligation to report in this circumstance, but one may be ethically justified in breaching confidentiality. Consider if Michael were not called to court but had material evidence that could prevent a criminal conviction against Philip. Michael faces an ethical dilemma—does his obligation to confidentiality override the interest in avoiding a wrongful conviction? There is no clear law on this matter. A clinician faced with this issue should refer to her agency's policies and professional code of ethics and also consult her attorney and professional association.

---

[11]The use of cooperative interviews serving dual purposes is controversial. An investigative interview follows a different path than a therapeutic interview. When the two are used together, especially with young children, there is an increased likelihood that the information obtained from the young child is influenced by the context of the interview process. This may reduce the usefulness of the child's information for legal or forensic evaluation purposes (Cross, Jones, Walsh, Simone, & Kolko, 2007).

Consent to Disclose Information

Where confidentiality and privilege are recognized, these rights are owned by the clients rather than the clinicians. As a result, a client may consent to the release of confidential information or waive his right to privilege. Clinicians cannot demand confidentiality or privilege if the client has agreed to disclosure. Clinicians can talk to the client and attorney about their roles as helping professionals and explain how being compelled to testify as a witness could compromise their ability to continue to provide treatment services. The attorney and client can then factor this information into the client's decision about whether to consent to release of information or waive privilege.

The preferred practice for obtaining permission to release information specifies that the consent be informed, voluntary, signed, dated, and specific. Some agencies require specific forms (e.g., for health organizations subject to federal HIPAA laws, see *www.hhs.gov/ocr/privacy*).[12] To ensure that consent is informed, you should explain the consent in plain language, giving your client the opportunity to ask questions. In particular, let the client know whether and how the information may be used in legal proceedings. If there are any questions about the client's mental capacity, explore the client's ability to understand the nature of the agreement. Mental capacity can be affected by mental illnesses, substance abuse, or the stress of legal proceedings (Barsky, 2010). If there are legal complexities or questions about the client's capacity, consider providing the client access to legal advice before signing. Make sure the consent form is signed by someone who is legally authorized to provide consent. Both Philip and Paula would need to sign a consent form in order for Frieda to release information about the couple's therapy. For information about Debra, her clinician would need to know who had legal custody. In terms of specific details in the release, the consent should include the scope of the information to be released, by whom, to whom, for what purposes, and over what period of time. An oral consent may be required for pragmatic reasons such as time constraints. In that case, you should note the consent in your client records.[13]

---

[12]Note that HIPAA allows disclosure of records subject to a court order or consent of the client. Preferred practice is to ask the client for consent even if there is a court order.

[13]In cases where an individual is referred for evaluation or therapy by a third party such as the court, the referred individual might be advised to review the informed consent with his attorney. An individual referred by the court may be unable to provide voluntary informed consent in the clinician's office. The rationale is that signing the consent in the office may be the result of coercion—the signing party might feel compelled to sign the consent in order to please the court. Allowing the signing of consent to occur between the party and his attorney may avoid such appearance of coercion, although the clinician should recognize that the client may still feel she is attending therapy or the evaluation under some pressure.

To test for voluntariness of the consent, explore your client's reasons for signing the consent and the possibility of coercion or pressure. For court-mandated clients, disclosure to the court may be required as part of the court order. Although you cannot obtain purely *voluntary* consent from such a client, your client has a right to know what information will be shared and with whom.

In cases where privilege is requested, the request must come from the client or the client's lawyer, not from you as the clinician. If you are called to testify, find out ahead of time whether the client intends to claim or to waive her right to privilege. In certain instances a client is deemed to have waived her right to privilege, such as when a client introduces confidential information into a hearing or when a client sues her clinician. This allows the clinician to respond to statements or allegations made by the client concerning the therapeutic process. For example, if Philip based his defense on having progressed well in therapy, the clinician could be asked for her evaluation. If Paula sued Michael for malpractice, she could not deny his right to respond by claiming that the information was privileged. It is always safer to obtain written consent before providing testimony. If that is not possible, then ask to obtain verbal consent on the record prior to beginning testimony. If you are unable to obtain verbal consent, yet the judge orders you to testify, you have two options. The first is to state for the record your ethical responsibilities to obtain consent. If the judge still orders you to testify, you can provide such testimony or you can refuse. Such refusal may result in your being held in contempt of court or being subjected to other sanctions. Although there are some instances in which defying a court order may be appropriate, it is normally wiser to obey the court after appropriately informing the court about your ethical responsibilities and how complying with the court's request necessarily places you in violation of those responsibilities (APA, 2010, ss.4.05 and 9.04; NASW, 2008, s.1.07(j)).

How does a clinician handle confidential information that comes her way even though she has not asked for it? Consider an example where Evelyn has completed her court testimony as an expert witness. The court has made a decision about Debra's custody and visitation, but now Philip has gone back to court for an increase in visitation periods. Philip's lawyer, Alice, asks Frieda to release her updated treatment information to Evelyn. For the sake of argument, let us say that Paula agrees to sign the release of information. Should Frieda release her treatment information to the court's witness?

Frieda probably has no ethical issue, because she is responding to a request to release of records by both clients, Philip and Paula. However, what should Evelyn do? Here, again, we have an interesting ethical dilemma.

Evelyn is no longer collecting data, yet she receives data. Evelyn is no longer formulating her opinion for the court; she has completed her task, having already testified. Clinicians who specialize in custody evaluations know that high-conflict parents often relitigate. It is not unusual for a court to order an updated evaluation. Evelyn should probably do two things. The first is to file the information without reading it. The second is to write to the judge, with a copy to each attorney, asking for the court's guidance. In some jurisdictions Evelyn may need to write to the attorneys with a copy to the judge. However, Evelyn probably should do nothing more than file the information until she receives clear directions from the court—not from the attorneys. This is an important point. Evelyn is working for the court in her role as its expert. The instruction to perform further work must come from Evelyn's client, the court, not the attorneys. Although they may place a motion before the court requesting that Evelyn assess the new information, it is the court that should direct Evelyn's activities.

Freedom of Information and Privacy Legislation

Various jurisdictions have freedom of information and protection of privacy legislation (at the federal level, see the Freedom of Information Act, 5 USC 552).[14] These laws regulate access to records held by government agencies and some organizations that receive government funding. Whether an organization is covered depends on its contractual relationship with the government. The legislation tries to balance the interests of an individual's privacy, state security, the public's right to know, and freedom of expression.

Privacy legislation guarantees protection of privacy for certain types of information (e.g., the federal Family Educational Rights and Privacy Act, 2011, for student information). Agencies where the legislation provides specific privacy protection include schools, substance abuse treatment programs, public social services, venereal disease clinics, and other publicly funded medical service providers (Kagle & Kopels, 2008). Professionals who work in these areas cannot release information without explicit written consent of the person who is the subject of the records or upon an order of the court.

The process of applying for information under freedom of information laws is an administrative process with regional differences, so I will not describe the process in detail. Legislation and regulations explain who to contact for access to information, how to apply, and the criteria for granting and denying access (check state websites for the most recent legislation and guidelines). Agency policies should reflect these laws so requests can be processed fairly and efficiently. The fact that a client has obtained

---

[14]For more information about federal freedom of information laws and procedures, see *www. usdoj.gov/foia/04_3.html*.

information under freedom of information laws does not necessarily make you compellable as a witness. Freedom of information and compellability are treated as separate issues.

COMPELLING A CLINICIAN TO DISCLOSE

When an attorney approaches a clinician to provide information for legal proceedings, the attorney will generally prefer to enlist the clinician on a voluntary basis. Because of the clinician's professional obligations to his clients, he may not be able to disclose information without the client's written consent to release the information. Accordingly, if an attorney takes steps to legally compel you to disclose information, you may wish to challenge a subpoena or motion to compel. Remember, just because you have been subpoenaed does not mean that you must provide what is requested by the subpoena. You are legally required to respond to a subpoena. One appropriate response is to file a "motion to quash." In it, you may explain to the court why protection of your client's confidential information is critical to maintaining the integrity of the therapeutic relationship. It might be useful to present an argument concerning why the need to protect the information is more important than the need to disclose the information. The legal system often examines the relative merits or weights of conflicting arguments. If you can make a strong case about the harm or detriment caused by the disclosure, such an argument might outweigh the value of disclosing the information, or at least disclosing the information in the manner requested by the attorney asking for the information.

If the court agrees with your argument, then you may not have to disclose any information. Alternatively, you may file a "protective order"[15]

---

[15]Under the U.S. Code Title 28, Federal Rule 26(c)(1),

> The court may, for good cause, issue an order to protect a party or person from annoyance, embarrassment, oppression, or undue burden or expense, including one or more of the following:
> (A) forbidding the disclosure or discovery;
> (B) specifying terms, including time and place, for the disclosure or discovery;
> (C) prescribing a discovery method other than the one selected by the party seeking discovery;
> (D) forbidding inquiry into certain matters, or limiting the scope of disclosure or discovery to certain matters;
> (E) designating the persons who may be present while the discovery is conducted;
> (F) requiring that a deposition be sealed and opened only on court order;
> (G) requiring that a trade secret or other confidential research, development, or commercial information not be revealed or be revealed only in a specified way; and
> (H) requiring that the parties simultaneously file specified documents or information in sealed envelopes, to be opened as the court directs. (*www.law.cornell.edu/ uscode/html/uscode28a/usc_sec_28a_02000026----000-.html*)

under which the court may limit what information you need to share or may agree to review the information *in camera* (in private) in order to determine whether the information should be shared in public court. If the court orders you to provide the requested information, you may state for the court record that you have an ethical obligation to maintain the confidentiality of the communication, but that you are providing the information in accordance with the court's order (APA, 2010, s.4.05; NASW, 2008, ss.1.07[j] and 3.09[c]). There are times when you may feel strongly about an issue and decide to disobey the order of the court for moral reasons. In doing so, you would put yourself at peril, legally and ethically. Legally, if you are in contempt of court, you could be fined or imprisoned. Ethically, you could face discipline or expulsion from your professional regulatory organization.

Before you respond to any request to provide information to an attorney or the court, stop and think about how disclosure of this information may fit into the larger picture. In some cases, you may be relieved to receive a court order because it takes the burden off you to decide whether to disclose. For example, Michael could have had concerns about Frieda's methods of practice, but the Carveys may not have provided permission to release any information about such concerns. No matter how strong Michael's feelings may be about the importance of reporting Frieda to a licensing board or professional association, if the client holds the privilege of the communication and decides not to consent to release such information, Michael has no choice but to respect the wishes of the client. On the other hand, if Michael were compelled by court order to disclose information about Frieda's practices, then he would be allowed to discuss his concerns in a forum that encourages scrutiny and responsibility.

Some clinicians feel unsettled about being compelled by court order to release information. They may feel anxious about testifying. They may feel concerned about their own work coming under attack. They may feel uneasy about having to provide information about a client and the effects such disclosure may have on the therapeutic relationship.

There are a variety of ways a clinician may be required to provide testimony or to disclose records. These include warrants, subpoenas, and applications for disclosure, production, or discovery. You should obtain legal advice if you plan to challenge any of these processes. Different tribunals have different degrees of authority to compel witnesses. Typically criminal courts have the greatest authority. Some tribunals have no authority to compel witnesses.

Warrants

A search warrant is a court order permitting police to search a particular location or property to investigate a crime. The police may gather evidence for use in subsequent criminal proceedings. In order to receive a warrant, police must show probable cause that a crime has been committed. The court may restrict the scope of the search in order to limit infringement on civil rights. Warrants are generally not used to gain access to a client's records.[16] If you as a clinician are not a suspect in an investigation, you are less likely to be presented with a search warrant than to receive a subpoena or an application for discovery.

Subpoenas

A subpoena is a summons requiring you (the recipient of the subpoena) to appear before a court or other hearing at a particular date, time, and place to give testimony for a particular case.[17] A subpoena may also require you to bring relevant records and documents to a hearing. You may not have to testify or disclose your records upon receipt of a subpoena, but you should respond either through compliance or a legal challenge. If a subpoena is issued by a court, then the subpoena is equivalent to a court order; often, subpoenas are issued not by the court, but by an attorney or other person acting as an officer of the court. A subpoena issued by an attorney or other officer of the court is not equivalent to a court order; you may not have to testify or turn over your documents unless the subpoena has been challenged and upheld by a court. Consult with your attorney to help you decide whether to provide the information required by the subpoena or to respond with a motion to quash, request an *in camera* review, or pursue some other remedy (NASW, 2008, s.1.07[j]; Polowy, Morgan, & Gilbertson, 2005).[18] Refusal to comply with a subpoena is considered contempt of court, with possible punishments including fines or incarceration. On the other hand, if you disclose a client's confidential information without proper authorization from the client or order of the court, you are placing yourself at risk of a malpractice lawsuit, sanctions from a professional association or state licensing board, or penalties imposed by the Office of Civil Rights for violating the Privacy Rule of the Health Insurance Portability and Accountability Act (1996, Parts 160 and 164) (Bernstein & Hartsell, 2005).

To illustrate, consider a situation in which one parent, Philip, asks his family counselor, Frieda, to provide her clinical records so he can use them

---

[16]Police are most likely to use warrants to search an accused person's case files if the person is currently incarcerated or has been incarcerated.

[17]The term "subpoena" is generally used in criminal hearings; other types of proceedings may issue a "notice to attend" or similar instrument. For simplicity, the term *subpoena* is used throughout this volume. Chapter 6 also discusses subpoenas that require submission of client records.

[18]If you are providing health services, then the Health Insurance Portability and Accountability Act (1996) may specifically require that the patient be provided with written notice of the subpoena and an opportunity to raise objections with the court or administrative tribunal.

in an upcoming family court trial. The other parent, Paula, refuses to provide Frieda with consent to release such confidential information. Philip's attorney, Alice, subpoenas Frieda's treatment notes and assessment information. Frieda realizes that failure to respond to the subpoena may result in charges of contempt of court and penalties. On the other hand, Frieda has an ethical responsibility to keep Paula's information confidential. So how can Frieda respond to this dilemma?

Let us say that Frieda files a motion to quash and the judge determines Frieda needs to turn over the information to Alice in spite of Paula's continued refusal to release Frieda to do so. Although Frieda should respond to the court's order to release the information, she also has a responsibility to provide an explanation of her professional ethics and responsibility that is read into the formal record of the trial. In this statement to the court, Frieda says, "I have informed the court of my ethical responsibility to maintain the confidentiality of my professional communications with Frieda. Confidentiality is a cornerstone of my practice, as it offers clients a safe and trusting environment to discuss difficult personal issues. Given my professional ethics, I do not agree with the court's decisions, though I will reluctantly comply with the court's order."

If you are served with a subpoena, you may not have to turn over your files nor speak with the attorneys for either party prior to your attendance at the hearing (NASW Legal Defense Fund, 2009). However, *depending upon your role*, you may decide to meet with a "friendly attorney" or to share information prior to the hearing. Cooperating with an attorney may facilitate settlement and help both you and the attorney prepare for the hearing. If someone other than your client's attorney issues the subpoena, you should inform your client that you have received a subpoena. You may also need to contact your client's attorney upon proper consent. The attorney and you may discuss what steps you plan to take. If the client provides oral consent for you to testify, obtain a written authorization specifying that the client waives privilege and confidentiality.

If your client does not have an attorney and you receive a subpoena for her records, advise the client to obtain independent legal advice. If your client intends to claim privilege, be careful about providing information to the attorneys in advance of the hearing. If you provide information to the attorney for one party, that attorney may have to disclose the information to the attorney for the other party.

There are three potential advantages to being subpoenaed:

- Because the subpoena requires you to testify, you may be viewed as a more objective witness than if you were to cooperate voluntarily with one side.
- If you receive a court-issued subpoena (or an attorney-issued

subpoena that is challenged and upheld by the court), then you are protected from a client's claim that you breached confidentiality when you testify.

- If the subpoena specifies that you are being asked to testify as an expert, then legislation in most states requires that you be paid. If you are subpoenaed by one side, it is that side's responsibility to pay your fees. If you are subpoenaed by the court, it may be the responsibility of the court to pay your fees.

A party can bring a motion to quash the subpoena on the grounds that the information is privileged, the file is irrelevant, or the subpoena had a technical deficiency (e.g., not complying with state rules regarding the wording of the subpoena). Alternatively, a client may claim privilege at the hearing to prevent a clinician from being compelled to testify. If there is a specific statutory law that says the communication is privileged, then the court should automatically honor this privilege. If there is no statutory privilege, then the judge has the discretion to decide privilege on a case-by-case basis (as described earlier). One factor is whether the information is needed to determine the case, as balanced against the interests of protecting the confidentiality of the professional relationship. Factors that weigh in favor of making the information available to the court include the seriousness of the issues (e.g., a criminal case with charges of murder) and the lack of other sources of evidence. Factors that weigh in favor of excluding the evidence include the following: people should be encouraged to make use of certain professionals; confidentiality is required to maintain the relationship; the community values this type of relationship; and the harms caused by disclosure are greater than the related benefits. This last factor may be the primary issue to be determined. Another criterion is whether the information to be presented provides information that is more probative than prejudicial. That is, is the information to be presented to the court important to the factual basis of the case, or is it more likely to elicit an emotional response from those who would hear it (such as jurors) that might color how they view the client?

Consider a case in which Philip is charged with physically assaulting Paula. If Philip had been participating in an anger management group, the group facilitator might have information that could help the prosecution prove that Philip committed the alleged offense. In spite of this benefit, a court might be hesitant about compelling the clinician to testify. Such a disclosure would surely discourage Philip (and others like him) from seeking therapeutic help for anger and violent behavior. Because other sources of evidence are available, including Paula's testimony and physical evidence of assault, the harm caused by forcing disclosure is greater than its benefits.

Even when a clinician is compelled to disclose information, there are ways to limit the harm from disclosure. For example, the attorneys could meet with the judge in her chambers to decide whether particular information should be disclosed and, if so, how. The judge could restrict the scope of the questioning to topics that are most relevant and least disturbing (e.g., the minimum necessary). Further, she could limit who is present at the hearing or prohibit publication by newspapers, television, and other media. For client records, the court may allow the clinician to submit a summary rather than the whole file. Alternatively, the court may limit disclosure to only those parts of the file that are directly relevant to the case. These decisions are based on balancing the client's right to privacy, the public's right to know, and the accused's right to a fair trial. As noted above, this area of law is full of controversy and in a state of flux. Accordingly, obtaining legal advice would be wise, should you or your client have questions about a particular case.

Under the USA Patriot Act (2001), the Federal Bureau of Investigation may apply for a court order to obtain client records for the purpose of investigating possible terrorist activities. Note that this type of subpoena is different from a traditional subpoena to provide records to court. Under the Patriot Act, if a clinician receives a subpoena, the clinician is not allowed to inform clients that the FBI has requested their records. This means that you may need to turn over your records without client notification or consent.

Other Applications for Disclosure, Production, or Discovery

After a legal proceeding has been initiated, a party may bring forward other types of applications to compel a clinician to disclose confidential information. Applications for pretrial disclosure, production of documents, or discovery are intended to enable each party to access information that may most affect its case.[19] Further, a defendant in a case is entitled to know the case that may be brought against her, so there are no surprises at the hearing. These pretrial disclosure processes may make it easier for the parties to settle the case before trial. (Discovery processes are discussed further in Chapter 10.)

In criminal proceedings, an accused party initiates a disclosure application by serving the clinician or her agency with the application. It will state what documents are being requested and the reasons for the request.[20]

---

[19]Note that in criminal cases, only the defense can request and receive disclosure. The defense does not need to reveal its case to the prosecution, except in rare cases.

[20]In most cases, the prosecution just hands over copies of all of its documents. This makes it unnecessary for an application for disclosure to go before a judge.

The client and the prosecution should also receive notice, so that they can speak to the issue. A judge will hear the application. Although you are not required to attend the hearing to determine disclosure, you need to decide whether to appear in court and whether to have an attorney represent you. You may have concerns about the impact of disclosure on your client (e.g., stress, embarrassment, loss of trust). You may also have independent concerns (e.g., whether the records identify other clients, such as family or group members; your ability to produce the documents; whether the records will be used to impugn your reputation). In some cases, professional associations and victim advocate groups have asked for standing to present arguments in such hearings or have helped pay for a clinician's attorney.

The court will deal with arguments about the relevance of the documents and claims for privilege. Since the Supreme Court ruling in *Jaffe v. Redmond* (1996), the clinical records of psychotherapists have been deemed privileged. However, for client records where privilege is in question, the judge may privately review the documents as part of her decision-making process. If the judge determines certain records should not be disclosed, they may still be kept in a sealed envelope and retained by the court until all court proceedings are exhausted. Retaining the documents allows the court to access them if issues are raised during trial that require disclosure. Find out in advance whether the court wants your original records or whether copies are acceptable. If the court requests originals, be sure to keep copies for yourself.

When a criminal court considers an application for disclosure, it must balance the client's right to privacy and the accused's right to a fair trial. The defense must establish that information contained in the records is "likely to be relevant" to the legal issues in the case and "material to the defense." Courts have said they will discourage fishing expeditions as well as obstructive and time-consuming requests for information. This is a particular concern where the defense is harassing a victim-witness.

When assessing whether client records must be produced, a court may consider the following factors:

- The extent to which the record is necessary for the accused to make a full answer and defense.
- The probative value of the record (i.e., the soundness of the information as evidentiary proof).
- Whether a client could reasonably expect the record to remain private.
- Whether production of the record would be premised on any discriminatory belief or bias.

- Potential harm to the client's dignity or privacy arising from production of the record.
- The terms of any statutory provisions that provide for confidentiality or privilege of information for certain licensed clinicians, or in specific contexts such as drug and alcohol programs, mental health settings, domestic violence shelters, and schools (Dickson, 1995).

To minimize intrusion into privacy if a court orders records to be produced, the judge may edit what may be disclosed, limit who may have copies, and specify how copies will be returned to their original custodian when court proceedings are completed.[21] If pretrial production is ordered, this information will probably be admissible in court during trial; however, the attorneys, parties, or witnesses may challenge admissibility again during trial.

CONCLUSION

You do not want to be caught off guard when an attorney or client initially raises a concern that has legal implications. Basically you need to consider four questions:

1. "What are my legal and professional obligations in terms of client confidentiality, privilege, and protection of individuals from harm to themselves or others?"
2. "How do I respond to a complaint in a manner that is most likely to satisfy the complainant's concerns without putting myself or others at risk [psychologically, physically, legally, or financially]?"
3. "When information about a client is requested, should I provide the information voluntarily or refuse until I am required to do so by law [e.g., through a court order and upon risk of being held in contempt of court]?"
4. "Should I contact my attorney, supervisor, colleague, insurer, or professional association for advice and support?"

Watch for red flags in your everyday practice that suggest that you should seek legal consultation. In some situations the need for legal advice is quite obvious: being served with a claim, subpoena, or other legal

---

[21]Bring copies and your original records to the hearing. If you are prepared to testify that the copy is an exact (true) one, then the judge may allow you to keep the originals and provide copies to the other parties.

document; being confronted by a client who is hostile or otherwise demonstrates a proclivity to litigation; and identifying a situation where you may have caused emotional, physical, or financial damage to a client. Other situations will require your best judgment call—for example, a father coming into treatment to talk about what children need when living with only one parent, or a mother refusing to allow you to read relevant documents on advice of her attorney. Err on the safe side.

Ideally, you will have a trusted attorney on retainer who is readily accessible for consultation. In addition, your practice will have established policies that provide guidelines for confidentiality and how to respond to various legal contingencies.

Chapter 4

PREPARATION FOR LEGAL PROCEEDINGS

Assume that you have agreed to cooperate with a "friendly attorney" who has contacted you as a potential witness and that you have dealt with any concerns about confidentiality.[1] In some situations, the attorney will inform you about the time and location of the hearing, but provide little other information. If your role as a witness is relatively minor and straightforward, this may be sufficient. For example, Michael may be called to testify about his knowledge that Philip and Paula attended mediation. If the rest of Michael's information is deemed privileged,[2] meeting with the attorney in advance may be unnecessary. If you are called as a witness and believe that a meeting with an attorney would be useful, do not hesitate to ask for one. There is always a balancing act required. In this case, the balancing act is between the need to consult with the attorney and the costs of such a meeting to your client. Remember that the attorney is being paid by her client for time spent on the case. So if you ask for a meeting, it will cost your client money. Consider ways to avoid running up costs: make a list of topics for discussion in advance, communicate via e-mail or telephone rather than in person, keep discussions focused, and minimize travel

---

[1]This chapter focuses on preparations for fact witnesses. Additional preparations for expert witnesses are handled in Chapter 7.

[2]As explored further in Chapter 3, privilege refers to a legal concept that protects certain witnesses from being compelled to testify about information learned in a special relationship, such as an attorney–client relationship and some therapist–client relationships (depending on the applicable laws in each state and for each profession)

when you do meet in person.[3] Attorneys often prefer meetings at their own offices.

Before meeting with the attorney, review your case notes and ensure that they are in order. "Tampering" with notes may be considered an obstruction of justice, so do not make changes to original documents, including whiting out, deleting, or destroying them. Missing pages and different writing styles are easy tip-offs to tampering. If you need to make corrections or additions, then write your new notes in a way that clearly shows they were added after the fact. State your reasons for the corrections or additions and include the date when you recorded them. These steps will show that you are not trying to conceal something. Prepare an executive summary for yourself as a way to focus your thoughts and describe the order of events. Bring notes, documentation, and questions that you want to discuss with the attorney.

When you arrange a meeting, ask the attorney about her purposes for the meeting. Typically, if an attorney wants to meet with you at this stage, it is to gather information to build her case, to test your credibility, and to determine whether to call you as a witness. Your information may facilitate a negotiated agreement or be used at a trial of the issues. It is often useful to ask the attorney to define a set of questions that she wants you to address. This would allow you to consider your answers prior to meeting.

This chapter begins with a description of the processes of gathering information and the decision about whether to call a clinician as a witness. The latter part of this chapter illustrates how a clinician can prepare for a particular legal proceeding once he knows he is going to be called as a witness.

GATHERING INFORMATION

When gathering information, the attorney wants to know as much about the case as possible.[4] Accordingly, she will ask for information that is both favorable and unfavorable to her client's case. Both you and the attorney have a mutual interest in finding out "what really happened," although either of you may have a propensity to color the truth in favor of your

---

[3]Some law firms try to contain legal costs by employing junior attorneys for the preparation phase. A junior attorney may have more time to spend and provide competent services. If you are working with a junior attorney and have any concerns, raise them with the junior attorney first, but do not hesitate to contact the attorney who is ultimately responsible for the case, if need be.

[4]This section describes an in-depth process of gathering information. In many cases, due to time, cost, and other practical considerations, this process is abridged.

client. When you meet with the attorney, be clear and deliberate about the role you are playing—are you an advocate for your client, a fact witness, or an expert witness? Even when acting as an advocate, if you were to lie or withhold certain information, you would likely be acting unethically or illegally.[5] Further, such actions may come back to haunt you in later proceedings.

To facilitate information gathering, the attorney will ideally engage you in a way that enables you to open up and recall events as accurately as possible. An effective interviewer will begin by asking general questions, followed by closed or focused questions to elicit more detail. Accordingly, the beginning of the interview will provide the best opportunity to give an overview of information you think is relevant. Because focused questions may sometimes lead to a distorted view, try to remember the facts as accurately as possible and avoid the temptation of telling the attorney exactly what you think she most wants to hear. It is much better to confront the attorney with adverse or qualified information at this stage than to allow surprises to arise at later stages of the proceedings.

As the attorney asks more focused questions, you may become aware of the issues that are important from a legal perspective—what evidence is needed to defend against fraud, discrimination, deportation, negligence, breach of contract, or whatever issue is at stake. An attorney builds his case by identifying the relevant legal issues and the evidence required to establish the allegations or defense. The parties may agree on some facts. If the case goes to a hearing, each side only has to prove the facts in dispute. If the information you provide is solid or indisputable, you may not have to be called as a witness, as both parties will likely accept your information as fact. Such agreement is called a stipulation. The parties may stipulate that your information be admitted as evidence without asking you to testify.

The attorney may try to obtain your version of what happened by taking you through a historical reconstruction of events in chronological order. Since most adjudications focus on what happened in the past, the attorney will want to know what information you have concerning critical incidents.

This area of inquiry may hold significant areas of concern for you. Typically, your testimony is about what a client has reported to you about an event that has occurred outside of the therapy office. Your so-called version of what happened, in fact, is your interpretation and recitation of what you have been told by the client about what happened. It is likely not

---

[5]Some would say lying or withholding information is always unethical. However, others would say there are some rare exceptions where a value higher than honesty can ethically justify dishonesty (e.g., to save a life) (Dolgoff, Loewenberg, & Harrington, 2009).

a direct observation of the alleged event in question. Do not get caught up in trying to argue for the truth of your client's version as repeated to you during therapy. Your knowledge is limited to what the client reported about an event. Your knowledge is about the client's representation of a specific event rather than about your independent impressions vis-à-vis the event unless you were present to witness the event itself.

In court processes, clinician-witnesses are not generally responsible for judging the credibility of other witnesses, including the credibility of their clients. The role of determining the credibility of a witness is left to the trier of fact, either the judge or the jury. The clinician's role is to provide information that may be helpful to the trier of fact. If you are admitted as an expert witness, you may provide testimony concerning the reliability of particular witnesses and their evidence (Skeem, Douglas, & Lilienfeld, 2009). If you are admitted as a fact witness, however, your role is to provide factual information. Technically, a fact witness may not provide opinions. Therefore, if you are asked to testify as a fact witness, you may be unable to act as an advocate. Since an advocate holds an opinion about the rightness of a particular perspective, the role of an advocate is to argue a position rather than act as an impartial witness. It is therefore not within the province of a fact witness to testify as an advocate.[6]

Although some attorneys are quite formal when they interview witnesses, this process is much different than being examined or cross-examined at a hearing. The range of information that you discuss with the attorney will be much broader than what would be permissible in a hearing. In private discussions with the attorney you are generally freer to reflect without as much concern for being clear, concise, and entirely consistent. The attorney will use these early discussions to determine which information is relevant, admissible, and necessary to be presented if the case proceeds to a hearing.

To enhance your ability to recall the therapy sessions, the attorney may ask you to review exhibits filed in court or go back through your notes. Such requests may be annoying if you believe that you have already related everything you know. However, if you comply with such suggestions, you may well be surprised at what else you remember.

In addition to asking you to reflect on your notes, you or your attorney might be tempted to use visualization or other recall aids to enhance your memory. The problem with using recall aids is that they may taint your memory, making your testimony more suspect at trial. Most clinicians are aware of the highly suggestible nature of memory recollection in young

---

[6]For further information about the definition and testimonial limitations of fact and expert witnesses, consult either the Federal Rules of Evidence or your state's evidence code.

children (Bruck & Ceci, 2009; Gould & Martindale, 2009). There also is considerable research indicating similar suggestibility for adult memories (Loftus & Ketcham, 1991). Thus, providing testimony about information that was retrieved using a memory aid such as visualization or hypnosis may leave you open to attacks on the reliability of the information, as well as on your credibility as a professional who appears unaware of relevant research pertaining to information retrieval and recall. Bottom line: stick to what you know and what is in your notes.

You may be asked to relate specific incidents and examples by breaking up large events into smaller components. The seemingly mundane detail requested by attorneys may frustrate you. Remember the level of detail a witness can provide is used as evidence that the witness recalls an event accurately. If an attorney focuses on discrete events, you may feel she is losing sight of the big picture. Although the attorney will have reasons for her line of questions, this is a time when you can raise your concerns about the broader picture. For example, Alice may ask Frieda questions about isolated incidents in which Paula made threats toward Philip. Frieda may need to help Alice consider the broader context of these outbursts: Paula's reaction to separation, fears that her daughter would be abducted, and her limited knowledge of her legal rights.

It is important to remember that when people do not recall details of events they often fill in the blanks with information that makes sense either from the perspective of today's recall or based on knowledge of situations that are similar to those of the particular event. Unless you have a clear memory represented in written notes, you are on somewhat shaky ground in providing such testimony. We know from memory research that human beings tend to fill in blanks with information drawn from their experience in similar situations. We also know that such memory completion tasks may make one feel as though one is accurately representing the past event—and yet be highly inaccurate. For example, drawing on the memory research on mothers and children, we know that when asked to immediately recall their young children's statements, mothers were notoriously inaccurate in recalling the statements verbatim. They were very good at recalling the general meaning of the statement—called gist memory—but they were very poor at recalling the specific words accurately (Bruck, Ceci, & Francoeur, 1999).

The conclusion is that taking contemporaneous notes during a session and providing only the information drawn from those sessions during testimony best serve clinicians.[7] The further away from the event, the more

---

[7]Research indicates that even verbatim contemporaneous notes are susceptible to numerous mistakes when matched against audio recordings of those same interview sessions (Lamb, Orbach, Sternberg, Hershkowitz, & Horowitz, 2000).

likely that the memory of the event has been affected by other experiences. It is difficult to testify about your memory of an historical event, given that your memory may be clouded by months or years of intervening therapy with the client as well as therapy with other clients. Be prepared for an attorney to challenge your memory as well as your professional awareness of memory functioning, suggestibility, and note taking.

The attorney may ask about practices and events that are of such a normal course that you do not even remember doing them. As a common practice, for example, you as a therapist may routinely screen for suicidal and homicidal ideation. Nonetheless, your notes may not indicate you did a screening unless during the session there was an indication of a crisis. In such circumstances, information on general practices will be useful for the attorney if she wants to establish that the client was not homicidal.

This is a critical point to scrutinize. If your testimony includes that you followed your usual and customary procedures during a treatment session (including screening for suicidal and homicidal ideation), then your written notes should reflect this. If you do not have a written record of such inquiry, be careful that your testimony differentiates between your general practice and the specific practice behaviors reflected in your notes for this particular case.

Try to separate what you know firsthand from what you know from other sources. This may direct the attorney to other sources of evidence, including witnesses, records, or documents. If you are reluctant to testify, identifying other sources may provide an opportunity for the attorney to find a more willing witness. Ideally, you will talk with these potential witnesses about their willingness to testify *before* you provide the attorney with their names and phone numbers. It is a professional courtesy to provide colleagues with such notice, so they can be prepared for a call from the attorney.

To facilitate information gathering, it is helpful if the attorney is familiar with scientific knowledge from your field of clinical practice. Sam, for example, can help to educate the attorney for his child protection agency about current research findings about the physical and psychological attributes most closely associated with child maltreatment. It might also be important to provide the attorney with rival but plausible alternative perspectives that undercut or contradict the current conventional wisdom. In this way, the attorney can be made more knowledgeable about the strengths and weaknesses of current research as well as possible professional controversy that may surround the research (e.g., prediction of dangerousness). This incremental knowledge will enable the attorney to ask more informed questions. Although you may feel knowledgeable about the law, be careful about wresting control of the information-gathering process from the attorney. Telling a lawyer how to do her job may be analogous to a client who comes to you with a little knowledge about psychology and then tries to tell you how to conduct psychotherapy with him.

Just as it is helpful for an attorney to understand your scientific and professional knowledge, it is also helpful for you to enhance your knowledge of the relevant laws. As a witness, you can focus your evidence more appropriately if you know what information is significant from the attorney's perspective. Ask the attorney for information about case law, statutes, and local rules that are relevant to your testimony.[8] Also, ask about what *not* to say on the stand. In a personal injury case, for example, an attorney might advise a witness not to testify about his conclusions, as these might adversely affect the size of the monetary award.

Familiarity with one another's jargon will help you avoid miscommunication, particularly when legal definitions of terms differ from psychological or sociological meanings. Remember to ask questions about how attorneys use words that appear familiar to us as mental health professionals. For example, when Art talks to Evelyn about "competence," Evelyn initially thinks he is referring to her professional competence as an evaluator. As the conversation continues, she discovers Art was referring to Debra's mental capacity and legal decision-making status. Asking for definitions will help clarify what specific information you are being asked to discuss. For another example, consider the term *reliability*. In legal parlance, when an attorney asks about the reliability of eyewitness evidence, he is asking whether the eyewitness's memory, recall, and honesty is worthy of being trusted. In psychology and behavioral sciences, reliability may refer more specifically to consistency within an experiment; for instance, one can prove strong inter-rater reliability if different raters using the same psychometric test arrive at the same answer. When interacting with attorneys, do not assume that just because you are both using the same words that you are necessarily speaking the same language or communicating the same thoughts!

SENSITIVE INFORMATION

Even when you have a client's permission to discuss confidential information with the attorney, be cautious about *how* you share sensitive information.

---

[8]See "Websites for Legal Research" in the Resources section for a list of websites to help clinicians access this information themselves. Although you may be able to do some of your own legal research to gain a general understanding of the law, specific legal research requires training to ensure you are accessing the most current, relevant laws. One of my favorite free-access legal websites is *www.law.cornell.edu*, which allows you to search for statutes, case law, and dictionary definitions of legal terms.

Set conditions, as needed, on how that information might be used. For example, if you share information about your client with her attorney, is the attorney permitted to share the information with the client? Do you have an ethical obligation to disclose such information to your client before you talk with the attorney? Assume Sam is concerned about Paula's safety. To protect her safety, he asks the attorney not to tell Philip where Paula is staying. If you need to establish terms of confidentiality for the sake of someone's safety or mental welfare, then negotiate and document these terms before disclosing sensitive information.

In a variation, if you share opinions rather than simply facts with the attorney, do you have a responsibility to share those same opinions with your client? Do you have an obligation to discuss those opinions with your client *before* talking with the attorney? In determining how to approach these questions, be clear about your primary responsibility. As a clinician, your primary responsibility is to your client. Therefore, any opinions expressed to your client's attorney should be discussed first with your client, both as a matter of ethics as well as a matter of common courtesy. By reviewing with your client all that you expect to say to her attorney, you define the limits of what you will discuss and provide an opportunity to work with your client on how such information is to be presented to someone outside of the treatment session. This type of review provides the client with a greater sense of safety and trust.

Conversely, an attorney may be unable to tell you everything about a case due to attorney–client privilege or for strategic reasons. The attorney may have investigated you before the interview to explore your knowledge and motivation. She may not want to tell you too much in order to hear what you have to say untainted by any information she may provide. Another reason an attorney may not share information or strategy with you is to avoid problems in cross-examination. If the attorney shares strategic information with you, you may be required to disclose that information during cross-examination. If you find the attorney is withholding important information from you, feel free to inquire about the reasons for doing so.

THE DECISION TO CALL YOU AS A WITNESS

During the information-gathering process, the attorney will assess whether to call you as a witness. At this point, there is no ownership of witnesses. If the attorney who initially interviews you decides not to call you as a witness, the attorney for the other party may still call you. Whether you respond to the second attorney's call depends on the nature of the relationship between you and the first attorney. If you have been hired by the first attorney, any communication acknowledging your involvement may be privileged. If you have not been hired by the first attorney, you may be free to talk with the second attorney.

Two questions will determine whether you will be called as a witness: Do you have useful evidence, and will you make an effective witness? In terms of the first question, the attorney will consider whether you have any observations that are vital to proving his case. (The attorney may also want you to present opinion evidence, as described in Chapter 7 on expert witnesses.) The attorney will have to decide whether any other sources can provide the same information as you and compare the strength of each source. For example, if the choice is between a live witness and written information, the attorney may decide to enter the documents as evidence, because the attorney can never be sure what a witness will say on the stand. More than one source of information may be needed to prove certain facts, so you could be called to attest to the information in a document or to corroborate the testimony of another witness. Although some hearings go on for months or years, most hearings are short-lived, typically taking hours rather than days. There are also pressures to keep costs down, which may limit the number of witnesses to be called. Finally, the attorney should consider whether the tribunal will make certain inferences if a particular witness is not called to testify.

As noted in Chapter 2, an effective witness is one who is *credible*. To assess your credibility, the attorney may consider your motivation, perception, memory, and communication skills. See Figure 4.1 for examples of issues that the attorney may explore.

- *Motivation*: How cooperative will you be as a witness? How objective are your information and beliefs? Do you have a financial or emotional interest in the outcome of the case? Will you be perceived as having biases toward one party or the other? How do you define your therapeutic role (e.g., supportive, confrontational)? Have you been engaged in dual relationships with the client or other stakeholders in the case?

- *Perception*: How accurate is your perception of what happened (e.g., accuracy of sight, hearing, interpretation of stimuli)? What were the effects of environmental and circumstantial factors affecting perception (e.g., lighting, noise, fatigue, stress, or biases from the clinician's theoretical perspective)? Did you observe the information directly, or is it secondhand information?

- *Memory*: How accurate is your recall? How certain are you about your facts?

- *Communication skills*: How well can you articulate your recollections? Are you able to focus on the facts? How well do you communicate under pressure?

FIGURE 4.1. Assessing credibility as a witness.

To ascertain your credibility, the attorney will not ask these questions directly, but will look for subtle indicators: Do you tend to agree with the questioner? Is your story consistent? Do you have past experiences that may color your perceptions? How have you testified in previous cases? While your interview with the attorney in private is not a cross-examination, questions about your credibility may help prepare you for cross-examination at a hearing. She may ask you, for example, "How do you remember this client so clearly?" Try to be direct and honest with the attorney. Consider an information-gathering meeting between Alice and Frieda. Frieda might become defensive if Alice asked about her methods of assessment. If Frieda can be open about the deficiencies in her assessment, Alice can help with how to confront them to minimize embarrassment when Frieda is testifying. If Frieda discloses her biases, Alice and Frieda can deal with these, possibly deciding to find a less biased clinician to testify instead of Frieda.

The attorney may be blunt with you concerning whether you will be a useful witness. You may find this uncomfortable. In most legal processes, attorneys decide who will be called as a witness.[9] If you believe that you should be called, but the attorneys indicate that you will not, secure legal advice to determine whether there is a means for you to participate in the hearing (e.g., by preparing an *amicus curiae* [friend-of-the-court] brief).

On the other hand, you may be reluctant to testify. If you want to dissuade the attorney from calling you as a witness, you could exhibit poor memory, poor clinical skills, or evidence contrary to the attorney's case. If any of these portrayals is fictitious, consider the potential consequences.[10] Even leaving aside the ethical questions and professional obligations, consider whether you will really achieve what you intend. For example, a sexuality therapist might consider "intentionally forgetting" everything that happened in her clinical intervention with a particular client who would not want information about her sexuality divulged in court. Does this really advance the client's interests? If the therapist's performance of incompetence is accepted, how will this affect the therapist's reputation in the community and with the professional regulatory association? Are there any alternatives to protect the client's interests? Could the therapist talk to the attorney about her reluctance to testify?

Even if an attorney initially decides to call you as a witness, you may not actually have to testify. The case may settle before or even during a

---

[9]For investigatory processes, an investigator or tribunal may decide whom to call as a witness.

[10]Consequences for dishonesty may include being sued by a client or other individual who suffers as a result, being charged with fraud or obstruction of justice, being fired or disciplined by one's employer, and being disciplined by one's professional association. Also consider societal obligations as a citizen to act in a manner that promotes social justice.

hearing. Alternatively, the other party may admit the facts to which you were to testify, negating the need to call you as a witness.

SIGNED STATEMENTS

There are times when an attorney may request that you sign a statement attesting to the information you provided. A signed statement serves several purposes. If the statement is about a recent event, it may be used later to refresh your memory or to support your evidence. Providing a written statement ensures that you focus your thoughts and commit to a specific version of what happened. On the downside, a signed statement may be used to find inconsistencies in your evidence at a subsequent hearing. The statement could also make you feel that you cannot add to or change your testimony later on. If you do want to make changes, advise the attorney as soon as possible.

Do not feel pressured into signing a statement. Let the attorney know if you need more time to think about what happened or to go over your records. Ask the attorney to prepare a summary of the important facts and give you a copy to review with your agency or attorney. You can then suggest changes and sign the statement only when you feel completely comfortable with the specific language used. If you discover an error in your original statement, it is better to add truthful amendments than to try to appear infallible. As an alternative to a signed statement, you could request that your information be documented through an audio or video recording.

PREPARING FOR A HEARING

Assume you have been subpoenaed or have agreed to participate as a witness and that you are now ready to prepare for testimony. Some attorneys believe too much preparation can hurt the effectiveness of a witness; a witness who is too polished may not come across as credible, while a witness who knows a good deal about the law may second-guess his attorney's strategies. However, an informed witness has a greater sense of control over the process and the capacity to be a better witness. The potential consequences in legal proceedings are too important to risk learning by "trial and error." As a clinician, you endeavor to be competent as a practitioner. In your role as a witness, there is no less reason to strive for competence. In this section we deal with the following components for competence as a witness: What knowledge do you need, what skills can you practice, and how can you psychologically and emotionally prepare yourself? This section also delves into ethical issues that can arise in the context of preparation.

A variety of factors will affect the amount of preparation you will need for a particular case, including your past experience, familiarity with legal processes and issues, confidence in public speaking, reaction to time pressures, outstanding emotional issues, the importance of the issues to be tried, and whether the proceedings will be televised. Regardless of whether you are involved for the first or thousandth time, do not underestimate the value of preparation.

Knowledge

You could ask the attorney calling you as a witness, "What do I need to know to prepare for the hearing?" The attorney may have standard written or oral information to provide you. If you create your own checklist, you can ask informed questions and assume more responsibility for your preparation. In this section I discuss the informational aspects of testimony preparation that may assist you, including information about the hearing process, roles of the participants, rules of evidence, substantive law, case facts, and clinical theory.

The Hearing Process

Although you can learn about the hearing process by asking questions or by reading an excellent book on the topic, observing a similar hearing ahead of time is invaluable preparation. You will gain a feel for the room and the players that can best be found through personal experience: who sits where, how witnesses are called, how witnesses approach the stand, should the witness sit or stand while providing testimony, when does the court take a recess (break), and what is the manner of decorum in the courtroom. Most court processes are open to the public. Some hearings are closed to respect the privacy of participants, for instance, in some child welfare cases. If you ask a clerk or administrator responsible for the hearing, you can often gain admittance to observe a closed hearing for the purposes of professional education. Arrange for someone familiar with the process to attend the hearing with you to point out subtleties and answer questions you may have. Make appointments to meet with various participants in the legal process: investigators, district attorneys and their prosecutors, public defenders or legal aid officials, administrative personnel, or members of the tribunal. Offer to have lunch *with* them (*buying* them lunch may be construed as a payoff or inappropriate influence). You can use such meetings not only to learn about the process but also to develop a positive rapport with key actors prior to being involved in an actual case with them. You can thereby establish your professionalism, competence, and interest in being a good witness.

At the most basic level, you need to know *where* the hearing will take place, *when* you are expected to be there, and even where you can park your car. Courts generally post dockets, which are daily schedules that you can check for the time and room. Find out from your attorney if you need to let a clerk or bailiff know that you are present and what your role in the case is (e.g., plaintiff or witness). You may be permitted to enter the courtroom immediately, or you may be asked to stay in a separate room for witnesses. Your attorney may want you to arrive early to allow for a final briefing or for last-minute settlement negotiations. For expediency, some attorneys refrain from meeting with clients or witnesses until just before the hearing. Although you may encourage your attorney to prepare you in advance, you may need to cooperate with last-minute preparations.

Find out how long you will be expected to wait, the probability of any extended delay, and whether you should wait in the hearing room or outside. Delays can be caused by witnesses not showing up, the testimony of others going overtime, and adjournments for assorted reasons. Bring reading or work that you can do while you wait, though be careful about what you carry onto the witness stand as an attorney may try to bring this into evidence. It may also be prudent to limit what you bring into the courthouse so that you do not have any problems going through metal detectors and security checkpoints. Although you may have little choice about when you will be called as a witness, advise the attorney of the times when you absolutely cannot attend and when you are most readily available. An attorney has ethical obligations to inconvenience witnesses as little as possible and to provide sufficient notice for hearings or other processes. You could ask the attorney, as a matter of "professional courtesy," to telephone you an hour before you are to testify, so you do not have to wait at the courthouse all day. Maintain contact with the attorney prior to your testimony in order to keep up with any changes.

For obvious practical reasons, the best time to be scheduled as a witness is the first thing in the morning. Everyone is fresh and able to focus on your evidence. Also, there is less opportunity for something unforeseen to happen and cause delays. For tactical reasons, other concerns may prevail. For example, the opening and closing witnesses are generally assumed to have the greatest impact on the judge and jurors.

Ask whether any restrictions prior to giving testimony apply to you. Frieda could be asked to stay outside of the hearing room until it is her turn to take the stand. Michael could be asked not to have any further discussions with Philip or Paula. Sam could be sequestered, that is, kept away from the hearing and any other possible sources of information about the case (e.g., media or people involved in the case). The purpose of such restrictions is to ensure that one witness is not influenced by what else is said in or about the hearing. Excluding a witness from the hearing room prior to her testimony is a common procedure. The other restrictions are used sparingly because of their costs and impositions. If a case is likely to attract media attention, ask for advice about how to deal with reporters. Should any reporter actually approach you, a simple "No comment," will normally suffice.

If you are anxious or if this is your first time testifying, consider bringing a support person to sit with while waiting to testify, preferably someone who is calm, reassuring, and sufficiently familiar with the proceedings to answer last-minute questions. If the person is your attorney or an agency colleague, he may also be someone to debrief with afterward (to review your performance on the stand, provide feedback, and help you process any emotional blows). Some clinicians offer to support their clients by sitting with them during the hearing. Although sitting with a client may be desirable from a clinical standpoint, consider possible implications. If Frieda sits with Philip in a custody proceeding, she may appear biased against Paula. Alternatively, Frieda may decide to sit with Philip at a circle sentencing process[11] to demonstrate that she supports him. Consider whether escorting your client will distract you from your function as a witness.

Identify what you need to bring to the hearing. In some cases, the attorney will have organized all the documents you need and filed them with the clerk. You should not bring anything to the stand unless you have arranged to do so with the attorney, because anything you bring to the stand could be examined and admitted as evidence. Check whether any of the following should be filed in court, or whether you should bring them: case notes, client records, relevant books or articles, electronically stored data, and your curriculum vitae.

Roles of Participants

Try to gain a sense of who will be present at the hearing, where everyone will be located, and what their roles will be.[12] In a typical hearing, the *judge* or person chairing the proceedings[13] sits at the front and center of the room, perhaps on an elevated dais. The area where the judge sits is called *the bench*. A *court clerk* and a *court reporter* sit in front of the judge. The clerk (or registrar) assists the judge, ensuring appropriate people are present,

---

[11]This process is an alternative to standard criminal justice proceedings that is used most often in Native American communities.

[12]Knowing the name of each key person may also be useful, since people generally respond more positively when you address them by name (e.g., "Mr. Li," rather than "Sir" or "Counselor"). This also demonstrates that you have a good memory.

[13]For example, administrative judge, justice of the peace, magistrate, referee, commissioner, or hearing officer.

carrying out administrative procedures for the hearing, marking exhibits, and swearing in witnesses. The role of the court reporter (or stenographer) is to create a record of the entire court proceedings. The court reporter may prepare a typed or written transcript during the proceedings, or make an audio or video recording from which a verbatim transcript of the proceedings can be prepared. A *court bailiff* is also stationed near the front of the courtroom. The bailiff's role is to help maintain orderliness in the court: calling court to order, asking people to rise when the judge is about to enter or leave the courtroom, leading jurors in and out of the courtroom, escorting witnesses to the witness stand, ensuring observers remain quiet, and performing administrative tasks as requested by the judge. Sometimes the bailiff is also responsible for swearing in witnesses.

The location where you will testify, the witness stand, is typically in front of the judge and slightly off to one side. Ask your attorney whether you will be standing or sitting when providing your testimony. In most jurisdictions, witnesses sit in a witness box. Find out if you will be speaking into a microphone to amplify your voice or if you will need to speak loud enough to be heard without a microphone. If there is a jury, then the jury box is usually in front of the judge and on the opposite side of the witness. There may be separate tables for each party and their attorneys to sit, located between the judge and the public gallery. A railing or low dividing wall (called *the bar*)[14] separates the area where the court officials and attorneys sit from the public gallery. As a nonparty witness, you will probably sit in the gallery before you are called to testify. If you are testifying as an expert witness, you may be allowed to listen to and incorporate trial testimony into your own testimony. As a fact witness, you may be sequestered to prevent your being influenced by other testimony. Again, ask your attorney in advance to determine where you should wait until you are called. If you do not have a chance to speak with your attorney, you could ask a court clerk.

Security guards or officers may be present. Certain officials in the room may have hidden call buttons in case there is an emergency. If, as a clinician, you are aware of potentially dangerous behavior by a client, consider advising your attorney to arrange for appropriate precautions.[15]

---

[14]Being "called to the bar" refers to the licensure of attorneys who are then permitted to sit in front of the bar in the courtroom and act as legal counsel for their clients.

[15]Clinicians have received death threats from clients who were angry about the information they expected the clinician to introduce into evidence. If you receive threats from a client, do not hesitate to consult with others, such as your attorney or supervisor or the client's attorney, to help assess the threat and to determine what actions to take. Simply refusing to testify would not be an ethical way to resolve the problem.

The judge or equivalent is responsible for chairing the process, ensuring that decorum is maintained, and ruling on any procedural issues. Judges may ask witnesses questions. Depending on the type of tribunal and the issues involved, some adjudicators assume a more active and investigative role. Ask your attorney about the specific predilections or preferences of the judge before whom you will appear. Your attorney may have judge-specific suggestions for how you present yourself and your testimony, as well as for preparing you for the tone that the judge tends to establish for the trial. If there is no jury, the judge also hears the evidence and legal arguments, makes findings of fact and renders decisions by applying relevant laws to the facts, of the case. If there is a jury, then the jury is responsible for making findings of fact, while the judge focuses on managing procedural, evidentiary, and legal issues.

Parties are individuals or institutions that have brought the matter to trial (e.g., a plaintiff or an applicant) or are being brought to trial (e.g., a defendant or a respondent). Each party may represent himself or herself. This is called acting *pro se*. In more formal hearings, parties generally use attorneys. In some proceedings a party may use a nonlawyer advocate. However, in most court proceedings an advocate must be licensed to practice law.

In her role as an advocate, the attorney is expected to decide the legal theory of the case, what evidence to present, and how to present it. She will determine which witnesses to call and the order of the evidence. She will examine the witnesses she calls and cross-examine the witnesses the other party calls. She may object to questions from the other party based on rules of evidence. As a witness, you may feel that you have little control over this process. The more familiar you are with the law and the greater the trust you have built with the attorney, the greater your opportunity to work on a more equal basis with the attorney, at least at this preparation stage. For example, Sam may have suggestions about what evidence tends to be persuasive with a particular judge, or Evelyn may be able to suggest questions that Alice can ask her. The attorney and clinician should recognize the strengths and limitations of the other's training and background, as well as the need to differentiate their roles.

The primary role of a witness is to present information, honestly, under oath or affirmation. An oath or affirmation refers to promising to tell the truth. With a traditional oath, a court bailiff asks witnesses to place their left hand on the Bible, raise their right hand, and respond to the question, "Do you swear to tell the truth, the whole truth, and nothing but the truth, so help you God?" Today, the use of a Bible or other religious texts for taking oaths is uncommon in the U.S. The use of an "affirmation" has become more widespread as it is not based on a particular religious belief system or Bible, for instance, "Do you solemnly swear or affirm under penalty of law that the testimony you will give before this court shall be the truth, the whole truth and nothing but the truth?" The appropriate response is, "I do." If a witness intentionally misleads or lies to the court, the witness may be guilty of the offence of perjury. Under the U.S. Code § 1621, perjury is punishable by a fine or imprisonment up to 5 years.

Rules of Evidence

Evidence is information presented at a hearing to substantiate facts that must be proved before dealing with the legal issues raised by a case (e.g., facts needed to prove refugee status, malpractice, etc.). The basic rule of evidence for witnesses in court[16] is that they may testify only about facts *within their personal knowledge* regarding issues that are *legally relevant* to the case. (Expert witnesses may provide opinion evidence as well as facts; see Chapter 7.) You can skip down to the next section if you want, because evidentiary decisions are complex and ultimately the responsibility of the judge and legal counsel. If you can weed your way through this section, however, it will help you understand what makes "good evidence" and how you can tailor what you say in order to maximize its impact. While actually on the stand, you do not want to become preoccupied with the rules of evidence.

Evidence can be classified in different ways:

- Testimonial versus documentary versus real.
- Direct versus circumstantial versus hearsay.
- Fact versus opinion.

Testimonial evidence is information presented under oath by a live witness at the hearing. *Documentary evidence* consists of client files, written assessments, affidavits, or other records filed or entered into the proceedings at the hearing (see Chapters 6 and 8). *Real (or physical) evidence* includes things that "speak for themselves," for example, a person who shows the court she still has scars or bruising, a picture of a house, or a tape recording of a session. Multiple sources of evidence are often used to corroborate the validity of one another. For example, Sam's records show that

---

[16]Depending on the type of proceeding, there are different standards for what information can be admitted. I focus on court proceedings in this section, as the rules of evidence in this realm are most developed. Even if "questionable" evidence is admissible in other proceedings, information that follows strict rules of evidence will generally have the greatest impact. Criminal proceedings tend to enforce evidentiary rules most strictly. Family court and child protection proceedings tend to be less formal. Administrative and legislative hearings vary greatly but are generally less rigid than criminal hearings about evidence.

Philip behaved in a cooperative manner during his assessment. Sam could also testify to this observation. As a witness, you may be asked to testify about the authenticity of a document or object in order for it to be admitted as evidence ("Yes, these are my records. I recognize my signature"). If there is no controversy of the authenticity of a document or a particular piece of physical evidence, the opposing attorney will allow its admission without requiring a witness to testify about its authenticity.

Direct evidence is information that establishes the proposition without requiring inferences. Consider a case in which the prosecutor wanted to prove that Philip assaulted Debra. If Paula observed him assault Debra, she could provide direct evidence by testifying about what she observed.

Circumstantial evidence requires inferences to prove the proposition. Consider Paula's evidence that Debra had bruises following three weekend visits with her father. Inferences are based on generalizations: children do not generally get bruises only on weekends. Research knowledge can be used to link circumstantial evidence with the propositions trying to be proved: What are the most common causes of bruises for children of Debra's age? Direct evidence is stronger evidence than circumstantial, because contrary inferences can be drawn from circumstantial evidence. A lot of information presented at a hearing is circumstantial. If there were strong direct evidence, then the case would probably be resolved without the need for a full hearing of the issues.

Hearsay evidence is secondhand information offered for the truth of the statement. The person testifying did not directly observe the events being described, and only knows what she has heard from someone who allegedly observed the events. As a general rule, hearsay is inadmissible in court because the person who made the statement is not on the stand and cannot be questioned to check the truth, accuracy, and meaning of the words or their context.

The admissibility of hearsay evidence is particularly confusing because its admissibility often depends on how the information is to be used. Consider a situation where Paula disclosed to Frieda that Philip repeatedly hit Debra. Frieda might not be allowed to testify about what Paula said in order to prove that Philip abused Debra. Frieda might be allowed to testify about what was recorded in her notes. That is, Frieda might be allowed to testify about the fact of the statement being in her notes but not about the truthfulness or falsity of the statement. Paula would be a better witness for this purpose because she is the one who says she observed the alleged abuse. However, if there were a defamation suit against Paula, Frieda could testify that she heard Paula make that statement in order to prove that Paula made those statements.

Several exceptions to the hearsay rule exist. These exceptions arise in contexts where the hearsay statements tend to be reliable. For example, an admission by the accused tends to be reliable because the accused would have no incentive to lie about something that goes against her own interests. Consider a situation in which Philip told the social worker, Sam, "I hit Debra with a shoe when she wouldn't eat dinner." Sam would be permitted to testify about Philip's admission. On the other hand, Sam might not be allowed to testify that Debra's teacher told him that Philip hit his daughter. Another hearsay exception that has particular relevance to clinicians concerns business records, including case notes or progress reports. Records made in the "ordinary course" of clinical work by clinicians at or near the time of contact with the client are admissible even if they contain hearsay. Because the records were kept out of routine rather than in contemplation of a legal action, the contents of the records are likely to be reliable. Other hearsay exceptions are made out of necessity in that there may be no other way to prove certain facts.

An additional hearsay exception relating to expert witnesses is of particular importance to mental health professionals who are asked to provide opinion evidence. Expert witnesses are allowed to rely on and present second-hand information even though it might otherwise be excluded as hearsay (*United States v. Leeson*, 2006). Rule 703 of the Federal Rules of Evidence explains that the information must be of a type reasonably relied upon by other experts in the field:

> The facts or data in the particular case upon which an expert bases an opinion or inference may be those perceived by or made known to the expert at or before the hearing. *If of a type reasonably relied upon by experts in the particular field in forming opinions or inferences upon the subject, the facts or data need not be admissible in evidence in order for the opinion or inference to be admitted.* Facts or data that are otherwise inadmissible shall not be disclosed to the jury by the proponent of the opinion or inference unless the court determines that their probative value in assisting the jury to evaluate the expert's opinion substantially outweighs their prejudicial effect. (emphasis added)

Many tribunals have recognized that putting children on the stand to testify is not in the child's best interest (Skeem et al., 2009). In some cases a clinician will be permitted to interview the child and present the child's statements in the hearing on behalf of the child, notwithstanding the general rule against hearsay.[17]

---

[17]In *Crawford v. Washington* (2004), the U.S. Supreme Court examined limits on the use of hearsay evidence in light of the constitutional right of an accused "to be confronted with the witnesses against him," under the Sixth Amendment. Although this case was not specifically about hearsay evidence from children, it has had a significant impact on how child testimony may be brought into court by forensic experts who have interviewed the child.

An informal exception to the hearsay rule occurs when a tribunal admits hearsay evidence related to facts that are uncontested or unimportant to the ultimate decisions to be made. Often, for the sake of convenience, it is easier to permit hearsay rather than to call additional witnesses and require strict proof of every fact.

When you are a witness, try to focus on direct evidence. If the only way you can answer a certain question is by hearsay evidence, you may say that you have no direct knowledge. On the other hand, you could provide your hearsay evidence (in a confident, matter-of-fact tone) and see if any of the attorneys object. If the evidence is ruled inadmissible, do not take it personally. You provided the best information you had. Some attorneys will strategically ask questions that they know will lead to an inadmissible response. Even if the answer is ruled inadmissible, the impact of the response may already have achieved its purpose. After all, it is hard for an adjudicator to completely forget—or rule out of mind—what he has just heard.

Fact evidence is information that is attested to from firsthand observation, perception, or experience. For example, Evelyn could testify about what she heard, saw, felt, smelled, tasted, and experienced when she conducted a home visit. She does not need to make interpretations or inferences to present this evidence. "I saw Debra run into her room. Then I heard a loud crashing sound. A few seconds later, I could smell smoke.... "

Opinion evidence includes beliefs, thoughts, interpretations, or recommendations that go beyond simple facts. Evelyn gathers fact evidence by interviewing the parties and conducting home visits with each parent and Debra: for instance, Philip lives in a one-bedroom apartment; Paula lives in a three-bedroom house; Philip does extensive travel for his work; Paula works at home. Given all the factual information that Evelyn collects, she expresses an opinion that Debra's best interests are served by a residential placement with her mother. Only "expert witnesses" are permitted to provide such opinions (see Chapter 7). Other witnesses are limited to testifying about facts, enabling the judge to draw her own inferences, conclusions, and recommendations.

The best evidence is direct, credible, and original. If a fact can be proven in more than one way, then the attorney should lead with the best evidence (e.g., an original document rather than a photocopy, or firsthand evidence from a direct witness rather than hearsay). Evidence that is admissible may be afforded different weight by the adjudicator. As a witness, you will want to present information in a way that is not just admissible but also persuasive.

The legal standards for what is relevant (or material) in the case may be quite different from what you as a clinician think is relevant. That is, what is legally relevant may be different from what is psychologically relevant.

Consider the story of a man who stole a loaf of bread to feed his family. A clinician may believe that the man should not be found criminally responsible due to extenuating circumstances. Lady Justice, however, wears a blindfold to signify that justice is blind. Accordingly, whether the man was hungry when he stole the bread has no legal relevance to the question of whether he committed the crime.[18] During the initial hearing, his clinician may not be allowed to offer testimony about his family circumstances. In criminal trials character testimony is generally inadmissible. However, if the defendant is found guilty, the law does permit testimony about character to be admitted into evidence. Such potentially mitigating evidence may be brought forward in the clinician's presentence report or in direct testimony. While the clinician may find such distinctions artificial or unfair, they are of great importance from a legal perspective. To determine what evidence is relevant, you need to know the legal issues in dispute as well as become familiar with your state's civil and criminal evidence code.

Judges may rule that certain evidence is inadmissible because admitting it would be too "prejudicial" or would go "against public policy." Prejudicial evidence is information that is relevant to the legal issues,[19] but admitting such evidence presents too great a risk of swaying a jury's decision making based on irrelevant or emotional factors (e.g., viewing a graphic photograph of an injury may have some relevance for proving a the plaintiff had an injury, but the emotional impact of the image may sway jurors to find the defendant liable simply because the injuries looked so gruesome). Public policy concerns may include encouraging people to settle and encouraging people to seek help for psychosocial concerns. Thus a judge may rule evidence of negotiation sessions and evidence from counseling sessions inadmissible (even if there is no specific statute protecting such communications) on the grounds of public policy. Given the discretion that judges have surrounding the admissibility of evidence, ask an attorney if you have questions concerning the likelihood of a judge admitting or rejecting certain pieces of evidence.

Substantive Law

To be an effective witness, a clinician does not need to be familiar with the legal basis of the case. That responsibility lies with the attorney. Still, you may benefit from becoming more familiar with the law because:

---

[18]Once again, there are important exceptions to the rule. For example, courts have considered "battered woman syndrome" as a valid defense for some women who have assaulted or killed abusive spouses.

[19]Relevant information may be referred to as evidence that has "probative value."

- You work in an area where you are frequently involved in legal processes.
- Knowledge is self-empowering.
- You can use your legal knowledge to explain certain information to your client.[20]
- You may feel less stress if you know what is happening.
- You can work with attorneys on a more equal basis.
- You may become a more circumspect and effective witness once you understand the legal concepts about which you are testifying.
- You may prepare for testimony differently once you understand the legal concepts about which you are testifying.
- You may better assist the friendly attorney in preparing direct examination questions for you.
- You can better prepare for cross-examination and better understand the limitations of your testimony.

Becoming competent in an area of law is not easy because it requires an understanding of the overall system, its underlying principles and processes, as well as case law precedents and recent rulings. For a basic primer in law, refer to textbooks designed for psychiatrists, social workers, or other clinicians (Bernstein & Hartsell, 2005; Brayne & Carr, 2005; Brewer & Williams, 2005). The American Psychiatric Association, National Association of Social Workers, and other professional associations provide law notes, legal briefs, and other legal information to their members (Pace, 2011). University programs for these professionals sometimes offer degree courses, field internships, continuing education courses, or seminars in law-related issues (Fernandez, Davis, Conroy, & Boccaccini, 2009). The primary sources of law are statutes, regulations, and case law. However, these sources tend to be hard to access and difficult to understand if you are unfamiliar with "legalese." Law librarians and online services are useful sources of information, should you need to conduct a search of relevant statutes, administrative codes, or case law.[21] Also, check state and federal government websites for legal information that is specifically written for nonlawyers (see the Resources for a list of websites and gateways). Your agency could enlist an attorney or informed clinician to provide a seminar on a specific topic (e.g., human rights legislation and proceedings). In preparing for a particular case, ask the attorney who intends to call you

---

[20]When providing an explanation of a legal concept to a client, remind your client that you are *not* providing a legal opinion. Refrain from providing any interpretation of law. Such behavior may be viewed as the unauthorized practice of law. Be safe and defer to your client's attorney.

[21]See "Websites for Legal Research" in the Resources section.

as a witness if there is certain legal information that you should have. He may be able to suggest particular sources of information, such as precedent cases, articles, videos, online trainings, or seminars.

As a general framework of how to organize your learning about a legal issue, ask first for the *relevant legal principle*. Read about the principle and the various interpretations placed on the principle. Once you understand the principle, ask for information about *statutory obligations*. Request relevant federal and state statutes. Digest their meaning. Integrate the meaning of the federal and state statutes with the general principle of law that you initially learned. Then ask for specific *case law* that addresses the specific issues about which you are being asked to testify.

Many people find memorizing the principles and statutes to be more challenging than reading case law drawn from a state appellate or supreme court decision. The reason is that case law decisions tell a story, while legal principles are framed within historical precedents or legalistic theory. One learns law from case decisions through the narrative of the parties' competing stories. Behavioral science research suggests that people often recall more information and generally learn better from narrative than from almost any other form of teaching (Clark, 2010). For many clinicians, once they learn the story that leads up to the court's decision, they are better able to recall the important aspects of the case that are relevant to their testimony.

Each witness's testimony may be viewed as a piece of a puzzle that the attorney is trying to present to the tribunal. Ask how your evidence fits into the bigger picture. Ask about the possible outcomes, desired outcomes, and likely outcomes of the hearing. Find out what evidence the case may turn on. If the attorney says that you may not be allowed to know such information until after the trial, try to understand the attorney's reasoning. Consider a divorce case in which Michael would be called to testify about his mediation with Philip and Paula.[22] Michael would be interested in why his testimony is significant and what types of orders the judge might fashion, depending on her findings. Initially, Michael may think that the attorney wants him to testify about the access arrangements agreed to in mediation. However, from a legal perspective, the status quo may be more important than what is on paper. Accordingly, the attorney may want Michael to testify about the access arrangements that the parties reported were put into practice rather than those to which they tentatively

---

[22]In many jurisdictions Michael would not be allowed to testify in his role as mediator except in very limited circumstances (e.g., to defend himself in a malpractice suit or if all parties agreed to waive any confidentiality or privilege for the mediation). For specific details in your own jurisdiction, check with your attorney and professional association.

agreed. With knowledge of the real issues in the case, Michael can prepare more effectively.

Although it is important to understand what particular laws say, it may also be important to understand how certain judges actually apply the laws. In family law, for example, a particular judge may be making custodial decisions based on the "approximation rule" (i.e., that custody and access arrangements after separation should be made to approximate the parenting arrangements during marriage), even though the statutory requirements say that the judge should make decisions based on the best interests of the child. Knowing the biases or decision-making history of a judge may help in creating a more effective legal strategy.

Facts and Theories

As a witness, your primary obligation is to answer questions as honestly as possible. If you are able to answer a question, do so. If you lack the knowledge to answer a question, then an honest answer is to admit, "I do not know." You are not expected to know all the facts of the case. You can enhance your value as a witness if you take time to review your information ahead of time, ensuring that you know what you are supposed to know. For example, if Frieda were called to testify about her therapy with the Carveys, she should review her file and notes in advance of the hearing. This review will enable her to refresh her memory and organize her thoughts. While Frieda may be able to use her notes at the hearing, her evidence will come across as more credible if she testifies from memory.

If you have participated in oral depositions, written interrogatories, or other pretrial processes (Chapter 10), review the transcripts or records of these processes to refresh your memory. If there are any inconsistencies between your pretrial evidence and testimony you plan to present at trial, plan how you will handle questions about such inconsistencies. Evelyn might have formulated a different opinion about Debra's needs after submitting her original custody evaluation: "In my original custody evaluation, I noted that Debra felt a strong affiliation with the Baptist religion. When I conducted the evaluation, her parents had recently separated and Debra was feeling resentful toward her father, including his wishes to take her to his church. Now, it is 18 months since the separation. In a recent follow-up meeting with Debra, I have noted that she is much more comfortable participating in both of her parents' churches."

It may be useful to prepare a point-form summary of important facts that need to be presented. Share this summary with the friendly attorney and try to organize direct examination around those points. The attorney may have specific suggestions about the most effective way to present your information. Do not be shy or passive if you have other ideas about how to present your testimony. Engage the attorney in a frank discussion, valuing the attorney's legal expertise while also asserting your expertise as a clinician. Do not try to memorize your testimony word for word, as you will not appear genuine and are more likely to stumble through your answers.

In some cases you may be asked to gather specific types of facts for a hearing. For example, Evelyn may be asked to provide a broad psychosocial assessment, or Sam may be asked to assess Debra for exposure to maltreatment. Your information-gathering process must be thorough enough to withstand the rigors of cross-examination (see Chapter 5). If you qualify as an expert witness (Chapter 7), you must have a sound knowledge of the theory you used to assess or intervene in a particular case. To prepare for a case, review all literature on which you intend to rely during your testimony. Also, you should review and consider plausible *alternative* hypotheses that may be suggested by the data from your evaluation or treatment.[23] Be prepared to discuss the literature that supports the rival hypotheses and be able to present a cogent, logically consistent argument for your advocacy of one interpretation over another. If you intend to cite a particular study or reading, you may end up being tested about your knowledge of this source in significant detail.

If you are providing expert testimony, you may need to prepare the attorney by educating her about the nature of your role, your qualifications, the type of opinion evidence you are competent to provide, and the type of opinion evidence that you are not competent to provide. You may also need to educate the attorney about the science behind your clinical expertise or research, for instance, what are the theoretical and empirical bases for your assessments, what is a reasonable level of certainty for making clinical assessments in your field of practice, and to what extent are your assessments are based on generally accepted practice within your field. Some attorneys may be used to working with witnesses from professional backgrounds similar to yours. Others may have little exposure to or understanding of your professional role, skills, and expertise.

Because knowledge is limited to what you can recall, consider using strategies designed to enhance your memory. For example, in the ordinary course of practice, take notes during your interviews and leave time between

---

[23]According to the Specialty Guidelines for Forensic Psychologists (CEGFP, 2011), psychologists are ethically obliged to examine rival, plausible alternative hypotheses in order to provide the court with the most comprehensive set of information and opinions possible.

sessions to reflect on each case. Use diagrams, pictures, or visualization[24] (imagining a scene or event in your mind) to reinforce your memory. For example, Sam could use a genogram to graphically display the members of the Carvey family and the relationships between them. If you bring such graphic aids to court, make sure you have enough copies to provide to each attorney and the judge. During your testimony, indicate that you have prepared a visual aid and offer that aid to the court. Do not hand anything to the judge. Simply state to the friendly attorney that you have available copies and would like to refer to the graphic during your testimony. There will likely be some discussion and/or examination of the document before it is handed to the judge. If there are no objections to its being presented to the judge, the friendly attorney will offer the document to the judge. If there are objections to its being handed to the judge, you may still continue to rely on it. However, no one else may be able to see it, and you may be called on to provide more a detailed description of its usefulness than if each party were able to examine it for herself. Often, the attorney will bring copies of exhibits to the court, but make sure you know who is responsible for bringing which documents.

At the time of the hearing, ensure that you are well rested, relaxed, and sober, since fatigue, anxiety, and drugs can interfere with recall.

Skills

While clinicians are skilled at communication, the type of communication emphasized in clinical practice differs significantly from the type of communication required in testifying. In delivering psychotherapy or other clinical services, the clinician facilitates the process, asks questions, and uses active listening skills. At a hearing, the attorney facilitates the process and asks questions, and the clinician uses information-providing skills. Whereas therapeutic interventions by clinicians generally occur in a private context in which the clinicians try to develop a safe environment for disclosure, a hearing is open to the public and the atmosphere during cross-examination is adversarial.

Observation and practice are the primary means of preparing for the unique environment of a hearing. In addition to observing a live hearing, review educational videos or transcripts of similar hearings. Rehearsing testimony with your attorney is perhaps the best way to prepare. This type of preparation ensures that you will not be in the position of providing

---

[24]Earlier, I mentioned that visualization should not be used for *recall* purposes as such use of visualization may not lead to accurate recall. Here, I suggest using visualization to reinforce a recent event, helping to *fortify your memory*.

answers to questions that are beyond your knowledge. You cannot control the questions that are asked of you. The friendly attorney should be able to monitor the other attorney's questions and raise objections when inappropriate questions are posed.

During direct examination, it is unlikely that the attorney will ask questions that are inappropriate or difficult to answer. The same is not true of the cross-examining attorney. Because opposing counsel has not prepared with you, it is likely that some questions will be posed that are outside the scope of proper examination. The cross-examining attorney usually asks questions related to information raised during direct examination, so be careful not to open the door during cross-examination to a topic about which you have not offered testimony on direct examination.

To ensure that you are well prepared for testifying, role-play both the examination by your attorney and the cross-examination by the opposing attorney. Role-playing can reveal at least three important aspects of testimony. First, it can shed light on gaps in information and will guide you toward what additional information you need to gather prior to trial. Second, a role-play will reveal inconsistencies in your testimony. Knowing how to present your information more consistently will add to the perception of you as a credible witness. Third, a role-play in which you are being cross-examined will provide you with opportunities to learn how to deal with aggressive and maybe even unfair questioning techniques. Consider a role-play in which the attorney asks yes/no questions and will not permit the witness to explain her answers by exhorting, "Just answer the question, yes or no?" The role-play permits the witness to experience the frustration and anger with such tactics in a safe environment, with an opportunity to work through these emotions before having to provide testimony in a real court.[25]

The attorney may coach you about how to streamline testimony, organize relevant material, and articulate clearly. The attorney may help you identify aspects of your testimony that are vague, unduly complicated, or incomplete. Some clinicians wonder whether it is appropriate for an attorney to tell them how to testify. Ethically, an attorney is permitted to help a witness with the *manner of testifying* but should not direct the witness about *what to say*. The line can be fuzzy, such as when an attorney suggests certain wording that has slightly different connotations. During trial

---

[25]Depending on the importance of the case and who is paying the attorney's fees, the attorney calling you as a witness may or may not be willing to spend time role-playing with you. To gain role-play experience, you could contact a local law school to see if they have a moot court or trial advocacy program. The school may be interested in having you role-play so its students can gain practice working with mental health clinicians, while you will gain experience being examined and cross-examined as a witness.

preparation, Sam uses the word "mistreatment," but Alice suggests that he substitute the word "abuse." Sam should ask about the significance of this change. To test whether you should adopt a suggestion, there are two things to consider. The first is whether the reframed statement accurately reflects the meaning and context of your original statement. You must feel comfortable that your response would be honest and accurate. A second concern is whether your statement properly reflects the literature. That is, are you using terms that are consistent with how mental health professionals use the terms? For example, do you know whether hitting a 13-year-old across the hands with a ruler is a reasonable discipline response by a parent to the child's misbehavior? The attorney may want you to talk about the father's alleged physical abuse of the child because such a characterization might help the mother's argument for relocation. Do you label this as abuse? Do you label it as maltreatment? Do you describe the research on the use of spanking with young children?

Begin with the presumption that the attorney will (1) act in good faith and (2) present an argument that most favors her client's position. Be prepared for occasions when you will be faced with an ethical conundrum. If you have evidence that runs contrary to a client's case, the attorney is more likely to pass you over as a witness than to ask you to testify and lie. An attorney is ethically permitted to suggest what to emphasize and what points to answer only if asked. It is not ethical for an attorney to knowingly lead false evidence or to ask you to distort or suppress evidence (American Bar Association, 2010, Rule 3.3). Your options for such requests include complying with the attorney, consulting with the law society or your professional association, and speaking with your attorney. If an attorney discovers that she has unintentionally led misleading evidence, she also has a duty to rectify the misunderstanding with the court and opposing counsel.

For clinicians, honesty is a core professional value. However, some clinicians place other values ahead of honesty. Radical clinicians, for example, may be willing to lie to protect a client or to advance a greater social cause (e.g., a clinician who supports euthanasia may lie to protect a person who assists in a suicide, even though assisted suicide is illegal in most states). Be aware of the potential consequences—for you, your client, and others—in order to make an informed decision.[26]

For those who place personal rather than professional values, ethics, and behavior at the top of the list, it is important to recognize two important aspects of these choices. First, driving a personal agenda in a court of law under the guise of a professional view hurts all clinical professionals

---

[26]For an outline of the consequences, see Footnote 10, this chapter.

involved in the system. The system learns to mistrust those who disingenuously represent themselves as representing their profession yet push a personal agenda without clearly articulating to the court that their expressed views are not a reflection of their profession.

Second, representing one's personal agenda to the court as if it were a professional agenda may be, at its core, an immoral action founded on deception and, or omission. As Lavin and Sales (1998) eloquently describe, the moral foundation of mental health expert witness testimony is an allegiance to a truthful representation of the research, the ethics, and the clinical experiences that inform our decision making. A moral advocacy position would be based on an accurate representation to the court that the information being presented represents a personal rather than a professional agenda. It would acknowledge that only one side of an argument is being presented rather than informing the court of rival, plausible alternative points of view and their reasoning.

If you choose to advocate for one side of an issue, it is ethically appropriate to let the court know that this is how you are presenting your arguments. This lets the court know that, regardless of how compelling your argument, you are not presenting a comprehensive view of a particular controversy. Alternatively, you could present alternate sides of an argument and then indicate your opinion to the court, based on all the reasoning you have analyzed and presented.

If you have a practical understanding of legal processes, you may be able to help the attorney strategize. For example, Evelyn has presented evidence before a particular judge on numerous occasions. She can suggest what type of presentation tends to be most persuasive to this judge and what type of argument falls on deaf ears. Frieda used to work for the human rights tribunal and knows that they prefer to resolve issues through negotiation. Following trial preparation, Michael identified significant issues that he did not have an opportunity to address. He suggested that Alice ask certain questions to afford him this opportunity. Together they created a list of questions, identified the order in which they would be asked, and each carried a copy of the questions into the courtroom. Alice used her list for direct examination.

In some cases, an attorney may hire a trial consultant to prepare witnesses. The consultant, often with a forensic mental health background, helps the witness testify in a confident, clear manner (Neal, 2009). Consultants can explain court processes and answer logistical questions. Ideally, consultants are familiar with the unique processes and personalities in the venue where you will be presenting. Consultants act as coaches, providing witnesses with opportunities to rehearse, receive immediate feedback, and gain reassurance (Brodsky, 2009). As with an attorney, a consultant may assist the witness with how to present information, but should not coach the witness to lie, make up facts, or intentionally mislead the court.

Unfortunately, rehearsing is an area of preparation often neglected by attorneys. In many cases, the costs of extensive witness preparation is prohibitive unless the dispute is over large sums of money, the lawsuit is politically charged and interest groups are raising money to support their cause, or the parties in the lawsuit have very deep pockets. If you want more intensive preparation than the attorney calling you as a witness is willing to provide, you can practice on your own or with a colleague who is knowledgeable about testifying. Ask your colleague to give you feedback from the perspective of a judge or juror who does not have your professional background or experience. Practicing in front of a mirror or using video can help you reflect on your total presentation. Focus on your physical positioning when you talk. Listen for your tonal quality. Consider appropriate eye contact with the judge and jury, as well as the attorneys. Wait patiently for each question to be completely posed and for any possible objection to the question. Then examine how you respond to *friendly* as well as *challenging* questions. Look for consistency in your response style.[27] Look for the appearance of openness and honesty. An essential goal as a witness is to be perceived as transparent. The message you want to communicate is that you have nothing to hide. You want to convey the message that you know what you know and that there are many things you do not know. When challenged about your responses, you may admit that you might have responded differently if different information had been presented to you. You want to convey the message that you are open to being wrong, yet you did the best you could with the information and resources you had at the time you did it.

Determine the type of image you want to convey to the decision makers, for example, objectivity, alliance with the disadvantaged, sympathy, or expertise. Different images may be desirable for different cases. How you present yourself should reflect the image you have decided to portray, from how you dress to how you speak and gesture. Dress professionally, but also comfortably. Bring layers of clothes, such as a sweater or jacket, so that you can maintain comfort even if the courtroom is too warm or cold. Develop a communication style that works best for you. For example, Michael may be naturally rational and subdued. A highly passionate presentation may not come across as genuine for him. He will have little problem coming across

---

[27]For example, when testifying, Michael has a tendency to speak slowly and calmly when responding to Lori's questions. To the jury, he sounds very confident and convincing. When the opposing attorney asks questions, Michael tends to speak more quickly and in an agitated tone. The jury interprets Michael's anxiety as a sign that he is hiding something.

as thoughtful and reliable. He will need to make special effort so as not to appear too distant or abstract.

MENTAL PREPARATION

One of the most common concerns among clinicians called to testify is the anxiety that it provokes (Brodsky, 2004). Stress can derive from a range of sources: not knowing what to expect; fear of looking bad on the stand; anxiety about public speaking; concerns about the consequences of a poor outcome of the case; or lack of confidence in your abilities as a witness. Label your fears and determine what type of preparation is needed.

Observing hearings and role-playing will help you to become familiar and comfortable with the process. Feel free to ask your attorney "stupid" questions. She will appreciate having an informed witness rather than someone who feigns wisdom. Find out how long you will be on the stand[28] and how grueling it might be. Ask about the worst-case scenario. Michael might think that his mediation skills will be put into question. Alice can reassure him that his competence is not a relevant issue and that is not why he is being called to testify. If his competence were likely to be called into question, Alice and Michael could strategize about how to deal with this possibility. Some witnesses fear that they will get burned in cross-examination; however, cases are usually won or lost on the facts of the case. Your best protection is to be aware of the facts and speak honestly. Most examinations are dry affairs, with relatively straightforward questions and matter-of-fact answers that leave little room for theatrics. Surprise testimony and witnesses breaking down on the stand are only common on television and in the movies. Prepare yourself with positive self-messages for when you take the stand: "I am not on trial. I am a competent clinician. As a practitioner/researcher, I know more about this issue than the attorneys, judge, or jury. I can get through this hearing as long as I remain calm and collected. I have nothing to hide."[29]

Make use of universal strategies for dealing with stress, such as a proper diet, good physical health and activity, rest, breathing exercises,

---

[28]To be safe, multiply the attorney's estimate for time on the stand by two. Although her direct examination may be exactly 30 minutes as estimated, you may be cross-examined for a longer period of time than expected. Often, the more important your testimony is to the case, the longer the period of cross-examination. Also, allot time for possible redirect and recross-examinations.

[29]In the 1990s, a character called Stuart Smalley on the television show *Saturday Night Live* repeats a daily affirmation, "I'm good enough, I'm smart enough, and gosh darn it, people like me!" Although this particular affirmation was used for laughs, daily affirmations have been proven effective in fostering positive beliefs and behaviors.

meditation, and taking breaks from other stressful activities. Use your support network and build additional support. Given the potential for embarrassment, some people tend to withdraw socially when they are embroiled in a legal conflict. Consider whom you can rely on for support without breaching the client's right to confidentiality.

If you feel anxious about remembering key facts, ask the attorney if you may bring notes to the hearing and refer to them during your testimony. Bringing notes may alleviate the stress of having to remember very detailed or specific information. If you are being called as an expert witness, you may be asked to help develop a binder of documents for use in court. These documents may include assessment tools, case notes, psychosocial reports, and journal articles that you may be using to support your opinion evidence.

Consider who will be present in the courtroom and how they might react to your testimony. If you are providing testimony in support of a person charged with rape, for instance, the alleged victim and her family may attend the trial. Will you provide them with direct eye contact, or will you try to avoid looking at them? If you perceive they are angry with you for defending a rapist, how will this affect you? Whether you feel sympathetic or defensive, you will need to find a way to remain calm and collected. You might remind yourself that your job is not to determine guilt or innocence, but to provide your evidence as honestly and clearly as possible. If you feel anxious or fearful about the prospect of testifying in front of people who will resent your testimony, talk through your emotions with a clinical supervisor or trial consultant.

Plan ahead for what you will do in the final hour or so before you testify. If you have no plans, you may end up pacing aimlessly or obsessing about what might happen on the stand. Having explicit relaxing exercises or planning to review specific materials prior to testifying can reduce feelings of anxiety during this time (Brodsky, 2009). You could also bring a newspaper or something to read if you need to wait outside the courtroom. As part of your final preparation, ensure that you are well rested and mentally alert. Be selective about what you eat and drink so that you do not become "gassy" or require frequent restroom breaks. Avoid the use of drugs as relaxants since they tend to affect memory, recall, and ability to articulate clearly.

PREPARING YOUR CLIENTS

In addition to preparing yourself for a hearing, consider whether you need to take steps to ensure that your client is also prepared. The attorney calling you as a witness might ask you not to speak with your client before a hearing to avoid conflicts or other legal complications. Even in such cases, you may have an ethical obligation to ensure the client has access to another clinician or an alternative support system (APA, 2010, s.10.10; NASW, 2008, ss.1.15 & 1.16). Discuss your ethical obligations both with the attorney and with the client. Make sure that any referral you make for your client does not compromise your relationship with the attorney. Also ensure that your relationship with the attorney does not compromise your ethical responsibility to your client.

For clinical reasons, you and your client should discuss the impact of your acting as a witness on your relationship with your client. Let the client know that you will be a witness and be honest about what you will say to the tribunal. If a conflict exists between you and the client, acknowledge the existence of the conflict and the difficulties of being involved in a legal process. Empathize with the client's feelings of anger, frustration, disbelief, sadness, or betrayal. You may find that disclosing negative information to a client in a frank manner can lead to positive changes. If Frieda plans to testify about Paula's limitations as a parent, Paula can take steps to deal with these limitations. A client may change her behavior to try to influence your testimony and recommendations. You may be concerned that confronting a client in this manner infringes on a client's right to self-determination. Consider, however, whether it would be less of an infringement to wait until the hearing for the client to hear your information or recommendations.

If you are serving the court in a forensic role (e.g., as a custody evaluator), then you may be prohibited from sharing your forensic report with the parties prior to trial. If you are in doubt about whether you can share the report, check with the court. If you are in a clinical treatment role, you should not be in a position of preparing a report for the court unless the parties have agreed in advance or there is a court order for treatment that includes reporting responsibilities to the court. In cases where you have both treatment and reporting roles, it is generally appropriate to review your written report with the parties prior to submitting the report to the court.

If you are serving in a clinical role and you have prepared a report to submit to an attorney, you may wish to talk with your client as well as the attorney about the contents of the report. In addition to dealing with feelings, your client may need to rethink whether to proceed to a hearing. The manner in which you present your report can either encourage settlement or aggravate the level of conflict (Barsky, 2007b). Let the client know your understanding of how your report will be used in the hearing. Advise your client to talk with her attorney about how your report is expected to be used. Then, if appropriate and legally permissible, you should remain open to the client's right to dispute your report's contents. The client may be able to provide suggestions for how to reword the document to make it less embarrassing or troubling. If your client works with you to reword some of the information, be prepared to defend your reasons for allowing the client to influence you as well as your reasons for allowing the client to change the words that reflect your professional judgment. Such challenges often focus on your lack of certainty, your alliance with the client rather than alliance with the truth, and your apparent bias in favor of your client. The bottom line is that your credibility may be challenged during cross-examination, making it appear that you have sold out your professional integrity to protect your client. Whether this is a fair representation or not, it is often used as an attack on your decision to allow your client to change your work product.

Remember that your client may not know the legal implications of including or excluding certain information and may need to be referred for legal advice. Although you may be hesitant to be the messenger of bad news, your report is more likely to have a harmful impact if your client first learns of its contents from her attorney, from filed documents, or at the hearing rather than from you directly.

In fact, an argument can be made that as a treating clinician, your report about your client should be discussed first with the client before being forwarded to the attorney. This is because your client holds the privilege of the communication and allows you to release information to others only upon informed consent. Your client cannot provide fully informed consent if you have not first discussed the contents of the communication with her! Therefore, if you are in a treatment role, you should discuss with your client what you intend to release and how it will be worded prior to its release. Anything less is likely not informed consent and may place you in an ethical as well as a legal conundrum. You should also inform your client that, should the case go to trial, you do not have control over the questions asked and the types of information that you may be required to divulge while testifying.

You may be able to downplay some of the adversarial aspects of an adjudication. Frieda, Paula, and Philip are all concerned about Debra's best interests. All of them want the judge to make a fair decision. Frieda could explain to Philip that they have an honest difference of opinion about what is best for Debra and that an impartial judge can help them decide what to do. Avoid becoming entrenched in a particular position. As a clinician, you do not have a personal interest in a specific outcome. You are presenting the best information you have to help an adjudicator make the best decision possible. Your priority as a witness is to provide information in an impartial and credible manner. Your goal is *not* to try to "win the case" or "prove others wrong."

You may be able to provide the client with information about the hearing process, but be careful not to provide legal advice. Ensure that your client has been advised to obtain counsel if she needs guidance or representation. Remember to record your advice in your treatment notes, complete with the date you discussed the issue and your client's stated position. Once the client obtains counsel, record the name and address of the attorney in your records. If your client refuses your advice, record in your notes the reasons why and consult with a colleague and/or an attorney about how best to handle any current or future requests for your treatment notes.

In some cases you may believe your client should not be present at a hearing because of the negative psychological impact. For example, a client who is suicidal may be pushed into crisis if she were exposed to testimony about the manner in which she was sexually assaulted. A child may not have the ability to understand or emotionally process the testimony that she may be exposed to during a hearing. If you are concerned about the impact of your testimony on your client, you may be able to adjust the manner of your presentation rather than try to exclude your client from the hearing. You may be faced with a dilemma if altering your testimony to protect your client detracts from your ability to be open and honest as a witness. Some clinicians are overly protective of their clients or underestimate the possibility of positive therapeutic impact of exposing a client to difficult information. A survivor of sexual abuse may actually benefit from sitting through a trial, so long as she has sufficient preparation and support.

If you harbor such concerns about your client's ability to be exposed to your testimony, raise this issue with her attorney. You may also need to consider whether your testimony will adversely affect or fatally injure your relationship with your client. Should these issues present themselves, consult a colleague or your attorney for advice.

Another area to discuss with your client is what will happen after the hearing. Can you resume your clinical relationship? Does the client want to be referred to another clinician? Can you help the client to deal with various potential outcomes? In some cases clinicians are helpful in implementing the terms of a court decision (e.g., supervising terms of access, providing assessment or therapeutic services, or monitoring implementation). Most tribunals do not have the power to order a person to attend counseling. However, if you discuss the possibility of clinical intervention with a client in advance, the client may agree to a consent order stating that the client will attend specified therapy sessions.

Make sure that any directive you receive from the court clearly indicates your reporting responsibilities. If you are to provide treatment updates to the court, make sure that there is sufficient information in the court's order about how such communications are to occur. If you are to provide treatment to the client and provide no information to the court, it may be wise to have the order specify that the litigant (rather than the court) is your client. In this way issues of privilege and confidentiality are clearly established in the order.

CASES INVOLVING CHILDREN

Children may be involved in court as witnesses, victims, offenders, or subjects of the decision making in family law and child protection cases (Bottoms, Najdowski, & Goodman, 2009). When legal cases involve children, clinicians should attend to their special needs and developmental issues, including their vulnerability to manipulation or abuse, level of cognitive functioning, ability to distinguish fantasy and reality, verbal skills, memory retrieval, and suggestibility[30] (Ceci & Bruck, 2006). When serving in a therapeutic role, clinicians are trained to engage with clients by tuning in, demonstrating empathy, using active listening skills, and acting as an ally for the client. Unfortunately, these very behaviors may contaminate information gathered from a child that the clinician may want to use as evidence in a subsequent hearing (Meyer & Weaver, 2006). Thus an effective interview from a therapeutic perspective may be ineffective from a forensic perspective. If a treating clinician is asked to testify concerning information received from a child, the clinician should explain that she was not acting in a forensic role and that there may be some limitations on the trustworthiness of the information. For instance, if an attorney asked Frieda to testify about Debra's relationships with her parents, Frieda could explain, "Debra provided many positive comments about each of her parents. However, since I was acting as a therapist rather than a forensic expert, I used a lot of questions that focused Debra on the strengths of her parents." Clearly, if a clinician asks about a parent's strengths, the child's responses are affected by positive framing of the question.

When a mental health professional interviews a child for forensic purposes, the professional should be specially trained in how to gather information in a manner that not only warrants its admissibility in court, but also ensures the evidence will be given due weight by the judge or jury. The professional must be able to elicit and truthfully report on the

---

[30]There is considerable debate in research literature concerning the memory and suggestibility of young children, with views ranging from *children's memory and suggestibility is so suspect that courts should not give any consideration to their evidence*, to *children's memory and resistance to suggestions is so strong that their credibility should not be questioned*. The truth lies somewhere in the middle.

child's perception of relevant events. Strategies to minimize distortions in children's memories and to maximize the accuracy of their information include:

- Starting with easy questions to show interest in the child, to build rapport, and foster trust.
- Keeping questions short, grammatical construction simple, and vocabulary familiar.
- Matching the content of questions to the child's knowledge and experience.
- Using open, exploratory questions ("Please tell me about ..."), rather than questions that might be perceived as applying pressure or challenging the child's honesty ("Don't you remember when you ... ?").
- Providing neutral feedback or support for the child's efforts, but avoiding praise for providing certain content.
- Avoiding authoritative or judgmental language, facial expressions, or body language.
- Inviting the child to share as much information as possible.
- Going through events in simple, chronological order.
- Allowing the child more time to process information and to respond than you might ordinarily allow for an adult.
- Avoiding contaminating influences such as false information, stereotypes, and instructions to visualize or imagine (Brewer & Williams, 2005; Melton et al., 2007).

Consider videorecording your forensic interviews so they may be reviewed by the court to ensure you interviewed the child properly. To ensure the dependability of evidence from children, some states have enacted laws that regulate who can gather information from child witnesses and what types of safeguards they must implement to protect children from harassment, manipulation, or undue pressure. Child custody evaluators have also developed standards of practice to promote ethical, effective practice (Association of Family and Conciliations Courts [AFCC], 2006).

The specifics of gathering information from children go beyond the scope of this volume, as there are textbooks and educational programs to train forensic experts on how to interview children for different types of court cases (Braaten, 2007). General factors to consider when gathering information from children include the number of interviews, types of interviews, interviewing methods (highly structured, semistructured, flexible), emotional tone, status of the person conducting the interview (social worker, police, teacher), whether to meet the parents separately or together with the child, and use of various information-gathering devices (e.g., observation of behaviors, or interactions, feedback from collaterals, play, art, and use of instruments to measure particular psychosocial phenomena) (Gould & Martindale, 2009).

Interpreting information from children may be particularly tricky. Children think and speak differently from adults. A clinician may believe that a child is giving inconsistent responses to questions, but from the child's view there is no inconsistency. Consider a young child who reports she traveled very recently, but when describing the story, the trip actually took place 2 years ago. The child may not be lying, as her perception of time may not be fully developed.

Assume that during Sam's investigation, Debra hints at being sexually abused but then turns silent or keeps saying "I don't remember." Her responses might indicate fear of her father, but they could also indicate shyness, lack of understanding, or difficulty retrieving memories. Children's performance in providing information is highly variable, so it may difficult to interpret the meaning of a child's communications with a high degree of certainty. If you are using interpretive techniques such as play or artwork, then make sure you are using a recognized model of forensic practice, supported by research on scientifically informed evaluations rather than simply your professional intuition or hunches (see Chapter 7).

In some cases, you may be asked to help prepare a child for testifying. Your role is not to coach the child on what to say, but rather to help the child prepare emotionally. Determine how the child will be testifying—in open court, behind a screen separating the child from the defendant, or on video. Help the child identify any concerns about testifying. Refer legal questions to an attorney or guardian ad litem. You may also need to act as a liaison between the attorney and child to help the child understand the legal process and the child's role as a witness. Providing a child with a plan for follow-up after giving testimony may be particularly helpful: who will meet the child after testimony, will they be able to debrief immediately or is there a possibility that the child will be recalled for further testimony, and who can help the child with any anxiety or other issues that may arise during the testimony.

In child abuse cases, clinicians should be aware that a child may be retraumatized by being interviewed, testifying, going into a scary courthouse, or having to face the offender. To mitigate or preempt the negative effects of such processes, consider the use of forensically sensitive courthouse tours, testimony provided through closed-circuit television, and other best practices that have been developed by child witness support programs (Cunningham & Stevens, 2011; National Children's Advocacy Center, n.d.). Forensic work with child victims of abuse is a specialized area of practice that requires dedicated training and supervision.

* * *

Regardless of whether a case involves children or adults, preparation as a witness is vital to your effectiveness in providing testimony. Make sure you know the legal issues involved in the case, as well as how your role as a witness fits into the overall case. Do not be afraid to ask your attorney questions well in advance of any hearings. Discussions 15 minutes prior to a hearing, outside the courtroom door, do not provide you with sufficient time to prepare. If you will be testifying as a fact witness, know your facts and review your notes to refresh your memory. If you will be testifying as an expert witness, review the opinions that you will be providing as well as the research or other information on which your evidence will be based. Ask your attorney what types of questions to expect during cross-examination and practice your answers. In addition to preparing for how you will testify, make sure you are well rested and psychologically prepared. Simple strategies such as checking out the courtroom and parking in advance will help put you at ease for when you will be testifying.

Chapter 5

ORAL TESTIMONY AT TRIAL

If you are thinking, "Halfway through the book and you're just getting to the hearing?" please consider how long it takes in real life to get from the first notice of a court action to the actual trial. If you have just started reading the book here because you will be in court tomorrow, you may have missed some important information and should probably go back to Chapter 1. It could be a late night ... irrespective of how you arrived here, the purposes of this chapter are to familiarize you with what to expect at a hearing and to provide guidance for testifying. This chapter begins with a description of the examination-in-chief, more commonly called the direct examination. I then present "The Top 10 Hard-and-Fast Rules for Witnesses." As will become readily apparent as you read on, even hard-and-fast rules can be soft and slow. I will then take you through the process of cross-examination and provide suggestions for how to deal with challenges that may arise during your testimony.

This chapter provides a repertoire of strategies from which you can draw. Rather than follow them by rote, consider the underlying reasons for each suggestion and whether these reasons apply in your situation. This process is similar to the use of microskills, intentional interviewing, or ethnosensitive practice (Ivey et al., 2010). Each tribunal has a unique culture. When a reflective clinician enters work with people from another culture, she takes responsibility for adjusting her use of self in order to present in a culturally appropriate manner through control of her verbal and body language. As you decide how to present yourself at a hearing, consider your role and the purpose of the hearing. To simplify the discussion, I will focus on a clinician who is called to testify about her observations while working with a client, leaving the discussion of opinion evidence and expert testimony to Chapter 7. As a fact witness, the clinician's primary role is to present her evidence in a factually accurate and credible manner. You may have additional intentions, in which case you may adjust your presentation accordingly.

To appear credible, you should determine the best way to demonstrate candor, impartiality, trustworthiness, respect, expert knowledge, and confidence (Brewer & Williams, 2005). For example, honesty may be demonstrated by steady speech, consistent messages, and poised body language. Fidgeting, shifting your eyes, contradicting yourself, and perspiring may be perceived as signs of dishonesty or fabrication. However, in different arenas or with different decision makers, you may need to tweak your manner of presentation. Direct eye contact in some cultures is a sign of attentiveness; in other cultures, it is a sign of disrespect. Just as different ethnic groups operate with different cultural norms, so do different legal systems or different courtrooms within the same jurisdiction.

Think about your audience and, in particular, the decision maker(s) at the hearing. What type of information will be most persuasive to this audience—scientific facts, emotional appeals, anecdotal information, moral arguments, eloquent storytelling, or information that has the support of a larger group (e.g., a petition or endorsement from a professional group)? How can you present yourself in the most effective manner? Effectiveness as a witness depends on total presentation of the person including preparation, knowledge of relevant material, dress, appearance, communication style, and confidence. Some decision makers will be impressed by one style, whereas other decision makers will be impressed by another. In a trial without a jury, tailor your evidence to the judge, keeping your testimony factual, concise, and rational. In a jury trial, you might try to connect with jury members by including more details and emotional content.[1] "The best testimony sends the audience home informed and cleansed from resolving the conflict that has led to the trial" (Brodsky, 2004, p. 27). In other words, try to convey your evidence so clearly that you make the decision easy for the judge or jury.

DIRECT EXAMINATION

Perceptions of your credibility begin even before you answer any questions. As you sit in the courtroom before being called to the stand, maintain your composure and remember those positive self-messages from Chapter 4 to calm anxiety and promote confidence. Ensure that your cell phone or other

---

[1] If an attorney objects and the judge sustains the objection, you may need to forego the emotional content and focus on a rational approach.

electronic devices are turned off. If you have been asked to bring any papers or electronic files, make sure they are readily available. As your name is called, be prepared to rise and walk confidently toward the stand. Direct your eye contact toward the judge, jury, or the stand where you are headed, rather than toward either of the parties. As you take an oath or affirm to tell the truth, continue to convey your poise.

As noted in Chapter 1, the direct examination is conducted by the attorney who calls the witness to testify. In general, this attorney cannot suggest specific answers to her questions. The reason for this rule is to avoid allowing an attorney to put words in the witness's mouth. Further, this attorney cannot impugn his own witness.[2]

These rules of direct examination have three primary exceptions. First, attorneys are given latitude to ask leading questions to guide a witness quickly through uncontroversial issues: "Your name is Michael Elliot?" "You are a mediator with Elliot and Associates?" "You were hired by the Carveys to mediate the terms of custody and access with their daughter?"

The second exception concerns "hostile witnesses." Attorneys usually call witnesses who are either neutral or sympathetic to their clients' interests. In some situations, an attorney will call a witness who is adverse in interest. If the tribunal deems the witness hostile, then the attorney conducting the direct examination will be permitted to ask questions as if it were a cross-examination (discussed below).

A third exception germane to clinicians is that someone appointed by the court to provide an assessment may be cross-examined by both parties. Since an attorney calling you as a witness should have discussed his questions and your testimony with you ahead of time, the direct examination should be relatively straightforward and free of surprises.[3] Starting with a direct examination gives you time to gain comfort on the stand. If your evidence were entered into the court record solely through documents, you would not have time to get acclimated to testifying before being subjected to challenging or even hostile questions in cross-examination. An examination usually begins with questions about who you are (e.g., name, professional role, employer, educational qualifications) and how you came to have information relevant to the case. Following these introductions, the attorney leads you through your story, typically in chronological order. To entice the judge or jury into listening and processing your testimony, try to construct your narrative in an interesting manner. Provide a rich description of the

---

[2]"Impugn" refers to attacking the credibility of a witness or calling her testimony into question.

[3]During this stage, witnesses are more likely to surprise an attorney with new information, rather than an attorney surprising the witness with a fresh question. Either type of surprise should be avoided.

relevant people and events. On the other hand, guard against becoming too flowery or straying from the truth, both of which may affect perceptions of your credibility. Ensure that your storytelling relates directly to the legal issues in dispute. The friendly attorney will focus primarily on evidence in support of her case. However, she may also ask questions that raise evidence contrary to her case, knowing that such evidence will likely come out in cross-examination anyway. By surfacing the problematic evidence during the direct examination, you have greater control than if it comes out in the cross. Further, by presenting both favorable and unfavorable evidence, you are showing that you are balanced and honest.

While some judges and tribunals are passive, others ask their own questions during either the direct examination or the cross-examination. Show them the same respect you do other questioners. You do not have to agree with the suggestions put forward in a judge's questions. However, such questions may be particularly important because they indicate the focus of the decision makers' interest. Their questions also give you the opportunity to help them with the information they need to make a particular decision.

It is appropriate to provide information counter to a judge's belief. For example, a judge may ask a question that suggests a poor understanding of current research. In the Carveys' divorce case, the judge asks about the potential harm to a 13-year-old girl having overnight visitation with her father. Evelyn describes three recent research articles that help the judge see how his ideas concerning the risks of overnight visits are not supported by current research. "With all due respect, Your Honor, this research suggests that overnight visits are beneficial to the child, particularly for someone of Debra's age." Whether such testimony affects the judge's personal biases is another story and an important question to keep in mind. You might be able to teach the judge something new about current research or treatment techniques. However, that does not mean the new knowledge will change the judge's strongly held personal beliefs.

The following 10 rules apply regardless of who is asking the questions.

Rule 1: Tell the Truth, the Whole Truth, and Nothing but the Truth

Honesty is the most basic rule of giving evidence as well as a legal commitment you make by giving an oath or making an affirmation. Although telling the truth seems so basic that no explanation is needed, be aware of certain traps. In particular, when you are asked a question, you may feel obliged to answer in a way that will reflect well on yourself or your client. After all, if the attorney asks you a question, he must think that you have a good answer. However, honesty may require admitting that you do not have one. *If you do not know the answer to a question, say so. If you do not remember the information requested, say so.* It is better to appear ignorant or admit to having an imperfect memory than to be caught trying to cover up what you really do not know. On the other hand, do not say "I don't know" or "I don't remember" just to avoid a difficult or embarrassing question.

Be forthright about evidence that goes against your preferred case. Do not feel obliged to rationalize damaging facts or to show reluctance to concede a point in favor of opposing counsel. A short answer may be better than a long explanation because it will downplay the importance attributed to the answer. Sam might admit, "Yes, Philip has cooperated with my investigation," even though this point may argue against Sam's belief that Debra needs protective services. Avoid the temptation of exaggerating or fabricating details to support your primary evidence. Even a small distortion or misrepresentation can lead the judge or jury to question your overall honesty and credibility.

Testify about what you observed even if it does not conform to other testimony that has been presented. Do not become overly invested in being right or ensuring that your point of view prevails as the truth. Different people can have different observations, perceptions, and memories. It is up to the tribunal rather than the witness to reconcile these differences. The other person may be wrong. You may want to discuss discrepancies with your retaining attorney outside of the hearing and *after* you have completed your testimony. Talking about your testimony during a break is inappropriate. Once you take the stand, you should not talk about your testimony except when being questioned. Even after you have completed your testimony, you may want to avoid contact with the attorney or client in the courthouse. If you are seen talking with them, the judge or jury may view this as an indication of bias.

A troubling situation may arise if your client or another witness testifies about something that you know to be untrue. During your testimony, focus on the facts and information you have, as well as the basis for these facts. Rather than testify that the other person is lying, establish the truth of your version. Labeling someone as dishonest may be perceived as an *ad hominem* (personal) attack and should be avoided. Professional codes of ethics suggest we should show respect to all people (APA, 2010, Principle E; NASW, 2008, Ethical Principles), even if we believe they are not telling the entire truth.

Certainly there may be situations where a witness comes across as not completely honest. As a professional clinician, do not let unconscious biases creep into your testimony. If Frieda feels sympathetic toward Paula, Frieda may exaggerate evidence in Paula's favor or downplay evidence against her.

Frieda's testimony that "During the marriage, Paula provided *all* of Debra's parenting" could be an innocent embellishment that hurts Frieda's credibility and sets her up for cross-examination. If Frieda is asked whether she is biased toward Paula, Frieda may be tempted to say that she is objective and nonjudgmental. On the other hand, it may be more honest for Frieda to admit that, yes, she does like Paula as a person and thinks she has demonstrated many positive parenting skills. By admitting her sympathies in a manner appropriate to her clinical role, Frieda maintains her credibility more than if she denied that she possessed any prejudices.

There are times when you may be tempted to stray from the absolute truth or withhold key information. As author of this text, I cannot condone lying under oath. If you are tempted to stray from the truth, be sure to consider the potentially dire consequences of doing so—as well as alternative means of achieving the same objective. I firmly believe that, if people think through the consequences and alternatives carefully, they are more likely to be honest.

Rule 2: Convey Professionalism and Genuineness

If you are called to testify in your professional capacity as a clinician, consider what style of presentation may be expected of you. Typically, professionalism implies formality, knowledge, skill, and objectivity. Each professional is an individual, so professionalism does not mean presenting in a stiff or staged manner. Figure out *who you are as a professional*, and be yourself (James, 2010). You will come across as more credible when your demeanor is true to who you are.

Although you should avoid overdramatizing, professionalism need not rule out your testifying in a warm and dynamic manner. Use your public speaking skills to convey your information in an engaging fashion, for example, by using inflections in your voice, vivid language, natural hand gestures, and personalized testimony. Bring out your charisma through your body language and manner of speaking. Your testimony will have little impact if the decision maker falls asleep during your delivery. Include sensory details—what you heard, smelled, or felt—to bring your testimony to life and give the decision maker a graphic picture to remember. Research on mock juries suggests they are strongly influenced by the manner—and not just the substance—of what is presented (Neal, 2009).

It is appropriate to advocate for a position forcefully, provided that you have a solid research or clinical foundation for such advocacy and you genuinely believe what you are saying. Such advocacy may also best be presented by offering alternative rival positions and then explaining how the current data are best interpreted through the position *you* advocate.

Rule 3: Respect the Formalities of the Tribunal

Legal processes tend to be staid, rational proceedings with comparatively few theatrics. Attorneys and witnesses are inclined to dress conservatively[4] as a sign of respect for the solemnity of the process and the serious issues at stake. Although tribunals vary greatly in their formality, all legal processes have rituals. Many court rituals revolve around how to show respect for the judge. While the designation of judges differs among courts, trial judges in most courts are addressed as "Your Honor." If in doubt, "Judge" is generally acceptable.[5] Respect for judges is demonstrated by standing when a judge addresses you, when she walks into the room, or when she gets up to leave. If you need to leave in the midst of a hearing, bow slightly to the judge before opening the door. Decorum tends to be less formal when the hearing is not conducted by a public court judge. Mr. and Ms. are usually the favored forms of address for other people, such as the attorneys or parties to an action. Entering or leaving the hearing while it is in session may be prohibited. A final rule of respect is to avoid arguing or flagrantly disagreeing with the decision maker.

Many rules in hearings are the same as those learned in kindergarten (Fulghum, 1988): play fair, don't hit people, no speaking when it's not your turn, no gum or food, no joking around, ask for a brief recess if you have to go to the washroom, and remove your hat when you come inside. While the rules should be taken seriously, there are some exceptions that your kindergarten teacher might not have accepted: passing notes discreetly; drinking water during your testimony; using humor to make a point (occasionally and respectfully); and donning religious headwear, such as yarmulkes or turbans.

When you are asked to take the witness stand, sit properly. Do not swivel or rotate in the chair, nor rock back and forth. Avoid moving about needlessly. Look at the attorney asking the questions and then provide your answers either to the judge, the jury, or the attorney. If the witness chair is bolted to the floor, you may need to lean forward to place your documents on a desk or platform.

Rule 4: Speak Slowly, Loudly, and without Hesitation

Ensure that you speak slowly enough for the tribunal recorder and others to record your testimony accurately and completely. Consider spelling

---

[4]Although you may need to dress conservatively, also try to dress comfortably. This will enable you to look and feel comfortable and confident, and you will also be able to focus more intently on the substance of your testimony.

[5]In the Supreme Court of the United States, a judge is called "Justice."

unusual names and words to help those taking notes or recording your testimony. Your pacing may depend on the conceptual difficulty of your information and the nature of your audience, but is generally slower than normal conversation. Pause briefly before answering a question to allow the other attorney time to register any objections and to give yourself a moment to think about how to articulate your answer. If you need time to think, take control by saying, "Let me consider my answer for a moment." Then take a moment to formulate your response. If you need more time, you could also ask for additional time to think. Taking the extra time demonstrates that you are taking the question seriously. Some witnesses use covert ways to buy time to think, for example, by asking the attorney to repeat or rephrase the question, dropping a paperclip and reaching down to pick it up, or providing information that does not really answer the question. Such strategies may work but can be distracting or might suggest that you are trying to avoid the question. Pausing too long or too often may appear as uncertainty or insincerity. Clear and fluid speech tends to impart greater confidence in what you are saying. This does not mean you have to give the perfect speech, since perfect speech may sound over-rehearsed and also lack credibility.

Anxiety may lead a person to hurry his answers. If you feel pressured into answering, take a deep breath and answer at a comfortable pace. Most legal proceedings are very methodical. The tribunal will not expect you to rush your responses: "I have affirmed to tell the truth, so please allow me a moment to collect my thoughts and make sure that I respond in a complete and accurate manner."

Gauge your volume to be loud enough to be heard by everyone in the room. If you will be using a microphone, practice with one ahead of time to become familiar with the optimal volume and distance from the microphone. You may also need to talk into a microphone that is for recording purposes rather than amplification.

Rule 5: Provide Clear, Concise Answers

Attorneys usually advise their witnesses not to volunteer unnecessary information, make speeches, or go off on tangents. Brief answers enable the attorney calling you to lay a foundation of information to build a case. Keeping answers short may also prevent you from getting into trouble by saying something you will regret during cross-examination. Use stress-reduction strategies to stay calm, as anxiety may cause you to ramble or lose track of your intended answers.

Closed-ended questions can often be answered with a simple "Yes," "No," "That is correct," or "That is not what I observed." Avoid indefinite terms such as "From what I can remember," "So far as I know," or "I guess so." These comments put unnecessary qualifications on your answers and weaken the impact of your testimony. Handling a yes/no question with a negative in it can be tricky. "Didn't you screen your client for suicidal ideation?" A simple yes or no answer is ambiguous. A preferred answer would be "Yes, I did screen" or "No, I did not screen." Be careful about questions that contain double negatives such as "Isn't it true that you did not attend the movie that night?" Rather than a "Yes" or "No" response, use a more complete sentence, such as "I did attend the movie that night."

Gear the level of your language to your audience. Your goal as a witness is to communicate your information in a manner that the decision makers can easily understand. When the decision makers are professionals from your field of clinical practice, then technical, professional language is appropriate. But when the decision makers are unfamiliar with the jargon used in your profession, then scrupulously avoid its use. If you need to use technical language, be prepared to define your terms in plain language. If you use a lot of psychobabble, some people will view your artful obscurity as detracting from the importance of your testimony—as well as your credibility.

Colloquialisms and slang not only detract from professionalism but also may have ambiguous meanings. The phrase, "One look at his mug and I could tell he was a bad-ass gangsta," could be interpreted in a number of ways. If you are asked to quote what a client said in your presence, however, do not be embarrassed if you need to use obscene or impolite language.

Be careful about speaking through the use of gestures or body language (e.g., nodding yes or no). People may be unable to see your gestures, and it is hard to record nonverbal responses. If you do answer with a gesture, the attorney may describe your gesture so that it is included in the transcript of the hearing. Rather than saying, "It was this big ... " and holding your hands out to demonstrate, describe the size in inches, centimeters, or other standard measures. Gestures and changes in the volume of your voice can be used to emphasize points and to make your testimony sound more interesting, but they should not be used to change the meaning of your testimony. In print, "Yeah, sure" is recorded as total agreement—even if you intended to say it *sarcastically.*

Although the "hard-and-fast" rule says to keep it brief, occasional elaboration on key points can significantly strengthen your testimony. The extent to which you can recall detail indicates the quality of your memory and the accuracy of your testimony. Frieda's recollection of important sessions with the Carveys will naturally carry greater weight, for example, if she can accurately place them by specific dates, times, and locations. "Philip and Debra arrived at my office at 9:10 A.M. It was a rainy day, and

I remember that Debra's shoes were soaking wet." Use your best judgment concerning when it is advantageous to be concise and when it is preferable to provide details that go beyond the immediate questions and legal issues.

Rule 6: Let the Attorney Lead the Questions

During examinations, attorneys are responsible for asking the questions and witnesses are responsible for answering them. Because clinicians are used to facilitating communication, they often find this division of roles to be stifling. It is hard to resist helping out an attorney by providing information that you think is important, regardless of the question asked. Yet you may be rebuked for trying to lead the examination in a different direction. The time to work with the attorney on the lines of questioning is during preparation. Once you are on the stand, allow the attorney to maintain control of the interviewing process. During preparation, you may ask the attorney to provide you with some open-ended questions, such as "Before closing, what additional important information do you wish to add?"

Answer all questions unless one of the attorneys states an objection that is upheld by the tribunal. If you start to provide an answer and one attorney states an objection, pause until the matter has been discussed and ruled upon. Once said, a statement has lasting impact, regardless of whether the judge rules the evidence inadmissible. As a witness, do not participate in the discussion between attorneys about whether the information should be admitted, so that you appear neutral. On occasion, you may be asked to leave the hearing while the objection is discussed. This procedure ensures that your evidence is not tainted by the debate over admissibility. You have no need to worry if you are asked to leave. After the attorneys make their arguments concerning the objection, the tribunal will either ask you to answer the question or ask the attorney to proceed with other questions.

If you have rehearsed the direct examination, be careful about anticipating questions. Listen carefully to each question and ensure that you understand it before answering. The attorney may decide to vary the line of questioning from how it was originally rehearsed.

Rule 7: Just the Facts, Ma'am/Sir

The primary role of most witnesses is to testify about facts. Only witnesses who qualify as experts can provide opinion evidence. Accordingly, if you are called as a fact witness, focus on concrete, observable, and specific information. Consider if Frieda were asked about what she observed when she interviewed Debra. To say "Debra was traumatized" involves an interpretation or opinion. If Frieda were asked just to provide facts, she could describe the actions and events that led to her conclusions, all without explicitly stating her opinion: "When I asked Debra about her father, she became silent. She turned away from me and began to quiver." These statements allow the judge or jurors to interpret the facts for themselves.

If you are a treating clinician who has been called as a witness, it may be particularly useful to restrict your testimony to factual information. As a treating clinician, you are interested in maintaining a positive therapeutic alliance with your client. If you focus on factual evidence, you may be able to continue to work with the client. If you provide opinions that go against the client's interests or wishes, the client may be more likely to distrust and disengage following the trial (Madden, 2003).

Avoid language with subjective interpretations. "The meeting was long" could mean 10 minutes or 10 hours, depending on whose perspective you consider. Use objective measures wherever possible. If your evidence strays from direct, factual observations, the opposing attorney may raise an objection on the basis that the evidence is "hearsay" or "opinion evidence." The attorneys may argue over the objection, but it is the judge who rules whether to *sustain* (uphold) or *overrule* the objection. As a witness, it is not your role to argue whether or not a certain piece of evidence is admissible. Once the judge rules, you will know whether you can continue with your answer.

Sticking to the facts does not mean that your testimony should be dry or tedious. Consider using language that will have an intellectual or emotional impact. Use descriptive language that enables the decision maker to better visualize the events being described. Rather than saying "Philip's house was a mess," Frieda could describe the stench of the beer in the carpets, the fuzzy blue mold inside the refrigerator, and the unlaundered clothes strewn across the living room.

Rule 8: Demonstrate Confidence and Maintain Your Composure

Research suggests that individuals who convey confidence are more likely to be believed than those who display nervousness, hesitancy, defensiveness, or doubt (Brodsky, 2009). Confidence may be demonstrated through a moderated, stable tone of voice, clarity in speech, moderately paced speech, willingness to acknowledge a degree of certainty (without demonstrating absolute certitude or cockiness), smooth narrative statements, good body posture (e.g., sitting erectly with shoulders relaxed, or leaning slightly forward with hands on your lap), hearing accurately and responding appropriately, and an explicit statement of your credentials and knowledge. Ultimately, it is more important to appear natural than to try to fit into someone's standard of the perfect-looking witness. In other words, rather than getting flustered about having perfect posture, language, and so on, simply relax. Remember, too, that judges and juries often expect witnesses to have some level of nervousness and imperfection. If you appear overconfident or the manner of your presentation is too perfect, the judge or jury may interpret your testimony as good acting rather than credible evidence.

To remain cool, collected, and confident during your testimony, use the anxiety reduction strategies described in Chapter 4 (e.g., self-talk, taking a deep breath). While difficulties in maintaining your composure are most likely to arise during cross-examination, you may also be confronted by difficult questions during the direct examination. Attorneys as a whole suggest that you should not take such confrontation personally, since each attorney is just playing his role in an intentionally adversarial process. Regardless of their intentions, you may feel that you are being unfairly attacked. Unfortunately, if your response is overly defensive—demonstrating testiness or outright hostility—some decision makers may construe such defensiveness as a sign of a lack of integrity, certainty, or professionalism on your part. Avoid defensive responses that will hurt your credibility such as hedging, stalling, arguing with the questioner, sounding overly apologetic, raising your voice, interrupting the questioner, or providing rationalizations for mistakes or omissions. You might try a matter-of-fact response, such as "Yes, I did not verify whether this client was eligible for social assistance. In hindsight, obtaining such information would have been a useful step." On the other hand, wisecracks and sarcasm are totally inappropriate. For example, "No, I am not a quack psychiatrist—but thank you for asking" sounds both unprofessional and petty. Omit the crack about "thank you for asking"; sarcasm inevitably backfires.

Maintaining a calm and confident demeanor does not imply that your testimony should lack emotion. If Frieda were defending the efficacy of her therapy, describing her interventions in a rational manner would doubtless be best. If she were challenged about her concern for Debra, however, her emotions might naturally be evidenced—through vivid descriptions and tone of voice—in describing the effects of abuse on Debra.

Although you may not be permitted to have a break just because you are facing difficult questions, there are situations in which it is appropriate to ask for a break in order to regain your composure, such as if you are very tired, not feeling well, or need to use the washroom. Tribunals are reluctant to interrupt the flow of testimony due to a belief that honest responses are more likely if you have to respond immediately. If you are in the midst of a key sequence of questions, the tribunal will call for a break only if you are in acute discomfort.

Rule 9: Maintain Eye Contact

Provide direct (but not piercing) eye contact with the attorney who is asking questions. Periodically, you may look at the judge or jury to demonstrate that you are telling them your story. Occasional glances at your client or at other parties in the courtroom may make your presentation seem more natural, so long as these glances are not overlong or distracting. If you peer intently at your own attorney when answering another person's questions, you will look as though you are being coached. If you are able to periodically observe the judge or jurors, you can assess their reactions: do they seem to be following what you are saying; do they look bored, irritated, or confused? With so many people in the courtroom, you cannot possibly keep track of everyone's reactions. Do not get distracted by reactions in the courtroom, as your attention needs to focus on the attorney's questions and how you will provide concise answers.

Rule 10: Use Notes to Refresh Your Memory

Ideally, you have a perfect memory and can accurately recall any information you are asked. In the real world, you cannot remember every contact you had with a particular client over the past 10 months, and perhaps not even what you had for breakfast today. If you maintain good clinical records (as outlined in Chapter 6), you may be able to use them during your oral testimony.

If you want to use your notes during a court proceeding, ask the judge, "May I refer to my notes to refresh my memory?" The judge may ask the following questions to qualify your notes: "Are these your own notes? When were these notes made? Were the events still fresh in your memory when you made these notes? Since you made these notes, have you made any additions or deletions?" Ideally, you can answer honestly that the notes were yours, you made them immediately following your contact with the client based on notes taken during the session, the events were still fresh in your memory, and you have not made any changes to the notes. The judge will allow you to use your notes to refresh your memory, provided that you made the notes contemporaneously with the events recorded and that you are using the notes only to refresh your memory rather than to replace information that you do not currently remember. You must also be prepared to provide the relevant notes or file to the court. Bring originals and several copies. Noncourt tribunals are generally less strict about the preconditions for using notes.

The primary advantage of using your notes is that you can check for details such as dates and times. Providing such details can enhance your credibility and demonstrate that you have maintained an accurate record of events. The main disadvantage of relying on your notes is that, once you refresh your memory or introduce any part of your notes, you may be cross-examined on all the notes in your record. You may also waive any privilege. During preparation, review your notes with the cooperating attorney to determine whether they are complete, accurate, and able to withstand cross-examination. You can then decide whether using your notes is a good idea.

If you decide to use your notes, avoid relying on them too much, since this may indicate that you do not have a current memory. Reading notes also tends to be monotonous and uninteresting. If you are able to answer questions accurately without notes, your testimony will tend to be more persuasive. If you can give more precise answers by using your notes, however, doing so adds to the credibility of your answers.

Using notes to refresh your memory is different from entering documentary evidence (including notes) into the record of the hearing. If you use notes just to refresh your memory, then only your oral testimony goes into the record. If your notes are entered as an exhibit, then they also form part of the official record of the hearing.

CROSS-EXAMINATION

The purposes of cross-examination are to test the reliability, accuracy, and credibility of testimony provided in the direct examination. The cross-examining attorney may try to elicit inconsistencies and weaknesses in the witness's earlier testimony. The attorney may also try to bring out additional information favorable to his client.

During cross-examination, the attorney may ask leading questions, suggest answers, and impugn the witness. Because it involves such risks, cross-examination is the aspect of legal proceedings that clinicians fear most. After all, clinicians can occasionally be made to look derelict or incompetent during that phase of the proceeding. True, you might even mess up a case for your client. But remember, pitchers often give batters too much credit. You can psych yourself out and create more problems for yourself than anything the attorney can possibly conjure. If you are honest, relaxed, and prepared, the risks entailed in cross-examination are low. If you provide a solid direct examination, the opposing attorney may have little to cross-examine. Prior to the hearing, your retaining attorney can help you identify the likely focus of cross-examination and prepare you to respond most effectively.

Try to think of cross-examination as a safety check that helps to ensure that your evidence is thorough and correct (Heilbronner, 2005). You would not want the court to operate on false or faulty information. Clinicians are not opposed in principle to safety checks (e.g., the use of second opinions in clinical diagnoses and interrater reliability checks in social research). It is natural to feel some anxiety during cross-examination. Few people really enjoy it, but the risks of cross-examination should not be blown out of proportion. The vast majority of cases are won or lost on the facts rather than one witness's performance on the stand. If you have strong facts, it may even be impossible to blunder badly enough to lose the case.

Research on juries suggests that witnesses come across as more credible and convincing when they provide direct eye contact and respond strongly (confidently), without becoming confrontational (Brodsky, 2009). When faced with challenging or potentially embarrassing questions, look directly at the attorney. Answer assertively and honestly. Do not tell yourself that you have to answer perfectly. If you stumble in your testimony, know that you can correct the error. "To ensure that my testimony is as accurate as possible, I'd like to clarify my last answer ... "

I will take you through a number of different tactics that you *might* face in cross-examination. Do not be overly concerned. These are for demonstration purposes only, to help you prepare for the worst. Many cross-examinations are straightforward, without devious maneuvers, malicious insinuations, or tricky questions. Cross-examining attorneys often treat their witnesses courteously, wanting to show the judge, jury, and witness that they are being respectful and reasonable. Cross-examination can be risky for the cross-examining attorney, since antagonistic tactics can backfire. If an attorney badgers a witness, the judge and jury may demonstrate further sympathy for the witness and his testimony. Attorneys are also conscious of their reputation, so using cheap tricks to manipulate or discredit a witness could have long-standing repercussions for the attorney's image (American Bar Association, 2010, Rule 3.4). Further, litigation attorneys are trained not to ask a question unless they already know what the answer will be. Better safe than sorry, as the adage goes. Because of this conservative attitude toward questioning, it is unlikely that you will encounter the most callous tactics. I will start with some of the more forthright tactics before progressing to methods that may cross the border of ethicality.

Tactic 1: Challenging Credibility

Challenging the credibility of a witness is one of the most common uses of cross-examination.[6] Questions may be raised to indicate that your

---

[6]For challenges to the credentials of expert witnesses, see Chapter 7.

perception (e.g., hearing) was faulty, your memory is inaccurate, your views are based on limited information, or your testimony is dishonest. Direct questions such as "Are you lying?" or "Did you really see that?" are unlikely. You are more likely to face indirect questions. For instance, "It's been over a year since you last spoke with Debra?" may be used to indicate your memory may not be so good after a year. There is nothing devious about this type of question. You can answer it honestly and allow people to draw their own conclusions. "That is correct." Similarly, if it was dark and you had difficulty seeing, then it was dark and you had difficulty seeing.

Consistency is key to whether your evidence will be believed. To impugn your credibility, the attorney could question exaggerations in your testimony, facts inadvertently or purposely omitted during the direct examination, or inconsistencies in your evidence. Were your direct examination to be perfect, it would include no exaggerations, omissions, or inconsistencies. However, testimony is rarely perfect, and you should avoid defensive responses. If you have committed one of these errors, keep your composure. Clarify your evidence in a "matter-of-fact" manner. "Yes, I did drive Paula home. I forgot to mention that in my original testimony." If there is a reason for an apparent inconsistency in your testimony, state the reason. "Perhaps I can explain the confusion. Philip acted as if he was intoxicated, but that was at our first session. At the second session, he acted sober."

Credibility can also be challenged by focusing on discrepancies between your evidence and that of another witness. State what you believe to be the truth. If you have a rational explanation for the discrepancy, then state it. "My observations may be different from Frieda's because I started working with the family 3 months after they last saw Frieda."

If your credibility is successfully impugned, the attorney who called you to the stand may undertake an effort to rehabilitate your evidence during the redirect phase of the examination. For instance, if the cross-examination has suggested that your memory has faded, she can ask you to refer to your notes to demonstrate that your oral testimony is consistent with what you wrote at the time of the event.

Tactic 2: Establishing Doubt

As noted in Chapter 1, different standards of proof are required in the various types of cases. In criminal trials, for example, the prosecution must prove its case "beyond a reasonable doubt." Accordingly, when an attorney is cross-examining for the defense, he may be trying to create just enough doubt to stave off a conviction. "Is it possible that someone other than Philip was responsible for Debra's injuries?" Well, anything is possible. Although you may agree that the attorney's proposition is "possible," you should also note how unlikely it is and your reasons for this. "Debra said the injuries occurred when Philip pushed her down the stairs. The injuries were consistent with her story. I could find no motivation for Debra to lie, so it is highly unlikely that someone else caused the injuries."

In responding to attacks that attempt to establish doubt, be careful not to talk about the ultimate issue. In a criminal law case, clinicians are not responsible for deciding guilt or innocence. In fact, the language of the behavioral sciences does not include concepts such as guilt or innocence. Our language is the language of probabilities and relative likelihood. You may wish to talk about your estimate of the likelihood that an event may occur or the probability that an individual might engage in a specific act—but never talk about the guilt or innocence of a party.

Another way to reduce the impact of facts that the cross-examiner tries to use to impugn your testimony is to show that one set of facts may have multiple interpretations. The attorney may ask, "You said that Philip was perspiring and appeared drunk. Doesn't perspiration usually indicate that someone is hot?" You may offer a response that suggests a rival plausible hypothesis that may reasonably explain the observed behavior. "Yes, perspiration could indicate someone is hot. In this case, Philip's presentation was more consistent with alcohol intoxication, as evidenced by his slurred speech, lack of coordination, and the smell of alcohol on his breath." Assert your interpretation with confidence, and do not respond defensively.

Tactic 3: Logic Funnel

When using a logic funnel, the attorney asks a series of questions intended to nudge the witness in a particular direction. By having the witness commit herself in earlier questions, she may be restricted in how she can answer later questions without contradicting herself (Brodsky, 2004). "Is it normal practice in your agency to screen for suicidal ideation?" (Yes.) "So, you are supposed to screen in every case?" (Yes.) "Then you should have screened in this case?" (Yes.) As you are being led down this funnel, answer honestly. If you are feeling squeezed toward the end of the funnel, take a few steps back: "I said that it was our standard practice to screen for suicidal ideation, and I would have done so in an ordinary case. This was no ordinary case, however, because ... " Alternatively, you might recognize that you should have assessed for suicidal ideation and did not. Your response could be: "I should have performed such an assessment in this case. I did not perform that aspect of the assessment in this case." Such a response is honest, simple, and provides the needed information without becoming defensive.

Sometimes the logic in the line of questioning is only apparent on the surface. You may be able to distinguish your responses to different questions in the sequence without necessarily appearing to be inconsistent. This type of questioning may strike one as manipulative and may result in your feeling very cautious. Be on guard against feelings of anger or frustration during such questioning, and do not permit such feelings to adversely affect your testimony.

Tactic 4: Leading Questions

Leading questions suggest a particular answer to the respondent. They are used to encourage the witness to agree with the attorney's propositions. "From your opening testimony, it sounds as if you try to maintain very accurate case notes; wouldn't you agree?" Rather than confront you in a blatantly adversarial manner, the attorney is more likely to get positive responses with a friendly approach and by asking easy questions first. The attorney may present a series of "yes-able" questions that put the witness in the habit of agreeing. She may also ask a series of innocuous-sounding questions to create a smooth sequence of questions and answers, lulling the witness into a false sense of security. To remain alert, consider each question independently. Take pauses. Change the speed and intonation of your voice.

Guard against the power of suggestion. If you do not agree with the attorney cross-examining you, say so. People who have a tendency to agree and avoid conflict must particularly pay heed. When you are asked a suggestive question, feel free to use your own words rather than accept the terms used by the questioning attorney. Sometimes, attorneys use mental health terms such as "borderline" or "antisocial" in inappropriate manners. If an attorney asks you about "dysthymia" and you respond with a comment about "depression," your choice of words might have significant implications. Consult with your attorney ahead of time about the type of language you should use, particularly with respect to legal and mental health terms. Also, if you are asked to describe something with a particular word and you disagree with the use of the word in the context of the question, do not use the word. Your testimony reflects *your* beliefs and opinions. Use terms that accurately reflect *your* ideas. Do not allow either attorney to mold your ideas to fit their theories. No one is more responsible for your choice of words, their intended meaning, and the effect they have on the court than you. Choose your words wisely!

Finally, be attentive enough to correct questions based on faulty assumptions. Evelyn testified that Debra had nightmares, whereupon the attorney followed up with the question "Was Debra more likely to have nightmares about her father following a visit?" The attorney had effectively changed Evelyn's testimony by adding that the nightmares were about her father. Evelyn testified only that Debra had nightmares, but the follow-up question assumed that the nightmares were about her father. Evelyn should clarify this before responding about the frequency of the nightmares. She might say, "I testified that Debra had nightmares. I did not say that she had nightmares about her father. I did not say that she had nightmares upon returning from visits with her father. I apologize to the court if my testimony was unclear. My testimony is that Debra reported that she had nightmares."

Tactic 5: Feigned Ignorance or Pleasure

Attorneys sometimes present themselves as ignorant and ask naïve questions. They may also shower the witness with flattery. These behaviors may put the witness at ease, as though the attorney had suddenly turned benign. The attorney may be fishing for evidence or trying to get the witness to open up. "Social work is a very noble profession. Can you tell me how you're able to be so caring and giving, even when you're working with parents who have abused their children so terribly?" Remember to answer the questions concisely. Continue to respond in a respectful manner, even if the attorney's questions sound increasingly simple-minded or convey a sense of incompetence. Be aware that the attorney has not suddenly changed sides, and that she is likely to know much more than she is indicating through her chosen behavior.

Another feigning ploy used by some attorneys is to display pleasure with the witness's response even though it seems to go against the attorney's case (Brodsky, 2009). Assume Sam testifies, "Paula needed to take a cultural diversity course," and Philip's attorney, Alice, responds slowly and with a big grin, "Verrrrry interesting. Paula needed to take a cultural diversity course. I see. ...." That information may go against her client's case, but the manner of presentation suggests this information is harmful to Philip's case. As a witness, Sam should not be thrown off by Alice's seemingly incongruous smile and tone of voice. He might simply respond in a matter-of-fact tone, "Yes, that's correct. Paula took a cultural diversity course."

Tactic 6: The Cutoff

Prepare for the possibility that your testimony will at some point be interrupted by the attorney during cross-examination. Cutoffs are used to stop you from providing further information that is detrimental to the attorney's case. Remain polite. The tribunal or your attorney may intervene to provide you with an opportunity to complete your response. If necessary, ask the tribunal, "May I finish my answer, Your Honor?" If you have started to answer a question with "Yes" or "No" and the attorney stops you from completing your answer, you could politely ask the tribunal, "May I qualify my answer?" Because the tribunal wants accurate and complete testimony, it has an interest in allowing you to provide the qualification. If you were to ask the cross-examining attorney for permission to qualify, the likely answer would be "No," as the attorney realizes your qualification is likely to go against her case.

Tactic 7: Rapid Fire

In a tactic related to the cutoff, an attorney may ask questions in a machine-gun-like fashion. While this manner of questioning may simply be a way to speed up the process, it is more likely an attempt to get you to speak without having time to think about how to formulate your responses. Pace yourself deliberately. Frame each question clearly in your own mind, and answer each with due deliberation. Do not permit the opposing attorney to dictate the pace of your testimony.

In combination with rapid-fire questioning, some attorneys try to use intense eye contact with the witness. Intense eye contact makes it more difficult for some witnesses to slow down the pace and think. Remember that you can break intense eye contact by looking away. Looking up while you pause, for instance, demonstrates that you are thinking or trying to recall a visual memory. This will also break the spell that the lawyer is trying to place on you with the intense eye contact.

Saying something like "Let me think about my answer for a moment" takes control away from the attorney and places it squarely with you. If the attorney attempts to rush you, you might say something like "I am providing the best, most thorough answers to your questions so that I am most helpful to the court. Please, allow me to complete my answers."

This brings up the 5-second rule. It is a simple idea. During cross-examination, once you are asked a question, give the friendly attorney time to raise an objection before you begin to answer. Wait a moment and look over at the friendly attorney to see if she is preparing to object. If no objection is raised, then answer the question. If an objection is raised, do not offer any information unless and until you are ordered to answer the question. You do not want to open the door on an area of inquiry that is outside the scope of your prepared testimony.

Tactic 8: Intentional Ambiguity

Intentional ambiguity is designed to confuse the witness and lead the witness to admit something that she did not intend. Ambiguity can be created through the use of language that has double meanings, through statements based on false assumptions, or through purposely complicated questions. Remember to listen carefully to each question so you can make sure you understand it, detecting problems related to ambiguity—intentional or otherwise. If Alice asked Sam, "Didn't you interview Paula and find that she was depressed?" then Sam would have to contend with two questions and one negative. Break complicated questions down into simple components and answer each question in sequence. "You have asked me two questions. The answer to the first is that I did interview Paula. The answer to the second question is that I am not an expert in diagnosing depression and did not report that Paula was depressed." Keeping your own statements simple helps to eliminate the possibility of being misunderstood.

On occasion, an attorney will make a speech rather than pose a question. Witnesses, not attorneys, are supposed to provide the evidence. If you do not hear a question in the attorney's comments, ask for the question to be clarified. When the attorney finishes his speech and looks to you for a response, you might say "I did not hear a question, Your Honor" or "I do not understand what you are asking of me."

Sometimes an ambiguous question is a "loaded question," meaning that the question attempts to discredit the witness by suggesting negative implications whether the witness agrees or disagrees. For example, the question "Isn't it true that psychologists have not reached consensus on the root causes of human behavior, so that further research is needed?" unfairly attempts to have the witness confess to a deficiency (Brodsky, 2004). The appropriate response to this type of question is to admit to the part that is true and then strongly rebut the part that is not true, as in, "This is a complex question that requires a complex answer. Yes, it is true that psychologists require further research to help explain many aspects of human behavior, but it is also true that there is strong research to support the premise that children like Debra are more likely to flourish when there is a lower level of conflict between divorcing parents." If the attorney insists on a "simple yes or no answer," politely explain that you could answer yes to one part, and no to another part, but that you need to clarify each part of the question in order to answer them honestly and accurately. You may further explain, "It would be a violation of my oath as a witness and my professional ethics of integrity to give a false or misleading yes or no answer."

The tribunal may frown on such tactics as rapid-fire questioning and intentional ambiguity that are designed to confuse the witness. They detract from the purpose of the hearing, which is to establish the truth. If the tribunal does rebuke an attorney for such tactics, do not to take any pleasure in such a rebuke—at least not outwardly!

Tactic 9: Implying Impropriety

Some questions are designed to imply that you have done something dishonest, such as "Have you spoken to anyone about the answers you are giving today?" A witness may feel that if they have discussed the case, then they may have breached some code of confidentiality or rule about evidence in court. If you have spoken to the attorney about your testimony before the trial, you should let the court know this. It is perfectly appropriate for a witness to discuss testimony ahead of time; the attorney may assist with *how* you present your information, but the substantive content should be what the witness knows about *the truth*. In addition, you may have discussed the case with the client, your supervisor, and others; so what?

Another question that can throw you off guard is whether you are being paid to testify. If you are working in an agency and going to court is part of your agency duties (as for a probation officer), admitting that you are being paid by the agency does not impeach your credibility. If you were hired to provide an assessment for the court, you should not be embarrassed to admit this fact (see "The Roles of Experts" in Chapter 7). However, it should be made clear that although you are being paid to perform particular duties, you are not being paid to provide any *particular* testimony. You are being paid for your time to perform such duties, not for your testimony. A direct and nondefensive response is the best way to respond to a question that attacks your integrity. "I was paid $450 per hour for 5 hours of evaluation services. This is my standard rate for evaluation or clinical services. The attorney paid my retainer up front, so my findings and testimony were not contingent on my findings or the evidence that I am providing today." You might also note your commitment to honesty under your professional code of ethics (APA, 2010, Principle C; NASW, 2008, s.4.04), and that it would be dishonest to provide inaccurate testimony in exchange for money or gifts.

Tactic 10: Rattling the Witness

There are a variety of ways to rattle a witness, most of which are of questionable ethics (American Bar Association, 2010, Rule 3.4). Remember, however, that a good, tough question is not an unethical question. If a question is tough because it goes beyond your knowledge, you may have to admit that you do not know the answer. If the question is tough because you do not want to disclose harmful testimony, you may have to bite the bullet and provide the information requested: "Yes, I was present when my client was euthanized."

Ridicule, insults, sarcasm, and intimidation are questionable tactics. These techniques often backfire because the tribunal is inclined to disapprove of the attorney's tactics, resulting in greater sympathy for the witness (Larson, 2008). If an attorney antagonizes you, you will be less likely to cooperate with her questions. Also, the clinical and legal communities are small. If an attorney treats you poorly in one case, you may refuse to cooperate with her in the future. Still, some attorneys use these tactics and you might as well be prepared.

Intimidation can occur when the attorney uses close physical proximity, piercing eye contact, or a loud voice. If your space is being violated, feel free to move back if possible (remember, some witness chairs are bolted to the floor). To avoid threatening eye contact, glance toward the tribunal or gallery (but not down, since this implies you have something to hide). Do not try to match the attorney's volume nor try to speak over him. Maintain your composure. Try dropping the volume of your voice to de-escalate the situation.

Monitor your emotions and presentation at all times when testifying. This includes monitoring your voice tone, volume, and quality. Use the cognitive strategies discussed earlier, reminding yourself to keep calm and focused. Understand why the attorney might be trying to intimidate you; for example, he might be abrasive with all people or might have developed a false idea that attorneys have to be intimidating to carry out their role in an adversarial court hearing (Brodsky, 1991). Sit back and allow the attorney to rant and rage. You can counter with a calm, matter-of-fact response that shows that you remain in control of your testimony despite his theatrics. Keep your answers brief. If an attorney were to ask, "Shouldn't you be embarrassed about providing an opinion based on such flimsy research evidence?" your answer might be a simple, "No."

Do not let ridicule or insults throw you off. Normally it is best to ignore them. You might feel that you want to say something like "Would you like to continue insulting me, or do you have questions that are relevant to the case?" However, it is usually best to allow the other attorney or the judge to respond to such inappropriate challenges during cross-examination. Avoid the temptation to enter the fray. Maintain your professional composure and focus on what you need to present to the court. Your attorney may step in: "Objection, Your Honor. Counsel is badgering the witness." In some instances, the tribunal will protect you from such tactics, regardless of whether anyone objects.[7] If a question is meant as an insult, you may ask the judge whether you have to answer it. Generally, leave objections to these types of questions to your attorney. Recall your techniques for dealing with anxiety and other feelings. Remind yourself that you are doing

---

[7]If you do not have an attorney watching out for you during the proceedings, the tribunal is more likely to take active steps to protect you from abuse.

a good job and that you are trying to be helpful and honest. Concentrate on staying calm and in control. While the attorneys and judge discuss the objection maintain focus on your own testimony (the information you plan to relate to the court) rather than getting caught up or sidetracked by their quarrels.

In extreme cases, you could file a complaint against an attorney for unprofessional behavior. Although attorneys are supposed to advocate strongly for their clients, they are not supposed to engage in dishonest, harassing, or condescending behavior (refer to your state bar association for its code of professional responsibility). The court transcript may serve as evidence against an attorney in a subsequent professional disciplinary hearing.

Sometimes, an attorney will try to impugn your credibility by asking personally intrusive questions about your sexual orientation, political affiliation, medication use, religion, or other matter that the attorney hopes to exploit. In a divorce case, Evelyn might be asked if she were divorced and what happened in her marriage. Such questions are objectionable if they are irrelevant or intended primarily to intimidate or discredit you on inappropriate, prejudicial grounds (Federal Rules of Evidence, 2010, Rule 403).[8] You might ask the tribunal, "I am here in a professional capacity; can you help me with how I am supposed to reply to personal questions?" If the question is permitted, you are placed in a difficult situation. If you do not answer, you may be found in contempt of court or you may appear to be hiding something. You may decide to answer the question directly and matter-of-factly to minimize the impact of these questions and focus on the real issues of the case. You do not want to appear defensive (Larson, 2008). If inappropriate evidence is allowed into the hearing, this may create grounds for a subsequent appeal of the decision. Another strategy would be to preempt such attacks during the direct examination. Frieda could disclose up front that she has a criminal record for possession of marijuana, or Sam could disclose that he had been reprimanded by his social work association 5 years ago for a breach of client confidentiality. By revealing potentially embarrassing information during the direct examination, the witness steals the thunder (or strong emotional impact) that it may have had if the opposing attorney brought the information to light during cross-examination (Brewer & Williams, 2005).

Different attorneys tend to use different types of cross-examination strategies. Ask the attorney calling you as a witness if there are particular strategies that the cross-examining attorney likes to use, so that you can be

---

[8]In *Cheatham v. Rogers* (1992), the Texas Court of Appeals allowed examination related to the personal psychotherapy treatment of a court-ordered evaluator.

prepared (Heilbronner, 2005). For instance, if an attorney tends to draw misleading quotes from a clinician's case records in order to impugn the clinician's credibility, the clinician can prepare by reviewing the case notes in advance and bring them to the hearing for quick reference.

HEARINGS WITHOUT ATTORNEYS

Some legal processes are less formal and do not require the use of attorneys. The advantage in such a situation is that you have more control over your testimony. However, it also means that you need to prepare yourself and your evidence by selecting the relevant issues, determining the order of your presentation, and deciding what evidence to emphasize. The tribunal in such hearings may be more active and may even try to assist you with your testimony. The rules of procedure and evidence are likely to be less strict, providing you with greater latitude about what to say and when. Still, your evidence will have its greatest impact if it meets the tests of credibility described above, particularly evidence that is based on firsthand knowledge and is directly relevant to the legal issues raised by the case.

It might be useful to obtain copies of the rules of evidence for such a hearing prior to attending. Review these evidentiary rules with your attorney or talk with colleagues who have attended similar proceedings.

TECHNOLOGY AND PROVIDING EVIDENCE

Traditionally, legal proceedings required live testimony with all participants present in a single hearing room. The use of technology is gaining greater acceptance in legal processes as a means of bringing people and evidence together more efficiently. Closed-circuit television, videoconferencing over the Internet, and telephone conferencing allow people to retain the "live" part of the hearing, even though some of the participants are not in the same room. Audio and video recording of testimony have more limited use, as they are past recordings and do not allow for cross-examination during the live part of the hearing. However, such recordings are used in selected circumstances, for example, to interview children in a less threatening environment than at a live, public hearing in a formal courtroom (Bottoms et al., 2009).

If you are going to provide testimony through one of these means, practice using the technology so that you can become accustomed to it and present yourself more effectively. For instance, audio recordings and telephone conferences are limited to verbal testimony. Ensure that you are communicating clearly without the use of body language or other visuals (unless you have sent visuals such as pictures, genograms, or graphs to the remote location ahead of time). Even video technology is limited inasmuch as the focus of attention is determined by whomever is operating the camera rather than by people individually, who are free to focus their attention on anyone in the room. Consider the setup of the room where you are being recorded to ensure there are no distractions and to convey the sense of professionalism intended. While you want to be conscious of the microphone and camera, do not overplay to them. If you are recording your testimony to be played at a later date, try to use one continuous production. If you start and stop the recording, the decision makers may wonder what you have cut out.

Check to see whether there are any statutory or case laws in your state about how to use technology for the purposes of gathering or presenting evidence. These laws may address continuous versus discrete recordings and their admissibility. Further, these laws might differentiate between video and audio recordings.

AFTER THE CROSS

After cross-examination, the attorney who conducted the direct examination can ask further questions to clarify your responses, clear up inconsistencies, or deal with other problems raised in the cross-examination. The attorney cannot raise new issues that should have been raised in the direct examination, nor can she ask leading or suggestive questions. Questions beyond the reexamination are rare. When you are dismissed from the stand, return to your previous seat in the hearing room. Remain there until the next break in the hearing.

When you are dismissed from the witness stand, you may thank the attorney and judge, and nod to the jury and the parties. Do not try to engage people in conversation as you leave the stand. Continue to display confidence and professionalism in your facial expression, body language, and stride as you step down, leaving the judge and jury with a positive final impression. Remain in the courtroom unless you are told that you are dismissed and you will not be needed for further testimony.

When most witnesses leave the stand, they feel a sense of relief. Some feel dissatisfied. Others even report "posttestimony depression." You may feel you did not get a chance to tell your whole story, or that you could have done a better job—if only.... Some clinicians fantasize for days about what they could have said or what they wish they had been asked. Others feel that they spent too much time preparing, given the limited questions and cross-examination that actually occurred. Certainly, it is better to be over-rather than underprepared. If you were subjected to personal attacks, you may feel angry or embarrassed.

If you remain in the courtroom until the end of the proceedings, you may hear the opposing attorney or other witnesses put down your testimony, contradict you, or make negative assertions about your integrity and credibility. As the "Serenity Prayer" from Alcoholics Anonymous (n.d.) suggests, take responsibility for what you can do, but when there is something that you cannot control, let it go. You can take control of presenting your evidence honestly, clearly, and with confidence. You cannot control what others say afterward. Further, take heart that the judge or jury may believe you even if others question you or your evidence throughout the rest of the court proceedings.

Debriefing is important. For legal issues, you may wish to consult with your attorney. For emotional or clinical issues, you may wish to debrief with a colleague. In rare instances you may be recalled as a witness. Check with your attorney to see whether you need to avoid discussions until the case is over.

When you next meet with the attorney, you can discuss how well you presented your evidence and ask for tips on how to improve. At a later date, you may even obtain a transcript of the hearing in order to review your performance. Your attorney can help you interpret the results of the hearing. If Sam's evidence were to be challenged in a child protection hearing, it might seem as though the attorney was trying to make Sam appear incompetent. If the attorney succeeds, the court's decision about the child may not be as Sam had recommended. Still, the court cannot impose punishment on Sam (unless he has committed perjury). Instead, the court weighs the value of the evidence presented by Sam as having less importance than other, more relevant or persuasive evidence. Although this type of experience is stressful, it is important to separate your best efforts from the verdict by a decision maker whom you do not control.

In some cases, you may never learn the results of the legal proceedings. For instance, if the parties settle a case before the court gives a final ruling, the parties might include a confidentiality clause that prohibits them from disclosing the terms of the agreement to others. In other cases, you may be too busy to follow up with the case, for instance, by calling your former client or the attorney who called you to testify. If you are curious about the outcome of a case, you could also check news reports or public court records. Ideally, you will have an opportunity to discuss the outcome of the case with the attorney who called you as a witness, so you can ask for feedback not only on the outcome, but also on the effectiveness of your testimony and recommendations for future cases.

Cases do not necessarily end at the conclusion of the hearing. Remember, if a party is unhappy with the results of a hearing, there may be grounds for appeal (e.g., the tribunal was biased or certain procedures were not followed). In some cases an attorney may not even intend to win at trial; to establish a new precedent, cases often need to progress to an appeal for a higher tribunal to make the decision. You may also undertake extralegal avenues of recourse, such as advocating to the government for changes in the law or public policy.

Usually, at the end of "round 1," it just feels good to have your oral testimony over and done with.

Chapter 6

CLINICAL RECORDS

Now that we have a picture of what happens at a hearing, let's take a step back to look at how to organize one's clinical practice in a way that best facilitates effective participation in legal processes. This chapter focuses on how to maintain clinical records that may end up being used in court or other adjudications. Remember, as a treating clinician, your primary purpose is to help the clients you are serving. Still, when creating, organizing, and storing your clinical records, you should do so with an eye to the possibility that your records may be used in a legal proceeding.

Broadly defined, records include intake forms, confidentiality agreements, case progress notes, assessments, termination summaries, appointment books, statistics and research, psychological tests and inventories, pictures drawn by clients, photographs, billings, videos, e-mail correspondence, and any other information stored on paper or electronically by the clinician or agency (Federal Rules of Evidence, 2010, Article X).[1] Comprehensive record management practices are crucial because they:

- Help the clinician remember important information by maintaining accurate treatment information and ensuring appropriate case continuity with each client.
- Facilitate supervision and case consultation.
- Enhance accountability of clinicians and programs to clients, funders, licensing bodies, and other stakeholders.

---

[1]Different privacy and access to information legislation may have different definitions for what is included and not included as a protected record, so you may need to check the wording of the relevant legislation for your context of practice (Kagel & Kopels, 2008).

- Track the effectiveness of various interventions, facilitating clinical evaluation, program evaluation, and evidence-based practice.
- Assist clinicians in preparation to be witnesses.
- Provide documented evidence for legal actions, based on observations that were fresh in the clinician's mind at the time of recording the information (including documentation of risk management practices).
- Facilitate negotiation and settlement of legal cases.
- Support a clinician's defense in a malpractice suit by articulating the clinician's actions and client responses, as well as the rationale for assessment and intervention decisions.
- Satisfy legal requirements for regulated agencies and professionals.

Good records protect clients and the public, as well as the clinician.[2] In clinical settings where every interaction or intervention has legal implications, clinicians may be required to adhere to different standards of record keeping. However, one cannot predict when a case may end up in legal proceedings, so "law-friendly" record keeping should be used universally. Each agency has unique recording requirements. In developing record-keeping policies, identify the most recent laws and codes of ethics relevant to your situation. Consult an attorney when reviewing your agency's organization of records, the content of records, and client rights. Check also with your state association ethics or legal committee chairperson for current expectations within the state. Finally, some state and national associations publish a legal reference guide (e.g., Hays, McPherson, & Hansen, 2010).

THE ORGANIZATION OF RECORDS

The organization of records includes how information will be gathered, entered into the system, preserved, and disposed. Most agencies open a separate file for each client and maintain an ongoing record of all contacts. Determine whether you should create separate files for each member of a client family, for each member of a therapy group, or for different services for the same individual. When considering separate files for services provided to the same individual, bear in mind the laws, agency policies, and ethical standards regulating your field of practice and profession (APA, 2010, ss.4, 6; NASW, 2008, ss.1.07, 3.04).

---

[2]Consult your professional association for ethical standards and practice guidelines that pertain to record keeping within your profession. Record-keeping guidelines for forensic professionals tend to require a higher level of clarity and organization than record keeping for treating clinicians (CEGFP, 2011).

Frieda prefers to use one file for a whole family or group because it is more efficient and enables her to describe systems information and group dynamics. However, if her file for the Carvey family is subpoenaed in a case involving Philip, she will have difficulty protecting Paula's confidentiality. Frieda may be ethically compelled *not to release information* about Philip because it contains information obtained from interviews with Paula. Without consent from both parties, the clinician may not be allowed to release information from a family session pertaining to only one person without violating the confidential relationship with others in the family for whom the therapist has no permission to release the information. One solution to such a quandary may be to provide a treatment summary that describes Philip's concerns while maintaining a confidential shield around information obtained from other people in the family session.

Another option is a hybrid approach. You could create a separate file containing sensitive or confidential information for each individual in a group or family, as well as a more general file for group or family processes. Developing separate files for the same client may be appropriate in cases where some information is likely to be used in a legal proceeding but other information about the same client has less legal significance. For example, if Paula were to receive witness preparation support and vocational counseling from the same agency, separate files could be opened for each service. Information gathered by the witness preparation clinician may be subpoenaed. By opening a separate file for vocational work, this information may be protected from disclosure. A tribunal may allow certain sections of a file to be released while allowing other information unrelated to the case to remain undisclosed. However, the manner in which notes were originally recorded may make this approach impractical, particularly if the clinician interweaves facts about separate individuals and services in one case record.

Maintaining separate clinical files and releasing only those files that you as the treating clinician deem appropriate is a tricky issue. First, you need to be certain about the type of information requested by the subpoena. A *subpoena ducus tecum* requires that you provide all information about the client from all existing files. If the subpoena is less extensive in its breadth, then you may be allowed to provide limited information. Do not make a decision about what you can and cannot legally and ethically release without consulting an attorney as well as state laws and your professional ethics code.

Generally, whoever gathers information should be responsible for entering the information into client records. This includes information obtained from both clients and collaterals (family members, employers, teachers, other clinicians, attorneys, etc.). Adjudicative processes give preference to firsthand information. If a receptionist gathers intake information, then the receptionist rather than the clinician should record this information with the receptionist's signature to acknowledge who recorded the note and when. If a clinician gathers information but has a secretary type her notes, then the clinician should review the typed notes to ensure that they are an accurate record. Notes should be signed by the person who gathered the information, warranting that the information is accurate. For electronically stored notes, you may use an electronic signature. The timing of note taking can have great legal significance. Ideally, notes should be made contemporaneously with the events being recorded (i.e., during a session with a client, immediately following, or within 24 hours). Evidentiary rules assume that information recorded contemporaneously with the events is more likely to be accurate, as they are fresh in the person's memory (Federal Rules of Evidence, 2010, Rule 803(5) and (6)). Behavioral science research supports the fact that notes contemporaneously taken are more accurate than those recorded at a later time, even if it is later the same day. In Lamb et al.'s (2000) study, verbatim notes taken by highly trained interviewers were compared with the audio-recorded versions of the interviews. The researchers found that even those interviewers with extensive training in *verbatim* note taking often got it wrong. The moral of the story is that accurate recordings are critical. If you are preparing testimony for a forensic report, it may be wise to record all your interviews electronically as this provides easier access and referencing.

Record the date of the event as well as the date that the record was made and signed. If the notes were not made contemporaneously with an event, note the reason for this. Frieda may not have entered her notes right away because she escorted Debra to the hospital on a medical emergency. If you follow a consistent practice of note recording, you can attest to your ordinary practice even if you do not have a distinct recollection of how a particular note was recorded. Be aware that notes recorded after an interview are likely to represent your general recollection of the session rather than your verbatim memory of specific statements. Therefore, when recording notes from a session after the fact, be careful about how you document the clients' statements. If you can accurately recall the client's statements, then you may provide direct quotations. If you only remember the general gist of the conversation, then be honest and indicate that you are summarizing or paraphrasing, rather than providing a direct quotation.

Organizing one's notes meticulously may give them greater credibility. More than a few clinicians have been embarrassed during cross-examination by sloppy notes. Notes should be word-processed or handwritten in ink, in a consistent format. The use of White Out should be avoided because that could indicate that the records have been doctored. If you need to amend notes to add facts or correct an inaccurate statement, identify clearly the date of the correction and the reason for the change.

Word-processing software allows clinicians to include numbered lines for notes that are to be used in court proceedings. Numbering the lines suggests a higher level organization, which may add to the court's perception of your credibility. For example, rather than saying that a note is referenced halfway down the page, you could say, "The material to be reviewed is found on line 17 of page 6 of my notes." Now *that* organizational scheme looks impressive!

Records should be stored in a safe place to ensure confidentiality and to prevent tampering. If and when they are destroyed or disposed of, it should be done in a secure fashion, for example, through use of a shredder. The length of time that records should be retained may be specified by your funding source, by legislation, by state licensing regulations, or by the code of ethics for your profession (see NASW, 2011, for links to record retention laws in various states). For hospitals and health care facilities, legislation typically requires retention of records from 3 to 10 years. Also, consider limitation periods for the types of actions that are more likely to arise from your practice. For example, civil lawsuits generally must be initiated within 2 to 6 years of the event that gave rise to the suit, depending on the state and the relevant statute of limitations. In some instances, lawsuits may be initiated beyond the general limitations period. If a client is not aware of an injury right away, the limitations period may begin when the client becomes aware. In certain cases involving a child as the injured party, a lawsuit may be initiated when the child becomes an adult, even if the general limitations period has expired. For serious criminal charges, there is no time limit. Consider whether the information in your files may be useful in potential actions, including a malpractice suit brought against you.

Storing information on electronic data systems permits its quick and efficient transfer. It also provides compact storage of large quantities of information with easy retrieval. This technology can save time and enhance the presentation of your case if it goes to a hearing. However, technology has pitfalls. Consider how to prevent tampering with information, computer viruses, lost data, and unauthorized access to client files. Both attorneys and computer programmers struggle with how to ensure that stored data are safe and accurate. Use digital or hard-copy backups as well as passwords and encryption to protect sensitive information. Video and audio recordings also require safe storage to prevent problems with unauthorized access and tampering. Finally, consider how to *permanently* erase information from disks or tapes; an unsuspecting clinician could easily forget that computers have "undelete" software that can restore data they thought they had destroyed.[3]

If you communicate via the Internet, be careful about what you say, as well as how you send and store the messages. In spite of firewalls, encryption, and password protections, it is possible for e-mail and other electronic messages to be intercepted, either over the Internet or by hacking into someone's computer and stealing a password. Ensure that all written communications are fashioned in ways that anticipate their potential use in court under circumstances in which you would be asked to explain their meaning. Text messages and other client data stored on cell phones, cameras, iPads, iPods, or other electronic devices may also be subject to subpoena. Some clinicians refuse to communicate via certain forms of technology in order to avoid risks to confidentiality and privilege.

THE CONTENTS OF RECORDS

The perfect records for use in adjudication would be word-for-word transcriptions from audio recordings, sworn testimonials, and videos of all client interactions. However, because your primary role is as a treating clinician, these types of recording methods would prove overly burdensome in practice. Unless your primary role is to gather evidence as a potential witness, the contents of your records should be based primarily on what is clinically relevant and ethically required to provide competent clinical services. Because of our focus in this volume, the following section highlights legal rather than clinical or therapeutic issues in discussing the contents of records.

When working in a nonforensic clinical setting, you will typically restrict your collection and documentation of personal client information to that which is directly pertinent to the purposes of your clinical relationship (APA, 2010, s.4; NASW, 2008, s.1.07). By retaining only the information necessary to determine and deliver appropriate services, you can protect client confidentiality in an environment where the evidence maintained might be illegitimately used to hurt or embarrass your clients. In forensic contexts such as probation and child protection, clinicians have a specific role in documenting behavior that may later be cited in evidentiary proceedings (Kagle & Kopels, 2008). Accordingly, forensic professionals

---

[3]Consider using software specifically designed to permanently erase records. Also, check your hard drive and external storage devices for temporary files that contain confidential information. When disposing of a computer, the safest ways to destroy all files are to reformat or physically demolish the hard drive.

are likely to have much more extensive notes. When Sam investigates an allegation of child sexual abuse, he needs to document who is alleged to have assaulted whom, who is alleged to have witnessed the assault, when it was alleged to have happened, where it was alleged to have taken place, and what the details of the alleged assault were (e.g., whether it was sexual and, if so, where the victim was touched and how; whether weapons were used; the physical and psychosocial impacts on the victim). The level of detail required for Sam's records may go beyond what is required for therapeutic purposes. To ensure that the appropriate information is gathered and recorded, Sam needs to know the legal requirements for a conviction in criminal court or for intervening in a child protection case (e.g., is a medical examination required to support a conviction?). The manner in which evidence is gathered is also critical. In particular, cases involving children have been challenged because the clinician asked leading questions and, as a result of poor interview techniques, adversely influenced the child's information (Ceci & Bruck, 2006; Cross et al., 2007). Clinicians who work as forensic experts require special training and knowledge (see Chapter 7).

Whatever the job-related context, clinicians should keep concise records and follow a consistent system for collecting information. If certain information is deliberately omitted from a record, consider stating the reasons for doing so on the record and be prepared to defend your reasoning to an examining attorney, if need be. During mediation, Philip and Paula may discuss past marital infidelities but may ask Michael not to record them. Michael could note that historical information about the marriage was omitted at the request of the clients. If you use codes or shorthand, follow a key that explains these notations, use the codes consistently, and include the key in your records. In the interests of clarity and integrity, avoid using codes or shorthand that cannot be understood by others reviewing your notes.

Contents of Progress Notes

Various agencies use different forms for progress notes. The following framework for progress notes uses the SOAP format (Kagel & Kopels, 2008). This format is particularly useful for legal purposes, as it separates four types of content: Subjective, Objective, Assessment, and Plans:

- The date and time of the meeting.
- Location of the meeting or type of contact (office, home visit, telephone, e-mail, Web-based chat or videoconference; text message).
- Brief summary of the purpose, agenda, or activities for this session.

- List of people present and people who were supposed to attend but did not.
- *S = SUBJECTIVE:* Summary of key content from the clients' perspectives, for instance:
  - What did the client say? What did other people say?
  - Thematic phrase that summarizes the session (e.g., frequent fights with spouse during past week).
  - Direct quote from the client that is significant to the issues discussed (e.g., "I purchased a gun last week, but I'm not planning to use it just yet").

- *O = OBJECTIVE:* Summary of key content from an independent third person's perspective, for instance:
  - Clinician's direct observations without interpretations (e.g., significant body language or client behaviors, not interpreted ... just the facts).
  - Information or facts that support or contradict what the client has stated.
  - Assessment tools used—methods, tests, and questions, but not results (which go under assessment).
  - Clinical interventions and client responses

- *A = ASSESSMENT:* Evaluation of client concerns, strengths, needs, and problems based on an analysis of the subjective and objective information that you gathered, for instance:
  - Assessment or clinical hypotheses—how do you, as a clinician, make sense of the subjective and objective data (based on the information under the Subjective and Objective categories, what is your clinical opinion of what is going on; applying what you know in terms of theory and assessment of the information presented by the client).
  - Explanation of client's current situation.
  - Possible diagnoses.
  - Key risks and ethical issues, such as homicidal ideation, suicidal ideation, child abuse and neglect, elder abuse and neglect, intimate partner abuse, client involvement in legal proceedings, or client lacking mental capacity.

- *P = PLANS:* Statement of what the clinician(s) and client(s) have decided to do to address the client's concerns and needs, as identified in the assessment, for instance:
  - Treatment plan (or service agreement), including the responsibilities of the client, the clinician, and agency, and the rationale for each intervention or component of the plan.

- o Homework that a client has agreed to complete.
- o Commitments by clinician to gather information, advocate, broker referrals, coordinate services, monitor and evaluate progress, provide follow-up support, and so on.
- o Services offered that the client rejects (including reason for rejection of services).
- o Issues to be discussed in future sessions.
- o How key risks and ethical issues were addressed or will be addressed (Barsky, 2010).

- Signature (if you did not write the progress note on the same day as the contact or meeting, also indicate the date that you wrote and signed the progress note).

The SOAP method of record keeping is particularly helpful if your notes are subpoenaed. The court can easily differentiate which parts of your notes are based on firsthand observations (the subjective and objective content) and which parts are based on opinion (the assessment and plans). Proofread your notes before signing them to check for grammatical and spelling errors, as well as for contradictions or inaccuracies that could raise questions about your professional competence should your records be entered into evidence in court.

If a client indicates suicidal or homicidal ideation—thoughts about harming herself or others—document this information and how you responded (e.g., whether you conducted a risk assessment, devised and had the client agree to a safety plan, referred the client for a second-level assessment, had the client dispose of drugs or a weapon, or warned a potential victim). Ensure that you also document issues such as child abuse, where there is a legal obligation to report. In using client statements as evidence in a proceeding, direct quotations have greater weight than paraphrasing. If you are unsure about the truth or basis of a client statement, include some details in your notes: "Paula appeared angry when she said she wanted 'to do Philip in,' but indicated upon extensive interviewing that she had no plan or intention of carrying out any harmful acts." If the clinician wanted to protect Paula further, she could simply state, "Paula expressed anger because of Philip's threats," omitting any reference to Paula's own threats. If you are working in a forensic setting, consider documenting *corroborating evidence*, that is, obtain and record more than one source of information to support your assessments and opinions (e.g., information received from the client, the client's spouse, and the client's physician). Also remember to document supervision meetings and consultations with risk management personnel or other clinicians. Documented use of supervision or consultation may be particularly helpful in a malpractice lawsuit, as you have demonstrated that you took appropriate steps in consulting with others.

Because adjudications base decisions on facts (especially direct observations), speculation and secondhand information contained in client records may be of little use. For clinical reasons, it is important to record opinions and assessments. State these as opinions or assessments rather than as facts: "A possible interpretation for Debra's nightmares is ... " Including the observations underlying your assessments and impressions can be useful clinically as well as in adjudication: "Debra disclosed that she continued to have nightmares about .. ." By noting the source of your information, you and others can reexamine your impressions at a later date to see whether they are supported by other information brought to trial.

Avoid using labels, particularly ones that perpetuate stereotypes or other negative connotations about a class of people. Rather than referring to a person as a "schizophrenic," you could describe the person as "having schizophrenia." If the person has not been formally diagnosed by a properly qualified clinician, then describe the person's hallucinations, delusions, or other indications you observed rather than attaching the diagnostic label.

Secondhand information is often used for clinical assessments even though it might be considered unreliable in legal cases. For example, Sam might gather information on Debra from her teacher and physician. If secondhand information is useful to you for clinical purposes, include it in your records, but note the source of the information.

As with oral testimony, your records will have greater credibility if the information is free of bias and jargon. Some agencies, such as child protection services, have a specific obligation to maintain "full, fair, and balanced records." For example, Sam should include both positive and negative aspects of Philip's parenting relationship with Debra. While judgmental and bigoted language should be avoided in all cases, not all clinicians have a legal obligation to maintain balanced records. Frieda's theoretical perspective focuses on client strengths. Her records will reflect this, deemphasizing client weaknesses. Other clinicians may omit damaging information about a client in order to protect the client, should a legal action arise. Although making such omissions may be legally permissible, consider whether it is clinically wise. (Note the discussion on thwarting disclosure, below.)

Be careful about making comments—written or verbal—concerning third parties. Such statements may increase the risk that your files will be subpoenaed by the third party about whom you allegedly made comments. This may damage your client's right to privacy. Further, you may be challenged for going beyond your authority, since the third party is not your client.

Contents of Critical Incident Reports

A critical incident report is a written statement used by agencies to document specific events that entail significant losses, physical or psychological harm, conflicts with the law, or risks to life or property (National Center for Critical Incident Analysis, n.d.). For instance, an agency may require clinicians to document violent activities or threats by clients, sexual improprieties or other acts of malpractice by staff, patients with indications of serious infectious diseases, infringement of client rights, or suspicions of child abuse and neglect. Critical incident reports should include information about the event, the context of the incident, who was involved or affected, precipitating events, client behaviors contributing to the event, injuries or losses incurred, how agency staff responded to the event, use of legal or clinical consultation, and plans for ongoing monitoring, evaluation, and follow-up. Critical incident reports are typically kept separate from client files and therefore may not be subject to a subpoena that is limited to a client's file. Critical incident reports may also be protected as privileged under tort claims and medical malpractice legislation, so you should check with an attorney before releasing such reports.

CLIENTS' RIGHTS

Clients should be aware of what will be kept in their records and what will not be kept, the policies for disposal, and provisions for gaining access to their records. Your agency should have procedures for clients to contest, correct, or revise the contents of their records, as well as policies to ensure that clients are aware of their rights.[4] The Health Insurance Portability and Accountability Act (1996), which applies to most health and mental health services, has specific provisions for patient rights, including a client's right to her own records.

All issues pertaining to confidentiality and disclosure should be documented in the client's records. Ideally, you have entered into a written service agreement with your client at the outset of providing treatment, explaining the client's right to confidentiality and the exceptions to it (described in Chapter 3). Before disclosing information to other people or agencies, you have asked the client to sign a consent form authorizing you to release such

---

[4]Different legislation governs different contexts of practice. At a federal level, consider the Health Insurance Portability and Accountability Act, the Freedom of Information Act, the Privacy Act of 1974, the Family Educational Rights and Privacy Act, Confidentiality of Alcohol and Drug Abuse Patient Records Regulation, and the Child Abuse Prevention and Treatment Act. Consider also state laws governing schools, hospitals, corrections, and the mental health professions.

information (APA, 2010, ss.4.05 and 9.04; NASW, 2008, ss.1.07 and 1.08). If the consent to release information is provided only orally, due to practical considerations, be sure to document this in your case notes. Then, have your client sign the written document as soon as possible. Any documents released to another agency should include a proviso that the information not be re-released without written permission from the client.[5]

During the intake stage of work with a client, the client has not yet entered into a service agreement. Because issues regarding confidentiality have not been settled between the agency and the client, the agency should limit documentation at the intake stage. When Michael received a call from Paula for mediation services, he documented the names and telephone numbers of the parties as well as the general nature of the issues to be mediated. He did not accept any historical information about the Carveys' situation nor the positions of the parties, preferring to wait until the parties had agreed to mediation and provisions regarding confidentiality. By doing so, he avoided setting himself up to be called as a witness in case the Carveys did not go ahead with mediation.

Consider situations in which disclosure in a legal proceeding is more likely to arise, for instance, a clinician who works with incest survivors, where disclosure is delayed and the clinician plays a role in bringing a formal report to the police. Pay particular attention to the contents of the records and the extent to which certain information can be damaging to your client if a case proceeds to a hearing. If clients keep diaries or prepare artwork as part of your intervention, consider whether they should keep these records in their own possession. If these documents are not in your possession or control, then you do not have to submit them if your records are subpoenaed. However, the same documents could be subpoenaed from your client.

USING RECORDS AT A HEARING

Records may be brought into evidence at hearings in three ways. The first method, use of reference notes to help refresh the clinician's memory, was described in Chapter 5 (Federal Rules of Evidence, 2010, Rule 612). In order to use notes to refresh your memory, the notes must have been made

---

[5]The provision not to re-release information without the client's written authorization may not apply when you release your case file to an investigator or evaluator who is preparing a report to the court. By definition, when documents are released to an investigator or evaluator for the court, the released information becomes part of the court's file and is available to be examined by the attorneys and the court.

contemporaneously with the events recorded, and you must have an active memory of the events at the time of the hearing.

The second method of bringing notes into a hearing arises when the witness has forgotten the events recorded. The notes may be entered into evidence as "past memory recorded." This type of evidence is not as persuasive as evidence provided when you use notes to refresh your memory. If you do not have a current recollection of the events, the contents of the notes cannot be challenged through cross-examination. Your notes may be unreliable as evidence, since they were developed for clinical purposes rather than for litigation. The information in clinical notes is often based on hearsay rather than sworn testimony and direct observations. Further, facts and opinions may be intermingled, and the information in your notes may be taken out of context. However, by following the guidelines suggested in this chapter, your notes are much more likely to withstand the legal tests of credibility even if you do not have a current recollection at the time of the hearing.

The third method of bringing client records into a hearing occurs when court admits them as "business records" (Federal Rules of Evidence, 2010, Rule 803(6)). Business records are documents created in the regular course of business activity and not in contemplation of a particular legal action. Courts may also admit records into evidence if the original witness is unavailable (e.g., dead, incapacitated, or whereabouts unknown) and certain other criteria are met (Federal Rules of Evidence, 2010, Rule 804). These criteria include: the statement was made in contemplation of death, the statement was made for purposes of diagnosis or treatment, or the statement was part of records of regularly conducted activity (similar to the business records rule). Still, the weight given to evidence stated in such records may be suspect if there is no opportunity to cross-examine the person who wrote the records. If you are planning to leave an agency or move to another location, consider leaving a forwarding address for clients or others who may need to call you as a witness. Your professional obligations may continue even after you have ended your working relationship with a client or agency. Unfortunately, most clinicians would rather not be called as a witness after they have moved on.

Videos can be very persuasive in court. They can provide accurate, objective, and complete recordings of what happened. In an investigation of allegations of child abuse, for example, a video of a child's interview with a clinician will help determine the quality of interviewing experienced by the child and inform the judge about the accuracy of the child's statements, including whether the child's statements may have been influenced by the investigator's techniques (Orbach & Lamb, 2001). Videos may also have an impact on the perception of witness credibility. Observing a child witness in a properly conducted interview may have a significantly more powerful effect on the judge and jury than the testimony of the clinician who interviewed the child. The decision makers can hear the child firsthand rather than having to rely on the clinician's interpretations of the interview. Conducting interviews on video requires specific expertise. Otherwise, their validity can easily be challenged on the basis of improper or leading questions (Bottoms et al., 2009; Ceci & Bruck, 2006).

THWARTING DISCLOSURE

Treating clinicians often wish they could prevent disclosure of records. Some reasons are ethically justifiable, others not. Clinicians treating victims of sexual assault, for example, may be concerned that their clients will be subjected to intense scrutiny before and during the trial of the alleged perpetrator. Historically, defense attorneys could subpoena complainants' records from clinicians, crisis services, and transition houses in order to discredit the complainant by saying that she is emotionally unstable, tends to fabricate stories, or is motivated to lie because she is trying to hide having had sex with someone else. For the most part, current evidentiary rules prohibit use of evidence of the victim's past sexual behavior or alleged sexual predisposition, although there are some exceptions (Federal Rules of Evidence, 2010, Rule 412). Also, most states have laws granting privilege to advocates, crisis counselors, and transition house staff working with victims of domestic violence (American Bar Association, n.d.). Still, there are many other areas of practice where clinical records could be subpoenaed and the client could be embarrassed. Consider, for instance, a client who has received vocational counseling. The counselor's records may include information about the client's problems, including poor performance in school or prior work settings, irresponsible behavior leading to dismissal, or ethically questionable behavior. If a clinician wants to protect his client from disclosure of this type of information in a public legal process, there are several options, described below. Unfortunately, each option has major drawbacks. Before adopting any of these options, consult with your attorney, professional association, or other expert on law and professional ethics.

Minimal Records

To protect their clients, some clinicians resort to maintaining minimal records (e.g., limiting details to the name of the client, the problem presented, and the dates seen). They deliberately exclude any information that could harm the credibility of the complainant or embarrass her. Unfortunately, some of this information may be clinically important, legally relevant, and ethically necessary. Suicidal or homicidal thoughts, alcohol or drug use, and high levels of stress are just a few examples. Although minimal records may thwart disclosure in legal processes, they may not meet the standards required for competent clinical practice. Further, the clinician may still be called to testify about client information not included in case records. If you want to keep minimal records, ensure that these records are consistent with agency policy, laws regulating your agency, and your professional code of ethics.

Double Records

Some clinicians keep two sets of records—an official set and a personal set. The official set excludes potentially damaging information. The personal set includes all information, assessments, and speculations that the clinician uses for her own purposes. Although some clinicians believe that a subpoena applies only to the official records, all records are subject to subpoena. Some clinicians hide the fact that they have a set of unofficial records. However, if found out, failure to disclose all records can result in obstruction of justice or contempt of court charges against the clinician. The question raised by some clinicians is "How will anyone know?" The real question is, "What does your sense of ethics and risk taking tell you?" Few agencies or professional associations would officially condone hiding a second set of records. There is no ethical foundation for keeping two sets of records. Ethically as well as statutorily, one set of records is what is appropriate.

Coded Information

Some clinicians use secret coding to make parts of their records indecipherable to people unfamiliar with the coding. Some codes are so subtle that the reader does not even know that coding is being used (e.g., a double asterisk may denote past suicide attempts; "FLK" for funny looking kid). During a hearing you may be asked to explain your codes or shorthand. Some codes may not be directly significant to the case but may indicate bias, lack of respect, or lack of professionalism. If it appears that you have deliberately tried to mislead the reader, your credibility as a witness may be called into question.[6] Further, if someone else in your agency needs to refer to your

---

[6]TTFO is sometimes used as slang for "told to f**k oneself." If asked what the initials mean, the practitioner might say "to take fluids only." Patients have sued agencies based on derogatory notations in their records.

records, will she understand what you have written? As indicated earlier, if you know in advance that your case may be involved in a legal proceeding, you may have an ethical obligation to maintain clear notes without the use of code or shorthand. This will ensure that others reviewing your work—in court or otherwise—can understand the meaning of your records. If you want to use acronyms or abbreviations in records, the professional approach is to include a key that accurately explains the meanings of these terms.

Doctoring or Disposing of Documents

If there is no impending legal process, clinicians are free to amend their records. In many agencies, supervisors or agency attorneys periodically review case records and suggest changes to avoid future problems (e.g., to remove judgmental language, bias, or speculation). Clinicians are also free to dispose of records, within the policies of the agency and the standards of the profession. Michael's mediation association, for example, suggests that mediators maintain records for at least 6 months after mediation has been terminated. However, if a clinician is aware of an impending legal process or has been subpoenaed, doctoring or destroying documents can result in such charges as contempt of court or obstruction of justice, malpractice suits, and professional disciplinary actions. Once again, the question may arise, "How will anyone know?" Before shredding your files, you might want to explore the frequency with which fraudulently motivated shredding has been unearthed and exposed.

Even if you have no records, you may still be called as a witness. You may have limited value as a witness, particularly if you have no current recollection of the events in question. However, keeping records might actually help your client, since premature disposal of records can hurt your credibility as a witness. Finally, a clinician without records may be more vulnerable to malpractice suits (e.g., where a client later alleges that the clinician induced a false memory of abuse) or complaints before a licensing board for failure to comply with ethical standards of record keeping.

Lying

As noted throughout this volume, when clinicians are involved in legal processes they are expected to tell the truth. Depending on their priority of values, some clinicians may be tempted to intentionally lie to protect clients or themselves. Frieda believes her records will embarrass Paula, so Frieda considers telling Alice that she has already destroyed them. Sam does not want to be called as a witness, so he wonders whether to tell the court he has no current recollection of any of his notes (a convenient memory lapse).

These types of tactics can thwart disclosure. However, you risk charges of perjury and professional misconduct, as well as a negative perception for both you and your profession. Professional organizations, agencies, and judges will rarely condone lying, even if the witness honestly believes she has good intentions.[7]

Given the foregoing dilemmas, how does a clinician balance these risks and conflicting interests? If a significant part of your mandate is to collect evidence, then this takes precedence in the way that you gather and store information. If your primary role is that of a helping professional, then your records should be designed primarily to meet your needs as a treating clinician. Bear in mind the potential legal pitfalls. In many fields of practice there are few conflicts between the clinical and legal requirements for proper record keeping. In areas where conflicts arise, there may be no ideal solution.

---

[7]The types of rare examples include necessity (e.g., lying in order to prevent a person from being killed when there is no other alternative) or to escape pernicious treatment by a rogue state (e.g., Jews and other persecuted people who lied to escape Nazi Germany).

Chapter 7

EXPERT WITNESSES

In the first six chapters, we focused on the role of clinicians as fact witnesses. This chapter focuses on the role of clinicians as expert witnesses. Whereas fact witnesses provide eyewitness accounts (or direct knowledge) of facts at issue in a legal proceeding, a person who qualifies as an expert witness may provide opinions as well as fact evidence. Court proceedings tend to be strict about limiting opinion evidence to recognized experts. Other types of hearings may allow people to express opinions without necessarily requiring that the person be legally qualified as an expert.

The rationale for restricting most witnesses to direct observations relates to the division of roles in an adjudicative process. The role of a witness is to state her knowledge of the relevant facts. The role of the judge or other decision maker is to determine the truth, based on a hearing of all of the witnesses. To come to a determination, the decision maker needs to formulate opinions. If a witness was permitted to state opinions during the hearing, he could usurp the role of the decision maker. An exception is made for people who qualify as experts, the theory being that experts can assist the decision maker by virtue of their specialized knowledge, skills, training, education, and experience. To some clinicians, these distinctions sound unduly rigid. However, if you wish to play the game, you need to know the rules.

Clinicians come from a range of disciplines that allow them to assist tribunals through their expertise. Among the more commonly used experts in court are clinicians who specialize in forensic mental health issues such as forensic social work, forensic psychology, and forensic psychiatry. They may be expert in criminology, child development, human motivation, memory, mental illness, or family violence. Social workers might be called on to deliver assessments of individuals in relation to their families and other systems in their social environments. Psychologists, psychiatrists, and other licensed mental health professionals may be called in legal proceedings to provide an assessment of an individual's mental condition (e.g., competence to stand trial or existence of mental disorders that render the individual not responsible for his actions). Psychiatrists might render medical opinions, while psychologists might offer interpretations of psychological test data. Clinicians with social science expertise may be called to explain research methodology or interpret research findings. Just because a clinician is recognized by her peers as an expert does not mean that the clinician will be qualified as an expert in a legal proceeding. If a clinician does not qualify as an expert witness, she may still be called as a fact witness, with the ability to testify about facts but not provide opinion evidence. If you are called as a fact witness rather than an expert witness, do not take this decision as a personal slight. Your role as a fact witness may be very important.

The following sections describe the various roles of experts, qualifying as an expert, admitting expert evidence, and ways in which an expert may be selected for a particular case. In the latter sections of this chapter, we revisit the direct examination and cross-examination, with a focus on expert witnesses.

THE ROLES OF EXPERTS

A psychologist, social worker, psychiatrist, or other practitioner who specializes in gathering, preparing, or presenting information for legal processes is called a *forensic expert*.[1] Forensic experts may be hired by one party, hired by both parties together, or appointed by the court. The roles of an expert include a consultant, an educator of the court, and combined fact–opinion expert, as described below.

Consultant

A consultant is a forensic expert hired by one party to assist the attorney with analyzing, preparing, strategizing, and developing a case. The case may be part of an existing legal proceeding or it may become part of a

---

[1]Forensic experts require very specific training and experience. Because forensic work is so specialized, we would not be able to do justice to any particular field without writing a separate book on that field (e.g., Bartol & Bartol, 2008; National Organization of Forensic Social Work, n.d.; Skeem et al., 2009). If you plan to act as a forensic expert, this book provides a good foundation, but you need to proceed beyond this base.

proceeding that has yet to be initiated. A consultant may or may not be used to testify as a witness, although the attorney's letter of engagement should specify the consultant's role and whether there is a possibility that the consultant will be called to testify. A consultant who is not called to testify is sometimes referred to as a "nontestimonial expert." The functions of a consultant may include:

- Identifying issues, collecting evidence, and building the case (e.g., compiling diagnoses and reports from other clinicians).
- Evaluating evidence (e.g., reviewing the process used for psychological testing, critiquing the credibility of information provided by other expert witnesses who may be called to testify, evaluating the validity and reliability of research in the area).
- Assisting an attorney in determining whether a reasonable cause of action exists (e.g., whether the mediator, Michael, breached his ethical obligation regarding confidentiality).
- Identifying and evaluating negative factors in the case (e.g., what evidence goes against Paula's claim for custody of Debra).
- Preparing a technical report explaining clinical concepts in terms that can be understood by the attorney (e.g., providing a literature review on child alienation).
- Preparing questions to ask expert witnesses at the hearing for examination of friendly witnesses and cross-examination of opposing witnesses.
- Evaluating or interpreting expert evidence adduced during the hearing.
- Developing diagrams for presentation at the hearing (e.g., genograms to depict family relationships or graphs that illustrate research findings).
- Identifying precedent cases involving expert evidence.
- Advising about the selection of jurors (e.g., what types of questions to ask prospective jurors; what types of verbal and nonverbal cues to observe; how to interpret various responses, attitudes, or values).
- Preparing witnesses so they can present their testimony in an effective, persuasive manner.
- Assisting with jury selection by applying social science research to help an attorney determine which prospective jurors may be favorably predisposed or biased against one's case (Brodsky, 2009; Cramer, Adams, & Brodsky, 2009).

In most situations, a consulting expert cannot be compelled to participate in pretrial discovery processes or to testify at trial (Federal Rules of

Evidence, 2010, Rule 26).[2] The consulting expert's files and information are considered to be part of the attorney–client privilege (work–product). However, if the consulting expert becomes a testifying witness, the expert is subject to pretrial disclosures (National Institute for Trial Advocacy, 2006). To ensure that any research you do as a consultant remains confidential and privileged, do not share the research with anyone other than the attorney with whom you are working. If you need to work with other clinicians, research assistants, or research subjects as part of your trial preparations or consultation, have them sign an agreement binding them to confidentiality and privilege (Miller, 2009).

Before agreeing to act as a consultant, make sure that the case is a good fit for you: Do you have the required expertise, do you have the time to do effective work within the time constraints of the attorney and court, do you have a sense that you and the attorney can work well together, do you have sufficient comfort to work with the issues raised by the case (e.g., child sexual abuse, gruesome violence), and does the case raise any ethical issues for you (e.g., honesty, dual relationships, or cultural competence)? Consider a case in which Philip's attorney asks you to provide consultation on how to cross-examine Debra. He wants to you to provide psychological information on suggestibility and memory so he can impeach her credibility. The attorney offers you a generous fee, but you feel queasy about collaborating with an attorney to denigrate the testimony of a teenager who is already enduring a difficult divorce. Is it ethical to provide such consultation? Even if your code of ethics does not specifically prohibit such consultation, would you be able to live with yourself? How might your participation in this case affect your personal and professional reputation?

For a sample of a service (retainer) agreement for an expert witness hired in a consultant's role, see Appendix A. This agreement should establish the scope of the consultant's work, including what information should be gathered and assessed, what theories and procedures will be followed, and what questions the expert will address. The agreement should not indicate what finding the attorney hopes the consultant will reach (National Institute for Trial Advocacy, 2006). Note that even though a consultant is retained by one party, the consultant has a professional obligation to be honest and fair in his gathering information, assessment of the issues, and recommendations to the attorney. Consultants should guard against providing attorneys only with the information or conclusions that they want to hear. A consultant who fails to provide full and accurate information and recommendations puts himself at risk of malpractice in relation

---

[2]A relatively rare exception permits courts to compel disclosure of necessary evidence that the court cannot otherwise acquire.

to competence and integrity (APA, 2010, ss.2.03 & 9.01; NASW, 2008, ss.1.04 & 4.04).

Educator of the Court

During legal proceedings, either party may call expert witnesses to testify for the purpose of educating the court concerning a particular field of science, such as mental health, human behavior, memory, or domestic violence. An example of an impartial expert is an independent mental health professional appointed by the court to answer specific psycholegal questions for which the court needs an expert's opinion, for instance, how to assess a patient for mental competency or how to know whether physical restraints are necessary to protect a client. As an educator of the court, the expert does not need direct knowledge about the facts of the case. Rather than testifying about what happened or what the expert directly observed about the parties, the expert testifies regarding research, theory, and evidence from a field of science in which the witness has particular training, knowledge, and experience. Consider a malpractice lawsuit in which a family sues a psychiatrist for failing to provide appropriate assessment and intervention for a suicidal patient. An independent expert on suicide may provide testimony about the incidence of suicide within certain treatment populations (e.g., alcohol abusers). She may also comment about suicide risk assessment, referring to research studies, clinical literature, and local standards of practice for assessing and responding to suicidal ideation. However, if the expert has never treated or met the patient, the expert may not provide information about the facts of the case. Many experts who play the role of educator have academic backgrounds, including research, scholarly publications, and teaching. However, other experts have extensive practice experience that can be used to educate the court. In some cases, the testimony of an expert is the most influential testimony presented at trial (Bernstein & Hartsell, 2005; Tindall, 2003). Judges tend to go along with the evidence of an expert unless there is contrary evidence provided by another credible expert. Different expert witnesses may provide conflicting information, as long as they participate in an honest exchange of ideas that can be critically evaluated by the judge or jury. When different experts provide conflicting evidence, the judge or jury needs to determine whose evidence is more credible.

In order to serve as impartial educators, experts should strive to provide objective testimony, supported by reliable research and documentation (Tindall, 2003). Interviews with actual jurors suggests that impartiality (along with clarity of presentation and familiarity the facts of the case) has greater impact on perceived credibility than the expert's educational credentials or personality (Melton et al., 2007). As educators of the court, experts should avoid circumstances in which they may be viewed as a *hired gun* or *predisposed advocate*. The notion of a hired gun suggests the expert is being hired because the attorney knows the expert will provide evidence supporting a particular point of view. If an expert is hired by one party to provide evidence, the expert may experience covert and overt pressure to distort data to support an opinion or to select information that supports a particular position. However, an expert witness has an ethical and legal duty to educate the court—providing reliable and relevant information in an objective, impartial manner—regardless of who hired or appointed him (CEGFP, 2011).

Maintaining objectivity and scientific integrity may be challenging because attorneys may be looking for partisan experts to support their case and convince the trier of fact (Sales & Shuman, 2008). Regardless of whether an attorney hires expert witnesses to support a particular finding or position, the ethical responsibility of any expert witness is to serve the best interests of the court. The best interests of the court are served when the expert witness testifies honestly and accurately, rejecting junk science and putting forth the most valid and reliable information from the witness's area of expertise. Unfortunately, there are still some experts who sell their services to the highest bidder or will testify in favor of the people who hired them rather than testifying for the truth. Still, more often than not, a forensic specialist hired by one side will provide an honest appraisal of the accumulated data and derived interpretations.

Some experts become known for having particular opinions and becoming strong advocates for those opinions, for instance, being pro-life or pro-choice, supporting or opposing equal rights for gay men and lesbians, or attributing particular causes for autism or other mental health conditions. A *predisposed advocate* supports a certain position based on allegiance to a particular philosophy, affiliation, belief system, or set of values. For example, a predisposed advocate might be known to favor joint custody without regard to valid facts or research evidence. She would dutifully advocate for joint custody in Philip and Paula's case, ignoring or minimizing allegations of abuse, perhaps even distorting known facts. Providing such testimony as a predisposed advocate is unethical. Forensic specialists have a professional obligation to the court to present rival, plausible alternative hypotheses that might explain a set of data. If an advocacy position means presenting only the arguments for a particular view, then this would be unethical. Presenting only one side without even referring to alternative perspectives misleads the court into believing there is only one side to the argument. If an advocacy position means supporting a particular position or conclusion by presenting information in a balanced and honest manner, then this would be ethical (Barrett & George, 2005). Advocating for the truth and accuracy of your data is not the same as blindly advocating for a particular client or position.

For most judicial proceedings, the ideal expert witness takes an objective stance and serves as an impartial educator. To avoid perceptions of bias, it is preferable for the expert to be hired by the court rather than by one party. Often, this not the case, challenging the expert to be even more cautious in order to avoid perceptions of bias. Although attorneys or judges may refer to you as the "defense expert" or "expert for the plaintiff" you should act as "expert for the truth." Regardless of who hires the expert, ethical obligations require professional clinicians to act honestly, making sure they do not misrepresent available research or professional knowledge.

A clinician who sees herself as an advocate should be careful about how she presents herself, so as not to taint her credibility in a particular case or her reputation more generally (e.g., if she always provides the same type of recommendation, regardless of the specifics of a case). If you are purposefully acting as an advocate for a particular client or point of view, be honest about your position and also provide credible evidence to support your position. Consider an expert who has been asked whether a minor named Joey should be tried as an adult. The expert is a social worker who fundamentally disagrees with the practice of trying minors as adults. She could respond, "No, I do not support trying Joey as an adult. First, as a social worker, I do not support this practice in general because of the research on the negative effects on minors who are treated as adults within the court system [and cite specific research]. Second, in this particular case, Joey is already highly vulnerable, given his history of suicide attempts.... " Become familiar with the evidence and arguments of those who oppose your opinion so you can respond proactively to their points of view. For instance, "While proponents of trying juveniles as adults purport this practice will reduce crime and recidivism by giving harsher sentences, in actuality, these practices substantially increase recidivism ... "

Ponder a case in which a psychologist is hired to provide testimony concerning the accuracy of an eyewitness account. If she presents herself as a predisposed advocate, she might emphasize those memory and perceptual factors that suggest inaccuracy, such as the briefness of the exposure or the likely stress experienced by the eyewitness. If she assumes the role of an impartial educator, she will discuss all factors that affect eyewitness performance, including lighting conditions or a short retention interval (Tindall, 2003). During court proceedings, impartiality and the perception of impartiality are vital to the expert witness's credibility. In public policy or legislative proceedings, predisposed advocacy for a particular point of view may be more acceptable. Still, the advocate will probably be viewed as more credible if she bases her position on objective facts and valid research, rather than on emotional or ideological appeals.

If your practice primarily consists of clinical work and you have had little or no prior experience testifying in court, take heart: the lack of court-room experience may actually be advantageous. In research conducted with mock jurors, highly credentialed experts with extensive testifying experience court were perceived as less honest, less trustworthy, less likeable, and more annoying than witnesses with little testifying experience (Melton et al., 2007).

In some instances when you are hired as an educator to the court, the hiring attorney will be scrupulous about not talking directly with you, not providing you with specific information about the case, and not helping you prepare your testimony. Here, the attorney's aim is to foster the court's perception that you are free from bias about the case. If your role is to provide information drawn only from the research or clinical literature, then there may be no need for you to know anything about the case before the bench. If this approach is effectively implemented, the court may view your testimony as more objective than if you had been briefed on the facts of the case or had prematurely formed impressions about which side should prevail.

In order for experts to foster and maintain credibility in legal proceedings, they should avoid situations that give rise to perceptions of partiality or demagoguery: publishing articles based on ideology or prejudice rather than rigorous research evidence and rational thought; associating oneself with organizations that devalue science; or presenting testimony based on biased or incomplete information. As court educators, they should demonstrate that they are concerned about the truth, including being open to alternative theories, research findings, and practice strategies.

Note that even as an expert who is hired to educate the court, you may not have to testify. In some cases, an attorney hires an expert to conduct an evaluation and initially plans to call the expert as a witness, but later changes his mind. The attorney may have a number of reasons for not calling the expert: concerns about the quality of the evaluation or report, concerns about the ability of the expert to serve as an effective witness, dissatisfaction with the opinions or conclusions of the report, settlement of the case outside court, or a change in tactics for the trial. When an attorney changes her mind about calling you as a witness, ask for feedback. If there were any problems with your evaluation process or report, you may be able to address these. Some experts put tremendous time and effort into preparing to testify, only to learn that the parties have settled the case outside of court. Take comfort in the fact that your strength as a potential witness may have helped settle the case, saving you, your clients, and others from the aggravations of having to participate in a lengthy, adversarial trial.

Fact–Opinion Expert

In many instances, witnesses possess both factual knowledge and expert (opinion) evidence. The expert may possess factual knowledge as either a clinician or forensic practitioner who has worked with one or more of the parties involved in the legal proceeding. At the same time, the expert may be able to provide the court with expert information or opinions, linking the expert's direct observations with knowledge from her area of professional expertise. In the Carveys' case, Evelyn has been hired to provide a custody evaluation. When called as a witness, she may testify about her direct observations, including information she has gathered during interviews with Paula, Philip, and Debra, as well as information gleaned from observing interactions between each parent and child. The court will also permit Evelyn to testify about her areas of expertise, including child development, family transitions, and effective parenting. When Evelyn recommends that Debra's best interests would be served by living primarily with her mother, Evelyn's opinion is based on a linkage between her factual evidence and expert knowledge. A fact–opinion expert reviews all data—pro and con—and forms an opinion on the basis of the data, rather than simply putting forward the desired position of the side that is soliciting her services.

In contrast to Evelyn, who was hired as a forensic expert, Frieda was hired by the Carveys as a treating clinician. When Frieda testifies in court, she can attest to factual information, such as whether Philip and Paula attended counseling and whether she observed any violence between them. If she were qualified as an expert, she could give opinions about the nature of their relationship. However, she should be cautious about how she responds to questions that ask her to predict future violence in the family. Because she was hired as a treating professional, not a forensic expert, predicting future behavior falls outside her role (Butters & Vaughan-Eden, 2011).

An expert witness's testimony may be limited by the expert's ability to gather data and conduct an assessment in a comprehensive, unbiased manner. Assume that Philip hires a family and divorce specialist to rebut Evelyn's custody evaluation. As Philip's expert, the specialist meets with Philip and concludes that Philip should have custody of Debra, even though the specialist has never met Paula or Debra. Judges, attorneys, and clinicians have increasingly become aware that it is unethical to offer an opinion about child custody or access without having evaluated the entire family system (Gould & Martindale, 2009). In today's climate, Philip's expert would likely be challenged by the opposing attorney, citing statements in various codes of ethics and professional practice guidelines as well as published texts in the field of custody evaluation. Thus a hired gun's assessment that offers predictable opinions about custodial placement is likely to be given little weight by the judge.

Clinicians should avoid situations in which they play two or more roles with their clients (Butters & Vaughan-Eden, 2011). Such instances raise ethical issues in terms of multiple roles and potential conflicts of interest (APA, 2010, ss.3.05 & 3.06; NASW, 2008, s.1.06). In particular, if you have provided therapeutic services to a client, you should avoid performing forensic evaluations for the same person.[3] By engaging in dual roles, you may be opening yourself and your client to a number of risks.[4] First, as a therapist, your primary duty is to your client (Zur, n.d.). Your role is to support and advocate for your client (APA, Principle B; NASW, 2008, s.101). If you act as a forensic evaluator, then you may need to testify against the client's wishes. As a forensic evaluator, your primary duties are to the court and the system of justice, rather than to the individual client. How can you develop a therapeutic alliance with your client and still be able to provide an objective assessment for the court? Second, as a therapist, you offer your client confidentiality in order to provide the client with a safe place to discuss issues that may be legally or personally embarrassing. As a forensic evaluator, you should advise your client that any information you gather may be used in court. Under Rule 26(a)(2)(B) of the Federal Rules of Civil Procedure, forensic experts are required to provide the court with a detailed written report with all the expert's opinions and the facts on which they are based. A forensic expert cannot ignore relevant information gathered during a treatment process when presenting written or oral testimony as a forensic evaluator. Clients may be confused, at the least, and angry toward a practitioner who initially offers confidentiality for treatment purposes, but then shares information to the court as part of a forensic evaluation process. Further, if a forensic evaluator has served as a treatment provider, the court may question the evaluator's objectivity and give little weight

---

[3]Dual roles may be unavoidable in some situations, for instance, when a treating practitioner is the only person in the region who can provide the type of forensic assessment that the court requires, or when a forensic evaluator has to provide crisis intervention counseling to a client who is in immediate danger. Even in such extreme or unforeseen circumstances, the practitioner should take steps to minimize risks, such as clarifying role expectations, explaining the limits of confidentiality, and documenting why the practitioner accepted a dual role (Barsky, 2010).

[4]Note that it may not technically be a dual relationship for a treating clinician to act as a fact witness, as the clinician may be providing fact evidence to the court but has not entered into a second form of relationship with the client. Providing fact evidence with consent of the client or pursuant to a court order may still pose risks, so clinicians should clearly explain their potential roles as fact witnesses to their clients.

to the expert's information and opinions. Finally, a client may refuse to receive further services from a therapist who acts as a forensic evaluator and provides the court with embarrassing or damaging information.

For a sample Informed Consent Form that explains the role of an impartial forensic expert, see Appendix C; also, see Appendix D for a sample of an Initial Letter to Attorneys after an Appointment Order. Note that forensic experts often identify the attorney who is hiring them as the client, not the person who is being evaluated (Heilbronner, 2005). By identifying the attorney as the client, the expert is ensuring that the person being evaluated does not view the expert as her counselor, therapist, or professional helper. Further, the hiring attorney is responsible for paying the expert (although the attorney will obtain the money for the expert from the person being evaluated).

ADMITTING EXPERT EVIDENCE

Admissibility of expert testimony refers to whether the judge should allow an expert to provide the court with certain types of scientific knowledge, including psychological theories and research on the particular clinical interventions. For expert evidence to be admitted into a court hearing, the evidence must satisfy five legal standards: relevant, helpful, delivered by a properly qualified expert, based on sound scientific methods or professional experience, and reasonable degree of certainty. The evidence must also meet other rules of admissibility (or inadmissibility), such as exclusionary rules based on public policy.[5] The judge acts as a gatekeeper, preventing jurors from hearing expert evidence that is irrelevant, unreliable, prejudicial, or a waste of the court's time. The following sections describe the five legal standards for admitting expert evidence, as well as other potential grounds for exclusion.

Relevant

As with other forms of evidence, expert evidence must be directly relevant to the issues in the case (Federal Rules of Evidence, 2010, Rule 403). Relevance refers to the potential of a given piece of evidence to help prove or disprove one of the legal elements of the case. For clinicians, this means that you must know how your expertise and opinions fit with legal issues

---

[5]As noted earlier, administrative tribunals will generally admit expert evidence without using the court's strict guidelines for exclusion. However, the weight given to the evidence may be related to similar factors.

at stake. In a family law case regarding spousal support or maintenance, Frieda's testimony about Philip's personality trait testing would have no legal relevance. On the other hand, if the case were about child custody, then the personality test results could be relevant to his ability to parent Debra. By understanding the legal issues, you will be better able to focus your testimony on the key issues. By limiting evidence to that which is most relevant, you are helping the court determine the truth and make its findings of fact in a more timely, cost-effective manner.

Helpful

Federal Rule of Evidence 702 states that, to be admissible, expert evidence "must assist the trier of fact to understand the evidence or determine a fact in issue."[6] This rule limits the expert to providing opinions or recommendations that are beyond the expertise of the decision makers. Is there knowledge, skill, or information that a layperson does not have but would require in order to formulate an opinion or conclusion? In other words, an opposing attorney can challenge the admissibility of an expert's witness if the testimony would not help the judge or jury formulate the findings required for resolution of the court case. If the area of knowledge is already within the grasp of decision makers, then there is no need for an expert to provide the information. For example, common sense tells us that if a person purchases a gun one day and the very next morning he puts on a mask and shoots his wife while she is sleeping, the murder is likely premeditated. An expert would not be needed to draw this conclusion. In contrast, an expert's opinion may be useful concerning the chances that a given defendant might repeat engaging in a particular form of criminal behavior. One of the most common uses of clinicians as experts is to provide clinical diagnoses or assessments (e.g., for mental disorders, drug dependencies, or instances of family dysfunction).[7] Mental health experts may also testify about the psychosocial effects of traumatic brain injury, physical abuse, neglect, or other harmful experiences (Bartol & Bartol, 2008).

Another role for an expert is to explain theories and scientific information. But what if a court has been educated about a particular theory in prior cases? The concept of "judicial notice" is a legal principle that allows courts to admit a specific scientific theory or finding that is so well established that it is common knowledge and does not require independent

---

[6]For state courts, remember to refer to the state's rules of evidence. Many states use rules similar to the federal ones, but there may be significant differences from jurisdiction to jurisdiction.

[7]Within a forensic context, performing the assessment of a mental disorder may require forensic rather than clinical methods and techniques.

proof of its truth at the hearing. Battered child syndrome was once a highly debated issue in certain courts. Its existence has now been so firmly established by expert witnesses that some courts take judicial notice of it. If the court takes judicial notice of certain information, it is no longer necessary to call an expert witness on the matter.[8]

Delivered by a Qualified Expert

To be "qualified" as an expert, the witness must have a defined knowledge, skill, experience, training, or education in the area related to the opinion evidence that the expert intends to provide (Federal Rules of Evidence, 2010, Rule 702; Pace, 2011). A clinician may qualify as an expert in relation to some issues but not others (Skeem et al., 2009). If Sam were admitted only as an expert in child development and the impact of sexual abuse on children, for example, he would not be permitted to provide opinions about Philip's propensity toward physical abuse against his wife. Assessments for people from a particular cultural group may require specific training, knowledge, and experience with that group (Good, 2009). An expert with competence in ethnospecific practice can provide important services to tribunals as cultural interpreters. In the Carveys' custody case, an expert on biracial families could be called to testify about challenges that a child such as Debra may experience. As a qualified expert, your testimony is limited to the areas for which you have been admitted as an expert. If there are several areas that require your testimony, seek to be qualified as an expert in each area of your potential testimony.

There is no single test for who may qualify as an expert (Federal Rules of Civil Procedure, 2010, Rule 26). The court will generally consider the witness's knowledge, skill, experience, and education, as well as her ability to use judgment in a particular field of science (*Fitzgerald v. Commonwealth*, 2007). Historically, courts have been more likely to recognize clinicians as experts if they come from medicine or other legislatively recognized professions.[9] If a clinician is licensed or accredited by a professional body,

---

[8]In *Florida Department of Children and Families v. In re: Matter of Adoption of X.X.G. and N.R.G.* (2010), the Florida Third District Court of Appeal overturned a state law banning gay men and lesbians from adopting. The trial and appeals courts based their decisions, in part, on the testimony of child and family experts who opined that gay men and lesbians were as capable of being good parents as heterosexual parents. Adoption cases arising after this case may take judicial notice of this expert evidence rather than requiring new testimony about gay and lesbian parenting at each adoption hearing—unless another party with standing in the case raises an objection.

[9]Psychiatry is still often treated as the mental health profession with the highest status. Some tribunals defer to the opinions of psychiatrists. This may be particularly discouraging to a clinician who has more specialized experience or greater research support than the psychiatrist.

the court is assured that the clinician meets the standards for knowledge, skill, experience, and education required by that body. However, being a member of a professional association does not guarantee qualification as an expert, and experienced clinicians who are not regulated professionals may still qualify as experts. If you do not qualify as an expert, you may still be able to provide fact evidence that can be used to support the opinions of other experts. For example, Sam could report his observations of Philip's behavior, and a university-affiliated criminologist could interpret this behavior.

If you are going to be called to testify as an expert witness, a current *curriculum vitae* (c.v.) or professional résumé is essential. The information in your c.v. should be well organized, accurate, and complete. Because decision makers are provided with a copy that they take away, the c.v. carries a lasting impression. Do not inflate your credentials, since the c.v. is subject to cross-examination. Your c.v. should include the elements listed in Figure 7.1.

Gear your c.v. to the specific areas of expertise required for the types of opinions you will be providing. If Alice calls a therapist to testify about Philip's competence to stand trial, the therapist could highlight her most relevant credentials by including brief (or expanded) explanations of them. If your c.v. looks interesting, people are more likely to spend time reading it. Avoid trying to squeeze in too much information. White space is important if you want to encourage the reader to actually read your c.v. and reference important information.

In terms of the process at the hearing, the attorney calling you informs the tribunal that he intends to qualify you as an expert. Sometimes the other party will not contest the witness's expertise, and the process of qualification is straightforward. In this stage of the trial (sometimes called a *voir dire*), the attorney will take you through your c.v. and highlight areas most relevant to the opinions to be given. Your attorney can also deal with weaknesses in your background. Michael may have authored few articles or books, but this can be explained largely by the overwhelming time demands associated with his extensive hands-on experience and practice-related study of mediation.

The retaining attorney might ask you an open-ended question about your education and experience, in which case you should be prepared to summarize your background in an organized and detailed manner. The other attorneys may cross-examine you on your qualifications, for instance, asking questions to highlight qualifications that you do not possess or challenging the relevance or rigor of the qualifications that you have stated. The judge is responsible for ruling on whether you qualify as an expert who can express opinion evidence. Even if the opposing attorney admits you as an expert witness, your attorney may still take you through your

- Your professional title
- Books, research, or published articles
- Training and education (highlighting examples most relevant to the expert testimony you intend to provide)
- Positive book reviews or judicial comments on your work
- Degrees, professional licenses, and credentials
- Professional speaking experiences
- Years of experience (numbers of clients treated or evaluated, if relevant)
- Ongoing supervision or case consultation
- Employment history (including internships and paid professional work)
- Professional development and continuing education courses you have taken
- Supervisory experience
- Consultation work
- Provision of training
- Code(s) of ethics to which you prescribe
- Special awards or citations
- Courses you have taught
- Prior court experience (issues, representing which side, level of court, whether qualified as an expert, county and state in which you qualified)
- Membership and offices held in professional organizations
- Work under recognized experts
- Recognized specializations
- Methods of practice to which you prescribe
- Profession-related volunteer work

FIGURE 7.1. Elements of a *curriculum vitae.*

qualifications in significant detail to ensure your evidence will be given due weight. The judge may limit qualification questions if your expertise is not in doubt and there is no reason to expand on your qualifications other than to try to impress the jury. In some cases, your attorney can also lay a foundation for your expertise in particular areas, since the opposing attorney may try to narrow the range of your expertise. Having the attorney walk you through your c.v. gives you time to get comfortable on the witness stand while you discuss a relatively easy topic. No matter how often you testify, make use of an opportunity to review your credentials in some detail so that you can settle into the witness chair and become comfortable with the surroundings.

The manner of your presentation may be more important than your actual list of credentials. This is a time to be neither too humble nor too egotistical. Aim for tempered confidence and enthusiasm about your professional identification, qualifications, and specialized knowledge. A problem facing social workers, in particular, is that the profession and many agencies promote generalist practice. For example, Sam's child protection agency encourages its workers to be familiar with a broad range of child welfare issues rather than to pursue specialization in incest, medical neglect, and or other specific areas of child maltreatment. While a generalist background may be useful for clinical purposes, lack of specialization makes it more challenging for Sam to qualify as an expert witness. Client-centered clinicians face a similar dilemma. Because they view clients as experts in their own lives, client-centered clinicians often find it difficult or distasteful to provide diagnoses or "expert" recommendations for their clients. This view may limit such clinicians to providing factual evidence.

Whereas some clinicians shy away from being considered as experts, others may strive to enhance their ability to act as expert witnesses. By the time you are called to participate in a particular case, it may be too late to enhance your qualifications. If you want to qualify as an expert, ensure that you obtain the requisite education, experience, and certification. These credentials enable you to demonstrate that you have acquired the appropriate knowledge and skills for competence in your field. Research, teaching, professional presentations, publications, and active membership in professional organizations will add to your credibility, although they are not necessarily required to qualify as an expert witness (Tindall, 2003). If you plan to provide testimony on particular topics, focus your work on those areas of specialization. Strive for consistency in what you say or publish, as inconsistencies can undermine your perceived trustworthiness. Keep your knowledge up to date by reading journals or attending seminars and conferences. Demonstrate support for evidence-based practice by evaluating your own services in a rigorous manner, and by basing your assessments and interventions on scientific research (National Registry of Evidence-Based Programs and Practices, n.d.). Working with recognized experts can enhance your reputation. Developing strong professional relationships with colleagues in your field of practice is also important, since they may be called on to evaluate your competence as a clinician and as an expert witness.

Based on Sound Scientific Methods or Professional Experience

Although clinicians are frequently called to provide expert evidence, much debate surrounds what expert evidence should be admitted, how it should be used, and whether it is reliable and valid (Skeem et al., 2009). Testimony based on psychological tests, diagnostic tools, social assessment instruments, clinical procedures, practitioner consensus, and theoretical concepts from psychology, social work, and related disciplines may be subjected to challenges before a court admits such testimony. Until the 1990s, the primary challenge for expert evidence was based on the Supreme Court's decision in *Frye v. United States* (1923). The *Frye* standard suggests that expert evidence is only admissible if it is based on a theory or research finding that has "general acceptance in the particular field in which it belongs." Although the *Frye* standard is still used in some state courts, it has been replaced by the *Daubert v. Merell Dow Pharmaceuticals, Inc.* (1993) test in federal court and in many states (Munson, 2011). The *Daubert* test suggests that expert evidence should be based on information that is not only reliable and valid, but also obtained through sound scientific methods. In considering the admissibility of scientific evidence, the court may consider[10]:

1. Whether the theory or technique in question can be and has been scientifically tested.[11]
2. Whether it has been subjected to peer review and publication.
3. Whether the known or potential error rate of the scientific technique justifies its use.[12]
4. Whether it has attracted widespread acceptance within a relevant scientific community.[13]

This is not an exhaustive list of criteria, and the expert evidence does not need to satisfy all four standards in order to be admitted. Courts in some states have added other criteria in certain cases, such as the extent to which the expert is relying on subjective interpretations or whether the expert can reasonably account for using an alternative technique or approach (National Institute for Trial Advocacy, 2006). In *Daubert*, the Supreme Court referred specifically to scientific data. In *Kumho Tire Co. v. Carmichael* (1999), the Supreme Court clarified that the *Daubert* criteria also

---

[10]Although the courts are to take all four factors into account, research suggests that the fourth factor, general acceptance of the research in the scientific community, is still the most persuasive factor in terms of whether a judge will admit expert evidence (Wingate & Thornton, 2004).

[11]This may include the existence and maintenance of standards controlling its operation.

[12]The courts have not identified a specific cutoff point for error rates, nor have they differentiated between Type I and Type II errors (Skeem et al., 2009).

[13]Whereas judges did not have to assess the validity and reliability of scientific evidence under the *Frye* test, the first four *Daubert* criteria require judges to determine the validity and reliability of such evidence. Psychologists should be prepared to explain the rigors of their methodology in terms that judges without research or behavioral-science education can understand. Consider, for instance, how to explain the differences between internal validity and external validity, interrater reliability and test/retest reliability, or t-test and chi square.

applied to technical and other specialized knowledge (e.g., the knowledge that clinicians may gain through practice experience). The court may be able to apply a different standard to "soft sciences" such as psychology, in comparison to the standards used for "hard sciences" such as physics. In other words, any expert testimony must be based on rigorous methods, although the types of methods required may be different depending on the type of evidence being offered (see Federal Judicial Center, 2000, for an online guide that federal judges use to determine admissibility of scientific evidence).

When presenting expert information based on scientific knowledge, consider using methods, assessment tools, and definitions that have been accepted in precedent cases. Assessment tools, such as the MMPI-2, Wechsler scales, the Rorschach, and the MCMI-III, have been subjected to the court's scrutiny, and each has been determined to be a scientific instrument within the legal meaning of that term (Skeem et al., 2009). In contrast, courts have ruled that tools such as the House–Tree–Person and Sentence Completion Test are inadmissible because they have too inadequate a scientific foundation (Lilienfeld, Wood, & Garb, 2000). Also consider methods or tools that have received approval from professional associations such as the American Medical Association or American Psychological Association. Although experts may base their opinions on professional experience (as opposed to scientific research), they should consult their attorneys regarding whether experience-based or research-based evidence will be afforded greater weight by the judge or jury.

Whereas tribunals are generally willing to rely on diagnostic tools for assessment purposes, tribunals generally have less confidence in their use for predictive purposes.[14] A tribunal may have little difficulty accepting evidence, for example, based on a diagnostic tool used to assess whether Philip suffered from a mental illness. On the other hand, a tribunal will tend to be more skeptical about use of a diagnostic tool that purports to predict Philip's risk of reoffending. The question raised by the court should be whether there is any proof that experts are significantly better at predicting behavior than anyone else. In responding to this question, you would need to show how the research provides a reliable, relevant, and helpful set of predictions to be used by the court in its decision making.

The admissibility of certain types of expert evidence may be quite complicated, so you may need an attorney to advise you on the subtleties of the law. For example, in several jurisdictions, the concept of Parental

---

[14]Although courts tend to be skeptical about the predictive ability of psychological instruments, a few actuarial risk assessments, such as STATIC 99 (for sex offender risk assessment) and PCL (the psychopathy checklist), are usually permitted.

Alienation Syndrome is inadmissible, yet one can present testimony about behaviors that characterize alienation dynamics (Gould & Martindale, 2009; National Institute for Trial Advocacy, 2006). The issue with this concept is that, because the legal definition of a syndrome is often judged not to have been met, testimony about Parental Alienation Syndrome is deemed inadmissible. Legal definitions drawn from case law precedents may exist about several important psychological and social phenomena. There are legal definitions for "battered wife syndrome" that provide a listing of symptoms that have been legally recognized as constituting this condition. There are federal as well as state definitions for the "best interests of the child." There are also psychological and social dimensions drawn from case law when examining a parent's request to relocate away from the noncustodial parent.

To demonstrate that they can predict better than lay witnesses, clinicians need to show that their opinions reflect more than just personal values or speculative beliefs. It is easy for biases to creep into an assessment. During a custody evaluation, Evelyn might find that Philip is more cooperative than Paula and that Philip is more amenable to family therapy. Evelyn could easily interpret this finding in a way that supports Philip's claim for custody. But how does Evelyn know that these factors will make Philip a better custodial parent? Is she biased by her attitude toward Paula's resistance?[15] Maybe Paula does not need psychotherapy. Is Philip putting on a show for Evelyn, trying to look good in order to obtain a favorable assessment? Evelyn needs to be aware of her potential biases. Research literature might suggest questions that help to identify the possibility of faking, malingering, or dissimilation by a client (Skeem et al., 2009). Ideally, Evelyn's assessment tools will have ways to identify risks of deception. To substantiate your oral testimony, refer the court to your written reports, test results, or other documentary evidence for additional details (Chapter 8).

Reasonable Degree of Certainty

For opinion evidence to be admissible, the expert witness should be able to testify with a "reasonable degree of certainty." *Reasonable degree of certainty* is a legal term of art that is not a definitive number. Also, what constitutes a reasonable degree of certainty depends on the type of opinion

---

[15]When you interview a client for an assessment or ask the client to complete a psychometric test, the interview or testing may cause a client to be guarded or anxious (Braaten, 2007). These reactions may be natural. It is the situation that may be abnormal. Note whether the client's reaction is enduring or reactive. Is the client's responsiveness affected by the climate you have established during your interview or testing?

being offered and what is reasonable in the context (e.g., a reasonable degree of *medical certainty* may be different from a reasonable degree of *psychological certainty*). If Sam were to testify that there was a risk that Debra would run away from home, Sam may be asked how he came to this assessment and what level of confidence he has in rendering this opinion. When considering whether his level of confidence is "reasonable," the court should base its decision in the context of a social worker trying to predict the risk of running-away behaviors. Expert witnesses are not expected to be able to provide each opinion with 100% certainty. Indeed, providing such a definitive opinion (particularly prediction about future behavior) could be misleading and unethical. Clinical assessments are often inexact, so experts should avoid exaggerating the accuracy of their opinions. Expert opinions based on pertinent research may provide helpful information to a court even if the opinion is framed as a statement of probability rather than an absolute certainty (Skeem et al., 2009).

When reporting the results of empirical research, be prepared to explain various sources of uncertainty, for instance, limitations of the research methods and the concept of statistical error. Consider a study on the effectiveness of a particular treatment for depression. The study might suggest that 88% of clients who received the treatment showed significant improvement. The results may be clouded by limitations such as lack of random sampling or limited follow-up to ensure the improvements were sustained. Further, you may need to explain the limitations of statistical analysis. If the study used a t-test to compare the control and experimental groups, you may need to explain the risk of observing a difference when there was none, or of observing no difference even though there was one. Although the cross-examining attorney may try to use these limitations to undermine your credibility, you can explain how such limitations are to be expected within the social and behavioral sciences (Meyer & Weaver, 2006).

As a general guideline, an expert's level of certainty should be over 50% in order for the opinion evidence to be admissible. As to the question of "how much over 50%," judges and legal scholars differ. In most cases, you should be able to say that you are offering your opinions "with a reasonable level of psychological certainty,"[16] without having to specify an exact percentage of certainty. Remember also that different courts have different standards of proof. In a criminal hearing, for instance, if the prosecution relies on an expert who provides opinions with only 70% confidence, the court may have to acquit because there is reasonable doubt. In other words, just because an expert's opinion is admitted does not mean

---

[16]Or a reasonable degree of certainty within your particular profession or discipline.

that it has sufficient weight to prove the case for which it is offered. Admission of testimony and the weight given to it are separate questions.

Additional Grounds for Exclusion

Although expert evidence must meet the primary criteria for admissibility— reliable, relevant, and helpful—these are not the only ground for admissibility or exclusion. Expert evidence may also be excluded:

- If the probative value of the evidence is outweighed by the risk of unfair prejudicial effects, confusion of the issues, or misleading the jury.
- If the time necessary to present the evidence is incommensurate with its value, for instance, causing an undue delay, waste of time, or needless presentation of cumulative evidence (Federal Rules of Evidence, 2010, Rule 403).
- The opinions are outside the scope of the witness's expertise.

The main fear with expert evidence is that the fact finder will be unduly influenced by an expert witness. In some instances, the expert testimony may be relevant but confusing or emotionally charged. In other instances, the effect of expert testimony on the adjudicator may be out of proportion to its reliability. Consider Sam's testimony regarding possible risk of violence associated with Philip's current behavior. It is difficult to predict risk of violence with a high degree of certainty, yet a judge or jury may be tempted to believe that Philip poses a high risk to Debra's safety, even if this is not the evidence that was presented. Sam's task is to educate the court about how Philip's risk factors may or may not present a danger specifically to Debra. Accordingly, Sam should provide a frank explanation of the reliability of the expert opinions he is offering.

Tribunals often place a great deal of faith in the opinions of expert witnesses. A clinician can spend much more time than the tribunal studying and assessing an individual. The clinician is also respected for his special expertise. To illustrate the difference between how tribunals treat expert evidence and evidence from laypersons, consider the use of professionally prepared presentence reports versus victim impact statements. Victim advocates have argued that criminal courts give little weight to victim impact statements when sentencing. Often, the court will simply follow the report of the expert who wrote the presentence report. The statement drafted by the victim may be emotionally charged, use biased language, and be written with poor grammar and spelling. The presentence report may be written in a manner that is balanced, well written, and uses language that speaks to the concerns of the judge. If a clinician wants the victim's perspective to be given weight, the clinician could include this perspective in the presentence report.

In older cases, courts held that experts may not provide opinions in relation to the *ultimate issue* in dispute (e.g., whether someone accused of premeditated murder was guilty of "premeditated murder," whether an accused raising the defense of not guilty by reason of insanity was "insane" at the time of the alleged crime, or whether a parent involved in a child protection case is a "fit parent"). The rationale for this Ultimate Issue Doctrine was that the trier of fact (judge or jury) was responsible for making the ultimate decision and expert witnesses should not usurp this power. The Federal Rules of Evidence, Rule 704 (and similar provisions in state laws) modify the Ultimate Issue Doctrine, stating, "[T]estimony in the form of an opinion or inference otherwise admissible is not objectionable because it embraces an ultimate issue to be decided by the trier of fact." Although an expert is permitted to provide opinions related to the ultimate issue, they are still restricted from providing legal opinions or otherwise going beyond the scope of their expertise (Bush et al., 2006). Consider a case in which Frieda has been sued for malpractice. Another clinician would not be permitted to testify directly that Frieda's interventions constituted malpractice, as this is the ultimate *legal* issue before the court. The other clinician could educate the court about the components of malpractice, for instance, what is a reasonable standard of care for a family counselor in Frieda's position and whether Frieda's interventions fulfilled this standard of care. Given these opinions, the judge would need to determine whether Frieda's behaviors constituted malpractice. For criminal cases, Rule 704 specifically states that an expert may not "state an opinion or inference as to whether the defendant did or did not have the mental state or condition constituting an element of the crime charged."

Courts are now allowing experts to provide evidence closely related to the ultimate issue; however, they are strictly applying the rules of relevance and necessity. If the court is just as capable as the expert in drawing a conclusion, then the expert is permitted to provide facts or knowledge, while the court retains the responsibility for drawing the ultimate conclusion. If Evelyn were testifying about the credibility of the two parents, for instance, the court judge might ask Evelyn to withhold such opinions, as it is the judge's responsibility to determine which parent is more credible (Gould & Martindale, 2009). If an attorney asked Evelyn about the best interests of the child, she could provide evidence that operationalizes this legal concept and helps the judge determine what is in Debra's best interests: "At this point in her life, Debra is struggling with school and social relationships. She would benefit from living with a parent who can provide stability, educational support, and clear boundaries concerning appropriate and inappropriate behaviors."

Be careful about situations where an attorney may entice you into saying things that you are not authorized to say or have no foundation to say. Consider a criminal case in which the defense attorney asks a mental health professional whether his client had the capacity to commit murder. If the professional says, "The client is innocent," this is a legal opinion, not a scientific or mental health decision. Further, pronouncing a client innocent or guilty involves a moral judgment that goes beyond the mandate and expertise of a mental health professional. Providing such an opinion could lead to a complaint to the state licensing board for practicing outside her area of professional competence. Do not shy away from asserting the appropriate boundaries of your expertise. If you were asked about an appropriate sentence for a convicted offender, for instance, you could respond, "The appropriate sentence for this person is a matter for the judge to decide." Stay within your role. Offer your direct observations and information within your area of professional competence. Avoid the temptation of providing legal opinions.

SELECTING EXPERTS

The discussion on choosing witnesses in Chapter 4 focused on fact witnesses. Many of the same criteria apply for selecting expert witnesses: Is the witness credible? How good is his memory and recall? Will he be viewed as an objective information provider? This section highlights factors particular to selecting experts.

The level and type of expertise required depend on the type of expert evidence needed. For instance, predicting whether a sexual offender will commit another offense requires a higher level of experience than simply reporting on the general literature. Choosing an expert depends on the nature of the legal issues, the expected roles of the expert, who is selecting the expert, and whether the witness would qualify as an expert according to the factors described above (specialized training, experience, etc.).

In some cases a clinician is asked to provide expert evidence simply because she has been working with a particular client. This testimony would be expert testimony based on clinical knowledge rather than that drawn from a forensic evaluation. For example, Frieda knows the Carveys very well from her family therapy with them. She can provide both fact and opinion evidence. She was working with Paula and Philip before litigation was contemplated, so they may not have been enticed to sway her assessments for legal purposes. However, Frieda would need to testify about the limitations of her data, particularly focusing on how her data are drawn only from a clinical context. Her assessment may not have the breadth of information that might be obtained from a more comprehensive forensic evaluation.

In contrast, Evelyn was hired specifically to provide a custody evaluation, in light of impending litigation. In hiring Evelyn, Philip and Paula's attorneys would be looking for a professional with a reputation for neutrality, fairness, objectivity, and independence, as well as a reputation as a competent, respected evaluator. Although hiring an evaluator may lead to a settlement, the parties hiring the evaluator should also be concerned about how the evaluator would provide evidence, should the case proceed to trial. Ideally, an expert witness should have no prior connection with the parties involved in the dispute. The expert is hired for her expertise in forensic investigations and for her ability to provide opinion evidence in a professional, credible manner.

The evidence of an expert hired by both parties tends to carry more weight than that of an expert hired by one party. A jointly hired expert avoids the possibility of dueling experts with conflicting opinions. Both parties are also more likely to cooperate with the expert, since both parties view the expert as an impartial professional—at least until the expert issues her report and recommendations.

If an interdisciplinary team has been working with a client, the attorney may decide to call only one or two members of the team as witnesses. Often, this decision is made according to which member of the team will have the greatest status (e.g., the psychiatrist as head of the forensic team). However, the best person to provide the evidence may be the one who has had the most direct contact or has made the more critical observations. Even though Evelyn's supervisor may have better educational credentials, Evelyn is the one who conducted the home visits with the Carveys.

For some attorneys, the key characteristic sought in an expert is the ability to be a good educator. An effective expert is able to translate complex phenomena into language that can be easily understood. During preparation for a case, Alice may hire an expert to teach her about the current research examining how children are affected by exposure to child abuse. There may be research addressing the specific allegations raised in the present case. In such an instance, it would be appropriate for Alice to talk about the specific research and its applicability to the case before the court.

During the hearing, this expert may also be used to educate the tribunal on the same matters. An expert is helpful to the court to the degree that she effectively communicates new and complex information into language that makes good sense to the judge and jury (if any). If an expert uses a lot of complicated jargon, the meaning of the information may be lost;

alternatively, the judge may question whether the expert really knows what she is talking about or whether she is trying to conceal weaknesses in her testimony. Research suggests that many judges and jurors have difficulty understanding scientific terms such as reliability and validity (McAuliff & Duckworth, 2010). Therefore, an expert should be able to explain herself in plain language, without losing technical accuracy or talking down to the tribunal. She must be well respected for her expertise, but not pretentious, biased, or dogmatic. She must be able to be authoritative and convincing, but also pleasant and easy to listen to (Brodsky, 2004).

When an attorney selects an expert, he will prefer someone he feels he can trust and with whom he can work. This feeling may come from a prior working relationship or preliminary discussions with a new person. Different attorneys have different styles. An authoritarian attorney may prefer a clinician who provides her expertise as requested but does not try to assume a role in strategizing or directing the case. A collaborative attorney may prefer a clinician who takes a more active role in these matters. Sometimes, the clinician needs to develop trust before trying to participate as an equal partner.

While an attorney is assessing you as a potential expert, you should also be evaluating whether this is an attorney you want to work with: What is his reputation as a litigator? How does he treat clinicians? What position is he representing? How well can he communicate the intricacies of the law? Is he able to allay your fears about testifying? Is he willing and able to learn about your field of practice? Is he willing to incorporate your advice on matters within your expertise? If he decides to call you as a witness, will he allow you to answer truthfully, even if some information goes against his case? Given your style and how you see your role, consider whether the two of you are a good match. Think about whether the attorney has experience with cases involving your field of expertise. If not, you might suggest that the attorney work with a co-counsel with the required specialization to handle certain parts of the case. Finally, are you competent to provide the services requested? If not, refer the attorney to someone who has the required knowledge, skills, supervision, and experience (APA, 2010, s.2.01; NASW, 2008, s.1.04). Frieda may be expert in the research addressing psychological causes of sexual aggression, but a physician may be needed to speak to physiological causes.

In cases where the tribunal assigns an expert, the tribunal usually relies on the same professionals that it has used in other cases. The tribunal may have a certain roster of assessors or diagnosticians, or it may be affiliated with specific agencies (e.g., family court clinics, victim assistance programs, or psychiatric institutions). The most important criteria for the tribunal are generally the expert's level of expertise and perceived impartiality. The expert should not have any monetary interest or investment in a particular outcome. For example, because Sam works for the child protection agency, the court could not ask him to provide an *independent* assessment in a child protection hearing.

To identify recognized experts in a particular field, attorneys investigate a number of sources: court-affiliated services, similar adjudications that have used experts, professional journals and books, public presentations, universities or other research centers, professional associations, and presence on the Internet (e.g., websites, blogs, online videos of real or mock trials). If you want attorneys to know of your expertise, you may need to speak for, write for, or join these types of organizations. To facilitate being hired as an expert, assemble a professional portfolio including your curriculum vitae, publications, sample reports, and transcripts of past evidence. Check what information is available about you on the Web: are you cited by your professional organization in a positive manner, is there an embarrassing video of you from college on YouTube, or are there scholarly articles criticizing your work? If you can have inaccurate or embarrassing information removed, then do so (e.g., by contacting the publisher of the website or a regulatory organization that oversees the publisher). In some instances, you may have no control over what information, photographs, and videos are posted on the Internet. Still, knowing what is out there may help you respond to questions at trial, particularly if embarrassing information is raised to impugn your credibility.

When being interviewed by an attorney who may hire you as an expert, be prepared to answer questions pertaining to your personal life, social relationships, political views, and religious convictions. If you have any biases or conflicts of interest, disclose these before you agree to work as an expert (especially if you have any past or present relationship with any of the parties to the litigation). An attorney may have contacted you because she suspected you would be sympathetic to her client's cause. Alternatively, she may be looking for someone who is untainted.

CONTRACT FOR SERVICES

A clinician may be retained as an expert by the tribunal, by one party, or by both parties to an action. If the tribunal retains the expert, then the contract for services is with the tribunal. Often, courts and other tribunals will order or recommend that the parties retain their own independent experts. Clinicians are sometimes engaged as witnesses without any explicit contract for services. To clarify your role and avoid any miscommunications, preferred practice is to use a written contract for services. A legally drafted retainer (service contract) will ensure that everyone's legal rights and responsibilities are covered. However, your own letter confirming the parameters of your services may be sufficient.

Initially, an attorney may contact you by telephone or letter to explore whether you are willing and able to provide services as an expert. You might suggest a face-to-face meeting to exchange information and to negotiate a contract for service. While an exchange of letters or telephone calls may be expedient, an in-person meeting will help both of you evaluate how effectively you can work together. Topics that should be discussed and outlined in the retainer or confirmation letter include the basic facts of the situation, the attorney's undertakings, your obligations, remuneration for your services, and contingencies (see Appendices A, B, C, and D).

In terms of the basic information, the attorney should spell out the name of the party engaging you, the names of other parties involved in the dispute, the presenting problems, the legal issues, the facts agreed upon, and the facts in dispute. In a refugee hearing, for example, you could be hired as a consultant for a refugee claimant, Sadru Nadji. The presenting problem is that Mr. Nadji's original application for refugee status has been turned down. The legal issue is how to interpret refugee legislation. The refugee board may agree that Mr. Nadji would not be in any physical danger if he were returned to his country of origin. The primary factual issue is whether the refugee has valid concerns regarding psychological torture.

While the attorney may be able to provide you with most of the factual information at the outset, consider what other information or assistance the attorney should undertake to provide for you on an ongoing basis. The refugee's attorney could undertake to provide the expert with documents filed with the refugee board, advise of any progress in settlement attempts or legal proceedings, and arrange for the refugee's voluntary participation in a psychological assessment. You could also ask the attorney for a more detailed analysis of the legal context of the case.

To clarify the parameters of your obligations, the contract or confirmation letter should provide details of the various services for which you are being retained (e.g., consultation, literature review, empirical research, forensic evaluation, testifying). If you are hired to conduct an evaluation, the contract should specify the purpose of the investigation, procedures to be used for gathering information, the nature of the reports to be submitted, who will have access to the reports, and the time frames for information gathering and reporting (see Chapter 8 and Appendices A, B, C, and D). When the court appoints Evelyn, she forwards her retainer agreement and informed consent information to each attorney with instructions to review the information with their clients, Paula and Philip. Her retainer states that she will provide an independent custody evaluation examining areas pertaining to the psychological and social best interests of Debra. Her evaluation methods and procedures will include use of parenting questionnaires, in-office interviews with the parties and the child, psychological test data (including a standardized test for malingering), collateral interviews and record review, and direct behavioral observations of each parent with the minor child (Gould & Martindale, 2009; National Institute for Trial Advocacy, 2006). The scope of her evaluation will be guided by concerns relevant to issues before the court as stated in the court's order or indicated by a letter of agreement from the attorneys specifying the areas of concern to be addressed in the evaluation.[17] Evelyn will provide a custody evaluation within 3 months, including recommendations for custody and access. Evelyn will send the report to the attorneys and the judge with the understanding that the report may be used in court and that Evelyn may be called to testify.

Some experts perform investigations but are not called as witnesses. An expert hired by the aforementioned refugee might arrive at an unfavorable opinion. Although the attorney would not call this expert to testify at the refugee hearing, the information provided in the report could help the attorney know the case she is up against.

The retainer agreement should not specify that the clinician is being hired to provide a particular opinion. This would not be ethical and would create an easy target for cross-examination, as retainer agreements are subject to pretrial discovery. As emphasized earlier, as a forensic expert, you are not a client advocate. Unless you are court-appointed, the party(ies) who hired you can decide after you submit your findings whether to call you as a witness. If you believe an attorney is shopping around for a favorable expert, be careful about making any commitments that could damage your reputation in this case or in the future.

In some instances, such as a confidential mediation process, both parties agree at the outset that the information gathered by the clinician is not to be used in court or other adjudications. This encourages the parties to be frank and open in order to try to settle the conflict; the parties do not have to worry that the information could come back to haunt them if the case does not settle.

In addition to explaining your responsibilities, the retainer agreement could include what you will *not* do. Evelyn's retainer explained that she is not an expert in child abuse and that, if either parent had concerns about abuse, then the issues would be reported to child protection services

---

[17]See Gould & Martindale (2009) for a fuller explanation of formulating questions that guide custody evaluations.

to conduct an investigation. Evelyn would suspend her assessment until completion of the protection process.

Many cases involve more than one expert, either to provide corroborating evidence or to provide different types of expertise. If multiple experts are hired, your retainer agreement should define which expert is responsible for which information and functions. One expert may be designated as the coordinator of the work, who ensures that draft reports are shared before final reports are submitted. Each expert may be responsible to testify about the information he or she collected and interpreted. If you use a group model to conduct the evaluation, each expert needs to be clear about who is in charge. In the body of the report, as well as in oral testimony, the coordinator would need to clearly identify each group member's area of responsibility.

Sometimes an attorney will ask an expert to perform a preliminary assessment of the case and provide an oral report rather than a written report. In such cases, it is imperative that the expert and the attorney talk about the production of notes and other written material. The expert may be instructed *not* to take notes or produce any written materials so that there are no records that could be subject to a subpoena by the other party's attorney. Upon completion of the preliminary assessment, the expert may be asked to conduct a full evaluation or be told to stop work.

If the attorney plans to call you as a witness, ensure that the attorney plans to meet with you in advance of the trial. This meeting can serve a number of purposes:

- The attorney can educate you about the theory of the case, what issues are in dispute, and what each party is trying to prove.
- The attorney can help you with your role as a witness, including how to present your qualifications during a *voir dire* (as explained below) and how to present your facts and opinions in an effective manner.
- You can provide the attorney with feedback on his plans for leading your evidence, as well as suggestions for highlighting key points.
- The attorney can role-play the direct examination and cross-examination with you to prepare for the actual trial (Melton et al., 2007).

When you are hired by one side to perform an assessment, there may be times when you feel tension between the needs of a good evaluation and the wishes of the attorney. There is no singularly right or wrong way to approach this issue. You should be aware that the tension between the needs of the evaluator and the wishes of the attorney can produce dynamic and challenging exchanges. For example, an attorney in a criminal case may ask you to interview some people while not interviewing other people. As an evaluation expert, you may feel strongly that you need to interview people from both groups. The manner in which you and the attorney negotiate these differences may reflect on the quality of your report. Imagine having to testify that the reason you did not interview certain people was because the attorney who hired you said you must not interview them. How do you suppose the court would view your testimony? How do you suppose the court would view your independence and credibility?

No matter who hires you, you are in charge of how you conduct your evaluation. Make clear requests for information as well as access to collateral records and informants, and make those requests *in writing*. Even if you have been hired by just one side in a case, your ethical responsibility is to the court and the discovery of truth. Even if your evaluation never is presented to a court because the attorney views your results as harmful to his case, you should produce a document that reflects a properly conducted evaluation, not an evaluation that reflects what the attorney wanted. If you feel uncomfortable about what an attorney is asking you to do or say as an expert witness, stand firm on your professional ethics. In some cases, this may mean turning away business in order to protect your integrity.

Do not forget to negotiate terms of payment. If you are providing expert evidence pursuant to a subpoena, state regulations may restrict the amount that you can claim to recovery of specific expenses and a nominal amount for your time.[18] If providing evidence is part of your agency role, such as in a parole department, you may not claim remuneration in addition to your usual salary.

If you are hired as an independent expert, you will find that clinicians contracted as experts generally charge rates similar to or higher than their usual clinical rates. You should have a published list of charges. Some people charge one set of rates for in-office work and another set of rates for deposition and trial testimony. Your rates should reflect two factors: community standards and your level of expertise. Talk to other experts in your locality to see what they typically charge.

Your retainer contract should also specify recoverable expenses (e.g., travel costs, overhead, secretarial support, research assistants, long-distance telephone charges, copying, and postage). Be aware that it is common for clinicians operating in a forensic context to develop office business procedures based on a legal model rather than a clinical model. Charges

---

[18]In some cases, such as criminal trials, clinicians can be compelled to testify as fact witnesses without payment for services.

often include time for phone calls, note taking, consultation, and any other work-related operation associated with the legal case.

Terms of payment should depend on the time spent preparing for and participating in the legal process; for instance, will you be paid for spending all day in the courtroom until you are called, or will you be paid for 2 days of time that you have cleared of appointments so you could be available for court? Contingency arrangements (where payment depends on which party wins or whether the tribunal accepts the expert's testimony) may be unethical and can be used to destroy your credibility (Committee on Ethical Guidelines for Forensic Psychologists, 2011, Guideline 4.2). An expert should be paid for her time, not for a particular outcome (see Appendix B). Some forensic experts secure their services under a professional service agreement between themselves and the attorney, rather than between themselves and the client. Making the attorney rather than the client the primary person responsible for payment may increase the likelihood that you will be fully paid for your time (Heilbronner, 2005).

Provide the attorney with an estimate of the time needed to conduct your assessment and to perform other services. During negotiations, the attorney should make you aware of any monetary constraints, particularly limitations on what the client can afford.[19] Because legal proceedings are costly even without fees for experts, consider a sliding-fee scale based on ability to pay or pro bono (voluntary) services for appropriate clients.

A tough moral dilemma occurs when there are financial limits placed on the amount of time you put into a case. Do you accept a case for a fixed fee and perform all necessary functions, or do you accept a case and bill on an hourly basis, stopping work when the money runs out? Alternatively, do you negotiate a fee for a limited set of services? There may be no perfect solution regarding which path to take. It is never ethical to provide a less competent work product because there is less money to be had. Each service you provide needs to be provided at the highest level of your professional ability. What you might need to do is limit how many services you provide, but you should not shortchange an attorney or party because they do not have the money to pay. Once you accept an assignment, you have an ethical responsibility to fulfill it to the highest level of your professional ability.

Adversarial proceedings can become intensely competitive and

---

[19]Occasionally, experts' fees are covered by the client's liability insurance or subsidized by legal aid. The scope of services covered by such plans is limited. For a Supreme Court decision on fees for expert witnesses, see *Kansas v. Colorado* (2009).

combative. They may leave clients feeling dissatisfied, in spite of the best efforts of the attorneys and clinicians involved. Recovering your fees at the end of the process may be problematic. As noted above, many clinicians who engage in forensic work adopt a legal paradigm for business practices. That paradigm entails an upfront retainer that enables you to bill your services in advance of your work. When the money runs out, you stop work until the retainer is replenished. Such business arrangements should be spelled out clearly in your retainer agreement.

Those clinicians who do not ask for their fees as a retainer up front normally opt to bill periodically. The contract could specify the time frame for payment and the interest penalty for late payments. Maintain timesheets for all contacts with clients, attorneys, or other collaterals. Keep records for recoverable expenses. To ensure the court will view your testimony as objective, it is better to be paid in full prior to testifying. When you are paid in advance, it renders moot the inevitable attempt to link the contents of your testimony to purportedly incentivized after-trial payments: "Doctor, isn't it true that full payment for your services will occur only after you complete your testimony? Isn't it also true that if you provide truthful testimony today, you might not collect all the fees due for your work here today?"

Ask the attorney about contingencies, such as the possibility of a settlement or delays. Your function may end at the time that initial conclusions are provided. If the case settles or there is insufficient basis to proceed, how will your services be terminated? If the attorney decides to use another expert in your place, can the other party call you to testify? If the case is delayed, will you be responsible for updating the assessment prior to the hearing?

The foregoing discussion deals with a broader spectrum of issues than many retainers actually encompass. Develop your own checklist or standard agreement to ensure that you deal with the issues that are most relevant to your situation. Ideally, have your personal attorney look over your retainer agreement to determine whether it is comprehensive and legally enforceable.

DIRECT EXAMINATION

Most of the suggestions in Chapter 5 for oral testimony apply to not only fact witnesses but also expert witnesses. In this section we highlight four areas that apply specifically to expert witnesses: the elements of expert testimony; engaging the tribunal in a persuasive manner; providing opinions; and language with multiple meanings.

The Elements of Expert Testimony

Direct examination should be presented in a logical, step-by-step fashion. As noted earlier, the first stage of the examination is qualifying the witness as an expert. The attorney will take you through your curriculum vitae, generally in chronological order, and highlight the information that is most relevant to the types of opinions you will provide. Upon being qualified, your attorney will ask you to describe when and how you became involved in the case. To lay the basis for your findings and recommendations, describe your information-gathering process (e.g., where, when, and how you interviewed each person). If you used any diagnostic or assessment tools, explain their purpose and how they were administered. You may also be asked how the tools were developed, including how they were substantiated for the validity and reliability. Clarify whether you followed your discipline's generally accepted standards for gathering information. If you did not follow these standards, then explain why (the case at hand may not have been a standard case or you may have had to deal with a particularly resistant client).

Once you have identified the sources of your information, present your factual findings. These findings could include the perspectives and wishes of the people interviewed, data and findings from your psychological and psychosocial testing, interviews with collateral sources of information such as other clinicians, family members, and direct observations of the subjects of the case (in a custody case, this would be each parent with the child). Your factual findings form the foundation for the next element of your testimony, your expert opinions. Opinion evidence includes explanations of psychological and psychosocial phenomena, interpretations of the data collected, predictions based on research findings, and predictions based on your judgment as an experienced clinician.

Each opinion needs to be connected with a theoretical and factual foundation. Move from general to specific; outline what the general theory is, how the current independent data sources support or do not support different perspectives, and how you have chosen to interpret the data to support an opinion that favors a particular recommendation. You may then be asked to discuss each of your recommendations and conclusions in light of the described data.

In preparing for your testimony, make sure you are familiar with both the research that supports your opinions and that which contradicts your opinions. To preempt criticisms that could be raised in cross-examination, it is usually a good idea to identify possible gaps or inconsistencies in your facts and opinions. You may be able to explain how you dealt with these problems. In some cases, you may have to admit that your information gathering, theory, or research has certain weaknesses. After all, behavioral and social sciences are inexact disciplines.

Your written report (discussed in Chapter 8) could be entered as an exhibit. Your report should include any and all opinions that you plan to present orally. During the oral examination, you would summarize your report and highlight important information. Remember, during the direct examination, you will most likely be asked open-ended questions. Be prepared to go through your information in detail without too many prompts from the attorney, although some attorneys like to conduct parts of the direct examination with specific closed-ended questions. Preparation is the key to successful testimony.

Ask your attorney whether you might be asked about the testimony or reports of the opposing party's experts. If so, ask to review the transcripts of the testimony and a copy of the reports so you can prepare your critique of the expert's information gathering, theory, clinical methods, research methodologies, applications, or conclusions. Your critique should include both strengths and limitations, showing that you are not simply dismissing everything the other expert did or said, but considering all her work carefully and objectively. Maintain your professionalism. Avoid ad hominem (personal) attacks, such as calling the other expert a *quack* or a *sloppy researcher*. Stick to the facts, behaviors, and science behind the opinions.

Engaging the Tribunal in a Persuasive Manner

As an expert witness, *how* you present can be just as important as *what* you present. Research on persuasiveness suggests that expert witnesses are more likely to influence decision makers when they are perceived as interesting, likeable, trustworthy, knowledgeable, confident, and succinct (Brewer & Williams, 2005; Brodsky et al., 2010; Brodsky & Terrell, 2011). Building a positive rapport with the tribunal should begin with your first impression, including how you dress and comport yourself, and continue throughout your testimony.

To be *interesting*, express your story in a rich and colorful manner. Researchers and academics in highly specialized areas should be particularly careful to avoid sounding too high or too dry (National Institute for Trial Advocacy, 2006). A frequent mistake is for an expert witness to begin her testimony with a tedious recitation of her educational and professional achievements, putting the judge and jury to sleep just when she should be heightening their attention and interest (Commons, Gutheil, & Hilliard, 2010). Think about the best teacher that you have ever had and what made that person a good teacher. Effective educators use many different methods of presentation, not just lecture or recitation of facts. Narrative is an important element in effective education, and research suggests judges and juries often find qualitative evidence more persuasive than quantitative information (McQuiston-Surrett & Saks, 2009). Engage the judge or jury by telling a vivid story, giving everyone a detailed mental picture of the relevant people and the chain of events. If an attorney began qualifying Evelyn by asking what brought her into the field of child custody evaluation, she could respond with the following narrative:

> "I grew up in a family where my mother was a family law attorney and my father was a psychologist. As you can imagine, I learned about divorce and children's developmental issues from a very early age. I took particular interest in the mental health side when I began my undergraduate degree at State University 15 years ago. One of my psychology professors, Dr. Barbara Miller, was doing research on the impact of divorce on children within Latin American families, and she encouraged me to become involved as a research assistant ... "

Note how Evelyn provides information about her qualifications, but in the context of the story of how she came into her area of expertise. She adds personal life details to make the story interesting and to humanize herself. Evelyn guards against straying too far from her qualifications, or she may face objections that the testimony is irrelevant, wasting the court's time.

In addition to narrative, graphics or visual devices may enhance understanding and make your testimony more memorable. If you plan to use visual devices, check with your attorney to determine whether the court can accommodate these devices and to ensure that everyone in the court will be able to see what you are presenting. Computer technology allows for not only two-dimensional graphics and still pictures, but also three-dimensional images that can convey depth and motion. Some jurisdictions permit greater creativity than others. For example, some jurisdictions may allow Sam to show videos, live sculpting, or psychodrama[20] to illustrate family relationships. In other jurisdictions he might be limited to verbal reports—within which he could use imagery, metaphors, and analogies to help bring the information to life. In presenting his child protection assessment, Sam conveys a dramatic picture of Debra rather than a sterile report of an anonymous child in need of protection. He draws specific connections

---

[20]Live sculpting and psychodrama refer to methods of demonstrating interactions between people. Participants act out a situation so that observers and participants can gain a more personal understanding of the dynamics.

between child welfare theory and Debra's personal needs. She was not in court, so he brought along photographs. Although you could provide small handout information with your graphics or visual devices, a large poster or projection on a large screen may allow you to engage the whole courtroom more effectively. Avoid graphics or charts that are too complex or detailed. "Less may be more" when it comes to the amount of information that you want to include on any visual aid.

Note that even if you convey your testimony in an interesting fashion, the judge or jurors may exhibit bland or bored facial expressions (Heilbronner, 2005). Sometimes, the judge or jurors may seem unresponsive in their attempt to present themselves as unbiased, neutral, and rational decision makers. Other times, they may be tired, bored, daydreaming, cranky, preoccupied, or overwhelmed. Do your best to engage them, but do not become flustered if they seem inattentive or you do not observe positive reactions in their facial expressions or body language.

Vary the format of your answers and use pronouns purposefully. Stating, "From psychological research on sexual abuse, *we* understand that ... " tends to emphasize that this information is generally understood. In contrast, stating, "From my review of research on sexual abuse, *I* understand that ... " tends to personalize the testimony. Prefacing your comments with personal references such as "I think ..., " "I believe ..., " or "My conclusion is ..., " should be used strategically. If you use them too often, you may sound too full of yourself. Some subtleties, perhaps not so noticeable during oral testimony, may carry substantial weight in the proceeding's transcript (Brodsky, 2009).

To come across as *likeable*, demonstrate the highest levels of courtesy and consideration for the parties, their attorneys, the judge, and the jurors. People associate likeability with being kind, polite, respectful, friendly, and pleasant (Brodsky et al., 2010). Do not go overboard with friendliness (e.g., using cutesy nicknames or disclosing personal information that is unrelated to the case), as you want to maintain your professionalism and credibility. Although you may present most of your evidence in a calm, rational manner, do not be afraid to demonstrate warmth, empathy, caring, and concern. Avoid annoying habits such as scratching your nose, clicking your teeth, or tapping a pen. Use positive language and avoid negative labeling. Unfortunately, in their effort to appear knowledgeable, some experts sound condescending and disrespectful. For the most part, experts have good intentions, but they may be unaware of how their behavior is interpreted.

Avoid flippant and defensive reactions. Expressing frustration with a questioner who does not seem to understand your answers may come across as arrogant. Correcting a questioner who mispronounces technical terms may sound condescending. Criticism of other experts could be interpreted as disdain. To function as an effective educator, demonstrate patience with those who are learning. Be careful not to embarrass learners about areas beyond their current knowledge. All of us have something to learn. When we feel safe and respected, we are more open to learning.

To show that you are *knowledgeable*, do not be too humble about your qualifications. Highlight those parts of your education, training, research, professional accreditations, and practice experience that relate most closely to the types of opinion evidence that you will be presenting. Be thorough, but also concise. Explain complex concepts in language that the judge and jury can readily understand. Make reference to specific research and readings to substantiate your opinions. Ensure the flow of your evidence is logical and easy to follow.

To convey *confidence*, walk to the witness stand in a dignified manner, using a head nod, eye contact, or passing smile to acknowledge the judge and jury. Speak in a calm and fluid voice, provide the attorney questioning you with direct eye contact, and remain relaxed. Maintain your composure even if the testimony is not going exactly as you expected. Remember that you have been called as an expert witness because you have knowledge and experience that the judge and jury do not possess. Although you want to convey that you are self-assured, guard against displays of overconfidence. You do not want to come across as cocky, arrogant, inauthentic, or patronizing.

To demonstrate *trustworthiness*, communicate in an honest and direct manner. You want the decision makers to know they can depend on you for the truth. If other professionals, researchers, or experts support your testimony, cite these sources to bolster your trustworthiness (Brewer & Williams, 2005). If the facts or research are not clearly on your side, be willing to acknowledge such problems. Consider a commission of inquiry into the existence of racism in a school system. Politically, you may want to support efforts to reduce racism, but do you have sufficient research to back up such an opinion? If you do not have credible knowledge about this issue, do not profess to have it. If you have research that supports your expert opinion, but also research that conflicts, provide both types of research. This shows that you have nothing to hide and that you are willing to address areas of uncertainty and controversy. When considering how to demonstrate trustworthiness, think about people that you know you can rely on and what characteristics they portray.

To be *succinct*, prepare your key points in advance and focus on conveying those points concisely. Judges and juries may lose interest or think you are hiding something if you go off on tangents or use convoluted explanations. If you are relying on research, ensure you know your research methods well enough to be able to translate them into terms that can be understood by people who have not read the text or taken college-level research courses. For example, if you were giving evidence about the validity of a personality test, you could briefly explain validity as, "Does the test measure what it is intended to measure?" Similarly, for a simple explanation of reliability, you could explain, "Would another clinician using the same test come up with a similar finding?" Provide concrete examples to illustrate these concepts. As noted earlier, demonstrations are also useful educational devices. If you want to demonstrate the statistical principles of probability and the independence of events, you could use the simple toss of a coin. "What is the probability of getting heads? [Flip a coin.] It came up heads. What is the probability that it will come up heads the next time?" As an educator to the court, simplify, don't complicate (National Institute for Trial Advocacy, 2006).

Providing Opinions

Qualifying as an expert witness allows you to put your opinions on the record. However, you are probably interested not only in being heard but also in influencing the decisions to be made. Opinions based on intuition or gut reaction generally carry little weight. To maximize the influence of your opinions, present them with confidence and base them on factual evidence and persuasive theory. Avoid providing opinions that overreach your expertise. If Evelyn were asked, "How would you interpret Philip's personality test scores on the MMPI?" Evelyn might respond, "I am not trained in administering the MMPI or interpreting its results, so it would be inappropriate for me to provide an opinion."

Do not disguise a personal or political belief as scientific knowledge (Bush et al., 2006). Consider the impact of corporal punishment on child development. Many clinicians have a strong negative view—based on moral beliefs and personal values—on the appropriateness of spanking or other forms of corporal punishment. To be an effective expert witness, be prepared to discuss the research about use of corporal punishment, its limitations, and potential usefulness. For adjudicative processes, personal beliefs are weak substitutes for empirical evidence. Be aware of your personal beliefs and values so you can ensure they do not inhibit your ability to present expert evidence in an objective manner.

Present your opinions with conviction, using assertive language and vocal qualities. While you do not want to come across as arrogant or aggressive, also avoid conveying uncertainty by using wishy-washy language and self-deprecating remarks: "I'm just a psychologist, but if you really want my opinion, I think that Philip may not have been very nice to Debra. But then again, maybe ... " What is the likelihood that Debra was abused, and what information supports that conclusion? Couch your opinions in terms of their probability, as supported by the knowledge in your field: "Seventy-five percent of children with Debra's pattern of sleep disturbances reported having experienced sexual abuse." Clinical assessments often require some level of subjective opinion. As mentioned earlier, you do not need 100% certainty, or any other specific percentage, to express an opinion: "Based on the facts outlined in my report, within a reasonable degree of psychological certainty,[21] I concluded that Debra was sexually abused." If confident in a belief, don't waver. If not, admit the information is tentative. A qualified opinion is better than a misleading opinion or no opinion at all.

As an expert, you may be asked for an opinion about the future behavior of a particular person. If you decide to provide a specific prediction, make sure it is based on an honest assessment of the research or other evidence you are presenting. If Sam were to say, "I am 100% certain that Philip will continue to abuse Debra," his statement rings false. Even with research-based instruments and keen assessment skills, clinicians cannot predict risk of abuse (or other human behavior) with 100% accuracy (Barber, Shlonsky, Black, Goodman, & Trocmé, 2008). Instead, Sam might testify, "When I administered the Risk Assessment Tool, I found that Philip was at moderately high risk of committing further child abuse." Sam could then explain how the Risk Assessment Tool measures risk and what is meant by "moderately high risk."

When offering expert opinion about *scientific information*, provide the court with an understanding of the research that supports your conclusions. On the other hand, if you are offering expert opinion about a *clinical issue*, the standard of admissible evidence may be somewhat lower (*Kumho Tire Co. v. Carmichael*, 1999). For example, claims based on research or theory should be backed up by current literature and research. If Sam opined that corporal punishment was harmful, he would need to be prepared with appropriate research to answer the question, "How do you know corporal punishment is harmful?" Bring an annotated bibliography of current and accepted literature that provides research on both sides of the issue.[22] Be prepared to explain competing ideas in the literature and how your interpretation in this particular case is more compelling than any other interpretation. Also be prepared to summarize the methods and findings of these studies as well as their limitations. When offering an opinion on a clinical issue (such as your assessment of Debra's ability to cope with

---

[21]For an expert who is not a psychologist, this phrase could be adapted to fit the person's discipline (e.g., "sociological certainty" or "criminological certainty").

[22]The attorney may have already submitted this bibliography and a compilation of key articles to the court as a paper file or as an electronic file.

her parents' divorce), your opinion should be supported by your clinical experience and judgment. Ideally, you should also use accepted theory and research evidence to substantiate your clinical judgments.

The basis of your opinion may be more important than the opinion itself since the tribunal needs a basis on which to evaluate, accept, or reject your evidence. Use concrete, specific, and observable facts. Stay away from such statements as "Paula is neglectful." There are two problems with such testimony. The first is that concluding that Paula is neglectful might be tantamount to addressing the ultimate issue to be decided in the case, which is the job of the judge (or jury), not the witness. The second is that the term "neglectful" is an interpretative statement that does not provide a clear description of behaviors that are of concern. It would be better if Evelyn could simply provide facts that support this conclusion: "When I arrived at the house, Debra was alone in the basement, playing with a loaded hunting rifle. I observed Paula watching television, occasionally yelling to Debra, 'Don't get into any trouble down there!'" These facts beg the tribunal to draw its own conclusions. By focusing on the factual basis rather than the actual opinion, you also avoid problems with the ultimate issue doctrine, described earlier. Inexperienced clinician-witnesses are particularly prone to stating conclusions without factual support. If you cannot identify observable facts to support your opinion, then consider whether it is well founded. You might be setting yourself up for a difficult cross-examination.

Opinions can be based on direct observations, case records, testimony presented in the hearing, hypothetical situations,[23] your own research, or professional literature. If you base your opinion on facts from your observations or readings of the case file, it is generally better to lay the factual foundation for your opinions first: "Based on the hospital records supplied to me, Mr. Carvey admits that he has not gone a day without drinking alcohol during the past 6 years. When he wakes up in the morning, he feels nauseous and his hands shake. These behaviors are similar to those reported in the literature as characteristic of people who are physically addicted to alcohol. Given this review of records and current behavioral science literature, it is my opinion that Mr. Carvey is physically addicted to alcohol." The witness might go on to explain the nature of physical addiction and how it is defined by withdrawal effects. If you base an opinion on facts that are in the records, make sure you have all of the facts. Nausea and shakiness can be caused by a variety of conditions. For example, did you happen to know that Mr. Carvey has multiple sclerosis?

---

[23]For example, Alice asks a child psychologist who has not seen any of the Carveys and has not heard any of the trial proceedings to provide an opinion about a hypothetical situation that closely resembles the picture of the Carveys that Alice has led in evidence.

If you lack direct knowledge about a clinical situation, you might be asked for an opinion based on a hypothetical situation: "Assuming that these facts are true, do you have an opinion? What is your opinion? What is the basis for your opinion?" In preparing for the case, review the hypothetical facts with the attorney who will present them. The hypothetical facts could be written down to ensure that they are accurately repeated during the direct examination.

Another method for introducing expert opinions is to call witnesses with factual information and have the expert listen to their testimony before calling the expert to testify. This approach can be tricky because the facts presented are not necessarily the facts proven. The expert witness may still have to respond to a hypothetical question: "Assuming Sam's testimony was true, what is your opinion about the impact of the abuse on Debra?" In order to remind the judge or jury that you are not accepting the truth of the hypothetical situations, you could restate the assumptions prior to offering your opinion: "So you are asking me to provide an opinion based on the assumption that Philip punished Debra by withholding meals. If that information were true, then ...."

Using multiple sources of information corroborates your evidence, giving it greater credibility (Austin, 2001). Corroboration is akin to the concept of triangulation in qualitative research (Denzin & Lincoln, 2011). Evelyn ratified the information gathered from personal interviews by reviewing prior assessments, by observing Debra's interaction with her parents, and by talking with people who have had direct observational knowledge of Debra's parenting such as teachers, coaches, and camp counselors.

To enhance the credibility of your opinion, describe the thought processes that led you to your opinion. Identifying the pros and cons of your opinion will demonstrate that you have considered alternative possibilities before arriving at your conclusion. When you analyze your opinion, consider other possible hypotheses, options, and variables. Consider an expert who has conducted a literature review on the causes and effects of psychological torture. Assume the expert found some research supports his opinions, but some research contradicts it. The expert could describe both the supportive and contradictory research, and explain why the supportive research is more persuasive. A balanced assessment is more believable than one deliberately limited to favorable data.

Language with Multiple Meanings

Communications in legal proceedings can be complicated by the fact that people come from different cultures: the dominant culture in the community, legal culture, professional clinical culture, and the cultures of minority participants in the process, to name a few. Each profession and each culture has its own language, even if everyone seems to be speaking English. In your role of expert-as-educator, you should adapt your language to communicate effectively with various participants (e.g., the decision makers, the attorneys, the parties, and the broader public).

During your preparation, find out who your target audience is. If the decision makers have a background in your field, use of technical language may be appropriate. If you come from a different culture than some of the participants, how familiar are you with their culture and patterns of communication? If you are not very familiar, consider using a cultural interpreter to help you prepare for your testimony. One of the questions that Evelyn is asked to assess in the Carveys' case is Debra's best interests in relation to her religious upbringing. To properly investigate this issue, it would be useful for Evelyn to know the similarities and differences between Baptist and Catholic teachings and traditions.

Legal definitions of particular words can vary significantly from what a clinician or layperson might expect. If a piece of legislation states that a cat is a dog, for the purposes outlined in the legislation, a cat is a dog. Federal drug regulations provide an interesting illustration of this type of legal fiction. The regulations list drugs in separate schedules, supposedly according to their level of risk (Drug Enforcement Administration, 2011). Schedule I substances are supposed to be the most toxic and riskiest substances, so the law imposes the strictest provisions on these substances, prohibiting possession and criminalizing production or sale of these substances. One of the Schedule I substances is tetrahydrocannabinol, commonly known as marijuana. Most substance abuse experts would agree that marijuana is less risky than many of the substances listed in other schedules—for instance, there are no known cases of a marijuana overdose. So, if you were asked about the relative risk of marijuana versus substances in Schedules II, III, or IV, how would you respond? Would you refer to scientific definitions of risk or legal definitions? The definition of Schedule I drugs also says that they have no currently accepted medical uses. Consider how marijuana has been used to treat a number of medical conditions, including nausea, vomiting, and lack of appetite for people with AIDS, cancer, and other illnesses. If you were asked whether marijuana could be used for medical purposes, would you defer to the legal definition?

Clinicians, too, have their own peculiar definitions. The *Diagnostic and Statistical Manual of Mental Disorders* (American Psychiatric Association, 2013) provides psychiatrists with specific criteria to diagnose mental disorders. In earlier editions the manual offered a definition for the term *psychopathic personality disorder*. In more recent editions, *antisocial* has replaced *psychopathic* as the preferred term. Does this mean psychopathic personality disorders no longer exist, or did they ever exist? Other conditions have remained the same but have different definitions. Perhaps this is not so peculiar, since all languages evolve. Reciting a technical DSM definition in order to educate the court about a mental disorder may not provide sufficient information for the court decision makers to fully understand the disorder. Expert witnesses may need to explain disorders in lay terms and perhaps with examples or analogies that the judge or jury can readily appreciate.

Communication problems tend to arise for words that have multiple meanings. If an attorney asked you about a client's mental capacity, would you know that he is referring to a term that has specific legal connotations? Is the attorney asking whether the client has the capacity to enter into a will, whether the client has the capacity to choose or deny medical treatment, or whether the person is legally competent to stand trial? The requirements for mental capacity differ depending on the legal issues at stake. As you are exposed to particular areas of law, you will become more familiar with legal concepts that relate to your field of practice. It is critical to discuss language issues with your attorney during the preparation stage. In some situations, the attorney may suggest that you avoid terms that have particular legal connotations. In other situations, she may encourage you to use legal terminology. If you do, make sure that you are well informed about its meaning.[24]

During the hearing, listen carefully for what is being asked. In a child protection hearing, Sam might be asked, "What makes you believe that Debra is in need of protection?" If state legislation defines "in need of protection" Sam needs to be familiar with this definition. In order to apply the legal definition to the question he is being asked, he needs to break down the legal constructs into plain language components and translate the legal question into observables. Thus, if "in need of protection" is defined as risk of sexual, physical, or emotional abuse and neglect," Sam needs to determine which type of abuse arose in Debra's case and what observable evidence he can present to support this determination.

You may also need to understand the relationship between the diagnostic categories and standards used for different legal issues. In criminal law, an accused person may claim that he is not guilty by reason of mental disease or defect (popularly known as an insanity defense; Comprehensive Crime Control Act, 1984). An expert witness who specializes in such cases must be familiar not only with the psychiatric criteria for diagnosing

---

[24]Consistent use of terminology is vital. Use the same words to describe the same concepts and use different words to describe different concepts. If you switch from talking about "abuse" to "assault" or "mistreatment," note that each term has different connotations.

a mental disease but also with the specific legal criteria for relieving an accused person of criminal responsibility. Given the challenges of using different sets of terminology, it is almost as if the expert needs to be multilingual.

CROSS-EXAMINATION

As with fact witnesses, thorough preparation and a sound direct examination are the best defenses for an expert witness during cross-examination. Expert witnesses are typically the most challenging type of witnesses to cross-examine. They have expertise that goes beyond that of the cross-examining attorney, giving the expert an informational advantage. An opposing attorney may choose not to cross-examine, particularly if the expert has shown that she is clinically and forensically competent and skilled at providing testimony. Still, it is prudent to expect that at least part of your testimony will be weakened in cross-examination and realize that perfect expert testimony is an unrealistic goal.

The primary focus for cross-examination of an expert may be to challenge the expert's qualifications and impartiality, as well as the factual and theoretical basis of his opinions.

Challenging Qualifications

If an opposing attorney challenges your qualifications, such a challenge is often made when you initially present your qualifications rather than after you have testified. That way, if you do not qualify as an expert, there is no need to go through your testimony. Even if you are admitted as a qualified expert, however, opposing attorneys can use cross-examination to try to narrow the scope of your expertise or to challenge your overall credibility. For instance, an attorney might challenge a social worker in a supervisory role for not having any recent direct practice with clients (Brodsky, 1991). Alternatively, an attorney might express utter disbelief that a supposed psychological expert had not read a particular research report. Note, the key to responding to cross-examination is to maintain your composure and respond in a nondefensive manner. Demonstrate your knowledge of relevant literature and practice issues. Confirm your expertise with confidence. Admit your limitations.

Assume that Paula's attorney, Art, is cross-examining Evelyn about her qualifications as an evaluator. Using an accusatory tone, Art asks, "Isn't it true that you have never studied adolescent drug use and you are not qualified to provide any authoritative statements about the etiology of Debra's drug use?" Evelyn has worked with some adolescents with drug-related problems, but basically Art's accusations are correct. Rather than quibble and get into a debate with Art, Evelyn agrees whole-heartedly, "You are correct. Adolescent drug use is not my primary area of expertise and you should not rely on me to make an absolutely authoritative opinion on the causes of Debra's drug use." By agreeing with the attorney, the witness defuses the potential conflict with the attorney, displaying honesty and likeability (Brodsky & Terrell, 2011).

Be cautious with questions that go beyond your expertise or statutory authority. In most jurisdictions, for example, only certain regulated professionals are allowed to provide a clinical diagnosis. Although you may be an expert, you are not the expert of everything! If you are asked a question beyond your expertise or authority, do not be embarrassed to say that you are not qualified or authorized to provide such an opinion. This approach is much safer than allowing the attorney to lead you down a garden path.

Challenging Impartiality

The opposing attorney may challenge your impartiality by suggesting bias in your information gathering, assessment process, report, or oral testimony. Even if you feel attacked, cooperate with the attorney, as cooperation will enhance your appearance of honesty and neutrality.

Some attorneys try to imply bias by asking the expert who is paying him. As recommended in Chapter 5, be frank about whether you have been paid for your consultation or your court appearance. Note that *you are being paid for your time, not for stating a particular opinion.* If you make your living as an expert witness, you may be questioned about this. If you always appear on behalf of a particular type of disputant (e.g., accused hate mongers), you risk being painted as biased in favor of that party. When Sam is called as an expert witness, he always represents the child protection agency. Although he always represents the same party, he can note that he does not always come to the same conclusion.

Expert witnesses, like all people, have biases. I am personally biased against hate mongering. Does that mean I cannot be objective in a case where someone is accused of this? If you are asked whether you have a bias about what should happen in a case, state your beliefs, based on your observations and expertise. Having an opinion—even a very strong opinion—does not constitute bias. The important issue is not whether you have a bias after your assessment but whether you brought pre-existing biases with you and whether they affected your approach to the task. Be open to considering new facts and avoid getting locked into an opinion so deeply that you are unable to simply think about other facts, opinions, or perspectives. The best defense against bias is self-awareness (Heilbronner, 2005).

Accusations of racial or cultural bias are particularly difficult to handle. Asserting that you are not prejudiced can come across as defensive. Consider whether you may have had such prejudices and what (if anything) you did to deal with them: "My clinical assessments are not simply subjective opinions or thoughts that just come off the top of my head. My clinical training and supervision has taught me to base my assessments on relevant data, such as ... and not to be influenced by stereotypes or other misleading attitudes." Many assessment tools used by clinicians do have inherent biases. Labeling a disproportionate number of African American students as mentally retarded and streaming them into special education, for example, has been challenged on the basis of cultural bias. Is there any literature that indicates whether the assessment procedures incur cultural biases? What precautions did you take to guard against bias in formulating your inferences, opinions, recommendations, or conclusions?

Challenging Factual Bases

If you were responsible for gathering information to inform your assessment, cross-examination could be used to challenge the thoroughness of your investigation—whether or not you followed reasonable standards from your discipline—and the strength of the information you relied on. Be familiar with standards for gathering information, including the recent literature, published protocols established by your agencies or associations, and current training and textbooks. If you have not followed established standards, be prepared to deal with questions about how you deviated and why. Be prepared to discuss how your approach provides a more thorough or more competent evaluation than if you followed established or conventional protocols.

If an expert is called to provide factual information and the client himself is not called to testify on his own behalf, the tribunal may wonder why the client is not taking the stand. A client may not be called to testify in order to protect the individual from difficult or embarrassing situations. Alternatively, the individual may not be a "good witness" due to uneasiness in public situations, limited communication skills, or poor memory. Some criminal courts have special rules permitting hearsay evidence to be heard from a clinician when a child or other victim has an impediment to testifying. Be aware that cross-examination may be used to suggest that your side is trying to hide something by not calling this witness. If there is a good reason that the person is not being called, it may be useful to disclose this reason. Before you disclose such information, be certain that the attorney wants you to provide such information to the court. Of course, even if the attorney does not want you to disclose such information, once you take the stand, you may be compelled to answer that question unless the attorney successfully objects to it.

In cases where you are asked to base your opinions on hypothetical situations or the reports of others, you have less control over the factual basis of your evidence. If you based your original opinion on a hypothetical set of facts, the cross-examining attorney may ask if your opinion would be different if there were additional facts (Melton et al., 2007). The additional facts may seem incredulous and you may have trouble accepting them. Remember that these facts are hypothetical. When you assume them, you are not agreeing with them: "The situation you are asking me to assume seems unlikely and is very different from that to which I have just offered in my testimony. However, if you would like me to include these variables in a different hypothetical situation, my opinion about this different circumstance would be ... " In order for your opinion to be used in the final adjudication, of course, the assumptions in the opposing attorney's version of the hypothetical would need to be proven.

If you received your facts from a secondhand source, you could be asked, "You weren't there when the riot erupted, so how do you know what happened?" Good question. A possible answer is: "That is correct. I was not there. I based my assessment on the reports of my associate, Dr. Johanna Perez." The rules of hearsay are relaxed somewhat for experts who have gathered information for an assessment. The court may look at whether the expert used standard methods and sources of information rather than require that court standards of admissibility be met. For example, is it common practice for a psychiatrist to rely on psychometric tests administered by a psychologist? If the factual basis of the assessment is in issue, the tribunal may require that the people who informed the expert take the stand personally so that they can be subject to live examination and cross-examination. The tribunal might also consider whether the source was likely to be honest. During an assessment, Paula might have an incentive to mislead Evelyn, so Paula's statements to Evelyn would be suspect. In contrast, an independent source such as Frieda has no stake in the outcome and no personal reason to mislead Evelyn. Thus Frieda's statements might be trustworthy.

There is no need to prove every single fact that the expert said she relied on. The weight given to an opinion, however, will depend on how well the factual basis underlying the opinion can be proven. To ensure that your opinions are given due weight, find out what the facts are before the hearing and whether evidence can be presented to prove those facts. You do not want to have your opinions undermined during cross-examination because the factual basis cannot be proven.

Some attorneys use nonverbal communication to add to the theatrics of cross-examination—rolling the eyes to cast aspersions about a particular response, repeating what the witness said in a slightly sarcastic tone to raise doubt, or making a casual utterance such as "uh-hmmmm" to lead the judge or jury think there is a hidden meaning behind what you stated. Maintain your professional composure. Do not become defensive. Do not give credence to the attorney's theatrics.

Challenging Theoretical or Research Bases

Technically, if an expert quotes someone else's research or articles, that information is hearsay evidence. Tribunals generally allow an expert to quote other people's work, provided that the work is well documented. The witness should be able to produce copies of the work, even though they may not be requested. If you are relying on literature for the theoretical basis of your opinion, use the original sources of information (i.e., the original theorist or the report of the original researchers). Your sources could easily be challenged if you rely on secondhand sources such as literature reviews or abstracts. How do you know the review or the abstract is accurate?

Theory and research can be challenged on the grounds that it is dated, unreliable, or invalid. To defend against these claims, be thoroughly familiar with the research you are relying on, as well as research that may go against your case. You may be asked, "Is the theory you used the only theory in current use?" Explain that there are other theories and why you chose to rely on this particular one. The weight attributed to your opinions will depend on a number of factors: Does the literature support your opinion? Is the research that you are relying on based on sound methods? Are your opinions consistent with scientific principles? Are your inferences logical? Are the assumptions reasonable? Is your process of reasoning consistent, explainable, objective, and defensible (Bush et al., 2006)? If an attorney quotes research but you are not sure the quote is accurate, you may ask to see a copy of the research. Some experts feel that attacks on their research or opinions shows contempt for good science and research, sensing the attorneys are motivated by winning a case rather than determining which research and theory truly provide the best evidence (Kolodinsky, 2010). To prepare for such challenges, look for criticisms of the research you are citing in other publications or by other researchers. Be ready to present the criticisms and your response to them. Identify whether there is consensus in the literature or among practitioners. If a major mental health organization has taken a stance on the debate, its perspective may be particularly persuasive. Also, investigate whether other courts or government commissions have cited or used the research that supports your expert opinions.

Assume your research and opinion evidence are based on solid grounds, but the attorney resorts to asking obtuse questions, challenging your ability to recall trivial details from a study you have cited. If the attorney requests information that is irrelevant to your opinions, state that the information is irrelevant and explain why. Guard against responding in a hostile or defensive manner. Remind yourself that your role is to provide the best evidence you can, regardless of the motivation behind an attorney's line of questioning: "I can attest to the overall methods and findings of the research based on my current memory. If you would like to enter the specific chi square and t-test statistics into evidence, I could refer to the study and read those data."

If you rely on part of a book or article, you may be cross-examined on the whole work. If a book is entered as an exhibit, you generally need to adopt the opinion of the book. If you agree with parts of the book and disagree with other parts of the book, be prepared to discuss your reasons for disagreeing with certain aspects of the work. Having research to support your position is always helpful. You may be cross-examined on any book that you refer to or that you admit is authoritative. As part of your preparation, ask your attorney which other experts will be called, what issues may arise, and what other literature they will likely introduce. Ensure that you are familiar with this literature and how it relates to your evidence.

Sometimes, a cross-examining attorney may try to impugn your credibility by asking challenging questions related to scientific methods, statistical analysis, or other highly technical information: "In your previous testimony, you mentioned the use of actuarial instruments. Could you explain how actuarial procedures are used to calculate risk of further abuse?" Ideally, you are able to provide a precise response based on your memory and understanding. If you need to refer to your notes, however, you could ask, "In order to provide an accurate response to this question, may I refer to an article in my materials?" Your materials may consist of a compilation of articles, test materials, charts, glossary definitions and reports, with an index and tabs so you can quickly access relevant information when faced with challenging questions.

If you are confronted with obscure references or quotations provided out of context, feel free to ask to see the book or reference. You might also want to ask the attorney to read the relevant quote so that you can respond to it. Be honest if you have not read a particular book or article. You cannot be questioned about readings or authors with which you are unfamiliar. According to evidentiary rules in some jurisdictions, an attorney cannot enter a journal article or other learned treatise into evidence unless the witness acknowledges the article as authoritative (Melton et al., 2007). Therefore, if you refuse to acknowledge a particular source as authoritative the attorney cannot introduce the source to impeach your evidence unless that attorney calls another expert to testify that the source is authoritative. If you know the source and truly believe it is a reasonable authority, you should acknowledge its authority. You can still critique the article or explain how your conclusions are valid, despite possible conflicts with what is stated in the article.

Another method of challenging expert evidence is to identify inconsistent statements. These inconsistencies could arise within your own testimony, between what you said on the stand and what you said previously, or between your testimony and information from others (including other witnesses, theorists, researchers, or common belief). If Sam has a theory about neglect that is inconsistent with common belief, he will have an uphill battle to prove his theory. Some people still believe the Earth is flat. If Sam's assessment practices went against what is said in traditional literature, he would need strong proof to demonstrate that his practices are valid or he would have to provide a more useful work product for the court.[25]

The cross-examining attorney may try to get mileage from the fact that you are not perfect, even if the inconsistency is not crucial to your overall testimony. Do not get flustered. Consider the possibility that you may be wrong (e.g., you may have made an error in judgment or missed a piece of information that the other side has uncovered and brought to your attention). Candidly admit a mistake rather than try to cover it up. If you have changed your opinion from a prior time, briefly explain why you changed it. Try to convey professionalism and confidence with your current statements. Your research may be more recent or more rigorous than the other research quoted. Explain the methodological soundness of your research in terms that the tribunal can comprehend. If an attorney tries to suggest that all of your testimony is invalid because of one small mistake, remain firm and confident about the testimony that is true and valid: "Yes, I misspoke when I said that I met Debra on February 7. Still, my testimony regarding the contents of the meeting on February 8 is accurate."

Sometimes attorneys will try to get a lot of mileage out of a small inconsistency or falsehood in your testimony: "I see! So you didn't really read the entire issue of the journal that you quoted. The statement in your deposition was false and misleading." A useful response is to admit the

---

[25]Consider the controversies over President Barack Obama's citizenship and religion. In spite of substantial evidence that he was born in the United States (he has a U.S. birth certificate) and that he is Christian (by virtue of his public declarations and involvement in Christian rituals and houses of worship), some Americans continue to question whether he is foreign-born and Muslim.

inconsistent and indefensible response with a brief statement (Melton et al., 2007) and then move to a more positive point that confirms your honesty, integrity, concern, and competence: "Yes, I read only the article by Gans and Helmond. This article relates directly to the issue of alienated children. If you think it would be useful for me to comment on the other articles in that issue, perhaps I could review them during a recess."

If the apparent inconsistency is not real, you may be able to clarify your statements or distinguish the contexts: "In the first case, I was quoted as supporting Theory X. In this case, I am relying on Theory Y. That is because the first case involved heroin abuse, and in this case Philip has been abusing cocaine." Your testimony is more credible if you correct past inconsistencies rather than avoid them or deal with them grudgingly. You might try to explain the inconsistencies during the direct examination to avoid the appearance that you are trying to hide something. If cross-examination has damaged your testimony, some of this damage may be reparable in the redirect. For example, your attorney can ask you to explain apparent inconsistencies, clarify your responses, or fill in the missing context.

Given that anything you say (or write) can be used against you in a future legal proceeding, be careful about how you express yourself publicly. Expressing controversial views may come back to haunt you.

Proof in law is different from scientific proof, although scientific methods and statistical probabilities are helpful in establishing proof in law. In law, the tribunal ultimately assesses whether the appropriate legal standard has been met. Consider an expert who is asked, "Are you certain, beyond a reasonable doubt?" The expert should use her own terms to describe her level of certainty about a particular opinion rather than the terminology that describes the legal standard of proof required. The language of a clinician professional might be "within a reasonable degree of psychological certainty." This avoids using the legal term "reasonable doubt." You want to convey confidence; however, you do not want to overstate your certainty since this could hurt your credibility. It all goes back to being honest, plain and simple.

Asking for an Inappropriate Opinion

If an attorney asks you for an opinion about something for which you do not have a sufficient basis to form an opinion, you may simply state that you do not have sufficient facts or information to express an opinion. In most instances, a judge will accept this answer and invite the attorney to move on to other lines of questioning. If the judge compels you to provide an opinion, you could preface your opinion by stating what types of information you would need to formulate a more valid or reliable opinion. If a family court judge pressed Evelyn to opine on whether Debra should be raised as a Catholic or Baptist, Evelyn might respond, "In my custody evaluation, I did not explore Debra's religious knowledge or identity, so I do not have sufficient information to provide an opinion on this matter. From my interviews with the parents, however, I understand that both mom and dad feel very strongly about their religion and would like to instill their values and beliefs in Debra. From my experience with other families, I know that children are able to manage being exposed to more than one religion. Given the information that I have gathered, I do not have any reason to believe that this would not be possible for Debra."

*   *   *

For a clinician who has never presented as an expert witness, the range of issues raised in this chapter may seem daunting. Take a deep breath. The central themes from this chapter are relatively straightforward:

- As an expert in mental health, a clinician may serve as a consultant to an attorney, an educator of the court, and a witness who can provide facts and interpret them for the court.
- You may not present opinion evidence in most court proceedings unless you are qualified as an expert.
- To be qualified as an expert, you need sufficient knowledge, training, supervision, and experience in the area related to the opinion evidence that you intend to provide.
- If an attorney asks you to serve as a forensic expert, make sure you understand the parameters of the proposed role and determine whether you can meet the attorney's expectations in a competent, ethical, and timely manner.
- When providing opinion evidence, ensure that you can provide sufficient factual, theoretical, or research support for each opinion.
- When testifying, present your information in an interesting, clear, concise, and confident manner.
- When responding to questions upon cross-examination, listen carefully to what you are being asked, maintain your composure, and answer truthfully.

Chapter 8

DOCUMENTARY EVIDENCE

with DIANE GREEN[1]

Although much of our discussion has focused on clinicians called to produce oral evidence, many legal proceedings are relying more and more heavily on documentary evidence, and in particular sworn affidavits or other written evidence.[2] For tribunals, the primary advantage of adjudicating on the basis of documentary evidence is speed, oral testimony being far more time-consuming than compiling written evidence. Written evidence also tends to be more focused than *viva voce* (live voice). In addition, documentary processes do not depend on the ability to get all of the parties and decision makers in the same room at the same time. Some clinicians prefer written evidence because they do not have to perform at a public hearing and are not subjected to on-the-spot cross-examination. Clinicians may also feel more comfortable with the narrative character of documentary evidence, in contrast with the question-and-answer format of

[1]Diane Green, MSW, PhD, is Associate Professor at the Florida Atlantic University School of Social Work. She received her MSW from the University of Central Florida and her PhD from the University of Texas at Austin. Her book credits include *Helping Victims of Violent Crime: Assessment, Treatment, and Evidence-Based Practice.* Dr. Green's research and scholarly interests include human trafficking, the stress and coping processes for victims of crime, restorative justice, the effectiveness of mental health interventions, and grief and loss issues.

[2]Documentary evidence refers to any document presented and allowed as evidence in a trial or hearing. Although historically, documents referred solely to information written down on paper, documentary evidence may also include information stored on cameras, video or audio recorders, smart phones, computers, the Internet, or similar media.

oral evidence. Among the drawbacks for clinicians are the time it takes to prepare documents and the inability to gauge how the decision makers are construing the information. On the stand, a witness can try to gauge how the judge or jury are responding to the testimony, and respond to any questions for clarification from the attorneys or judge.

In most legal proceedings a combination of written and oral evidence is used. For example, when Alice initiated divorce proceedings, she filed a petition, or legal application for the divorce, outlining the grounds for the application. Alice might also file written evidence from Frieda with the application. Frieda has a lot invested in what goes down on paper, because she is committed to certain facts and positions even though it is early in the legal process. It would hard for her to retract any statements made—particularly during oral cross-examination—because inconsistent statements could discredit her decisiveness, honesty, or professional competence. On the other hand, effective written evidence can be used to corroborate and strengthen her oral testimony.

Novice witnesses may assume that the need to make a strong case for their positions means they should not include disconfirming information in the written evidence. A parole officer who is recommending that parole be withdrawn might be inclined to include only negative information about the parolee. On the stand, the same officer might feel freer to provide balanced testimony about the parolee. In most instances, balanced information is preferable, regardless of whether the evidence is oral or written. Balance demonstrates the witness is objective. Further, including positive information is likely to leave the client feeling better about the process and the clinician. Clinicians who hope or need to continue to work with a client following adjudication do not want to win the case and lose the person. From an ethics perspective, including positive information fulfills the clinician's duty to show respect for the dignity and worth of all people (APA, 2010, Principle E; NASW, 2008, Ethical Principles).

In this chapter, we deal with three types of documentary evidence: affidavits, reports, and exhibits. The following section describes each of these types of evidence. We then outline the key elements of reports and provide suggestions for reviewing them. The final section revisits the issue of language and how to be careful about what you put in writing.

TYPES OF DOCUMENTARY EVIDENCE

Affidavits

An affidavit is a formal sworn statement of fact, signed by the author, who is called the *affiant* or *deponent* (i.e., the person who has knowledge of the information contained in the affidavit and is attesting to its truth). An affidavit must be witnessed and signed by a notary public or commissioner of oaths who certifies authenticity of the affiant's signature and oath on the affidavit (see Appendix E for a sample). An affidavit should also include the date and place that it is made. If a party wants to enter an affidavit into the records for a hearing, it must satisfy the rules of admissibility for that tribunal. For example, because of the rules against hearsay, the information should come primarily from the deponent's direct knowledge and beliefs. If an affidavit contains secondhand information, the source of the information should be stated: "I am advised by psychologist Fern Richards, PsyD, and do verily believe ... " If the other party to the proceeding does not contest this information, then the tribunal may rely on it. If the other party does contest it, then proof of Dr. Richards's information would have to come from her own testimony or affidavit. Tribunals normally recognize that mental health professionals often work as a team and that they should allow one professional to present the whole team's information in one document. Rather than paraphrase a coprofessional's report, another option is to attach the other professional's report as an exhibit to the affidavit.

Affidavits often require very specific information and formatting. For example, because an affidavit consists of personal observations, it should be written in the first-person singular voice (i.e., using "I" statements rather than "we," "the agency," or "the social worker"). Each statement in an affidavit is written as a separately numbered paragraph, for ease of reference at a hearing.[3] Attorneys frequently take responsibility for drafting affidavits. However, a clinician with extensive experience in similar cases may be able to draft her own, subject to review by an attorney or supervisor. Do not hesitate to ask attorneys or court clerks for sample affidavits, if needed, and other assistance. Even if an attorney plans to draft your affidavit, prepare a detailed written summary of your information to use as the basis for the affidavit. Before swearing to or affirming an affidavit, read it carefully. Do not be embarrassed or shy about suggesting changes for greater clarity and accuracy. You may have additional information, or you may have questions about the wording and its legal significance.

If you are preparing an affidavit that summarizes research, be careful to accurately describe the research. Sometimes an attorney may ask you to change the language you use to summarize research, subtly altering the meaning you intended to convey. For example, when writing an affidavit for a custody case, your original affidavit might refer to research on

---

[3]Many commonly used word processing programs have templates or standard format for legal documents, such as affidavits that allow for numbered paragraphs or lines. General affidavit forms from all 50 states can be found at *www.ilrg.com/forms/affidavt.html*.

"mother–infant" relationships. To avoid the appearance of gender-typing, the attorney may reframe your affidavit to refer to "caretaker–infant" relationships. If the research is based only on mother–infant observations and does not include data on and father–infant relationships, then using the gender-neutral term "caretaker" rather than "mother" may be misleading and should therefore be corrected.

Reports

The term "report" does not have a legal definition in the same way that an affidavit does. We are using "report" here to refer to any psychiatric, psychological, or social assessment prepared by a clinician for the purposes of a legal process. In contrast to an affidavit, a report is not a sworn document.[4] Tribunals may rely on information in a report if the information is not contested. If it is contested, then the author of the report may be required to provide oral testimony to prove its contents. Even though reports are not sworn, they can be very persuasive to the parties and the tribunal. A good report is impartial, thorough, well documented, and consequently unimpeachable in cross-examination. If your report is particularly strong in these respects, the parties may feel better able to predict the results of adjudication and may well settle the case on their own. Accordingly, you can save a lot of blood, sweat, and tears (including your own) if you do your best work up front, in the report.

The range of possible reports includes presentence reports in criminal hearings, investigation reports in child protection cases, custody assessments in divorce cases, parental fitness evaluations in cases involving termination of parental rights, assessments for juvenile transfer hearings, mental competence evaluations for involuntary committal hearings, and social policy reports submitted to legislative hearings. Unless the matter is under federal jurisdiction (as in federal criminal cases), you will need to refer to state law for specific procedures and formal requirements for such reports. Some reports have few requirements for format and content. Other reports are regulated by statutes, regulations, or agency policies. Adoption laws, for instance, require the inclusion of certain information about adoptive parents in a home study, and adoption agencies have protocols for these reports that comply with the laws and expectations of the relevant tribunals. Clinicians can influence local guidelines by forming committees with attorneys, judges, or other tribunal members to develop better standards for specific types of reports.

---

[4]As mentioned above, a report may be attached to an affidavit, in which the affiant swears to its truth.

If Evelyn worked on an interdisciplinary team, how does the team decide which member should write the report? Reports generally should be written and signed by someone who qualifies as an expert. Although a report could be restricted to fact evidence, most reports also include opinions. If Evelyn worked with a student who gathered some of the evidence, Evelyn may decide to submit the report under her name to give credibility to opinions in the report. However, if the primary reason for submitting the report were to document certain facts, then the student who gathered the information would be the most appropriate signatory. Alternatively, both Evelyn and her student could sign the report, indicating their respective contributions.

If you know that a report is going to be used in a legal proceeding, ensure that it is written in a manner that is helpful to legal consumers. Attorneys and judges have often criticized reports by mental health professionals as being confusing, filled with jargon, hard to follow, and full of conclusions without sufficient factual basis (Melton et al., 2007). Use an introduction to summarize your report and break the report into a logical sequence of headings to ensure it is easy to understand and follow. Separate opinions (including interpretations, conclusions, and recommendations) from facts, and ensure that each opinion is substantiated.

Exhibits

Exhibits are objects that attorneys file with a tribunal to become part of its record of evidence. Examples of exhibits include reports, affidavits, case records, photographs, and clothes. As noted throughout this volume, the purpose of providing evidence at a trial is to educate the judge or jury about the facts in a case. As the saying goes, "Seeing is believing," so using visual aids in courtroom presentations can have a critical impact on the decision makers. Seeing a torn piece of clothes may be more convincing than just hearing about it. Exhibits may also be used as visual aids, making it easier to explain complex information. Clinicians may supplement their verbal evidence with a broad range of visual aids, for instance, charts illustrating statistical information, genograms illustrating the family structure, ecomaps illustrating the client's social environment, timelines of important events, maps of key locations, and diagrams portraying particular client behaviors.

If an exhibit is introduced during your testimony, you may be asked to identify the object and how you are familiar with it. If a client left cocaine in your office and the cocaine was introduced into evidence, you would be asked whether you are familiar with this object, where you found it, whom it belonged to, and how you know this. You also may be asked to attest to the chain of custody since you initially found it (e.g., if you gave it directly to the police or if others at your agency have handled it). If you collect any objects that you believe may be used as evidence at a future hearing, maintain notes about how you obtained the evidence, keep it in secure custody to prevent tampering, and be sure you can trace possession of the object. If you are asked to submit clinical records, bring three copies to the hearing—one for each party and one for the court. The court may permit you to submit "true and correct" copies of the originals, so that you can maintain the original files (Bernstein & Hartsell, 2005). Ask your attorney if you should bring the original, or whether copies are sufficient.

ELEMENTS OF REPORTS

The format and key elements of a report vary, depending on the nature of the legal and clinical/forensic issues, the requirements of the tribunal, and the contract between the expert and the party who hires the expert to produce the report (whether that be one of the disputants, the tribunal, or a public agency such as a probation office or a public advocacy group). For certain types of reports, such as presentencing reports in criminal cases, the elements of the report may be defined by a particular statute or regulations. The format and parameters of a report should be established before you conduct the assessment so you can gear your investigation to the needs of the tribunal (see Chapter 7). Whatever format you use, ensure your report is succinct, clear, and error-free. Your professionalism and credibility are at stake. The following subsections identify topics that are typically included in reports (Braaten, 2007; Koocher, Norcross, & Hill, 2004; Melton et al., 2007).

Title of the Proceedings

If a legal case has been initiated, use the legal title of the case (e.g., *Philip Carvey v. Paula Carvey*). Identify the docket number[5] and the name of the court or other tribunal. If no case has been initiated, identify your report using the name of the party or parties that are the subject of your report.

Submitted By

Provide your name, address, and telephone number. Only include your e-mail address or other electronic contact information if you want to be

---

[5]"Docket number" refers to the number assigned by a court or other tribunal to identify the case file.

contacted through those means. Describe your agency and position. A brief description of your qualifications as an expert may also be included here. Attach your curriculum vitae as an appendix to the report to substantiate your qualifications as an expert, focusing on education, experience, and credentials that relate most closely to the expertise required for your evaluation and report.[6]

Purpose

Briefly state the purpose of the report (e.g., an independent custody evaluation, a presentence report, an investigation into charges of discrimination). Identify the presenting legal issues as well as the party(ies) hiring you to prepare the report. Describe the key circumstances surrounding the legal dispute and the referral to you, including the scope of your evaluation and any other instructions provided to you. If there is a court order or a consent order directing your work, cite the order and what the order says is the focus of your evaluative responsibilities. Describe any pertinent facts or assumptions that the referring party has asked you to make for the report. Ensure that the rest of the report is geared toward the stated purpose, so that you do not provide too much information or set yourself up for problems during cross-examination.

Identifying Information

Identify the individual(s), families, or groups who are the focus of your report. Provide names, addresses, telephone numbers, relationships to the legal action, and relationships to one another (e.g., mother of Debra, respondent in the action). For each individual, include the birth date, age, gender, birthplace, citizenship, and attorney acting on the individual's behalf. If the subject of the evaluation was voluntary, you may explain how you obtained informed consent. If the subject of the evaluation was involuntary, you may explain how you notified the subject about the evaluation process, including how the report could be used in court.

Materials Reviewed

List all documents you reviewed while preparing the report. Include the name of each document, the date of its creation, to whom it was sent, and by whom it was sent. If the document is a court document, indicate the title of the document and its date of entry.

---

[6]See Chapter 7 for contents of a curriculum vitae.

Positions of the Parties

State the original positions of the parties with regard to the primary legal issue(s) in dispute (e.g., Frieda denies professional misconduct; Paula is seeking sole custody of Debra).

Primer

Depending on the sophistication of the tribunal hearing the case, you may need to include a section designed to educate the tribunal about your area of expertise (e.g., the theoretical basis of your assessment, definitions of key concepts, information-gathering methodologies, explanations of actuarial data and their relevance to the legal issues). Some reports need to be framed within the psychological or social variables that have been established in case law (e.g., mental capacity to stand trial). When relying on a case law precedent, cite the specific case and include direct quotations explaining the psychological or social variables to be applied in your report.

Rather than including background information or definitions as a separate section of your report, you may find that integrating this information into other sections is more effective from an organizational perspective. Thus you could put a definition of standard deviation in a section explaining research methods, a definition of bipolar disorder in the section where you present your diagnosis, or a discussion of legal precedents when you are linking psychosocial information to the standards developed in these cases. When determining whether it is better to have a separate primer or to integrate this information in the rest of the report, try to place yourself in the position of a judge or juror who does not have your professional expertise and is reading this information for the first time.

Sources and Procedures for Gathering Information

Identify the sources of data that informed your report and list them in chronological order. Note that judges and juries will be concerned about the factual basis of your findings and opinions, so providing details of your sources of information is critical. These decision makers may give more weight to your findings if you had prolonged and varied contact with the relevant parties than if you met only briefly or if you did not have any direct contact with important sources of information (Melton et al., 2007). Indicate dates, places, and people involved in any interviews. Further, describe the procedures that you used to gather information, for example:

- Clinical interviews (unstructured, semistructured, or highly structured, including the standards or instruments used for structuring the interview, face-to-face, telephone, or online).
- Observations of the client (during a home visit, during supervised child visitation, etc.).
- Interviews with collaterals, such as family members, friends, or teachers.
- Physiological measurements.
- Psychological testing.
- Assessments of social problems, strengths, adaptations, and functioning.
- Self-reports or other report forms.
- Records from other professionals (e.g., physicians or other mental health professionals).

Briefly explain any specific procedures or protocols you followed to enhance the credibility of your reports, for instance, how you used a certain assessment format that avoided leading and suggestive questions, how you used a random selection protocol to avoid bias in selecting participants for a research study, or how you used an instrument that included questions to screen for malingering or other false information (Ceci & Bruck, 2006; Melton et al., 2007).

If you are providing a report concerning a person from a minority background, you may need to establish that your procedures were appropriate given the person's culture, religion, or other socioeconomic status. For instance, information about a person's experience with racism, homophobia, or other forms of oppression may be relevant to understanding the person's attitudes, beliefs, and behaviors. If you have used an instrument to assess the person's level of depression, indicate whether the instrument was normed for the person's cultural group. Ensure that you convey information pertaining to culture or other aspects of diversity in a respectful manner (Barrett & George, 2005).

Relevant History

Family or individual histories should focus on information that is relevant to the current issues in dispute. For example, a presentence report should include information about arrests and past convictions. A refugee report should focus on the claimant's treatment in his country of origin (Barrett & George, 2005). In a child protection case, the report should include evidence of abuse or neglect, developmental history, out-of-home placements, school, and medical history (Munson, 2009). The level and breadth and detail for your report will depend on the issues in dispute, as well as the parameters of the court order or contract authorizing your services.

Present Circumstances

Present circumstances could include a description of family dynamics, peer relationships, education, employment, and financial information, as well as other social, emotional, and physical data. Describe the subject's motivations and past attempts at change. Some reports require a full psychosocial history, including family composition and background, culture, religion, education history, employment history, medical history, mental health status, behavioral problems, criminal justice history, significant life events, social supports, stressors, strengths, spirituality, needs, disabilities or special challenges, and general social functioning. Other reports are focused on particular topics (e.g., a report on the current mental capacity of an individual). Provide balanced information, including both positive and negative elements. Use currently supported forensic methods and procedures in gathering information for the report (Bush et al., 2006; Greenfield & Gottschalk, 2009; Gould & Martindale, 2009). Avoid offering information that does not bear directly on the legal purpose for your professional services. Ensure that you have included all of the facts that enabled you to arrive at your opinion.

Interpretation of Data

Describe the relevant data from the following sources as they apply to the case:

- Interviews with each party.
- Results from psychological test data (including descriptions and summaries of standardized measurements that you used).
- Information from collateral record review and interviews with collaterals.
- Direct behavioral observations (e.g., if the report is about issues related to parenting competencies, then you might describe your observations of how each parent interacted with the child and how you interpreted these behaviors).

Interpret the data using language that can be easily understood by a person without your clinical or forensic expertise.

Integration of Data

Discuss the degree to which information obtained from different sources of data converge or diverge on specific conclusions. Obviously, a specific conclusion is soundest when all data sources support that conclusion, while it becomes more suspect when one or more data sources support divergent conclusions.

Opinion

State your opinion or assessment of the individual and/or the larger situation, based on the facts provided earlier in your report. As noted in Chapter 7, opinions may include inferences, interpretations of data, expert assessments, clinical impressions, and predictions of behavior or other social phenomena (e.g., the risk of a client committing suicide). Your opinions should be linked back to the stated purpose of the report (e.g., to determine the mental state of an alleged murderer, the best interests of the child, or the psychological harm suffered by the plaintiff). Do not provide opinions that go beyond your area of expertise. Although you may provide information about a criminal defendant's behavior, for instance, do not provide a legal opinion about the defendant's innocence or guilt. That is for the judge or jury to determine.

Qualification of Opinion

Evaluate the factors considered in developing your opinion. Identify the strengths and limitations of the basis of your opinion (e.g., the reliability and validity of instruments used; assumptions made; support in the research literature; noncooperation of a particular party, inability to interview a relevant person or obtain key documents). Indicate the degree of certainty with which you put your opinion forward. Use examples or analogies to illustrate complex points.

Offer rival, plausible alternative hypotheses. If you strongly believe in one interpretation of the data, then explain why you believe your interpretation is more strongly supported by the data than the alternative hypotheses.

Conclusions and Recommendations

Whether your recommendations are directed toward the tribunal or to the parties themselves should be negotiated when you are initially hired. State recommendations as suggestions rather than "orders" or decisions about what should happen. The parties and the tribunal can accept or reject whatever you suggest. Accordingly, it is important to provide a sound rationale for why your recommendations should be followed. Support your recommendations with empirical research and provide full citations. Indicate whether one or both parties are willing to comply with your suggestions. If you recommend an involuntary option, consider whether your recommendations are within the tribunal's dispositional authority (e.g., some tribunals are not allowed to order someone to undertake treatment). Offer alternative recommendations and provide the tribunal with your opinion of which recommendation(s) should be considered the most useful and why (i.e., the rationale for implementation of your suggestions). Be sure to justify each recommendation you make. If you have been hired to provide an evaluation of a client's condition but not to provide recommendations, then provide the evaluation without recommendations. When in doubt, ask the hiring attorney whether and how you should address the ultimate legal issue to be decided in the case (see Chapter 7). Do not provide opinions or recommendations that go beyond the scope of the court order or contract for services.

Evaluative Summary and Provisos

Highlight the key facts, opinions, and recommendations. In a presentence report, for example, include: the individual's motive for the crime, the precipitating factors, how the offense fits into the fabric of the subject's life, the individual's plans, and your recommendations for therapeutic intervention and sentencing.

You may also include any provisos or cautions about the use of the report, for instance, stating that the report is based on the information you received as of the date of the report and you are reserving the right to amend your opinion should you receive additional information. Other warnings may relate to the methods used to gather information. For instance, if you used tools that measured a particular psychological characteristic, you can use this information for descriptive purposes. If the tool was not designed to predict behavior, then it should not be used for such purposes.

Date and Signature

The report should include the date it was completed and the signature of the person who prepared the report. Prior to your signature, you may provide a concluding declaration such as, "I have conducted interviews, gathered information, analyzed test results, and reviewed reports in a manner consistent with [agency policy, standards of my profession, or state guidelines].

My report is based on full and honest disclosure of the information I have collected and opinions I have developed for this case."

Appendices

Your curriculum vitae and any other documents supporting your report may be attached as appendices. Be sure you have included all key materials underlying your assessment. Any updates and amendments should be prepared as separate documents.

PROOFING YOUR REPORT

Prepare and review your report with an eye to meeting both legal and professional clinical standards (see list of Ethics Codes & Practice Guidelines for Assessment, Therapy, Counseling, & Forensic Practice at *kspope.com/ ethcodes/index.php*). In addition, be aware of the idiosyncratic expectations of your intended audiences, for instance, a judge who is partial to empirical studies with large sample sizes, or who detests the use of a particular psychometric instrument. Check your report to ensure that it is readable, thorough, credible, impartial, and well documented. Use the questions in the Figure 8.1 as a checklist.

Review a draft of your report with an experienced clinician or your attorney. Even the most highly regarded expert can benefit from having a report reviewed by a professional colleague. For a sample format of a forensic report, see Figure 8.2. For a completed sample of a forensic report, see *www.barsky.org/clinicians*.

THE USE OF LANGUAGE

Your close attention to language is just as important when providing written evidence as it is in oral evidence. In fact, written evidence can have even greater impact than oral evidence, since the tribunal sees it before hearing oral testimony. During deliberations, the tribunal may also look back at the documents after hearing the oral testimony.

As with oral testimony, use clear descriptive language rather than jargon, slang, or colloquialisms. Rather than use subjective terms such as "inappropriate behavior," give concrete examples of the behavior (e.g., "Paula slapped Debra across her face."). Avoid equivocal phrases such as "it seems that" or "one may conclude." If the facts give rise to equivocal or

√ Is the language clear and concise?

√ Is the level of language used appropriate given the sophistication of the tribunal?

√ Have you used phrases such as "reported by" and "according to" when reporting information concerning matters for which you do not have direct knowledge?

√ Have you gathered or shaped the facts in a way that supports a predetermined conclusion? If so, how can you conduct a more objective investigation and ensure that your conclusions are sound (i.e., unbiased)?

√ Does anything in the report indicate bias (e.g., judgmental language, cultural insensitivity, lack of balance in fact finding)? If so, how can you correct the report to ensure that it sounds fair and impartial?

√ Does any of your information conflict with common sense? If so, have you adequately explained why *common sense* does not apply in this case?

√ Does the description of the case provide sufficient factual background to inform decisions that need to be made?

√ Does the report make any factual assumptions? Are there gaps in the information you have documented?

√ Are facts, opinions, and recommendations clearly differentiated?

√ Is there a logical connection between the facts, opinions, and recommendations? Is it explained in persuasive terms?

√ Does the report include only information to which you can testify honestly, confidently, and knowledgeably?

√ Are your opinions consistent with the research literature and with other reports? If not, have you provided adequate explanations?

√ Is the format easy to follow through use of headings, numbered paragraphs, an index, or tabs for long reports?[7]

√ Does the report clearly relate to the legal issues in the case?[8]

√ Are your charts, tables, and appendices easy to follow? Have you provided adequate explanations for them?

√ Does the report give an overall impression of professionalism (including spelling, grammar, language, format, and contents)?

FIGURE 8.1. Checklist for reports.

---

[7]For web-based reports, you could also use hyperlinks to help the reader navigate between related sections of the report.

[8]For example, a child protection report should not just provide an opinion about what a clean house is, but rather should connect this issue with the legal test for neglect.

I.   Introduction (title of proceedings, submitted by, purpose, evaluation questions, records reviewed

II. History (family and individual history, developmental history, criminal justice history, medical history)

III. Mental Status/Diagnosis/Clinical Impression (including substance dependency and psychological testing)

IV. Summary/Opinions/Recommendations

FIGURE 8.2. Sample format of forensic report.

contradictory conclusions, state them clearly. For example, "I observed X. This suggests either Y or Z. Y is more likely, because ... "

Check to see if any terms you are using have specific meanings in law (e.g., informed consent, mental disorder). If so, make sure that you use these terms appropriately. Some clinicians use standard forms for reports or affidavits. The primary advantage of standard forms is that they use tried and tested clauses, based on precedent. For example, an affidavit in support of a welfare appeal would need to refer to certain standards established in welfare legislation. Having standard clauses for the affidavit, a clinician can ensure that the required information is included, even if the clinician is not an expert in welfare laws. Although standard forms can be an expedient alternative, the main disadvantage is that the clinician may be unaware of the specific connotations or consequences of the language used. Another potential problem is that the issues in some cases do not fit within standard forms. The format for a presentencing report may be geared toward adult offenders, but what if you have a child offender who has been tried as an adult? Should you use the standard format, or should you alter it to accommodate the age of the offender? Standard forms should also be updated to ensure conformity with changing laws. If you use standard forms, ensure that you understand the meanings of all the clauses. Finally, consider using the standard form as a flexible outline rather than as a fixed format.

Consider who may see the report. If the case settles privately, the parties and their attorneys may be the only ones with access to it. How will they interpret the report? If the case goes on to court or another form of public hearing, then information in the report may be widely accessible. Consider how you can frame the report in terms that are least embarrassing without losing key information required by the parties and the tribunal. Finally, note the impact of the report on third parties. Will Debra have access to Evelyn's custody report now or when she grows older? Will one parent try to use information in the report to turn Debra against the other parent?

The purpose of your affidavit or report is to inform, not inflame. Even though adjudications are adversarial by definition, the role of a witness can be carried out in a nonadversarial manner. Be humane, balanced, and sensitive. Use language that is direct but has the least stigma attached. For instance, suggest referring a client for a mental health assessment rather than for a personality disorder assessment. Your choice of words can have a strong impact on the overall tone of the document and how it is received. A report stating that "Philip was disturbed" could be rephrased as "Philip was upset." Similarly, "Paula refused services" could be changed to "Paula declined service." Consider whether your document helps or hinders chances for an amicable settlement. If you are a clinician in a treatment role who has provided a clinical report and testimony, consider how your report may affect your ongoing relationship with the client. Take your report seriously. Your recommendations can have serious consequences for the parties. Your words can also have a lasting emotional impact on the parties, regardless of the tribunal's decision. Finally, when you are preparing for a hearing, consider whether you should review the report with your client and help the client process her feelings about its contents (covered more fully in Chapter 4). Once again, you may need to consult with an attorney or supervisor to determine whether it is appropriate to review a report with the client prior to forwarding it to the attorneys or court.

Chapter 9

CLAIMS AGAINST CLINICIANS

For the most part, when a clinician is involved in a case as a witness, the clinician does not have a personal interest in the dispute. The dispute concerns a client or others who have a professional relationship with the clinician. The clinician may represent an agency, such as victim services, child protection, or a human rights agency. A victim services worker, for example, has a strong interest in supporting the needs and wishes of clients who have suffered from criminal offenses against them. Likewise, a human rights investigator is interested in identifying and remedying human rights violations. Still, the clinician's interests are professional rather than personal. When a client threatens to sue a clinician, however, the clinician has a personal stake in the outcome of the case. Being sued puts the clinician in an ethically challenging situation. On the one hand, clinicians have a fiduciary ethical commitment toward their clients (APA, 2010, Principle B; NASW, 2008, s.1.01). On the other hand, clinicians have a right to defend themselves against false allegations. This chapter highlights the special concerns for clinicians as witnesses in situations involving allegations of malpractice.

Broadly speaking, a clinician commits malpractice when she causes harm to a client through improper performance of duties (Heilbrun, Matteo, Marczyk, & Goldstein, 2008). How "improper" is defined depends on the profession, how it is regulated, and the type of legal recourse that the client pursues. The criminal justice system is able to impose the most severe penalties, including fines and incarceration. "Improper" conduct in criminal law is defined primarily by offenses established under the federal or state criminal law statutes. Relatively few cases of misconduct by professionals amount to criminal offenses. Sexual assault, misappropriation of client funds (fraud), and unlawful confinement are among the most likely situations in which clinicians might be involved.[1] The primary avenues of legal recourse against clinicians are court actions and disciplinary hearings conducted by the clinician's regulatory association.[2]

COURT ACTIONS

Clients may initiate civil lawsuits on the basis of breach of contract for services, intentionally violating a client's rights, or negligence. Negligence (or malpractice) is the most common form of court action against clinicians. To establish negligence, the client must prove four points:

- The clinician owed the client a duty of professional care.
- The clinician breached that duty.
- The client suffered damages as a result of the breach.
- There is a reasonably close connection (or proximate cause) between the breach and the damages.

In most cases, the issue of a clinician owing a duty of care is easily established. By simply offering or advertising therapeutic services to a client, the clinician is holding himself out to be someone who can help the client through the use of particular professional services. Thus social workers, psychologists, and other clinicians owe clients a duty of care based on their professional training and experience. Sometimes the question of *who is a client* may be complicated (Barsky, 2010). As a mediator, for instance, Michael's clients are the parents, Paula and Philip. Although the focus of the custody dispute is Debra, Debra is not Michael's client. Debra has not retained Michael's mediation services. In contrast, as a clinician conducting child abuse investigation, Sam's primary client is Debra, not her parents. In further contrast, consider Evelyn's role as a custody evaluator. Given that Evelyn was hired by a court to provide a forensic evaluation, the court is her client. The subjects of the evaluation (Debra, Philip, and Paula) are not her clients, so this may prevent any of them from suing her for malpractice.

The standard of care expected of a professional is to behave in the same way as an ordinary, reasonable, and prudent professional with similar training and under similar circumstances (Reamer, 2011). Examples of

---

[1]These offenses often include clinicians who exploit vulnerable children, people with cognitive impairment, and the elderly, particularly in residential facilities such as nursing homes.

[2]Most client complaints against clinicians are dealt with informally, between the clinician and client, or through various mechanisms within an agency (e.g., complaints registered with supervisors; in-agency appeal processes). How you respond at an early stage often determines whether a complaint goes any further (as was explained more fully in Chapter 3).

professional standards of care that are common across different clinical roles include ensuring clients have an opportunity to provide informed and voluntary consent, respecting client confidentiality, maintaining appropriate boundaries with clients, and offering services within one's area of expertise (APA, 2010, ss. 3.10, 4.01, 3.08, & 2.01; NASW, 2008, ss. 1.03, 1.07, 1.09 & 1.04). Although some standards of care are similar across different professional roles, each type of clinician is expected to act in accordance with standards of care specific to her own profession and role.[3] Michael, who works as a mediator, is expected to live up to the standards of a reasonable mediator. Mediators are expected to respect a client's right to confidentiality (AFCC, 2000). If Michael disclosed the Carveys' domestic problems to Philip's employer without the Carveys' permission, Michael would be in breach of his duty to the Carveys. If Philip lost his job because of this breach, then Philip could sue Michael for damages (monetary compensation for the losses or injuries he incurred). However, the factual question may arise, "Did Michael's disclosure actually cause Philip to lose his job?" As a family therapist, Frieda is expected to live up to the standards of "a reasonable family therapist." Consider the fact that the Carveys separated even though Frieda offered to help them, utilizing a somewhat unorthodox form of intervention. What were Frieda's professional responsibilities? Did she fail to meet the standards of her coprofessionals in dealing with this situation? Just because therapy was not successful does not mean that Frieda was negligent.[4] Even if she was found negligent, was her negligence the proximate cause of the Carveys' breakup? Further, how would the court calculate emotional and social damages?

When one is a defendant in a legal action, knowing the issues in contention is crucial for preparing to be a witness. Ask your attorney to explain the nature of the legal issues and the type of evidence you can use to respond directly to these issues. Michael would not help himself if he focused his testimony on how he never intended to hurt Philip, since negligence does not depend on intent. On the other hand, if Philip gave Michael permission to speak with the employer, evidence to that effect would be crucial.

---

[3]Courts can impose standards of care even in situations where no express or definite standards previously existed. In order to reduce uncertainty, professional associations try to develop generally accepted practices for their members. The difficulty is that clinical intervention is partially an art rather than an exact science.

[4]Consider a case where the client threatens suicide. If a clinician makes a reasonable assessment and things still go wrong, the clinician has not been negligent. The court is more concerned about how the clinician made the decision rather than the specific consequences of the decision. How much time was put into making the decision? What theory, research, logic, observations, or ethical standards were used to inform the decision? Whom did the clinician consult to make the decision? Clinicians constantly make judgment calls. They are not expected to be perfect. Protect yourself by documenting the rationale for key decisions.

Whereas clients do not need to prove *intent to harm* for negligence lawsuits, they would need to prove intent for intentional torts or infringements of civil rights. In a fraud lawsuit, for instance, a client would have to prove that the worker intentionally misled, cheated, or took advantage of the client for personal gain. Examples of fraud may include deliberately charging Medicare or private insurance companies for services that were not rendered, deceiving a client into thinking he needed services that were not necessary, or purposefully misrepresenting the clinician's professional qualifications to attract clients.

Another form of lawsuit to which some clinicians are susceptible is *unauthorized practice of law*. To practice law a person must be a licensed attorney. For instance, a clinician may advocate for a client in many forums, but in a formal court setting, only licensed attorneys are permitted to provide legal representation for clients. The most common trouble spots for clinicians are providing legal advice and drafting legal documents (e.g., if Michael drafted the Carveys' separation agreement and advised them of the benefits of signing). If you are helping a client with legal issues, it is important to know the lines between attorney and nonattorney functions. In addition, keep records that document what you did and did not do. If Paula asked Sam for legal advice, he should document the request and how he responded. If Sam referred Paula for legal advice and Paula refused, he should note this in Paula's file. If Paula later claims that Sam provided legal advice, Sam will have evidence documenting the information he provided and actions taken.

Some clinicians are concerned that a client could sue them for defamation (or slander) based on statements made while acting as a witness. Defamation refers to untrue written or verbal statements that harm the reputation of another person. If you tell the truth on the stand, you are not liable for defamation. It is unlikely that you will be sued based on statements you make as a witness, as long as you act in good faith and without malice.[5]

DISCIPLINARY HEARINGS

The various clinical professions have different mechanisms for dealing with client complaints. At one end of the spectrum, some regulatory bodies have mandatory adjudicative hearings with broad powers of discipline (e.g., suspending or revoking licensure, placing conditions on practice, or requiring compensation for damages incurred by clients). Other professions have less formal dispute resolution processes, more akin to mediation or arbitration (see Chapter 10). Some fields of practice may not require a licensure or

---

[5]For child protection issues, elder abuse, and other forensic roles, state legislation may specifically protect clinicians from being sued.

certification, so enforcement of participation in disciplinary hearings is tenuous. Some clinicians are not associated with any regulatory body, and clients in that case have no recourse for professional discipline other than what is offered in court or by the agency employing the clinician. Given the high cost of participating in court processes, disciplinary hearings are more accessible than court for most clients.

Some clinical professions have their own codes of ethics and standards of professional conduct. These codes establish the line between proper and improper practice. Conduct that amounts to a criminal offense or civil cause of action generally falls within the purview of professional misconduct as well. Professional misconduct also includes activities not actionable in court. Some professions, for example, prohibit a clinician from engaging in sexual activities with a client. Even though the state generally stays out of the bedrooms of consenting adults, these professions believe that such a rule is required in order to protect clients from clinicians who may take advantage of clients' vulnerabilities and trust. What if Frieda's unorthodox intervention with the Carveys included surrogate sex therapy? If Frieda were a member of a profession that prohibited sex with clients, she would be guilty of professional misconduct, even though other professions might allow it.

Issues often dealt with in disciplinary hearings include: role boundary violations (Gutheil & Brodsky, 2008); inadvertent disclosure of confidential information; diagnostic errors; inappropriate child placement; abandoning a client; premature termination without appropriate referrals for follow-up; defamation; failure to protect a client or third party from harm; and using a treatment approach inconsistent with practice standards and evaluative research (Reamer, 2003). A clinician who inadequately prepares to present as an expert witness could also be liable for malpractice. This does not mean the expert guarantees her client will win the case. The expert must carry out her role according to the standards established by her profession. Evelyn could be subject to malpractice claims if she did not verify information used to support her assessment or if she allowed bias to interfere with an assessment. Experts must produce fair reports, regardless of which party hires them. Experts can express strong opinions, but they may be subject to professional discipline if they state conclusions without having a factual basis or without considering alternative theories (APA, 2010, s.9.01).

If a client complains to a licensing board, it is inappropriate to contact the client directly. There are two alternatives on how to proceed. The first is to respond to the licensing board with your explanation of the alleged issue. The second alternative is to contact an attorney and, together with the attorney, formulate a response to the complaint, with your attorney having all contact with the licensing board. Given the allegations against you, you may need to terminate services with the client. Still, you have an ethical obligation to ensure that your client has access to services. Talk to your attorney and agency supervisor about how you can offer services (perhaps through a referral to another agency), so that the client does not feel abandoned (APA, 2010, s.10.10; NASW, 2008, s.1.16[b])

It is important to understand that the primary function of a licensing board is to protect the public. It is not to protect you. The board wants to maintain the public confidence in your profession. The board is responsible for the proper examination of all legitimate complaints. You should take any complaints from a licensing board *very* seriously. No matter how you view the allegation, the licensing board will take all aspects of the allegation seriously.[6] Remember that some members of licensing boards may not have expertise in your particular area of practice. They may need to be educated about aspects of your work and/or case law precedents that support your position. This is another reason to obtain legal counsel. Your attorney may guide you toward legal avenues of response that are unknown to you.

AVOIDING MALPRACTICE ACTIONS

The best advice on how to deal with a malpractice suit is to avoid it. From the client's perspective, he perceives that he has been wronged—and he may be right. From your perspective, you want to practice competently, do good for your clients, and avoid harm. A legal action is costly, time-consuming, stressful, and harmful to one's professional reputation—even if you *win* the action. A malpractice action is not all bad. An action is a means of ensuring that your practice is accountable. If you believe in a client's rights to competent clinicians, there needs to be a system of checks and balances. If you are sued, you can look upon the claim as an opportunity to work out a problem identified by a disgruntled client. Most suits are settled before trial. If you are well prepared, even the court experience can be positive for you and your client. That said, you still want to avoid malpractice actions.

Even a competent practitioner who performs in a manner consistent with the standards of his profession can be sued for malpractice. Clinicians often deal with difficult situations and dissatisfied clients. A negative outcome may not be the result of malpractice, but an unhappy client may take action out of anger or frustration.

Figure 9.1 lists strategies for reducing the risk of malpractice lawsuits.

---

[6]As a member of the NASW National Ethics Committee, I have seen some social work responses to allegations that have been very appropriate, but others that are misguided. Professionals who do not respond appropriately to allegations may put themselves at risk, not just because of the original allegation of misconduct, but because of the problems in how they responded to the allegation (e.g., not responding in a timely manner, not responding directly to the allegations against them, or breaching the confidentiality of the professional review process).

- Ensure that you have the proper education, experience, and supervision for the type of clinical practice[7] in which you are engaged.

- Stay within your area of expertise.

- Avoid dual relationships or multiple roles, such as acting as a forensic mental health professional and treating professional for the same client.

- Use self-care strategies to ensure that you are able to perform your work in a competent manner, and taking proper recourse for challenges such as stress, fatigue, and burnout.

- Stay current with theory, research, practice, and ethical standards in your field, and ensure your assessments and interventions are consistent with these.

- Maintain timely, accurate, and thorough records of your assessment, interventions, and rationale for those interventions.[8]

- Have the client sign an informed consent form that discloses the type of treatment, explains client and clinician roles and responsibilities, identifies benefits and risks, defines confidentiality and its limitations, and describes the limits of confidentiality.

- If you plan to use a novel or unorthodox intervention with a client, be particularly careful about documenting the informed consent process and ensure that you offer the client alternatives (e.g., offering a referral to another agency if the client prefers a more traditional intervention).

- When a client raises a complaint, respond with genuineness, empathic understanding, compassion, and unconditional positive regard, permitting the client to vent anger without responding defensively (consider whether you should have this meeting alone with the client or whether to have a supervisor attend in order to observe the interaction and offer support).

- When faced with a challenging clinical or ethical issue, reach out for help. Know when to call an attorney, your professional association,[9] your liability insurance provider, a supervisor, or colleague for assistance with ethical and legal issues, and do not be embarrassed to ask for assistance.

- Consider the use of a mediator or other conflict resolution professional to help resolve conflicts in a collaborative manner (see Chapter 10).

- If an allegation is true, consider apologizing, admitting fault, and offering an appropriate remedy; depending on the severity of the issues, legal advice may be warranted first.

FIGURE 9.1. Strategies for reducing the risk of malpractice lawsuits.

---

[7]If you are acting as a forensic expert, make sure you have appropriate education, experience, and supervision for gathering, analyzing, and presenting forensic evidence.

[8]Because malpractice can include actions *not* taken, be sure to document actions you considered but did not pursue. Be prepared to explain the rationale not only for what you did but also for what you decided *not* to do (Barsky, 2010). Malpractice attorneys have a saying, "If you didn't document it, it didn't happen." (Happy Hospitalist, 2007).

[9]Some professional associations allow members to request advice on a confidential basis, particularly with respect to how to deal with ethical issues.

- Be particularly cautious with clients who have a proclivity for bringing legal actions (e.g., people with paranoia, competitive personalities, or a history of involvement in courts).[10]
- After participating in a court trial as a witness or a party to an action involving a client, meet with your supervisor or clinical team to determine the best course of action moving forward (e.g., continuing work with the client but with certain precautions, or referring the client to services at another agency).

FIGURE 9.1. (*continued*)

Although many of these seem obvious, some of them may be challenging to incorporate into everyday practice. Be vigilant. These tips will not only help you reduce the risk of being sued, but also help you defend yourself should a malpractice action arise. If you have acted competently, ethically, and judiciously, you will have strong facts behind you. You will have a much easier time testifying, since good facts make good evidence.

TESTIFYING

Whenever you are part of a legal proceeding, consider whether your conduct can be called into question. What is the purpose of the proceeding? What is the role of your evidence within it? Find out if you or your agency is being investigated. If Evelyn were to be involved in a forensic inquiry into a child's death, she should find out whether the inquiry could lead to criminal charges. Some tribunals are only allowed to offer recommendations. In rare situations witnesses can be granted immunity from prosecution. In other cases your testimony at an inquiry can be brought directly into charges against you. Although this section deals primarily with testifying when there are specific actions against you, the information also applies to cases where there is just potential for future actions.

Are there any case law or statutory privileges that prevent you from being compelled to be a witness? If a client initiates an action against you, the client cannot claim privilege to prevent you from testifying for your own defense. However, if a nonclient makes a claim, you may not be able to reveal confidential information pertaining to your clients. Some clinicians have legislative protection against lawsuits. Child protection legislation, for instance, may protect Sam from being sued for

---

[10]Some clinicians, concerned about allegations of sexual impropriety, avoid being alone with certain clients (e.g., by keeping a door open or having another person present).

professional negligence, so long as he does not act out of malice.[11] Under the principles of sovereign immunity, probation officers and other state-employed clinicians may also be protected from being sued. Federal and state tort legislation permit the government and its employees to be sued under certain circumstances, so consult an attorney if you need to know if your professional work is covered (Health Resources and Services Administration, n.d.).

Ensure that you have legal advice to guide you through the process. Although some disciplinary processes do not permit legal representation at a hearing, you can consult an attorney before the hearing or have your attorney try to negotiate a solution. Ask your attorney to explain options on how to proceed, as well as the advantages and disadvantages of each. Find out whether allegations against you mean that you need to alter your practice until the legal issues are resolved. Suggest the names of other clinicians who could be used to support your practices and ethical choices. Review the suggestions in Chapters 4 and 5 regarding preparation and oral testimony.

Because malpractice claims are challenges to your professionalism, presenting in a professional manner is particularly crucial. Be conscious of your dress, mannerisms, and choice of words. Tailor your language to that of the tribunal, whether it consists of coprofessionals or laypeople. Ensure that your notes and records are in good order. If the case is based on claims of ethical misconduct, ensure that you are intimately familiar with the code of ethics for your profession. If the case is based on negligence, study the current standards of care in your field. Finally, avoid defensive responses. This is particularly difficult since your conduct is the focus of the allegations. Remember that your assessments and interventions are being challenged, not your whole being. Focus responses on your thoughts and behaviors rather than defending yourself as a person.

COSTS OF A DEFENSE

The costs of defending an action may be paid from a number of sources: out of your own pocket, from your agency or its insurance company, or from your professional liability insurance.[12] Malpractice insurance generally covers the cost of lawsuits for unintentional acts. Fraud, sexual assault, and defenses for criminal charges generally are not covered. Insurance policies

---

[11]See *www.childwelfare.gov/systemwide/laws_policies/state* for links to child protection legislation in your state.

[12]For human rights issues or cases involving precedents that could affect your whole profession, you might be able to secure financial support or free legal services from civil liberties organizations or your professional association.

vary significantly, and you do need to read the fine print to determine what is covered and what is not. Some professional associations offer assistance in terms of representation, information, and referral. They have an interest in protecting the reputation of the profession. Check with your agency, insurance company, and professional association to verify that you have proper coverage—*before* you get involved in any legal proceedings. Then, if you ever receive notice of a malpractice suit or any other legal or professional action against you, notify your agency supervisor, your insurance company, and your own attorney as soon as possible.

RESEARCH NEEDS

When clinicians are involved in research, few think of producing knowledge to be used specifically as evidence in malpractice cases. How do we know what the proper intervention is for a particular situation? How do we know whether there is a causal link between certain types of clinician misconduct and negative client outcomes? How do we assess emotional and social damages suffered by a client? As forensic specialties develop, perhaps there will be greater focus on malpractice issues.

The study of ethics has a rich body of literature that ranges from the abstract and philosophical to the concrete and practical (Barsky, 2010; Corey, Corey, & Callanan, 2011). Most professions have a code of ethical conduct.[13] These codes vary in quality and continue to develop as new ethical challenges arise.

In terms of legal research, there is considerable case law on malpractice. Case law is difficult to access for people without a background in law. Information in some legal journals is more accessible to nonattorneys. Some malpractice textbooks and journal articles are specifically geared toward clinicians (*American Journal of Forensic Psychology*; Bernstein & Hartsell, 2004; *Journal of Forensic Social Work*; Reamer, 2003; Roberts, Monferrari, & Yeager, 2009). Still, much more collaborative research and development of educational materials could be pursued to narrow the gap between the legal and mental health professions.

---

[13]For the code of ethics of the National Association of Social Workers, see *www.cswe.org*. For the code of ethics of the American Psychological Association, see *www.apa.org*.

Chapter 10

ALTERNATIVES AND PRECURSORS TO ADJUDICATION

Although clinicians should be prepared for the possibility of testifying in court, they should note that well over 90% of civil and criminal cases are resolved through negotiation, mediation, judge-led settlement conferences, mini-trials, early neutral evaluations, or other alternatives to adjudication in court (Alternative Dispute Resolution Act, 1998; Bartol & Bartol, 2008). Alternative dispute resolution has been growing in popularity, both as a way to avoid the high costs of litigation and a way to promote collaborative problem solving (Barsky, 2007a).[1] In this chapter we deal with the role of witnesses in five types of alternatives and precursors to adjudicative processes: discovery processes, pretrial settlement conferences, administrative tribunals, legislative hearings, collaborative dispute resolution (including mediation), and problem-solving courts.

DISCOVERY PROCESSES

Discovery refers to a pretrial disclosure process where parties involved in a conflict are required to share certain types of information before the parties have a trial on the issues of the case. Discovery processes promote a safe, fair, timely, and economically efficient trial (Federal Rules of Civil

---

[1]The term "alternative" is a bit misleading in this context. The different types of dispute resolution processes are not mutually exclusive alternatives. Many can be used in conjunction with one another, or in sequence.

Procedure, 2010). Because both parties know the case against them, they can prepare more effectively for the hearing. Surprise witnesses and testimony make for good cinema, but a trial is supposed to be a fair process, not an entertaining one. Discovery processes often expedite settlement, because sharing information allows each party to assess the strength of its case. Even if the case does not settle, sharing information may settle some issues and enable the parties to stipulate (or admit) to certain facts. Such agreement preempts the need to call witnesses to testify on these facts. Information obtained through pretrial disclosure can be raised at a subsequent hearing. A witness can be challenged and his testimony possibly discredited if information provided during pretrial disclosure is inconsistent with information provided at the trial. Discovery processes vary among different types of cases and jurisdictions. The four basic types of disclosure processes are requests for records, oral depositions, written interrogatories, and requests for admission.[2]

Requests for Records

Requests for records (sometimes called "discovery of documents" or "commands to produce documents") generally occur before oral depositions, if any. The rules of the court require each party to provide a list of documents relevant to the issues in the case that are in the possession of the party or within the party's control. The list may be supported by an affidavit swearing that all relevant documents have been listed. Give each of your documents a unique name and number so you can easily refer to them at subsequent hearings, and to ensure that one document is not confused with another. The other party can then request copies of the documents. If a clinician's evidence is relevant, these documents may include the clinician's notes, reports, videotapes, computer records, and information stored on the Internet, cell phones, or other electronic devices (Bahadur, 2009). Documents in the possession of a party's clinician are considered to be within the control of the party. In some cases, parties may ask to inspect tangible evidence, such as blood samples or clothes.

---

[2]The examples of pretrial disclosure processes in this section relate primarily to civil cases. Pretrial processes in criminal cases include arraignments, preliminary hearings, and grand jury indictments. At an arraignment, the person accused of a criminal offense is brought before a judge who reads the charges and asks how the defendant pleads: guilty, not guilty, or no contest. The judge also determines whether the person should be held in jail or whether to release the defendant, with or without bail. At a preliminary hearing (typically held only in serious felony cases), the judge determines whether the prosecuting attorney has produced sufficient evidence to require a full trial. Some states use a grand jury indictment rather than a preliminary inquiry, in which a group of citizens (grand jury) determines if there is sufficient evidence for the case should go to trial. Witnesses do not provide direct testimony at these pretrial processes.

Some court proceedings require that each party specifically disclose the names of any experts to be called. They may also require that the party calling an expert provide a written report or statement summarizing the witness's credentials and intended testimony. If this information is not disclosed in advance, the party may be prohibited from calling the expert. Many states have statutory requirements or local rules for 14-day, 21-day, or 30-day notice prior to trial.

The exchange of documents under discovery is the responsibility of the parties to the court action. Clinicians have little control over the process. If a client requests documents for discovery purposes, consider whether the documents are confidential or privileged (see Chapter 3). However, since a client generally has a right to his own records, clinicians should honor a client's request for documents. If the client wants to claim privilege or challenge discovery of a clinician's records, then that is generally the responsibility of the client or her counsel.

The clinician's responsibility is in keeping good records on an ongoing basis. Knowing that your records may be requested during the discovery process, consider what type of information is important to include and how to frame it in a constructive manner (Chapter 6). If you are preparing a report as an expert witness, be aware that your report may be seen by the opposing party prior to trial (Chapter 8).

In order to decide which documents to make available to the other party, an attorney may ask you which documents might be relevant. If you leave out significant documents and the omission is later discovered, your credibility may be damaged. If you have lost certain documents, the attorney might ask how they became lost and where they are now. Are they in someone else's possession? Were they intentionally hidden? Were they destroyed? The examining attorney has plenty of room to try to cast suspicion on either your competence or your honesty.

Oral Depositions

Oral depositions are question-and-answer sessions that take place prior to a trial. Oral depositions are sometimes called oral interrogatories or oral examinations for discovery. Generally, only parties named in the legal action and their witnesses can be examined for discovery (expert witnesses, in particular, can expect to be deposed). Oral depositions are often conducted in the private offices of an attorney, court reporter, or special examiner, but may also be held at the clinician's office. Attorneys for each party are present in the room, along with one witness at a time. A special examiner or magistrate may be present to oversee the proceedings, as well as a court reporter, stenographer, transcriber, and/or technician to operate the video or audio recording equipment. Opposing parties may be present, but this is not necessary. The participants sit around a table. The witness (deponent) swears or affirms to tell the truth. The opposing attorney (or attorney who issued a notice for the witness to appear) is the first to ask the witness questions. The witness's attorney may interrupt periodically to advise the witness not to answer or to object to certain questions (e.g., based on privilege, irrelevance, or misleading form of question). If the witness's attorney objects to a question, the witness may be directed to answer the question based on an understanding that a judge will review the transcript at a later time and rule on the question's admissibility. The witness's attorney may also ask questions to clarify responses to the opposing attorney's questions. In some jurisdictions, the witness may go through both a direct examination and a cross-examination during the deposition. Typically, the attorney who plans to call a witness at trial asks few questions during depositions. The attorney does not want to share more information than necessary with opposing counsel.

As with all forms of pretrial discovery processes, the opposing attorney may use depositions to learn about the witness's evidence. The opposing attorney may also use depositions to assess the witness's strengths and vulnerabilities as a witness (Melton et al., 2007). If the witness comes across as confident and persuasive, the attorney may be inclined to settle the case before trial. If the witness has certain vulnerabilities, in form or substance, the attorney may determine which strategies she can use in cross-examination to exploit these vulnerabilities.

The amount of time for a deposition can vary from a few minutes to several days. Ask your attorney ahead of time for an estimate of the time required and the types of questions that you may be asked. If you are serving as an expert witness, you are likely to be asked about the foundations for opinions in your written report: what theory, experience, or research you are relying on, and what factors you have considered in reaching your opinion. Attorneys generally recommend that witnesses keep their answers brief and to the point when asked questions. Because the judge is not present for the depositions, you do not need to go into detail, educating or trying to convince the court that your view of the case is correct (Schwerha, 2009). You are merely providing the other party sufficient information to know about the primary facts and lines of reasoning that you may be presenting at trial. If you provide more information than necessary during a deposition, you may be opening up your evidence to more room for attacks on your credibility or the accuracy of your testimony at trial. Rule 30 of the Federal Rules of Civil Procedure (2010) governs the procedure for oral depositions related to federal court cases.

After making an oral deposition, ask to review the transcript of the deposition to ensure the stenographer or transcriber has presented your statements accurately. Review the transcripts carefully and ask your attorney to request any corrections before you sign the transcript to confirm that it is accurate. Making corrections at this point can save you embarrassment and loss of credibility at trial due to inconsistent or inaccurate statements found in the transcripts of the deposition. Note, however, that ordinarily, you may only make corrections to information that was improperly reported by the stenographer or transcriber. You may not correct information that you misstated by asking for your depositions to be rewritten as you would have liked them to have been stated (e.g., correcting any mistakes in grammar, factual information, or stated opinions). If you made a significant mistake in your testimony at the deposition, you could ask your attorney how to deal with this error, for instance, submitting an affidavit to amend your deposition, or waiting until trial to make a correction during your oral testimony. Ideally, you want to avoid mistakes during your oral depositions, as such mistakes are often raised at trial to embarrass or challenge the credibility of the witness (Brodsky, 2004).

Unless you have the client's consent, a court order, or other legal authority permitting you to disclose confidential information, you should not disclose such information during discoveries or any other pretrial process (see Chapter 3). Although you may feel protective of your client's confidential information, note how being authorized to disclose information during discoveries can be beneficial to both parties. Similar to discovery of documents, oral depositions provide each party with an opportunity to be aware of the other's case and avoid surprises at the hearing. Many cases settle following depositions. However, if the case goes on to trial, transcripts of oral depositions may be entered into evidence at the trial. This is particularly useful if a party makes certain admissions of fact or guilt.

In preparing for depositions, ask your attorney what information and documentation to bring as well as what types of questions you may be asked. You could also ask the attorney to role-play to give you experience with the question and answering process of a deposition. If you receive a subpoena *duces tecum*, you must bring the documents listed in the subpoena (e.g., client progress notes, psychosocial assessments, correspondence with the client and collaterals, your c.v.). If the subpoena does not ask you to bring documents, then you should not bring client records unless your attorney advises otherwise. Your primary responsibility in depositions is to tell the truth based on your knowledge, recollection, information, and belief. Do not try to use depositions to present favorable information in order to win the case. The opposing attorney may only bring out one side of the case. The time for your attorney to argue her case is during the actual hearing. You do not need to disclose information other than that requested.

Most of our earlier suggestions for hearings also apply to oral discoveries: prepare by reviewing your notes and reports; use your anxiety management strategies; provide clear and concise responses; answer only what you are asked; watch for questions based on faulty assumptions; do not argue; do not try to evade questions; ask for clarification if needed; and do not guess at answers. Because discoveries are transcribed, avoid the use of gestures and vague utterances, such as "uh-huh," to answer questions. If you lack firsthand knowledge of the information requested, state the information you have and its sources. Note that you cannot personally attest to its truth: "The psychologist provided me with these test results. I have no reason to disbelieve her, but I did not personally observe the administration of the tests."

Because the opposing attorney is interested in having you disclose information, the tone of a depositions is generally friendly or matter-of-fact. Still, ask your attorney about the usual demeanor and approaches of the opposing attorney. The opposing attorney may use challenging or suggestive questions, but this is not a cross-examination where the focus is on discrediting the witness. Questions tend to be detailed and dry. Neither the attorneys nor the witnesses show much emotion or dramatic performance. Deposition questions tend to cover a wider range of topics than those permitted at trial. Depositions may be used to fish for information to see what may be relevant for trial. You might be asked personal information, such as medical history, illicit drug use, divorce, reprimands or grievances at work, and arrests (Vogelsang, 2001). The attorney may be rummaging for facts that could put your credibility in doubt. You should be prepared for how to respond to these questions even if they may not be admissible at trial. If you are an expert witness making a deposition, remember that the client's attorney is not your attorney. Consider consulting an attorney who represents you prior to the deposition or ask your attorney to attend the deposition with you. In spite of the differences between depositions and trials, participation in depositions can provide witnesses with good experience in preparing for a trial.

There is no judge at a discovery to rule on the admissibility of questions (e.g., on the basis of relevance or privilege). The attorneys must work out any disputes on their own or take them to court, after the depositions. If your attorney directs you not to answer a question, follow her direction. Do not feel intimidated by an attorney who insists that you have to answer a question if your attorney advises otherwise.

For clinicians, one of the key areas of questioning is the source of information in client records and reports: what information did you observe directly; what information came from other professionals; what information are you inferring, guessing, hypothesizing, speculating, or assuming;

and how have you verified your information. Some questions may be aimed at establishing bias (e.g., whether you like or dislike the client). Other questions may be designed to confuse or provoke you into making inconsistent statements (Bernstein & Hartsell, 2005).

If you are asked to provide information and you do not know the answer, say so. You may also be asked to state why you do not know the answer, for instance, did you have the information but no longer remember it, or were you never privy to the information. If there is information that you do not have available at the discovery but can obtain later, you and your attorney may be asked to provide an undertaking (promise) to give the information in writing. If you are uncertain of the date of conducting a particular interview, for instance, you could be asked to undertake to find this information at your office and provide the information to the attorney by a specified date. Be careful about giving undertakings on matters over which you lack complete control. Avoid absolutes. Instead, promise, "I will use my best efforts to obtain the following records ... "

After the discoveries, transcripts will be prepared. Review them for accuracy with your attorney. The other party has a right to be advised of any inaccuracies or omissions. This review can also save you the embarrassment of making inconsistent statements at trial.

Because preparing for and participating in depositions can be time-consuming, consider including a clause in your service agreements with clients that requires them to reimburse you for time spent responding to subpoenas or participating in discovery processes. Ensure you have a written agreement for payment *prior* to participating in a deposition, including your hourly rate and when you will be paid (e.g., with a retainer in advance or payment by a specific date). Remember that if you are a salaried clinician and participating in legal processes is part of your regular job, you may not be able to bill extra for participating in depositions. If you are subpoenaed to participate at a very inconvenient time (e.g., during a family crisis or when you have critical client appointments), you could ask the attorneys to reschedule the depositions. You could also ask your attorney to file a motion for a protective motion of the court, asking the court to reschedule the deposition or to order one of the parties to reimburse you for the appointments you had to cancel (Bernstein & Hartsell, 2005).

Written Interrogatories

Interrogatories are similar to depositions in that both involve responding to questions from the opposing party prior to trial. Whereas depositions are oral questions and answers, interrogatories are written questions and answers. Also, whereas depositions questions are directed to the parties and their witnesses in the case, interrogatory questions may be directed to third persons who are not direct parties in the case. Rules of civil procedures in the state (or the United States if it is a federal case) prescribe how many people can be served to answer and how many questions may be issued (e.g., 25 to 60 questions per party).[3] Interrogatories are typically used in civil lawsuits, rather than criminal proceedings. Responses to interrogatories are made under oath or affirmation of the parties, typically notarized by an attorney or other person authorized to notarize documents. If you do not know the answer to a particular question, explain why (e.g., the question is about a matter that is outside your area of expertise, or the question pertains to information that was never shared with you). As with depositions, responses to interrogatories should be concise and truthful. Attorneys may assist with the wording of the responses, but the accuracy of the content is the responsibility of the witness who is responding. Before submitting your written interrogatory responses, have them reviewed by an attorney who represents you, rather than by an attorney who represents your client or another party.

Requests for Admission

Under a request to admit (or "notice to admit") one party specifically asks the other to admit or deny certain facts. By admitting certain facts, the issues at trial are reduced and the trial can focus on the key matters in dispute. You should review requests to admit with your attorney for advice about which facts to admit. In a case of physician-assisted suicide, you might have knowledge that the physician provided the patient with certain drugs; however, the attorney may have sound legal reasons for wanting this issue to be tried in court (e.g., the preponderance of evidence may not extend beyond a reasonable doubt). In civil lawsuits, there is a financial risk for not admitting certain facts that are later proven at trial: the court may order that party to pay the winning party's litigation costs. Usually, you can respond to a request to admit simply by an "admit" or "deny" response. You do not need to explain your response. If you are unable to admit or deny a fact because you do not know the facts or remember the events, simply state why you cannot admit or deny the requested facts: "I was not present when the patient died, so I am unable to admit or deny that the physician administered the lethal injection."

---

[3]See *topics.law.cornell.edu/wex/table_civil_procedure* for links to rules of civil procedure in various states.

PRETRIAL SETTLEMENT CONFERENCES

Following discoveries, but still before trial, many courts encourage settlement through pretrial conferences. These conferences are informal meetings between the parties, their attorneys, and the judge to try to resolve the dispute without the need for a full hearing. The attorneys for each party may be asked to provide an overview of the case. Witnesses are not present, and there is no formal presentation of evidence. Options for resolution are discussed. The judge may offer suggestions for settlement or indicate how he might decide certain issues, given the information presented at pretrial. If a trial is going to proceed, then the parties may be able to narrow the issues, streamline the process, and develop an agreed-on statement of facts.

Although a clinician who is a potential witness does not take part in the pretrial conference itself, the clinician does have a role to play.[4] Prior to the conference, the clinician may be asked to write out the main points of her evidence for the attorney to take to the pretrial. If this information is clear, objective, and persuasive, it may facilitate a settlement.[5] Even if you are hired by one side, consider how you can frame your information in a manner that is constructive for everyone involved. Evelyn might be able to offer custody and access options that give both parents a legitimate role in Debra's upbringing. Sam could offer examples of Philip's parenting strengths as well as concerns related to Debra's safety.

ADMINISTRATIVE TRIBUNALS

Whereas courts and other adjudicative tribunals are specifically designed to arbitrate disputes for conflicting parties, the functions of administrative tribunals—law making, policy development, law enforcing, and arbitrating—often overlap. The arbitrating role varies among tribunals, although there are similarities: interested parties have a right to notice of the hearing and a right to be heard. Some administrative tribunals use an adversarial process similar to that used by courts (outlined in Chapter 1). Others use a more investigative process. Rather than make the parties responsible for preparing and presenting testimony, the tribunal takes a more active role

---

[4]Some clinicians feel a lack of control, and even resentment, at being left out of pretrial processes, including settlement negotiations. If you have concerns about your role, discuss this with your attorney. You may be able to agree on the parameters of your respective roles or how to share certain information (e.g., helping the attorney prepare for a pretrial conference; participating in certain portions of discussions; receiving a brief of what went on at the conference).

[5]If your evidence is weak, that might also facilitate a settlement, but not in your favor.

in gathering information and investigating the case. Members of a human rights tribunal may interview the complainant and the defendant in a discrimination case. A board that reviews the status of patients involuntarily committed for posing a risk to self or others will enlist its own experts to provide diagnoses and recommendations.

Clinicians can play a variety of functions in administrative processes, including fact witness, expert witness, advocate, client support, or tribunal member (especially for issues related to mental health and capacity). Clinicians may take on the role of client advocate if the tribunal does not require attorney advocates. The process and powers of an administrative tribunal are established by legislation, regulations, and internal policies. You need to understand the regulatory process in order to work effectively in these systems. Unfortunately, training for particular tribunals is hard to come by unless you work within the system (e.g., if you are an employee of a human rights commission or a member of a parole board). If you have no direct experience within the system, it is worth speaking with people who do. Explore the following aspects of the tribunal:

- Functions of the tribunal (decision making, policy development, enforcement).
- Roles of participants (tribunal members, disputants, experts, witnesses, advocates).
- Type of information on which the tribunal can rely (investigative processes generally do not have strict rules on admissibility of evidence).
- Types of information that will be persuasive (fact, expert opinion, political belief, values, emotional pleas).
- Manner of presentation of information (oral testimony, private interview, written).
- Names of other clinicians who have been involved in a similar administrative process.

Whether you are examined at a public hearing or interviewed privately, be prepared to answer questions as honestly, objectively, and fully as possible. As with adjudication, good records and reports will make your job as a witness much easier. Public court judges are usually generalists in the sense that they deal with a broad range of cases. In contrast, members of administrative tribunals deal with a narrow range of cases. The composition of the tribunal may include laypersons, experts, or a combination. The information you provide and the language you use to explain it should be geared to the level of expertise of tribunal members.

LEGISLATIVE HEARINGS

Legislative hearings are used by governments to gather information to make public policy and law reform decisions (e.g., on mental health, child protection, or criminal laws). Input may be sought from particular experts, interest groups, or the public at large. Clinicians often organize themselves to present information, deciding on a particular position and combining resources to provide a persuasive argument.

Acting as a witness for the purpose of influencing legislative decisions can be quite different from acting as a witness at an adjudication. In preparing for legislative hearings, consider their purpose, the history of the law, the current law, and proposals under consideration (Vance, 2009). For your specific hearing, assess the type of information that will be most influential, whether it be professional expertise, anecdotal information (personal experiences of clients), political appeals, or positions with broad support (documented with petitions or letters; e.g., whether there is widespread support for a particular type of health care reform could be substantiated by an opinion poll conducted by an independent polling organization). Even if you are presenting as an advocate for a particular cause, objectivity is important to your credibility.

While truth and facts are important, decisions at legislative hearings are influenced largely by political factors, including how decisions will be perceived by voters and how these perceptions may affect upcoming elections. What goes on outside of the hearings is often more important than what goes on during them. That sort of advocacy goes beyond the scope of this volume.

COLLABORATIVE PROCESSES

Collaborative alternatives to adjudication include mediation, conciliation, family group conferences, and circle sentencing (in Native American communities). In each of these processes, a neutral third party brings interested parties together to work out mutually agreeable solutions to their conflicts. The third party has no power to decide or impose solutions on the parties (AFCC, 2000; Barsky, 2007a).

In some cases, only the immediate parties involved in the conflict are invited to participate in the process. Collaborative dispute resolution processes do not use "witnesses," at least not in the same way as adjudicative processes. However, clinicians may be brought into these processes in various roles. First, a clinician may be brought in as a support person for a client. In mediation, for example, Paula might be allowed to bring her clinician for moral support or to help her negotiate with Philip. Second, a clinician could be asked to provide an assessment. Paula and Philip could agree that Evelyn would conduct a custody assessment.[6] Evelyn would then provide a report that they would review in mediation. In preparing the report, Evelyn should consider the same suggestions as discussed for reports for adjudicative processes (as discussed in Chapter 8). In particular, the report should be written in factual, balanced, and resolution-focused terms. Third, a clinician could be asked to provide information from her previous work with the client. For example, Philip and Paula may have a dispute about Debra's parenting needs. Frieda may have useful and objective information. If the parties agree, this information could be brought into the mediation process to help them make a more informed decision.

To be an effective participant in a collaborative dispute resolution process, a clinician needs to understand how the process works. Collaborative processes focus parties on future plans rather than rehashing the past and assigning blame. Collaborative processes help parties work together for win–win solutions. Collaborative processes encourage parties to keep an open mind about how to meet their needs and interests. If your clients are involved in such a process, you can support these efforts by the way you provide information and model for your clients.[7] If you are asked to provide information for a collaborative process, find out whether the information you provide can be used at a later trial. For further information on collaborative conflict resolution processes, see *crinfo.com*.

PROBLEM-SOLVING COURTS

Although the legal profession has traditionally embraced an adversarial approach to resolving disputes, some lawyers are now embracing law as more of a healing profession that takes a more comprehensive approach to helping people (Daicoff, 2006). As part of this movement, various states have experimented with specialized courts designed to divert cases from traditional (adversarial) courts into courts that focus on problem solving. For example, a person charged with a drug-related offence may be diverted

---

[6]Before agreeing to conduct any type of forensic assessment without a court order, explore local state liability issues. In particular, find out whether you (as the evaluator) are covered by immunity or limited immunity statutes when working outside of the court system. In some states, a clinician is not fully covered.

[7]A fascinating movement is collaborative law, a practice framework in which lawyers are trained to use nonadversarial negotiation processes to resolve their clients' disputes. You may wish to explore how clinicians can work within a collaborative law framework by contacting your local chapter of the American Bar Association at *www.abanet.org*.

to a drug court that offers counseling, addiction treatment planning and services, drug use monitoring, referrals to community services, engagement of family members, and closely supervised probation. If the person successfully completes her treatment plan, the criminal charges are dismissed and she does not face criminal prosecution. Similarly, problem-solving courts may be used for domestic violence situations, providing services such as victim advocacy, support, perpetrator monitoring, and mental health counseling (Madden, 2003). Mental health courts have also been established to deal with people with mental illness who have had conflict with the criminal justice system (Polowy & Morgan, 2010). Evaluations of problem-solving courts show promise in terms of cost effectiveness, lower rates of recidivism, and enhancing access to treatment, although further research is needed (Bureau of Justice Assistance, n.d.). Further, some courts have made great strides in terms of accessibility, providing court staff who can educate the public about court procedures, lawyer referral services, and other support systems to help them through the process (Quinn, 2005).

Typically, clinicians do not provide oral testimony in problem-solving courts, although it depends on the model. More often, clinicians are responsible for providing written reports to the court or the probation officer. If you are invited to participate in a problem-solving court hearing, note that the rules of procedure and evidence are less formal than those in traditional criminal or civil hearings. If you are asked to participate in a problem-solving court process, ask specifically about your expected role and the type of questions you will be asked. If possible, observe another session in advance to familiarize yourself with the process.

Chapter 11

CONCLUSION

As we look to the future, there are many opportunities for clinicians not only to participate in legal systems, but also to assume more leadership and provide greater input into how these systems operate. In the past, the legal profession has assumed the primary role in designing formal dispute resolution systems. Lawyers and judges have taken charge of how cases are processed.[1] They have decided when and how clinicians should be brought into these processes. While some clinicians have learned how to work within legal systems, others have participated in legal proceedings with little knowledge and even less control. Since the 1980s, various clinicians have questioned traditional legal systems and have strived to chart a new course. They have helped develop innovative approaches to resolving legal issues and interpersonal conflict. Some clinicians have focused on how to protect the rights of women, children, ethnic minorities, immigrants, and other vulnerable populations. Others have focused on developing more equal partnerships with attorneys through interprofessional education, collaboration, and practice. Yet others have played pivotal roles in developing problem-solving courts, mediation, family group conferencing, and other alternatives to adversarial legal systems. Attorneys are also recognizing that dealing effectively with mental health concerns and social conflict requires interprofessional collaboration. Interprofessional associations such as the Association for Family Conciliation Courts have been very successful at bringing various professionals together for conferences,

---

[1]Judges, legislators, and court administrators also play key roles in how the legal system evolves and how cases are managed.

training, and policy development. But where do we go from here? The following paragraphs offer suggestions in relation to education, practice standards, research, and policy.

In order to enhance attorney–clinician cooperation we first need to bring them together. Separate education, training, and practice tend to spawn ignorance and stereotypes about the other profession (Taylor, 2006). Institutes of higher learning can bring attorneys and clinicians together through joint degree programs, joint courses, and joint field internships (Colarossi & Forgey, 2006; Fernandez et al., 2009). In the area of continuing education, joint workshops and seminars can also enhance interprofessional understanding and collaboration.

Interprofessional committees can be used to facilitate discussion and determine appropriate roles for attorneys and clinicians. In some jurisdictions, committees of judges, attorneys, and forensic clinicians have developed standards for gathering and producing evidence. Other clinicians, particularly unregulated ones, have had little input regarding their participation in legal processes. Higher standards of education, practice, and accountability may be necessary in order for these clinicians to gain influence. Clinicians from various disciplines need to work together, particularly for emerging roles such as parenting coordinators and forensic mental health consultants, which cut across traditional professional boundaries. When psychology, social work, family therapy, and other professions act independently to develop standards and gain legal recognition for their professions, they miss the opportunity to develop transprofessional standards. One area that begs for greater interprofessional cooperation is development of standards of practice for forensic mental health experts. Although forensic psychology has relatively well-developed standards of practice, professions such as forensic social workers, drug court counselors, supervised visitation practitioners, and child custody evaluators are in relatively early stages of developing model codes of ethics and evidence-based practice standards (Munson, 2011). In particular, practice standards should delineate the differences between the roles of forensic evaluators from the roles of treating clinicians, and address ethical issues pertaining to conflict of interest, informed consent, record keeping, and competencies required for particular forensic tasks.

On the research front, areas such as criminology, sexual deviance, mental disorders, substance abuse, child protection, and the validity of eyewitness testimony have received considerable attention. Unfortunately, there has been some disconnect between researchers and treating clinicians. Although forensic mental health has grown as a specialization, many treating clinicians have little knowledge or involvement with forensic research.

Psychotherapists, family counselors, and other treating clinicians could play a greater role in developing research questions and designs (Barsky, 2009). For instance, clinicians may be able to inform forensic researchers about issues they see with clients *following* their experiences with forensic professionals–what factors in the forensic evaluation process are related to positive growth and development, and what factors lead to greater anxiety, stress, and dysfunction? Legal scholars and behavioral scientists could also join forces to do collaborative research. A prime area for future research is a study of factors contributing to a clinician's effectiveness in particular types of hearings. Although there has been considerable grown in research on the roles of forensic specialists, there is still relatively little research on the roles and effectiveness of treating clinicians as witnesses. Within forensic practice, there is need for further legal research to explore the relationship between scientific standards (validity, reliability, probability) and legal standards (admissibility, credibility, and weight of evidence). Finally, research is needed to identify the unique contributions that attorneys and clinicians can each make toward the resolution of social conflict (Meyer & Weaver, 2006).

In terms of social policy, clinicians should continue to advocate for legal and judicial reforms in the spheres of criminal law, child welfare, juvenile justice, family law, mental health, and malpractice. Although some jurisdictions have replaced archaic technical language in the laws and legal documents with plain language, there is still much more we can do to can make the law and legal processes more accessible to laypeople. Promoting collaborative conflict resolution over adversarial trials can lead to improved social relationships and less costly resolution of disputes. Providing judges with better training in behavioral, emotional, and cultural issues can better sensitize them to the needs of the people they are serving. Courts have traditionally focused on problems and negative attributes, including fault, illness, mental disorders, neglect, abuse, and crime. Clinicians can help judges and attorneys pay more attention to the strengths, resources, goals, and aspirations of the parties. The notion of therapeutic jurisprudence suggests that suggests the legal system can have positive effects on the behavior, emotions, social welfare, and mental health of the parties involved in legal processes. Under this model, judges in particular need to assume a stronger administrative and rehabilitative role with respect to the people appearing before them (Quinn, 2005). Although there have been significant advances with projects such as drug courts, specialized domestic violence procedures, and other problem-solving processes, the constructive potential for therapeutic jurisprudence is much greater.

Throughout this volume, I have emphasized the importance of

conciseness. I will try to follow that advice in this conclusion. My primary advice for clinicians as witnesses can be summed up in four words:

Prepare, and be honest.

I trust that by reading this book you now have a better understanding of the roles that clinicians play as witnesses. While the breadth and depth of information on how to be an effective witness may initially feel overwhelming, your newfound knowledge and confidence will help you to survive and thrive while participating in legal processes. Take what control you can. As for the rest, may luck and/or your higher power be with you.

EPILOGUE

You may be wondering whatever happened to the Carveys, their clinicians, and the other professionals involved in this case. Sam's child protection investigation determined that allegations of abuse against Philip were unfounded. Both the child protection case and criminal charges against Philip were dropped. Philip and Paula returned to Michael for mediation. Emotional differences subsided when they began to discuss the reason Paula threw Philip out of the house, namely, that Philip was having an affair with their family therapist, Frieda. Paula and Philip initiated a complaint against Frieda through her professional association. Evelyn and Michael were brought in as witnesses during Frieda's disciplinary hearing and provided comprehensive, professional, and persuasive testimony. The tribunal revoked Frieda's license to practice family therapy. Philip and Paula agreed to a joint custody arrangement, based on the recommendations in Evelyn's assessment. In spite of all the preparation, Alice and Art were pleased that this case did not require a full trial of the issues. They were so inspired by Michael's transformative mediation success that they decided to pursue training in collaborative law and therapeutic jurisprudence. Debra has grown up and is attending university, with plans to become a forensic mental health practitioner. Frieda is no longer practicing family therapy. She has recently accepted a job with a reality television show, providing personal life coaching to unsuspecting participants.

GLOSSARY

This glossary includes definitions of terms used in legal contexts. Some words have additional meanings when used in other contexts.[1]

Adjudication. A process in which two or more parties present evidence and seek resolution of a conflict from an independent, third-party decision maker, such as a judge or arbitration panel.

Affidavit. A document containing information that is signed by a person who is swearing or attesting to the truth of its contents (see Appendix E for a sample).

Amicus curiae. Literally, a friend of the court (e.g., a clinician who is brought in to educate the court about a particular mental health issue; sometimes the *amicus* provides a written brief to provide the court with professional expertise on a topic relevant to the case).

Arbitration. An adjudicative process in which a private person or tribunal, rather than a publicly appointed judge, makes the decisions. Rules of arbitration may be governed by statute or contracted by the parties.

Bar. (1) Members of the legal profession. (2) A railing or partition in a courtroom that separates the public from the attorneys, parties, judge, and jury.

Bench. A seat or office representing the judge or panel of judges in a courtroom.

Burden of proof. A legal requirement establishing which party has the onus of proving particular facts in dispute in order to achieve the remedy being sought (typically, the plaintiff in a civil action and the prosecution in a criminal case).

Caveat. A caution or warning, often identifying a limitation in legal responsibility by the party declaring the caveat. For example, a clinician may assert that his

---

[1]For additional definitions, see *dictionary.law.com.*

model of intervention is effective but pronounce a caveat that he will not be legally responsible if the client does not follow certain specified instructions. A caveat may be provided to a client orally, but preferably it is in writing to ensure provide documentary evidence that the specific warning was provided.

Circle (sentencing) process. A process originally used in Native American communities to deal with people who have committed criminal offences. Various members of the community, including the offender, victim, family members, and clinicians, are brought together to discuss appropriate remedies and to offer support. The process is designed to be healing-oriented as well as rehabilitative and deterrent of future crime.

Civil law. (1) Laws that regulate affairs among both individuals and groups, including family law, contract law, property law, child protection, and the law of torts (civil wrongs including negligence and malpractice). Although civil law primarily regulates the affairs between private parties, government agencies may also be parties to civil actions. Remedies for civil law tend to be compensatory, whereas remedies for criminal law tend to be punitive and deterring. (2) The type of legal system that operates in Louisiana, Quebec, and most of continental Europe (derived from the Roman Civil Code), in contrast to the common law system in the United Kingdom and most North American jurisdictions.

Clinician. An individual who provides counseling, guidance, emotional support, or therapy to individuals, families, or treatment groups; as used in this volume, this designation includes psychiatrists, social workers, psychologists, clergy, and human service workers with or without professional education or status.

Common law. (1) Law that develops from judicial opinions, principles, and precedents identified in cases tried in court (in contradistinction to statutes or laws passed by the government). (2) The system of law in most of the United States, the United Kingdom, and Canada (in contrast to civil law, which is used in Quebec, Louisiana, and most of continental Europe).

Compellable witness. A person who may be required by law to attend a hearing and provide testimony.

Consent order. A declaration by a judge reflecting agreement among the parties who consented to the order (in contrast to a court order imposing a solution without consent of the parties).

Criminal law. Law that deals with remedies for offenses against the state, including fines, incarceration, and restriction of civil rights.

Cross-examination. A series of questions posed by an opposing attorney to challenge or discredit the witness's testimony or to bring out additional facts.

Defamation. An intentional tort or civil cause of action for making false statements that harm the reputation of another person. Defamatory statements made orally are sometimes referred to as slander. Defamatory statements made in writing are sometimes referred to as libel.

Defendant. The party against whom a claim, petition, or charge is brought. In some types of hearings, this party may be called the respondent. In criminal cases, this person is called the accused.

Depositions. Oral question-and-answer sessions used to allow each party to learn about the evidence that the other party may present at trial (sometimes referred to as a discovery process).

Direct evidence. Information provided orally in a hearing, by a person who was a firsthand observer of the information being attested (in contrast to hearsay).

Direct examination. The initial round of testimony provided by a witness in response to questioning by the attorney who called the witness (conducted prior to cross-examination by the opposing attorney).

Disclaimer. A statement designed to limit legal liability by advising others not to rely on certain information or not to use information for particular purposes.

Discovery. A pretrial process of sharing information between parties used to make each party aware of the evidence that the other party may bring to trial. Attorneys for each party ask the other party questions under oath. Questions and answers are recorded and may be used in the trial. Oral discovery processes may be called depositions. Written discovery processes are called interrogatories (an attorney presents a list of questions which the deponent answers in writing).

Expert witness. A person with legally recognized specialized knowledge that allows that person to provide opinion evidence at a trial.

Evaluator. Used generically in this volume to describe a mental health professional who performs a psychological or psychosocial assessment to be used for forensic purposes, but does not provide treatment services.

Evidence. Information that sheds light on the issues being tried (cf. Hearsay, Direct evidence).

Evidence-in-chief. *See* Direct examination.

Fact witness (also, called lay witness or eyewitness). An individual called to testify about matters the individual has observed or experienced firsthand. Unlike expert witnesses, fact witnesses are generally not allowed to provide opinions as part of their testimony.

Family group conferences. Meetings of family members and support persons, facilitated by a clinician. Family group conferences have been used to help family members take responsibility for dealing with child protection issues, child criminal behavior issues, and guardianship of elders at risk. Successful resolution within the family prevents the case from proceeding to court.

Forensic. Literally, of or belonging to courts or legal proceedings. Used in this volume to refer specifically to people from clinical professions who specialize in gathering and presenting evidence for use in legal proceedings.

Friendly attorney. Used colloquially in this volume to describe an attorney who does not represent the clinician but whose client's interests are consistent with the evidence and interests of the clinician. This is an attorney with whom the clinician will generally cooperate.

Hearsay. Secondhand information that a witness possesses through statements made out of court by another person (in contrast to direct evidence). Generally, a person can only provide evidence from direct observations, although there are several exceptions to the hearsay rule.

Hostile witness. A person who has been called to testify by an attorney who has adverse interests or expresses opposition to the party represented by the attorney. An attorney is permitted to cross-examine a witness that the court considers hostile.

Impeach. Challenge, accuse, or cast doubt, such as impeaching testimony to suggest the testimony is dishonest, lacking in credibility, misleading, or not to be believed.

Incarceration. Confinement of a person convicted of a criminal offense, in a jail, prison, or other secure custody setting.

Insanity. The legal status of a person who, due to severe mental impairment, is deemed by a judge not to be legally responsible for crimes committed.

Interrogatories. A pretrial discovery process in which an attorney presents a list of questions that the deponent answers in writing, used to help each party learn about the evidence the other party may lead at trial.

Judicial notice. A rule of evidence that gives judges discretion to accept commonly known information as fact without requiring the parties to prove the information by introducing evidence.

Jurisdiction. Power over a particular geographic area and/or over particular legal issues. For instance, a government presiding over a city, province, state, or country is empowered to pass laws over certain types of issues. Each state in the United States is primarily responsible for regulating health care, child welfare, education, and licensing of professionals, although some federal laws also affect these areas. The federal government has primary jurisdiction over national defense and international commerce. Responsibility for criminal law is split between state and federal governments. Different courts have jurisdiction (power) to make decisions for legal issues arising in different geographical regions and over different types of issues (e.g., a family court judge has jurisdiction to make decisions over divorce and child welfare issues, but not criminal law matters).

Legislation. Laws developed and declared in force by state or national governments (also called statutes or acts).

Limitations period. Length of time following a wrongful act in which a person can be sued or charged for that act; limits the period of time in which a claimant can initiate a legal action (generally 2 to 10 years). There may be no limitations periods for serious criminal offences, and exceptions for lawsuits involving vulnerable clients without mental capacity.

Malpractice. A wrongful act by a clinician or other professional in relation to performance of services. Legal recourse for malpractice (or professional negligence) requires proof that the professional breached a duty of care that was owed to a client and that, as a direct consequence, the client suffered damages.

Material evidence. Information that, if presented in court, could have a significant impact on the outcome of the trial.

Material witness. A person whose evidence is critical for the purposes of a trial. In some instances, a material witness can be held involuntarily to ensure attendance at the trial.

Mediation. A collaborative conflict resolution process facilitated by an impartial third party who has no decision-making authority. The mediator helps participants communicate, problem solve, and develop their own agreement.

Motion. A request made to the hearing by one of the parties to the action concerning procedural issues or interim relief (judicial decisions that affect the parties until the final decision in the trial is made).

Party. An individual, group, or institution involved in a dispute resolution process that has a direct stake in the outcome; one who brings a legal action or is named as a defendant in an action.

Plaintiff. The party who initiates a claim, petition, complaint, or charge, particularly in a civil lawsuit; in other proceedings this party may alternatively be called the petitioner, claimant, appellant (in appeal cases), or prosecution (in criminal cases).

Prima facie. Literally, on the first face or impression; refers to the sufficiency of information that is initially offered to establish proof unless and until the opposing side presents evidence to prove otherwise.

Privilege. A legal principle that may render information conveyed within a confidential relationship noncompellable in court. Although the attorney–client relationship is generally protected by privilege, privilege between clinicians and their clients cannot be assumed. It varies depending on the legal status of the clinician, the importance of the information to the hearing, and how the laws in each jurisdiction weigh the importance of protecting a particular type of professional relationship.

Pro se. An individual representing him- or herself, without legal counsel.

Probate court. A court that has special jurisdiction to handle legal issues pertaining to wills, trusts, adult guardianship, competency, and protection of vulnerable clients.

Res judicata. Literally, "the thing has been judged"; the legal principle that, once a matter has been decided in a hearing, the issue should not be raised again to be redecided. This principle forbids relitigation of the same issue.

Retainer. A contract with a professional (e.g., an attorney or clinician) establishing terms under which services will be provided and paid for; typically, the contract requires the client to advance specified funds to the professional prior to the services actually being rendered (see Appendix B for a sample agreement).

Sequester. Detain a witness or jury members in a protective setting during legal proceedings to prevent contact with others who may influence the detained individual(s) by speaking about the proceedings.

Sovereign immunity. Statute or common law doctrine that protects government and its agencies from civil lawsuits or criminal prosecution. The immunity from lawsuits may be absolute or limited to certain conditions.

Standard of proof. The degree of certainty required by law to establish a claim in court, for instance, beyond a reasonable doubt in criminal court, or on the preponderance of evidence in a civil court.

Standing. Recognition by a judge or tribunal that allows an individual or corporate entity to present arguments and information on its own behalf. If a witness is not a party to a proceeding, generally that person cannot provide information or arguments during an adjudicative hearing unless called as a witness by one of the parties or granted special standing.

Stipulation. A statement by the attorneys on behalf of their clients indicating agreement over a procedural or factual issue (e.g., a statement of which facts are agreed on, and which ones are open for dispute in court).

Subpoena. A legally enforceable demand for an individual to testify in criminal court or to submit documents or other evidence. Failure to comply with a subpoena may result in a charge of contempt of court, which may be punishable by incarceration.

Testimony. Evidence provided by a witness who swears or affirms the truth of the information provided.

Therapeutic jurisprudence. An approach used by judges, attorneys, and other court-related professionals to ensure that legal processes, laws, and decisions are more likely to foster positive, healing effects on the parties.

Tort. A civil wrong, or category of legal action, in which a party who suffered damages may sue another party for compensation or other remedies. Examples of torts include negligence, defamation, and nuisance (e.g., when noises or fumes emanating from one person's house disturb a neighbor's enjoyment of his or her property).

Trial. A full hearing of the issues by a court or other decision maker that results in a final decision regarding the factual evidence and legal issues being tried.

Tribunal. Used in this volume to refer to the decision makers in a legal dispute resolution process (including a single judge, a panel of judges, an arbitration board, a human rights commission, and other administrative or quasi-judicial decision-making bodies).

Undertaking. A promise to do something. For example, the attorney for one party may undertake (promise) to provide copies of the clinician's report to the other parties. Undertakings may be enforceable as contracts. Also, an attorney or clinician who gives an undertaking and fails to follow through on it may be subject to discipline by his or her professional association for breach of an ethical obligation.

Voir dire. (1) The process of questioning a prospective juror to determine appropriateness or bias as a juror. (2) The process of questioning a proposed witness to determine his or her qualifications (e.g., as an expert) or the admissibility of the proposed testimony. In jury trials, a *voir dire* may be held "in chambers" (i.e., the judge's private office).

Warrant. Legal authority granted by a judge or magistrate allowing police to conduct a search or arrest a person.

Witness. A person who provides information at a hearing, typically under oath or affirmation to indicate the person is attesting to the truth of the information.

Work product. Investigations, evaluations, test results, and other documents that clinicians (or others) create when helping an attorney prepare for a particular court case; such documents are generally privileged (i.e., exempt from discovery and not compellable as evidence in court).

Appendices

Appendices A through F contain sample documents. These samples illustrate the issues that should be covered in such documents. Still, each document needs to be tailored to particular cases, given the specific issues raised by the case and the local laws that apply. To create your own forms and documents, consult with a local attorney who has expertise in the fields in which you will be testifying as a witness. Appendix G presents topics and scenarios for further thought and discussion.

APPENDIX A. Service Agreement for an Expert Witness for Review/Rebuttal Services

The purpose of this Agreement is to explain the parameters of the role of [Name of Expert] as an expert witness for [Name of Plaintiff or Defendant in the case hiring the Expert], who is represented by [Name of Attorney representing the Plaintiff or Defendant], Attorney-at-Law, in the case between [List Names of Parties involved in the case and Court Reference Number, if any].

[Expert] agrees to review a copy of the evaluation report filed in connection with the matter referenced above. [Expert] will review the text of the report and examine its methods and procedures, test data from psychological tests (if available), and will provide the attorney-client an analysis of the report and of the evaluator's use of test data, conformity to current professional practice standards and guidelines, and use of forensic methods and procedures. [Expert] will provide opinions regarding both the strengths and deficiencies of the evaluator's work. There is no implicit understanding that [Expert]'s task is confined to identifying deficiencies.

If, on the basis of the information available, it appears that the evaluation was conducted appropriately and it appears that the conclusions drawn follow logically from the information considered, [Expert] will so inform [the Attorney-Client] either by verbal or written report. [Expert] will charge a fee for time expended and offer no additional services unless specifically agreed to in writing by [Expert] and [the Attorney-Client].

If, in [Expert]'s view, significant methodological errors were made and/or the report contains significant flaws, [Expert] will consider amending [his/her] service agreement to include assisting the attorney in preparation for trial, to assist at trial, or to offer expert testimony. If expert testimony is requested, [Expert] will prepare a written report to be used in [his/her] courtroom testimony.

[Expert] will *not* attempt to conduct a reevaluation. Because [Expert] is not conducting a comprehensive evaluation, it is understood that [Expert] will *not* offer an opinion concerning the comparative parenting competencies or custodial suitability of the parents. [Expert]'s testimony will focus on the analysis of the evaluation described above.

Fees for these services include a retainer in the amount of [Dollar Amount], payable on the date this agreement is signed. [Expert]'s work is billable at a rate of [Dollar Amount] per hour, and each hour worked is billed against the retainer. One-half of the retainer is nonrefundable. [Expert] will provide [Client] a statement of time billed on a monthly basis and at the termination of services. Should additional retainer fees be required, [Expert] will request these and [Client] will provide them in advance of [Expert]'s providing additional services.

Date [when agreement signed]: _____

Name of Attorney: _____ Signature: _____

Name of Expert: _____ Signature: _____

APPENDIX B. Fee Arrangement for an Expert Witness Who Is Called to Testify

The purpose of this Agreement is to explain the fee arrangements for [Name of Expert], who has been asked to testify as an expert witness by [Name of Attorney], Attorney-at-Law, who is representing [Name of Plaintiff or Defendant] in the case between [list Names of Parties involved in the case and court reference number, if any].

Fees for the Expert's services will be billed at a rate of [Dollar Amount] per hour for Preparation Time prior to trial, and [Dollar Amount] per hour for Attendance Time. Preparation Time includes time expended while corresponding with the court, consulting with attorneys, preparing for trial, traveling to and from meetings with attorneys, and other activities required for preparing to testify (including any time that has been expended on this case prior to signing this agreement). [Expert] will record all interactions and provide a detailed account upon billing the Attorney-Client. Attendance time includes all time spent in relation to attending at the court, including time spent going to and from court, waiting to testify, and providing testimony.

Fees for Preparation Time will be paid regardless of whether [Expert] is actually called to testify. If [Attorney] asks [Expert] to attend at court, there will be a minimum charge for 4 hours of services [Dollar Amount], regardless of whether [Expert] provides testimony on that day. [Expert] and [Attorney] acknowledge that [Attorney] has provided [Expert] with a Retainer of [Dollar Amount]. If, upon completion of [Expert]'s forensic services, monies are owed to [Attorney], [Expert] will refund the balance within 15 working days of the date of final billing. If the trial is continued, settled out of court, or otherwise delayed, the Retainer will be fully refunded, less fees for Preparation Time if notice is received at least 5 working days prior to the trial. Fifty percent of the "Retainer less fees for Preparation Time" will be refunded when notice is received at least 2 working days prior to the scheduled trial. Twenty percent of the "Retainer less fees for Preparation Time" will be refunded if notice is received less than 2 working days prior to trial.

If additional fees are charged, payment of outstanding fees will be paid within 30 days of the date of billing. If payment is not made within the specified time frame, [Expert] reserves the rights to charge interest at Prime Rate or to authorize the services of a collection agency or an attorney. All reasonable costs associated with their collection efforts shall be added to Attorney's bill.

All payments to [Expert] are for the provision of expert services as [identify professional background or expertise], and are NOT contingent upon providing particular opinions or upon a particular outcome of the case.

Date: _____

Name of Attorney: _____   Signature: _____

Name of Expert: _____   Signature: _____

APPENDIX C. Statement of Understanding to Participate in a Forensic Psychological Evaluation[1]

THE ROLE OF THE EVALUATOR

I [name of Evaluator] have been appointed by the Court to conduct an impartial forensic psychological evaluation. My purpose in conducting this evaluation is to gather information to enable me to formulate an opinion concerning what custody and/or visitation arrangement is most likely to be in the best psychological interests of your child[ren]. I shall strive to be accurate, fair, objective, and independent in gathering data for the purpose of this evaluation. I may present the information I gather and the recommendations that I reach to the Court or any other proceeding deemed necessary by the Court. Although the manner in which my fees will be paid has been determined by the Court, and although my fees are not paid by the Court, the work that I am doing will be done for the Court. Regardless of who pays an impartial evaluator, an impartial evaluator is expected to operate as though he or she was employed by the Court.

I do not presume that those whom I am evaluating are lying. However, I do not presume that they are telling the truth. Forensic psychologists are expected to secure verification of assertions made by those whom they are evaluating. Your cooperation will be expected as verification is sought of assertions made by you.

CONFIDENTIALITY AND PRIVILEGE

Principles of confidentiality and privilege do not apply within the context of an assessment such as the one being conducted. Information provided by you, regardless of the form in which it has been provided or obtained, may be shared with others involved in the evaluation. Such information may include your statements, video or audio recordings, diaries, correspondence, photographs, observations outside the interview context, and other such materials.

---

[1]Gould and Martindale (2009) suggest calling this form a "Statement of Understanding" for evaluations that are court ordered, as opposed to an "Agreement to Participate," which would be used if the litigants voluntarily chose to participate in the evaluation. This sample is based on the form presented in the first edition *Clinicians in Court*, with updates recommended by the Association of Family and Conciliation Courts (2006) and by Gould and Martindale.

By presenting information to others, verification of information provided can be sought and others can be afforded opportunities to respond to allegations that may have been made. Statements made by children may need to be cited in an evaluation report. It is important that you do not mislead your children. Do not tell them that what is said to me (the evaluator) is confidential. It is not. Information concerning your payments for my services (amounts, sources of payments, form of payments) also is not confidential.

Office and clerical staff from my office who become involved in aspects of your evaluation are bound by the same rules of confidentiality and exceptions to confidentiality as I am under this consent form.

The need may arise for me to discuss the evaluation with other professionals and/ or provide a copy of the final report to colleagues for their review and comments. In either case, all names and identifying information will be changed. In discussions with others who may assist in interviewing collateral sources, names are not changed.

FEES

Fees are determined through Court order or based on an hourly rate of compensation. My hourly rate of compensation is [Dollar Amount]. Note that I reserve the right to increase fees, with appropriate notice to you. Also note that fees for an assessment of this type are usually not reimbursable by health insurance.

A typical evaluation will cost between [range of dollar amounts]. In most cases, I will have expended some time prior to your receipt of this document. Fees are charged retroactively from the time that my services are initially requested and a file is opened. These fees do not include funds for work done after the evaluation is completed, such as additional correspondence, depositions, and/or trial preparation and testimony.

If, in my judgment, it is advisable that I consult with other mental health professionals, attorneys, or other professionals for purposes *other* than collateral information, time expended by me in such consultations will be billed to your account. If another professional is consulted for the purpose of a collateral interview and it is their office policy to charge for such interview time, the cost of this professional's time will be passed on to the person(s) financially responsible for the cost of the evaluation. I will not assume responsibility to pay for or forward bills for fees charged by other professionals who I consult for this evaluation.

Record-keeping requirements of forensic work make it necessary to log each telephone message and make a record of even the briefest telephone call. For this reason, there will be a minimum charge of [Dollar Amount] charged for any phone contact. All phone contacts will be charged at a prorated rate of [Dollar Amount] per hour.

Once an evaluation has been concluded, fees paid may be reapportioned according to the attorney's negotiation or the Court's direction. However, while the evaluation is in progress, I will not apportion fees based on what was done and for whom. All work relating to the assessment is done in order to obtain as much relevant information as possible and cannot be viewed as work done for one party or for the other. Similarly, fees cannot be reapportioned in a manner that involves assigning financial responsibility for fees associated with other services to the other party (e.g., fees for a separate evaluation).

There may be times when an individual being evaluated will be required to pay fees for time expended by me in obtaining and reviewing information that the individual would have preferred that I not obtain or review. Similarly, there may be times when the financially responsible party (parties) will be required to pay fees in connection with the evaluation of a third party whom the financially responsible party (parties) would have preferred I not evaluate.

If it should become necessary for me to report allegations of abuse/neglect to the Department of Social Services (DSS),[2] the financially responsible party will be billed for any time expended in filing the report, being interviewed by DSS, and so on. This may mean that a financially responsible party will have to pay for time expended in reporting him or her to DSS.

There may be times when the actions of one party will make it necessary for me to make phone calls and/or write letters. In calculating fees for my services, no distinction is made between time expended in administrative matters and time expended in evaluation activities. Fees for time expended in administrative activities are apportioned in the same manner as other fees. This includes time expended in addressing fee-related matters.

It is to your advantage to organize any materials you submit for my consideration. You are paying for my time, and more time is required to review material if it has been poorly organized. Any items submitted to me should be clearly identified with your name. This is particularly important in the case of photographs, audio or video recordings, diary pages, and notes. Any item submitted for my consideration will not be returned. All items submitted for my consideration will be placed in my file.

---

[2]Or other name of the appropriate government authority responsible for receiving reports of child abuse.

The performance of evaluation-related services by me does not cease with the issuance of my report. Fees for all postevaluation services such as correspondence, phone time, attendance at conferences, review of court orders, etc., are the responsibility of the party requesting the services, unless other arrangements have been made. In the case of postevaluation services performed for the Court, fees will be paid by the financially responsible party (or parties) identified in the Court order.

If I am called to testify at Court or to provide a deposition, you must pay for my preparation time and appearance. The scheduling of my testimony will be done in consultation with me and with appropriate recognition of possible conflicting personal and professional commitments. Your attorney(s) must provide me with notice of appearance indicating the approximate time of testimony. I will reserve this time for you and your attorney. I will not be on "standby." If you need my testimony, you will pay for either one-half day or one full day of my time. In this way, people toward whom I have other commitments will not be inconvenienced, as often happens in "standby" testimony. When you reserve my time, I am available to you at any or all of the time during that reserved time.

LIMITATIONS, RISKS, AND SERVICES *NOT* PROVIDED

The profession of psychology has not developed specific methods and procedures for use in assessing comparative custodial fitness, and neither the profession of psychology nor the State of [Name of State] has established specific criteria. The criteria that I employ and the methods and procedures I utilize have been chosen by me and reflect, in my judgment, the current state of the art in conducting child custody evaluations. I will respond to any questions you have about these methods and procedures during our initial evaluation session.

Please note that my report is only an advisory evaluation to the Court. The Court is not obliged to accept my recommendations. It is also possible, although not likely, that upon completion of a thorough examination of the issues, I may be unable to offer an opinion to the Court within a reasonable degree of psychological certainty. Fees for services already rendered will not be refunded under this circumstance or under circumstances in which completion of the evaluation becomes either impossible or unnecessary. If an evaluation has not begun, fees for time expended will be subtracted from any retainer and the balance will be refunded in a timely manner.

It is not possible to guarantee that an evaluation will be concluded by a specific date. Ordinarily, judges who have requested that forensic evaluations be performed wish to have the reports prepared prior to the commencement of trial. Though quite unlikely, a judge could begin a trial prior to receiving my report. In accordance with my professional standards of practice, I will not provide recommendations for interim custody and visitation.

I will take reasonable steps to minimize the distress associated with the evaluation process. Nevertheless, although more than 90% of the cases in which I am involved are resolved without judicial intervention, I must presume that there will be a trial and I will conduct myself accordingly. This means that information you provide will be questioned, and at times you may feel as though you are being interrogated rather than interviewed. In order to perform my Court-appointed function, I must be an examiner, not a therapist.

I cannot provide psychological advice or treatment services to an individual whom I am evaluating. If counseling or psychotherapy services are desired, please consult your attorney or other professionals for appropriate referrals. The pager used by my clinical partners and me is for emergencies of a *clinical*, not forensic, nature. The emergency number is *not* to be used at any time by anyone involved in a forensic evaluation. If you have an emergency, contact your attorney, physician, the police, the nearest hospital, 911, or an appropriately trained professional.

Psychologists are admonished by our ethics code to release test data only to individuals qualified to interpret them. Unless otherwise instructed by the Court, test data will be released only to a mental health professional with appropriate credentials and training who is competent to interpret forensic test data. Additional information concerning this procedure will be provided to you and/or your attorney if requested.

If any questions arise of a legal nature, you must consult with your attorney. It is inappropriate for someone not trained in the law to attempt to offer an opinion concerning legal matters. I will provide no such opinions.

PSYCHOLOGICAL TESTING

It is expected that when individuals being evaluated come to my office for the purpose of taking psychological tests, they will arrive unaccompanied. Spouses, children, companions, and friends can serve as sources of distraction. If someone must transport the test-taker, that person will be asked to leave and not return until the test-taker has completed all testing.

SUBMISSION AND RETENTION OF DOCUMENTS

Your attorney will often be able to anticipate what documents an evaluator is likely to require. Obtaining pertinent documents prior to the beginning of the evaluation will expedite the evaluative process. Documents you wish me to consider must be delivered in a manner that ensures their safe transfer into my custody. Under no circumstances are litigants or others to make unannounced visits to my office in order to deliver documents. With the exception of certain test-related data, it is my obligation to produce at trial all items that I have considered in formulating my opinion. Therefore, my policy is to retain all documents and materials submitted for my consideration.

You are strongly encouraged to make copies of any materials you intend to provide to me. If you neglect to make copies and if you later require copies, you will be charged for time expended in copying these documents. If, prior to trial, a written request is made that I copy and release items in my file for examination by an attorney or by another mental health professional, you will be charged for the costs associated with producing these copies.

OUT-OF-SESSION CONTACT

Out-of-session contact between you and me should be avoided. It is to your *disadvantage* to communicate information to an evaluator in an informal manner. Limit your phone contact with me to scheduling appointments and addressing other procedural matters. I will not accept any information from you that I deem relevant to the evaluation over the phone, in public spaces, through e-mail, or via other forms of electronic transfer.

OBTAINING INFORMATION FROM COLLATERAL SOURCES

Individuals being evaluated agree to authorize me to obtain any documents that I may wish to examine and to authorize communication between me and any individuals who, in my judgment, may have information bearing on the subject of the assessment. In most cases, information needed from professionals will be obtained by telephonic interview as well as review of their written files. Individuals who are likely to be advocates for one party or the other will be expected to provide information in writing. I reserve the right to contact these people by telephone for clarification and/or additional information. Some professionals may require you to sign a consent to release information to me.

I will be responsible for making all decisions regarding who must be evaluated, how extensively, and what information should be obtained and reviewed. There may be times when I will be asked to review information that I reasonably believe is likely to be more prejudicial than probative. There also may be instances in which I am asked to contact people whom I believe would be inappropriate to contact. I make the final decision about whether or not to pursue the information in such matters.

I reserve the right to consider any information regardless of the manner in which it has been obtained unless it has been obtained illegally. If I am asked to consider information that may have been obtained illegally, I will follow instructions from the attorneys if they are in agreement. If they cannot agree, I will request direction from the Court.

You may ask others to provide information about their direct observations of your parenting. It is your responsibility to explain to anyone from whom you solicit a letter that the information contained in the letter may be revealed to *any* of the individuals involved in the evaluation. This may include revealing information to your children in order to obtain their feedback and reaction. Your information or that of the collateral sources may be quoted in the evaluation report. Please ask each person to include his or her name, phone number, and address. I may wish to interview any or all of these people about their reported observations.

I will not accept any information via e-mail or other electronic transfers of information. I will not accept any information via fax unless it is from the attorneys or the Court.

CONTACT WITH ATTORNEYS

Once I have been informed that I have been appointed to conduct an impartial evaluation for the Court, I endeavor to avoid *ex parte* communications with the attorneys representing the litigants. Ordinarily, I meet with both litigants to review a draft of my report and will provide both of you with an opportunity to provide feedback before preparing my final draft and sending it to the court. Once my report is complete and has been forwarded to the Court, I will engage in discussions with the attorneys once they agree on a format for that communication.

ALLEGATIONS OF ABUSE/NEGLECT

I am required by law to report allegations or suspicions of child abuse or neglect, even if they have previously been reported. The penalties imposed on mandated reporters who fail to report such allegations are severe. If allegations are made, I will report them to the appropriate authorities, and my action in reporting them must not be interpreted as a display of support for the individual who has made the allegations. My action in reporting should also not be interpreted as an indication that I disapprove of the alleged actions of the person who has been accused. Most important, it must not be inferred that my reporting of such allegations suggests that I find them credible. It is the responsibility of the appropriate child protection authorities to determine the credibility of the allegations and whether to take further actions.

POSTEVALUATIVE DEVELOPMENTS

After I have met with the litigants to discuss a draft copy of my evaluation, I will take reasonable steps to avoid contact with the litigants and their attorneys. I will only deal with requests for follow-up evaluation services if requested in writing by both attorneys, or if ordered by the court. If significant time elapses between the issuance of my report and the date of the trial, I may request that the parties meet with me and/or undergo some type of follow-up investigation. If such a request is made, both parties must cooperate.

*   *   *

In accordance with the Health Insurance Portability and Accountability Act, Section 164.512(e)(l)(i), your signature on this document will acknowledge your understanding that health information that would otherwise be protected by confidentiality may be provided in the course of judicial or administrative proceedings. Once records are released by me to the court, to the attorneys, or other consultants retained by the attorneys, I no longer exercise control over who may access the information contained in those records.

I ask that you thoroughly review this document and that you seek guidance from your attorney in the event that any aspect of this document is not clear to you. The evaluation will not proceed until both parties have expressed their understanding of and willingness to abide by the policies and procedures set forth in this document.

Your signature below indicates that (1) you have received, read, understood, and will abide by my evaluation policies and procedures; (2) you are waiving privilege with respect to any information in my file concerning this matter; and (3) you are authorizing the release by me of information, including my evaluation report, to the Court, your attorneys, and other parties to which I have been directed to release the report by the Court.

Client's Name: _____ Client's Signature: _____ Date Signed: _____

Client's Name: _____ Client's Signature: _____ Date Signed: _____

Evaluator's Name: _____ Evaluator's Signature: _____

Date Signed: _____

Please sign both copies of this form and return one copy to me. Retain the other copy so that you can refer to it during the course of the evaluation.

APPENDIX D. Initial Letter to Attorneys
after Evaluator Received an Appointment Order

[Date]

1st Attorney's Name:
Address:

2nd Attorney's Name:
Address:

Dear [both attorneys' names]:

RE: [Names of Parties; Court Case Number]

I have received the [Date] court order signed by the Honorable Judge [Name of Judge], in which I have been appointed to conduct an independent and impartial child custody evaluation. I have also received materials from both attorneys in the above-referenced case. Before we begin the evaluation process, please review the six enclosed forms with your clients before they call for their initial interview.

1. *Statement of Understanding* provides an explanation of the evaluation process.
2. *List of Collaterals* asks the parents to list the names and contact information of people whom they consider to be appropriate collateral sources of information for the evaluation.
3. *Informed Consent for Collaterals* is to be provided to each collateral source. Each collateral source needs to read, sign, and return the informed consent form to me with his or her written statement.
4. *Questionnaire for Collaterals* must be given to each collateral interview source identified by the parents.
5. *Statement of Understanding for Nonparty Participants* is to be used if either of the parents is repartnered and if either new partner will be asked to participate in the evaluation; it should be signed and forwarded to my office.
6. *Parenting Questionnaire* (included as a paper copy as well as digitally to allow for word processing) must be completed by each parent and/or caretaker and returned to my office.

My initial interview will not occur until I have received a signed original Statement of Understanding from both parents. The retainer for the evaluation is [Dollar Amount]. Please forward the retainer along with your client's signed Statement of Understanding. Upon receipt, I will schedule the initial meetings with each parent. Please ask the parents to bring their completed Parenting Questionnaires to the initial session. Please also advise the parents *not* to bring the children to the initial session.

Finally, I ask that the attorneys decide which documents, pleadings, and other materials will be necessary to forward to my office. I am particularly interested in any documents that help me to understand the legal issues involved in the case. I ask that each attorney copy the other side with all correspondence and materials forwarded to my office.

Thank you for your cooperation. I look forward to working with you on this evaluation.

Sincerely,

[Evaluator's name]

APPENDIX E. Sample Affidavit

AFFIDAVIT OF JANE HENSON, PhD[3]
Re: State of New York v. Ronald Wells
Case No.: CR-987-983

I, Jane Henson, PhD, hereby state and declare as follows:

1. I am a licensed psychologist in the State of New York, and am engaged in private practice in the areas of forensic and clinical psychology.
2. So that the court might be familiar with my qualifications, I offer the following brief background. My full current curriculum vitae is attached to this affidavit and incorporated into this affidavit by reference.
3. I received a bachelor's degree in science with a major in psychology from New York University in 1988; a master's degree in clinical psychology from Columbia University in 1990; and a PhD in forensic psychology from Yale University in 1995. I am currently in private practice in New York City, where I have specialized in family violence and sexual assault cases as a forensic psychologist. I have presented workshops on forensic psychology at the New York State Bar Association's conference on psychology and the law, as well as at the American Psychological Association's annual conference.
4. I have conducted more than 180 forensic evaluations for domestic violence cases over a 12-year period. I have been qualified as an expert in forensic mental health, domestic violence, and sexual assault.
5. My reason for detailing these aspects of my practice and training is to summarize my qualifications. In no way am I speaking in fact or by implication on behalf of any of the above organizations or institutions.
6. I have been retained as a forensic expert by counsel for the Office of the Public Defender in Nassau County, NY.
7. I have been asked to review the behavioral science literature pertaining to intimate partner abuse, with a focus on battery and extreme cruelty.
8. I have not evaluated Ronald Wells or any other interested party to this litigation outside of the attorney for the Office of the Public Defender,

---

[3]The names and other information in this affidavit are based on a fictitious case. The format used for this example is drawn in part from affidavits constructed by Jonathan Gould and Noël Busch-Armendariz.

Wilma Unrau. Because I have not conducted an examination of any party to this litigation or the minor children, I do not know whether the conclusions drawn from the behavioral science literature review are applicable to the present situation. In order for a mental health professional to apply the conclusions drawn from the behavioral science literature to the *State of N Y v. Wells* case, a forensic evaluation of Ronald Wells and the alleged victim would need to be conducted. However, as guidance to the Plaintiff's attorneys and, potentially, the Court, the educative purpose of this review may provide useful guidelines about current behavioral science research and literature pertaining to intimate partner violence.

9. **Brief Overview of Intimate Partner Violence:** Relationships that involve intimate partner violence (IPV) do not usually begin with an abusive incident. Rather, relationships that later involve intimate partner abuse most often begin as romantic relationships. Originally described by Lenore Walker (1979), the cycle of violence in abusive relationships commonly consists of three phases: honeymoon, tension building, and acute battering . . .

10. **Impacts of Extreme Physical Abuse:** Although IPV often begins with name calling and verbal abuse, it may escalate to more physical violence, including grabbing, pushing, slapping, punching, and hitting. Abusive partners will often escalate their controlling behaviors in order to maintain their authority over their victims (Bancroft, 2002). Stark (2007) writes, "Exposure to severe violence so overwhelms the ego's defense mechanisms that a person's capacity to act effectively on their own behalf is paralyzed, producing a posttraumatic reaction or disorder such as posttraumatic stress disorder (PTSD) and a range of secondary psychosocial and behavioral problems" (p. 114). Roberts (2002) writes, "In chronic cases, the human suffering, degradation, and emotional and physical pain sometimes ends in permanent injuries to the victim or the death of the batterer or the battered women" (p. 78) . . .

11. **Factors Contributing to Domestic Homicide:** Research on why some female victims of extreme intimate partner abuse kill their male partners suggests that these women feel trapped in their relationships . . .

I hereby declare under penalty of perjury of the laws of the State of New York that the foregoing information is true and correct to the best of my knowledge.

DATED [Date] at New York, NY.

_____

Jane Henson

Sworn to and subscribed before me on [Date]

_____

Signature of Notary Public (plus Stamp with Seal and Number)

Print or Stamp Name of Notary Public _____

Personally known _____ or Produced ID _____ Type of ID _____

[attach list of citations and *curriculum vitae*]

APPENDIX F. Motion to Quash Subpoena

As with the other forms in this volume, this example is for general reference only. Consult with an attorney to draft a motion that applies specifically to the laws of your jurisdiction and the specifics of your case.

Case Number: 983-394

IN RE the matter of	)	In the Circuit Court, Broward County
	)	17th Circuit
Ewan Campbell	)	Fort Lauderdale, Florida

Motion to Quash Subpoena Duces Tecum

MS. NINA TRAN (Movant), a Licensed Clinical Social Worker practicing in Fort Lauderdale, Florida respectfully asks this Court to quash the Subpoena Duces Tecum ("Subpoena") served on Movant at the request of Mr. Ewan Campbell. The grounds for this motion are as follows:

1. On January 14, 2012, Movant was served with a subpoena from Mr. Campbell's attorney, Warren Pejorich to appear at his law office on February 19, 2012, "for a deposition and to produce all records relating to the psychosocial assessment and therapy provided to Ms. Zina Campbell, wife of Mr. Ewen Campbell."
2. Movant does not admit or deny having a professional relationship with anyone by the name of Zina Campbell.
3. Movant advised Mr. Pejorich that agency policy and the National Association of Social Workers (NASW) Code of Ethics (2008, Standard 1.07, available via *www.naswdc.org*) prohibit her from disclosing confidential client information, including whether or not Zina Campbell is or ever was a client.
4. Under Section 491.0147 of the Florida Statutes, communications between a Licensed Clinical Social Worker and clients are confidential and privileged.
5. Movant advised Mr. Pejorich that she would require written consent to release information and to waive privilege, or she would be unable to speak with him or participate in a deposition concerning any client.

6. There is no legal basis to compel Movant to participate in the deposition or to produce client records.
7. Movant respectfully asks this Court to quash the subpoena and issue an order for attorney's fees and costs.
8. In accordance with the NASW Code of Ethics, Movant is willing and able to comply with all orders made by this court with respect to the current matters under consideration.

Respectfully submitted, this 21st day of January 2012, by:

_____

Name, Signature, and Address of Attorney

On Behalf of Ms. Nina Tran, Movant

Appendix G. For Further Reflection

This appendix presents topics and case scenarios for further thought and discussion. You may find them useful for reinforcing your knowledge before getting involved in a legal matter. Some questions are designed to encourage you to explore local laws and ethical codes specific to your context of practice. Other questions are designed to help you think through ethical and legal conflicts. Finally, some questions are designed to help you synthesize and apply what you have been reading in the book. The questions are linked to each chapter. Practitioners may also continue the dialogue by emailing me additional cases and questions that I can post on my website. For additional information and suggestions for use of these cases and questions, see *www.barsky.org/clinicians* or email *barsky@barsky.org*.

CHAPTER 1

1. *Dual Relationships*: Dr. Vanity is a mental health professional who provided a presentencing report for Clyde, a man convicted of armed robbery. After serving 3 years in prison, Clyde calls Dr. Vanity to ask whether she can provide Clyde with psychotherapy. Clyde says he liked Dr. Vanity and believed that he could trust her more than any other mental health professional whom he had met. Dr. Vanity notes that her code of ethics suggests that she avoid dual relationships, but she is not sure whether there is a conflict of interest in this case because she has not seen Clyde for 3 years. Consider whether it would be ethical for Dr. Vanity to provide psychotherapy to Clyde. Refer to your profession's code of ethics for guidance. Identify the potential benefits and risks of deciding to provide Clyde with psychotherapy. Finally, consider what Dr. Vanity could do to minimize the risks should she choose to work with Clyde.

2. *Helping Whom?* Dolores has been hired by the court to provide a forensic evaluation of Werner, who is currently being held involuntarily in a mental health institution due to concerns that he might kill himself. Werner insists that he is fine and should be released right away. Although Werner has a history of suicide attempts, Dolores believes that he does not need to remain at the mental health facility at this time. Dolores wonders whether she should advocate for Werner by talking to his treating psychiatrists, or whether she should just wait until trial to present her information to the court. Who is Dolores's primary client? What ethical duties does she owe to Werner, to the court, and to Werner's psychiatrist? How should she resolve her question about whether to advocate on Werner's behalf or to wait until she testifies at trial?

3. *Treating versus Forensic*: Betty tells Priscilla (a psychologist) that her exboyfriend tried to strangle her with a belt. Which of the following responses would be appropriate for Priscilla if she were a treating psychologist? Which would be

291

appropriate if she were a forensic psychologist? Consider how the appropriate response relates to the psychologist's role.

   a. "How did that make you feel?"

   b. "Did anybody else see him try to strangle you?"

   c. "You must have felt terrified."

   d. "May I take a look at your neck to see if there is any evidence of strangulation?"

4. *Agent of Change versus Agent of Social Control*: The primary role of a treating clinician is to help clients achieve their goals. Some clinicians are concerned that when they or their colleagues act as forensic experts and provide testimony in courts, they compromise their roles as helping professionals: court takes time away from their role as helpers, clients begin to view mental health professionals as agents of the court and agents of social control, and clients are less likely to seek services or develop trust with clinicians who also serve as forensic experts. To what extent does forensic practice actually interfere with the provision of treatment services in an ethical, effective manner? If a clinician wants to engage in both forensic and treatment practice, what strategies can be used to minimize the risks of one role interfering with the other?

CHAPTER 2

1. *Other Professionals*: This chapter explored the relationship between clinicians and attorneys. Clinicians also interact with judges, police, forensic evaluators, and other officials that work within court and legal systems. Select one of these professions and identify the commonalities and differences between this profession and your own (especially roles, legal mandates, and ethical responsibilities). What are some of the ways your two professions can collaborate? What types of conflicts might you face in working with the other profession?

2. *Empathy and Impartiality*: Elka facilitates therapeutic groups for men who have histories of intimate partner abuse. One of her clients, Peter, has been convicted of assault and wants Elka to provide mitigation testimony at an upcoming hearing on sentencing. Elka has a strong sense of empathy for Peter, as he was subjected to physical abuse as a child and has had to overcome many obstacles in his life. On the other hand, she is concerned that Peter may continue to be violent with women in future relationships. Elka fears that her testimony may lead to a light sentence that would not deter Peter from similar assaults in the future. As a potential witness in a sentencing hearing, what roles should empathy and impartiality play in how Elka presents herself as a witness? What challenges might Elka face in being an effective, ethical witness?

3. *Defending an Alleged Sex Offender*: Assume that you have been serving as a therapist for Nick, a man charged with aggravated sexual assault. Nick's attorney has asked you to testify on his behalf. You believe your testimony will be overwhelmingly favorable to Nick's case. You are concerned, however, that Nick is guilty in the eyes of the public. You have seen very strong opinions expressed in local media and on the Internet, calling for Nick's castration, and worse. You fear that you will be ostracized for testifying in favor of a despicable human being. What strategies should you use to help prepare for this case—emotionally and socially—given your desire to remain a respected professional in your community?

4. *Role Conflict*: Polly is a psychologist who has been providing counseling services to Jared, a man sued for defrauding a health insurance company. Jared tells Polly that he cannot afford an attorney and he does not qualify for legal aid. Jared asks Polly if she can help him with the upcoming case because she is a good advocate and she has a lot of expertise in legal processes. How could Polly explain that she cannot provide Jared with legal advice or representation? Write four or five sentences that she could use, explaining the ethical issues and role conflict that would arise if she were to act as his attorney.

5. *Child Abuse*: Leila is an attorney who has hired Shawn, a social worker, to assist with family law cases. In one case, Shawn suspects the client is physically abusing the child. Leila tells Shawn not to report the abuse to child welfare authorities because Shawn is working in a law office and there is no legal duty to report for lawyers and their employees. What ethical issues does this case raise for Shawn and Leila? How should Shawn respond to Leila, and why?

6. *Video Response*: Go to the YouTube website (*www.youtube.com*) and search for "cross-examination psychologist" (or substitute social worker or another type of professional for psychologist). Select and watch a video of an actual or mock cross-examination. As you watch the video, visualize yourself as the expert witness. Write down your thoughts and feelings toward the cross-examining attorney.

7. *Comparative Roles and Ethics*: Read the first nine sections of the American Bar Association's (2010) Model Rules of Professional Conduct (available via *http://www.americanbar.org*). Compare the roles and ethics of an attorney to those of your own profession. How are they similar? How are they different?

CHAPTER 3

1. *Ethically Challenged*: An attorney calls you, stating that he has a client who has been charged with theft. The attorney wants to refer the client to you for addiction counseling, so when the case comes to trial, the client will be seen as cooperative, taking steps to address the underlying reason for the client's theft. The attorney requests that you send her monthly reports on the client's progress (Bush

et al., 2006). The attorney suggests that if all goes well with this case, he will have many more clients to refer to you. Assume you are in private practice and you need to secure additional clients in order to pay your bills.

a. What issues does this referral raise for you in terms of client confidentiality, informed consent, trust, bias, integrity, and dual relationships?

b. What factors should you consider in terms of whether to accept this referral?

c. When deciding whether to accept this referral, who should you talk to first: the client, the attorney, or someone else?

d. What type of arrangements between the client, attorney, and yourself would be ethical?

e. If you decide to accept this referral, what could you do to reduce the risks regarding conflict of interests and your professional integrity?

2. *Forensic Intake Questions:* A woman named Maryam says she would like to hire you to conduct a mental health evaluation. She claims she left her country of origin due to torture and is seeking asylum in the United States. She says she needs the evaluation for an upcoming hearing on her application for asylum. Assume that you are professionally qualified to provide such services. What questions would you ask and what information would you gather before deciding whether to offer such forensic services?

3. *To Call or Not to Call:* Najaf is a psychotherapist who has been providing solution-focused therapy to Charlotte, a woman who is suing her employer for wrongful dismissal. Charlotte wants her attorney to call Najaf as a witness to testify about the impact of her being fired. Her attorney thinks Najaf's testimony may be useful in proving psychological damages incurred by Charlotte. In using solution-focused therapy, Najaf has not conducted a thorough psychosocial assessment. Rather, he has helped her focus on how to make positive changes in her life. Najaf has taken extensive case notes on his meetings with Charlotte and has observed significant improvement. Najaf serves about 25 clients per week, so he has some difficulty remembering each client's situation and progress without his notes. Najaf strongly believes that Charlotte should be compensated for being unjustly fired and would like to advocate on Charlotte's behalf. Would Najaf make a good fact witness in Charlotte's lawsuit? How would the forgoing facts affect Najaf's ability to be an effective witness?

4. *To Testify or Not to Testify:* A prosecuting attorney wants to hire you as an expert witness to testify—in a favorable manner—about the use of criminal personality profiling in a murder trial. Assume that you have the required expertise, but you are concerned that the use of such profiling may offend your profession's code of ethics with regard to respect for the dignity and worth of all people, as well as social justice (fairness, equal treatment). You are also concerned that criminal personality profiling is not an exact science. On the other hand, you would be paid well for your services, and the attorney will simply find another expert if you do

not agree to testify. Analyze the ethical issues raised by the case, using your professional code of ethics, identifying alternatives, and determining which course of action is appropriate.

5. *Personal Threat*: An attorney subpoenas a psychotherapist, Patricia, to testify in a case to determine the mental status of a client, Vern, who has schizophrenia. Two days later, Patricia receives an anonymous letter stating, "Don't testify. Your children will regret it." What are Patricia's options for dealing with this threat? Explain which option is best, taking confidentiality, safety, respect, professional objectivity, and Patricia's role as a potential witness into account.

6. *Confidentiality Conflict*: Barb works as a social worker in a public defender's office, where she helps clients by providing psychosocial assessments, developing treatment plans, and securing treatment as alternatives to traditional sentencing. While interviewing Felix, a client charged with defrauding elders in a Ponzi scheme,[1] Barb discovers that Felix is continuing to defraud other elders. Police do not know about this second scheme. Barb wants to inform adult protective services so they can take appropriate steps to protect these unsuspecting elders. Barb's attorney-supervisor, Hillary, insists that she maintain confidentiality, as her work is governed by the rules of attorney–client confidentiality, which does not have an exception for reporting financial crimes. Barb argues that if she was not working in a legal office, she would be obliged to report the scheme as elder abuse. What are Barb's conflicting legal and ethical obligations, and what should she do in this case?

CHAPTER 4

1. *Reframing versus Manufacturing Evidence*: Assume you have been working with Donna, a client with severe depression who has recently been hospitalized involuntarily due to suicidal thoughts. Donna has hired an attorney to help her gain release from the hospital. With Donna's permission, you have been consulting with the attorney in order to prepare for testifying in support of Donna's release at an upcoming hearing. While role-playing a cross-examination with the attorney, you state, "Donna has a history of cutting herself, and she may continue to cut herself. Still, this does not mean that she is going to kill herself. She uses cutting to deal with emotional pain, distracting herself from emotional traumas arising from abuse that she suffered as a child." The attorney suggests, "Rather than talking about cutting as a way to deal with the emotional pain from past traumas, you should talk about cutting as a way that Donna exerts control over herself, which is more positive." Although this explanation is plausible, it does not fit with your

---

[1]A Ponzi scheme is a fraudulent pyramid investment scheme in which the perpetrator obtains money from investors but does not actually invest the money as promised. The perpetrator pays investors with their own money or money from additional investors, and continues to try to raise more money from new investors to pay prior investors.

initial assessment. How should you deal with the attorney's request to reframe your explanation of Donna's cutting, and why?

2. *Believability*: Select an event that you witnessed at least 3 months ago (e.g., something that happened at a party, in a class, or on the street). Try to recollect the entire scenario and develop a story that you could tell to describe the event. Write notes to highlight key points that you want to relate in the story, but do not write an entire script or try to memorize everything you will say word for word. Video yourself recounting the story without the aid of any notes. Critique the video in terms of what factors made your account of the event more believable and what factors made it less believable (consider your body language, facial expressions, hand gestures, voice tone, pauses, eye movements, choice of words, pacing, level of details, and story coherence).

3. *Be Yourself:* This exercise is designed to help you testify in a more credible manner by learning how to be yourself when acting as a witness. Video yourself in four successive segments of about 60 seconds each: (1) pretend you are testifying and your attorney asks you to describe your preferred model of intervention when working with clients who have a particular presenting problem (e.g., addiction, poor social skills, depression); (2) tell an interesting story about something that happened in your childhood; (3) describe one of the scariest moments of your life; (4) pretend you are testifying in court and the opposing attorney asks you to describe a situation in which you lied to a client or withheld important information. Review the four segments and try to determine how the "real you" presents (note any differences in demeanor, language, facial expressions, and manner of communication). In segments 2 and 3 you are relating personal stories, so these segments may demonstrate the more natural you. In segments 1 and 4, you are asked to play the role of a witness. You may repeat this exercise with different scenarios, with the goal of communicating naturally and authentically when you are acting as a witness.[2]

4. *Labeling Fears*: Take a moment to visualize yourself testifying and identify what scares you most about acting as a witness. Write down your fears. For each fear you have identified, identify a strategy that may be useful in overcoming such fear. For instance, you might identify your fears as follows, "I hate the thought of some attorney trying to attack my honesty or professional competence. I know that I'm good at what I do in practice, but I'm afraid the attorney is going make me look like a fool." Then identify what you can do to manage these fears, referring back to strategies described in this chapter.

5. *Attorney Trouble*: Stella is a street outreach worker who has been working with Yulian, an 18-year-old who has been charged with trafficking to minors. Yulian informs Stella that he has a court-appointed attorney named Mr. Bungle. He thinks Mr. Bungle will represent him well. Stella has met Mr. Bungle and has

---

[2]This exercise is derived from a drill that James (2010) suggests for preparing attorneys to deliver their opening statements in a trial.

strong reservations about his legal skills and motivation. Should Stella share these reservations with Yulian? How might her decision affect her roles as Yulian's worker and as a potential witness in the case?

6. *Guardianship Court*: Assume that you have been providing psychotherapy to an elderly client, Ms. Zarconia, with diminished physical and mental capacities. Ms. Zarconia's children want her declared mentally incompetent so they may be appointed as guardians on her behalf. Ms. Zarconia's attorney has subpoenaed you to testify, and Ms. Zarconia is willing to waive any privilege. In preparing for this case, what questions should you ask the attorney? In particular, prepare a list of questions related to the legal issues, what needs to be proven, the burden and standard of proof, your role as a witness, and the setup of the courtroom.

7. *Legal Standards:* Assume you have been providing supportive counseling to Clive, a young man who is cognitively challenged. You have been subpoenaed to provide testimony in a sexual assault case involving a nurse who had sex with Clive. The primary issue at trial is whether Clive has sufficient "mental capacity to consent to sexual relations." The attorney calling you says that you will be asked to provide your observations about the Clive's sexual consent capacity. Identify what factors a court will consider when trying to determine whether Clive has sufficient mental capacity to consent to sexual relations. Give four examples of direct, factual observations you could provide to help the court make this determination.

CHAPTER 5

1. *Cultural Considerations*: Patricia is testifying about a client who fled torture in North Korea and claimed refugee status in the United States. The client spoke no English, so she used a Korean–English translator. During cross-examination, an attorney asks Patricia how she knew the translator was conveying accurately what the translator said. Ideally, how should Patricia respond? What legal, ethical, and clinical standards should Patricia have considered at the time she conducted her interview with the client, and when she prepared to testify?

2. *Faulty Examination*: Read the following segment of testimony aloud. You will note that the witness's narrative sounds disjointed, incoherent, uninteresting, lacking sensory details, and inauthentic. Rewrite the narrative to correct these problems.

ATTORNEY: Please tell the court what you observed when you entered Ms. Chisholm's home.

WITNESS: The party which I was evaluating was seen sleeping in her bed. When I entered the room she rolled over. The next thing, she said she wanted to die. Oh my God! Earlier, as I walked through the living room and hallway I saw an empty bottle of whiskey there. The medicine cabinet was empty. Last time I visited, she had oxycodone. There were at least 16 pills. I knew she was at risk. My supervisor said she was OK, but I wanted to call the police. The police never came and now look what happened. Overdose. End of story.

3. *Ethics Issue*: Assume that you have been asked to present evidence in a malpractice lawsuit against a defendant whom you know personally, as well as in a professional capacity. The defendant, Dr. Pratt, is a psychotherapist who has been accused of making inappropriate referrals, specifically, referring clients to colleagues who provide him with commissions for making such referrals. The attorney asks you whether you have reason to doubt Dr. Pratt's integrity. Assume that you know Dr. Pratt has bragged about cheating on his taxes. How would you respond to the attorney's question about integrity? Would you disclose the information about Dr. Pratt's taxes? Why or why not?

4. *A Colleague's Misbehavior*: Assume you are present in a courtroom when another mental health professional is testifying. During the testimony, you find the other professional's language is judgmental and disrespectful to her client. You believe that the professional is acting in a biased, rude manner, reflecting negatively on your profession. What are your ethical and legal obligations, if any, regarding whether or how to respond to these concerns?

5. *Tough Cross-Examination Questions*: For each of the following scenarios, identify what makes the question difficult for the clinician to answer. Then, offer a "word-for-word" suggestion for how the clinician could answer the question effectively:

a. On cross-examination during a malpractice lawsuit, an attorney asks a clinician, "You failed to use cognitive restructuring for this client, didn't you?" The clinician provided aggression-replacement therapy in accordance with his training and agency mandate.

b. In a criminal case against a man accused of rape, the cross-examining attorney says to the accused's therapist, "You have testified that you have provided therapy to people who have committed violent crimes. Isn't it true, however, that this is the first client whom you have served who is a rapist?" Assume that what the attorney asks is true, but embarrassing to the witness.

c. In a hearing to determine whether a client should be maintained in a mental health facility, a clinician has testified that the client threatened to kill his former boss, who recently fired him. During cross-examination, the client's attorney asks, "Wouldn't you be angry at your boss if you were fired without cause? Wasn't the client's expression of anger an understandable response to the boss's own actions?"

d. In a malpractice lawsuit against a social worker, the attorney asks the worker, "Isn't it true that another social worker might have used a different, more effective intervention?" The social worker used a paradoxical intervention to try to help a client leave his abusive partner, but the intervention backfired when the client followed the worker's paradoxical advice.

e. In a mental health hearing to determine the mental competence of an elderly woman, the cross-examining attorney says to the psychologist, "You only spent 50 minutes interviewing this client. Isn't it true that in order to complete a full psychosocial assessment, you would need at least two additional interviews?" Assume the psychologist spent less time than usual, but still thinks her assessment is valid and reliable.

6. *Confidentiality after Trial:* During a trial, the state attorney questioned Inez (a social worker) about a client's involvement in gang-related activities. Although Inez asked to maintain the client's confidentiality, the judge ordered her to testify. After the case, news reporters ask Inez for further comments about the convicted client. Inez thinks that she can improve her client's public image by cooperating with reporters. What should Inez do, and why?

7. *Cross-Examination:* In following example, an attorney is cross-examining a clinician in a criminal case against a private residential treatment program for youth with anorexia. The charges include billing fraud and malpractice. Critique the clinicians' responses to the cross-examining attorney's questions. Identify the strengths and limitations of the clinician responses in relation to: clarity, ambiguity, plain language, relevance, honesty, confidence, arrogance, guessing at information, being argumentative, showing bias, evading questions, inappropriate body language, acquiescence, or providing testimony without having direct knowledge, and credibility. Rewrite the clinician responses to address the problematic responses.

ATTORNEY: *(holding up a transcript)* Ms. Yates, in your earlier testimony, you stated, "After we diagnosed Liz with anorexia, we designed a plan to help her eliminate unhealthy weight control behaviors." When you say "We," don't you mean the psychologist, Dr. Zaitz? You weren't actually the one to diagnose Liz.

CLINICIAN: That's an outright lie. Dr. Zaitz did not conduct the diagnosis. We work as a team.

ATTORNEY: Isn't it also true that you made your diagnosis based on Liz's records, even though you never actually saw Liz as a patient?

CLINICIAN: *(rolling her eyes)* I always follow agency policy. You know, just because I used records from other clinicians does not mean I did anything wrong.

ATTORNEY: Isn't it true that standard 9.01(b) of the American Psychological Association Code of Conduct says that assessments should be based on firsthand knowledge, not the records of other clinicians?

CLINICIAN: I really don't know. I haven't read that subsection lately. I suppose it could.

ATTORNEY: It's also interesting to note that you met with Liz's mother, but not with Liz. By interviewing the mother and not Liz, it would seem that your assessment is biased.

CLINICIAN: With all due respect, counsel, are you asking me a question or are you just providing your own testimony?

ATTORNEY: Well let me be perfectly clear with this question, and please give me a clear *yes* or *no* answer. Did you disclose to the court that you were put on probation when you started your job?

CLINICIAN: What are you insinuating? Everyone at this facility is put on probation ...

ATTORNEY: (*cutting off the witness*) Just answer the question, were you put on probation when you started your job, yes or no?

CLINICIAN: Yes, I suppose, but ...

ATTORNEY: I thought so ... I understand that you have had more than 140 clients this year alone. Have you ever mixed up information about one case with another?

CLINICIAN: (*shaking head from side to side for emphasis*) Uh-uh. Never.

ATTORNEY: So you're perfect?

CLINICIAN: Well, that's what my mother tells me (*smiles and laughs to lighten the mood*).

ATTORNEY: How do you know Liz's mother was telling the truth when she described her daughter's eating behaviors?

CLINICIAN: My job was not to analyze whether she was telling me the truth. My job was to gather information from everyone and make sense of it from a psychological perspective. If you really want to know, in this case, I looked into her eyes and saw the soul of an honest woman. Why would she lie? You must believe me when I say that I handled this assessment in a thorough and competent manner. I followed all the rules. We don't use lie detector tests.

ATTORNEY: You don't really have a current recollection of what happened during your interview with Liz's mother. You are basically just restating what is written in your progress notes. Could you please explain what types of information you include in your notes and what types of information you leave out?

CLINICIAN: I try to include everything that is relevant to the case. I don't leave anything out.

ATTORNEY: You said that you had additional records at your office. You seem to be withholding information from the court.

CLINICIAN: (*looks toward the ground*) I resent your insinuations. Integrity is my hallmark. I would never withhold information.

ATTORNEY: One last question. I understand that you are a gun owner. In fact, you have a collection of more than 20 guns. Isn't it true that you are a member and avid supporter of the National Rifle Association?

CLINICIAN: (*responding quickly*) If that's your last question, why bother even asking it? It's completely irrelevant. I am an honest, law-abiding citizen, and integrity as a clinician is my hallmark.

CHAPTER 6

1. *Local Laws and Ethics*: Identify the state legislation and professional codes of ethics that apply to record keeping within your profession and context of practice, for instance, hospital, hospice, school, or private practice. What do these laws and professional codes tell you about:

a. Information that should be included in your client records?

b. How records should be stored?

c. Requirements for release of client records?

d. When and how records should be destroyed?

e. Client rights to access records and request changes?

2. *Deficient Records*: Assume that you have written the following progress notes for an interview with an elderly client who was receiving insufficient care in a nursing home:

November 31—Met Mr. Shorts in his room. Appeared very distraught, nonverbal. Called nursing station to request help. Nurse did not come for a long time. Called head nurse for floor. Head nurse came immediately and saw client in distress. She called emergency services and asked me to leave.

Assume that your records, including these case notes, have been subpoenaed for an adult guardianship case involving Mr. Shorts. To prepare for trial, you are planning to meet with the attorney who has called you to testify. In preparation for your meeting with the attorney, your first task is to identify any deficiencies or concerns about the contents of your case notes. What concerns would you like to discuss with the attorney? What questions could you raise with the attorney regarding the possibility of correcting what is written in your case notes? What questions could you raise with the attorney regarding how to defend against concerns that may be raised during cross-examination on your records at trial? You do not need to answer the questions, just formulate relevant questions for your meeting with the attorney.

3. *To Note, or Not to Note*: Verna works for a vocational rehabilitation program. Many of her clients have been injured in work-related accidents and they may have legal actions pending against their employers. Although Verna's clinical records may be subpoenaed, her primary obligation as a treating practitioner is to provide vocational counseling services. Consider each of the following types of information and discuss whether Verna should include it in her files. Provide your reasons, making reference to your professional code of ethics and relevant legislation:

a. Verna believes that a client is fabricating a back injury in order to obtain compensation from his employer. Verna does not have concrete proof, but the client has disclosed playing football and doing heavy lifting while making renovations to his home.

b. A client tells Verna that her former boss was sexually harassing her and that she does not want to go back to that work environment, even if her disabling condition is cured.

c. Verna refers a client to an orthopedic surgeon to assess her condition and determine whether she needs medical treatment before returning to work. Two days later, Verna reads in the newspaper that the surgeon has been charged with Medicaid fraud and his license to practice may be suspended.

d. A client tells Verna that she is HIV positive. Her HIV status is irrelevant to the reasons that she is unemployed and requires vocational training.

e. Verna is trying to find a job for a client who has a history of alcohol dependence. The client says he is in recovery and provides her with a copy of a discharge report from an addictions treatment facility, saying that he has been able to maintain abstinence for at least 3 months. The client is concerned he may be discriminated against because of his addiction status, which the client claims is a disability protected by the Americans with Disabilities Act.

4. *Court-Ready Files:* Because any client you see may end up in court, should you treat all clinical records as if they were forensic case files, ready for trial? Consider the following scenario, including what are the benefits and costs of writing case records with an eye to their being used in court.

Hoshi provides integrative mind–body psychotherapy to help people with problems related to memory and concentration. Hoshi wants to protect the confidentiality of her clients, so she takes very limited notes on her clients and interventions with them. Taking limited notes saves her time and saves the clients' money, as she does not have to charge clients as much for her services. Hoshi's record-keeping practice consists of noting each client's goals, the number of sessions attended, and degree of goal attainment as measured by qualitative feedback from clients. She does not write a formal assessment or evaluation. One of her clients, Garth, is the plaintiff in a lawsuit against a pharmaceutical company, claiming that one of its medications has caused permanent brain damage and memory loss. Garth's attorney, Ms. Smart, sub-poenas Hoshi's case records, hoping to find evidence to support Garth's claim. When Ms. Smart reviews the records, she finds they are sparse and useless for the upcoming trial. When Garth finds out the records are sparse, he becomes incensed at Hoshi for not taking more comprehensive notes.

5. *Raw Test Scores*: An attorney, with the client's written consent, asks you for a copy of her client's raw scores on the psychological tests that you completed. The attorney says she needs the raw data in order to prepare an adequate defense for her client in an upcoming criminal trial. You believe that raw scores should only be released to a licensed psychologist because they could be misinterpreted or misused by others. What does your state law and professional code of ethics say about whether you should release the raw test scores to the attorney? What are the advantages and disadvantages of these laws and professional codes? How should you respond if a judge ordered you to release the raw scores to the court?

CHAPTER 7

1. *Weak Evidence*: An attorney representing the alleged victim of domestic violence asks Lavern, a psychotherapist who specializes in intimate-partner abuse, to testify about the veracity of a victim-witness's testimony when the victim-witness does not express fear of the alleged batterer (Kohn, 2003). Lavern would like to support the attorney's client, but is concerned that the research evidence on witness credibility in such cases is mixed. How should Lavern respond to the attorney's request? What concerns should she discuss with the attorney before agreeing to accept acting as an expert in such a case?

2. *Informed Consent*: Roger is a forensic psychologist appointed by a court to assess the mental status of a woman accused of infanticide. One of the psychological tests that Roger wants to administer suggests that the subject should not be told about the nature of the test. Roger asks you whether it is ethical to administer a psychological test without fully disclosing the nature of the test to the subject. The test itself is not risky, and the results are more credible if the client does not have too much information about the nature of the test prior to taking it. How would you advise Roger, and why? What does your professional code of ethics say about this situation?

3. *The Whole Truth?* Assume you are presenting expert evidence to the court concerning the effectiveness of harm reduction therapy for people addicted to nicotine. You provide evidence supporting your opinion, but you do not have a chance to discuss limitations of the research upon which you are relying (e.g., small sample size, lack of a control group, or insufficient long-term follow-up). Neither attorney nor the judge asks specifically about the limitations. At the close of your testimony, an attorney asks if there is anything else you would like to add to your testimony before stepping down. Should you describe the limitations of the research you have

relied on? Why or why not? What does your professional code of ethics say about this issue?

4. *Impugning a Colleague:* An attorney hires you as a consultant for an upcoming mental health status hearing. The attorney represents a client who is currently being held involuntarily in a mental health facility. The attorney asks you to provide any "dirt" you have on the psychiatrist at the mental health facility, so the attorney can impugn his credibility at the upcoming hearing. Which, if any, of the following types of evidence would you be willing to provide (assume you believe each of the following statements to be true):

a. The psychiatrist is having an affair with one of the nurses at the psychiatric facility.

b. The psychiatrist has a drinking problem, although this problem is not directly affecting the quality of care received by clients.

c. The psychiatrist has been censured by his licensing board for defrauding private insurance companies (e.g., by submitting claims for clients who did not meet the eligibility criteria for insurance reimbursement).

d. The psychiatrist's website suggests he is qualified to perform psychometric testing, but you know that he does not possess the appropriate training or qualifications.

Explain your reasons for providing or withholding such information, with reference to your profession's code of ethics. Remember, the hiring attorney is asking you for the information, not a court. What difference would it make if you were asked these questions on the witness stand, rather than in private consultations with an attorney?

5. *Faulty Testimony:* For each of the following scenarios, identify which of the following faults the expert witness has exhibited: providing information beyond her area of expertise, providing expert information without a valid research basis, allowing bias to influence her opinion, engaging in speculation of facts, or not following a generally accepted procedure for conducting research or an assessment. Describe what the expert would need to do in order to testify in an honest, objective manner, based on valid research and facts.

a. Walter has strong religious convictions regarding the importance of children being raised by a father and a mother who are legally married. During an adoption study, Walter recommends that a certain couple be rejected as adoptive parents because they are living together, but not legally married.

b. Theresa, a family counselor, is testifying at a hearing to determine whether a potentially violent man should be civilly committed into a locked mental health facility. Theresa testifies that the client will not pose a significant risk if he would only take his antipsychotic medications.

    c. Elida, a psychometrist, does not like the standard personality tests that are used by other psychometrists. When she conducts forensic evaluations, she uses a personality test that she has developed. She truly believes the test is valid and reliable, although she has not confirmed these beliefs through research.

    d. Roger prepares a victim impact statement for a criminal trial by interviewing the victim over the telephone. His agency's policy requires him to meet the victim in person. Due to time restrictions and a high caseload, Roger did not have time to schedule an in-person meeting. Roger honestly believes the telephone interview was sufficient.

    6. *Metaphors*: Witnesses may use metaphors to help explain information by relating an analogous idea or story. At their best, metaphors are interesting, relevant, and easily accessible to the intended audience. Try constructing metaphors to explain complex terms to a judge or jury in the following circumstances.

    a. In a child protection case, you are trying to explain how one of the parents exhibits Münchausen syndrome, fabricating physical illness in order to obtain attention.

    b. In the criminal trial of a defendant with alcoholism, you are trying to explain the difference between blacking out and passing out.

    c. In a malpractice lawsuit against a psychotherapist whose client burned down city hall, you are testifying about the benefits and risks of paradoxical interventions.

    7. *Cross-Examination Critique:* Review the following transcript of the cross-examination of an expert witness. Critique each of the witness's responses, indicating strengths and limitations. For each limitation, revise the response to correct the problems you identified. Examples of strengths include witness responses that come across as: clear, confident, concise, nondefensive, respectful, honest, technically accurate, interesting, or having a sound factual basis provided to support an opinion. Examples of limitations include responses that come across as: unclear, defensive, arrogant, disrespectful, dishonest, inaccurate, dull, having no factual basis for opinions, and speculating rather than objectively knowing. The scenario is a civil lawsuit in which Abdul is suing Roger for injuries suffered in a fight. Abdul alleges that Roger initiated the fight because of anti-Arab attitudes. Abdul also alleges that he was so traumatized by Roger that he is unable to work. Roger counters that Abdul is fabricating the traumatization and is perfectly able to work. Dr. Fell, the expert witness, has evaluated Abdul and has presented evidence that he is not malingering. The cross-examination by Roger's attorney, Ms. Wallace, begins below:

    ATTORNEY: In your earlier testimony, you stated that you received your PhD from Cloud Four University, a program that was rated in the bottom quartile of all psychology programs in the United States. Now I understand that most of your coursework was online and that your program was not accredited by the American Psychiatric Association.

WITNESS: Your question is confusing, Mr. Wallace. My PhD program was accredited, but not by the APA.

ATTORNEY: I'd like to ask some questions about how you tested Abdul for malingering. You said you used the Quingcon Malingering Instrument, or QMI. We've heard from other witnesses that QMI is no longer used by most forensic psychologists because of problems with reliability. So just how reliable would you say the QMI is?

WITNESS: Oh, it's very reliable. It's actually the most accurate tool available for measuring malingering.

ATTORNEY: What research are you relying on when you say the QMI is the most accurate measure?

WITNESS: It's not just my personal opinion. The company that developed the QMI has done its own studies to test reliability. I think the actual level of interrater reliability was a .70 correlation, which is perfectly acceptable within our discipline.

ATTORNEY: If I'm understanding you correctly, a .70 correlation means that different psychologists are likely to reach different conclusions 30% of the time. Hmm.

WITNESS: You're focusing on the negative. Different raters are likely to reach the same conclusions 70% of the time. Also, you should note that the content validity using Cronbach's coefficient alpha procedure establishes a reliability of $r = .98$.

ATTORNEY: Please help the jury understand what you mean by a Cronbach's coefficient alpha. It sounds like some sort of research psychobabble.

WITNESS: Basically, it is a mathematical calculation to determine the consistency of the questions within an instrument or test. The actual calculation would probably be meaningless for jurors who have not studied research statistics. As soon as I start mentioning alphas and chi's, it starts to sound like a bunch of Greek. But believe me, this is a generally accepted way to measure internal reliability of psychological instruments. It's all explained in my report.

ATTORNEY: OK, so you can't explain it in plain language. Let's move on. How much did Abdul's attorney pay you to testify today?

WITNESS: (*turning to the judge*) Your worship, Ma'am, that question is personal and irrelevant. Do I need to answer it?

JUDGE: Please answer the question.

WITNESS: My standard rate of pay for testifying is $325 per hour. My total pay for today will depend on how much time I spend in court.

ATTORNEY: So you won't be paid until after the attorney sees how well you have testified today.

WITNESS: (*initially in an agitated voice, then calmer*) What are you insinuating? As I'm sure you are aware, counselor, I am paid for my time. I testify in an honest, objective manner regardless of how much I am paid and when I am paid. My professional code of ethics requires me to testify truthfully. My pay is not contingent on what I say or how I say it.

ATTORNEY: Thank you. That's very helpful. (*turns to judge and winks*) Now I understand that Abdul's attorney met with you prior to trial in order to help you prepare and tell you how to testify.

WITNESS: That is correct. (*Smiles broadly and sincerely.*)

ATTORNEY: You mentioned that you diagnosed Abdul with posttraumatic stress disorder, or PTSD. Perhaps you could tell us about some of the weaknesses of the *Diagnostic and Statistical Manual,* which you used to make the diagnosis.

WITNESS: The DSM is like the Bible for the mental health professions. It is not perfect, but we have a lot of faith in it.

ATTORNEY: Do you recognize Dr. John P. Wilson as an authority on PTSD?

WITNESS: No, I don't. I know he has done some research in the area, but I have not read it.

ATTORNEY: So you haven't read his textbook on assessing psychological trauma, one of the most authoritative textbooks on the subject. Now, you say that you have extensive training on PTSD, but you don't have any specific training on PTSD among Arab Americans.

WITNESS: PTSD is PTSD. It doesn't differ from one ethnic group to another.

ATTORNEY: So you use a colorblind approach to psychiatric diagnosis.

WITNESS: No, I use the correct approach. Do you have any other questions?

ATTORNEY: One final question. Have you ever donated money to support an Arab cause or charity?

WITNESS: Yes, I have supported many Arab charities. I have also supported many African, Asian, European, and American charities. No disrespect, but what's your point?

8. *Mitigation:* Assume that you have been asked to testify as an expert in the sentencing phase of a capital murder trial. What do your state laws say in regard to *mitigating factors* that a court may consider when determining capital

punishment? (If your state does not permit capital punishment, you may do this exercise based on the laws of another state)

    a. How would you gather information in order to support your testimony regarding mitigating factors?

    b. What are your personal and professional views on capital punishment?

    c. What practical and clinical challenges may arise when you are gathering information, writing your report, or testifying in court? How would you manage each of these challenges?

CHAPTER 8

    1. *Attesting*: In an affidavit, a witness may attest to facts that he or she has directly observed. In general, witnesses should avoid attesting to information provided to them from other sources.[3] Review the following statements from the affidavit of a cognitive-behavioral therapist. Identify which statements are based on firsthand observations and which statements are based on secondhand information.

    a. I provided Ahmad with six sessions of cognitive-behavioral therapy.

    b. Between sessions, Ahmad would practice the positive self-messages that we introduced during therapy.

    c. After the sixth session, I discovered that Ahmad was becoming more abusive to his wife, not less.

    d. I discontinued therapy because I believed that it was not providing the intended effects.

    2. *Interview with a Professional*: Identify a type of forensic report that you may need to write in your future practice (e.g., a child protection worker's assessment of a sexual abuse situation, a parole officer's report on a prisoner applying for parole, a mental health professional's report on a suicidal client for the purposes of determining whether to involuntarily commit the client, or a human rights worker's report on alleged discrimination against a person seeking redress against an employer). Identify a professional in your community who has expertise in writing this type of report. Arrange for a meeting with this professional for the purposes of discussing how the professional gathers information and writes forensic reports. Ask for a copy of the template (headings) that the professional uses for reports. Also, ask whether the professional can share a copy of an actual report that is already on public record. After your meeting with the professional, critique the strengths and limitations of the template and/or actual report.

    3. *Actuarial versus Clinical Predictions*: Spencer has raped 14 women. A court is considering whether to declare Spencer a "dangerous sex offender." Your

---

[3]The witness may attest, "X told me that ... and I verily believe...." However, the truth of this information can easily be challenged.

role is to provide evidence concerning Spencer's risk of reoffending. What is the difference between an actuarial prediction and a clinical prediction? Which should you include in your report to the court, and why? Identify a tool that has demonstrated levels of validity and reliability, and is valid for the specific purpose of this judicial proceeding.

CHAPTER 9

1. *Malpractice in Adoption*: Mr. and Ms. Santana adopted an infant, Ella, in a closed adoption process. They did not have access to Ella's medical records, although they asked Amanda, the adoption worker, a number of questions, including whether the mother was using drugs or alcohol during pregnancy or had a history of mental health problems. Amanda responded that the mother did not have any history of substance abuse or mental illness. As Ella grew older, many developmental and learning issues arose. Mr. and Ms. Santana suspected these problems were related to medical information that Ella failed to disclose. In order to sue Amanda or her agency for malpractice, what would the Santanas need to prove? What is the difference between suing for malpractice (negligence) and suing for fraudulent misrepresentations?

2. *Suit by a Third Party*: Harriet is a psychologist who has been providing psychotherapy for Renita. Through the use of hypnotherapy, Harriet helps Renita recover a memory of childhood sexual abuse by her father, Brad. Renita discloses the abuse to various family members, causing great angst and division within the family. Some family members cut their ties with Brad, believing he is a sexual molester. Brad denies ever abusing Renita and sues Harriet for malpractice. What would Brad have to prove in order to be successful in his lawsuit? Given the facts as provided above, do you think Harriet is liable for malpractice? Why or why not?

3. *Faulty Referral*: A psychologist named Dr. Waters referred a client named Vern to a cognitive-behavioral therapist for help with depression. Vern's depression was more severe than Dr. Waters suspected, and Vern was not responsive to cognitive-behavioral therapy. Vern committed suicide after just 2 weeks of cognitive-behavioral therapy. Vern's family sued Dr. Waters for malpractice. Describe the roles that an independent psychologist hired by the family's attorney might play in the lawsuit against Dr. Waters.

4. *Risk Management*: Consider each of the following scenarios and identify what risk management strategies the clinician could have used in order to reduce the risk of being sued for malpractice:

   a. Polly-Anna is a parenting coordinator who has been helping Xavier and Roberta implement the custody and access order with respect to their son, Juan. One day, Xavier called Polly-Anna, expressing grave distress that Roberta was not allowing him to pick up Juan to take him to Mexico for a holiday. Roberta had previously agreed to this trip, but now claims that Xavier is planning to move to Mexico, keeping Juan with him. Polly-Anna agrees to meet Xavier and Roberta at Roberta's house to help them resolve this standoff. When Polly-Anna arrives, she asks Juan to play in the backyard so the adults can talk. During a heated session, Xavier excuses himself to go to the bathroom. Moments later, Roberta notices that Xavier has snuck out the back door and has absconded with Juan. Roberta threatens to sue Polly-Anna for malpractice, claiming it is her fault that Xavier abducted Juan.

b. Winnifred works for a family counseling agency that bills Medicare for services provided to its elderly clients. One day, Winnifred meets a client, Sanford, for an intake interview. In order to provide him with services, agency policy requires Winnifred to provide him with a clinical diagnosis during the first meeting. At the end of the meeting, Winnifred informs her supervisor that she was unable to determine Sanford's diagnosis because he was not very verbal. The supervisor tells Winnifred to use "adjustment disorder as his diagnosis because that covers just about anything." Winnifred reluctantly complies, fearing that she may be reprimanded if she does not comply. When Sanford finds out he has been labeled with "adjustment disorder" he sues Winnifred for malpractice and fraud, claiming she intentionally provided an inappropriate diagnosis in order to benefit herself and her agency.

5. *Components of Malpractice*: Select either Polly-Anna's case or Winnifred's case from Exercise 4. Analyze whether each of the components of malpractice are present. What would the client have to prove in terms of duty of care, breach of the duty, damages caused, and proximate link between the breach and the damages?

6. *Legal and Ethical Advice*: How much does it cost to obtain legal and ethical advice? Identify possible sources of free legal and ethical information and consultation. Check your professional association's website or call them to see whether they offer free consultations, as well as online information related to ethics and malpractice. Contact your liability insurance company or a company that insures practitioners in your profession. Ask about the types of information or consultation they provide to contract holders who have concerns related to malpractice. Finally, contact the lawyer referral service offered by the bar association of your state (*apps.americanbar.org/legalservices/lris/directory*). Ask the referral service for the names and contact information of attorneys in your locality who specialize in malpractice lawsuits. Find out the hourly rate, retainer fee, and an estimate of the total cost of defending a malpractice claim.

7. *Mandated Dual Relationship*: Keyon has been providing couple counseling to Yolanda and Quincy. Quincy was recently sent to drug court in relation

to a crime related to his drug use. When the judge discovered that Quincy was already seeing Keyon for counseling, the judge ordered Quincy to engage in 6 weeks of drug counseling with Keyon. According to the court order, Keyon is to provide the court with a report on Quincy's progress at the end of 6 weeks. Although Quincy originally agreed with the court order, Keyon is concerned. One the one hand, Keyon does not want to be in contempt of court for not following a court order. On the other hand, Keyon is concerned that providing couple counseling and individual drug counseling puts him in a dual relationship with Quincy. What should Keyon do, and why? Apply your own profession's code of ethics to your analysis.

CHAPTER 10

1. *Oral Deposition*: Review the following excerpt of an oral deposition and critique it in relation to the following factors: clarity, professional language, factual observations separated from opinions, objectivity/bias, and responding directly to the question. How might each of these mistakes hurt the clinician or the client in court? The case involves a lawsuit against a state attorney's office. The plaintiffs claim that the State Attorney's office has intentionally violated the rights of people charged with criminal offenses in order to convict people who were later determined to be innocent. The clinician worked for the State Attorney's office, providing consultation on how to interview suspects.

ATTORNEY: What are your professional qualifications?

CLINICIAN [deponent]: I have a PhD in forensic psychology from the University of Perplexia. I have completed a certification in forensic investigations with the State Attorney's office. In the 45 cases where I have presented forensic testimony, we have been able to convict the accused person in 44 of those cases.

ATTORNEY: Please explain your role with the State Attorney's office.

CLINICIAN: My primary role is to provide consultation to the legal team on how to interrogate people charged with felony offences. I provide group and individual training, including role-plays to teach the use of particular skills.

ATTORNEY: So your role is to help the State Attorney's office convict suspects?

CLINICIAN: Basically, yes.

ATTORNEY: When did you first become aware of any violations of rights within the State Attorney's office?

CLINICIAN: When the case hit the news. I think I was watching one of the cable news networks when I noticed that we were being investigated. Frankly, I was shocked.

ATTORNEY: In your training courses, do you ever suggest that the attorneys should use any forms of deception to elicit admissions of guilt?

CLINICIAN: Not exactly. I don't advocate any form of lying. In some instances, the investigators are told not to fully disclose everything they know about the case. That's not deception.

ATTORNEY: What is the difference between lying and withholding important information?

CLINICIAN: You're not understanding what I am trying to say. It's just that sometimes the investigators need to play dumb, you know, allow the suspect to tell the story.

ATTORNEY: If a suspect is not fully honest with an investigator, what types of pressure are investigators allowed to use?

CLINICIAN: We don't do torture, if that's what you mean. Sometimes, investigators raise their voices, or ask questions in a very assertive manner. We review videos on a regular basis to make sure that the investigators stay within the bounds of appropriateness. And no waterboarding . . .

ATTORNEY: Do you think that the State Attorney's office should be immune from civil lawsuits?

CLINICIAN: Yes, we need the protection of immunity in order to do our jobs and keep the community safe.

2. *Admission*: Regis is responding to written interrogatories when he comes across a particularly challenging question: "Do you admit that you told the client that Native Americans have lower rates of success than other Americans when it comes to alcohol addiction treatment?" Regis did tell her something to this effect. He had intended to provide the client with factual information. He is concerned that answering, "Yes," to this question is tantamount to admitting that he is biased or that he was showing disrespect to the client, who is Native American. What ethical and legal issues does this situation raise for Regis? What should Regis do before he responds to the interrogatory?

3. *Translated Sessions*: Assume that you have been working with a client who speaks Spanish, so your counseling sessions were conducted with the aid of a Spanish–English interpreter. During depositions, an attorney asks, "Isn't it true that you do not speak Spanish? Isn't it true that you had to rely solely on the interpreter to understand what the client was saying?" Assume that both of these statements are essentially true. During depositions, should you simply answer "Yes" to each question, or should you provide additional information? If so, what additional information should you provide?

4. *Conflict of Interest*: Betty, a clinical psychologist, receives a list of questions to answer for the interrogatories in an upcoming malpractice trial against another psychologist. The attorney for this psychologist plans to call Betty to testify that the psychologist acted in a prudent, ethical manner. Upon receiving the interrogatory questions, Betty realizes that the attorney for the plaintiff (client) is Betty's first cousin and good friend. What is the potential conflict of interest that arises in this situation, and how should Betty respond to these concerns? State any assumptions or contextual factors that may affect your decision.

5. *Willful Exclusion*: A custody evaluator named Harold has been asked to provide a list of psychological tests that he plans to rely on at trial. The attorney asks him not to include a particular instrument that measures parent–child attachment because that instrument has been successfully challenged as unreliable in previous trials. Harold believes the attachment instrument is reliable. How should Harold deal with the attorney's request to exclude the instrument? Assume that this is not the only instrument that Harold wants to use, but that he believes it contributes to his ability to make sound custody recommendations.

6. *Professional Review Hearing*: Zelda is a psychologist who has been providing psychotherapy to Eunice, a woman who experiences delusions of grandeur. Unbeknownst to Zelda, Eunice's son, Clarence, attends the same school as Zelda's son, Don. Don invites Clarence to a sleepover at his house. When Zelda asks Clarence about his family, she discovers his mother is her client, Eunice. Zelda prohibits Don from being friends with Clarence and to avoid all contact with him. Clarence tells his mother, who becomes furious and lodges a professional complaint against Zelda for breach of confidentiality and engaging in dual relationships. What steps should Zelda take to prepare for a professional review hearing? What types of evidence should she try to gather to support herself in this case? Which of the following types of information should she disclose at the hearing, and which should she keep confidential? Provide reasons for each of your answers:

   a. Eunice experiences delusions of grandeur.

   b. When Don invited Clarence to a sleepover, Zelda did not know that Clarence's mother was one of her clients.

   c. Zelda did not tell Don or Clarence that Eunice was a client.

   d. Eunice has not paid for her last session and Zelda has therefore terminated services.

If Eunice's complaint went to mediation rather than adjudication, what would Zelda need to do in order to prepare for effective participation in this collaborative process?

7. *Hoarding*: Brandy loves cats. In fact, she has 26 cats. She also hoards. Her house is filled with so much furniture and so many tchotchkes that it is difficult to move. Walter is a clinician who works for the Department of Health. His role

is to investigate situations where a person's living conditions pose a health risk to the person and/or the community. When Walter investigates Brandy's situation, he concludes that her house is unsanitary and that the state needs to intervene in order to protect Brandy's health. Brandy sues Walter for malpractice, claiming that his investigation was based on bias, improper investigation methods, and sloppy interviewing. In your state, would Walter be immune from such a lawsuit? What would Brandy have to prove in order to be able to sue him successfully?

RESOURCES

WEBSITES FOR LEGAL RESEARCH[1]

Campus Research Law: *west.thomson.com/westlaw/campus-research/default.aspx*

Code of Federal Regulations: *www.gpoaccess.gov/cfr/index.html*

Criminology: A SAGE Full-Text Collection: *www.sagepub.com/librarians/collections/crim.sp*

Index to Legal Periodicals: *www.hwwilson.com/databases/Legal.htm*

Legal Information Institute (LII): *www.law.cornell.edu*

LegalTrac: *www.jenkinslaw.org/collection/legaltrac.php*

LexisNexis Academic: *www.lexisnexis.com/hottopics/lnacademic*

MegaLaw.com: *www.megalaw.com*

Mental Health Law (including Blog re ethical dilemmas): *www.mentalhealthlaw.us*

ProQuest Criminal Justice: *www.proquest.com/en-US/catalogs/databases/detail/pq_criminal_justice.shtml*

State Government Websites[2]: *www.usa.gov/Agencies/State_and_Territories.shtml*

Thomas – Legislative Information from the Library of Congress: *thomas.loc.gov*

United States Department of Justice: *www.usdoj.gov*

Westlaw: *www.westlaw.com*

---

[1]Includes fee-based and institutional subscriptions. My favorite free-access website for legal research is Legal Information Institute.

[2]Provides links to the websites of each state. From state website, search for relevant statutes.

FORENSIC JOURNALS

Criminal Justice and Behavior
Criminology: An International Journal
Family Court Review
International Journal of Law and Psychiatry
Journal of Forensic Psychiatry and Psychology
Journal of Forensic Psychology Practice
Journal of Forensic Social Work
Journal of Research in Crime and Delinquency
Law and Human Behavior
Law and Psychology Review
Legal and Criminological Psychology
Psychology, Crime, and Law
Psychology, Public Policy, and the Law

PROFESSIONAL ASSOCIATIONS
WITH INTEREST IN FORENSIC PRACTICE

American Academy of Psychiatry and the Law: *www.aapl.org*
American Bar Association: *www.abanet.org*
American Board of Forensic Psychology: *abfp.com*
American Psychology Law Society: *ww.ap-ls.org*
American Society of Trial Consultants: *www.astcweb.org/public/index.cfm*
Association of Family and Conciliation Courts: *www.afccnet.org*
Child Welfare League of America: *www.cwla.org*
National Council on Crime and Delinquency: *www.nccd-crc.org*
National Institute of Justice – Restorative Justice: nij.gov/topics/courts/restorative-justice/welcome.htm
National Organization for Forensic Social Work: *www.nofsw.org*

REFERENCES

Alcoholics Anonymous. (n.d.). *Serenity prayer.* Retrieved from *www.aahistory.com/prayer.html*

Alternative Dispute Resolution Act. (1998). 28 United States Code 44. Retrieved from *www.gpo.gov/fdsys/pkg/BILLS-105hr3528enr/pdf/BILLS-105hr3528enr.pdf*

American Bar Association (ABA). (2010). Model rules of professional conduct. Retrieved from *www.abanet.org/cpr/mrpc/mrpc_toc.html*

American Bar Association Section on Legal Education. (2011). Standards and rules of procedure for approval of law schools. Retrieved from *www.americanbar.org/groups/legal_education/resources/standards.html*

American Bar Association. (n.d.). Statutory summary charts (Domestic violence resources). Retrieved from *www.americanbar.org/groups/domestic_violence/resources/statutory_summary_charts.html*

American Psychiatric Association. (2013). *Diagnostic and statistical manual of mental disorders* (5th ed.). Arlington, VA: Author. (See *www.dsm5.org*)

American Psychological Association (APA). (2010). Ethical principles of psychologists and code of conduct. Retrieved from *www.apa.org/ethics/code/index.aspx*

Association of Family and Conciliation Courts (AFCC). (2000). Model standards of practice for family and divorce mediation. Retrieved from *www.afccnet.org/Portals/0/PublicDocuments/CEFCP/ModelStandardsOfPracticeForFamilyAndDivorceMediation.pdf*

Association of Family and Conciliation Courts (AFCC). (2006). Model standards of practice for child custody evaluation. Retrieved from *www.afccnet.org/Portals/0/ModelStdsChildCustodyEvalSept2006.pdf*

Austin, W. G. (2001). Partner violence and risk assessment in child custody evaluations. *Family Court Review, 39*(4), 483–496.

Bahadur, R. (2009). Electronic discovery, informational privacy, Facebook, and utopian civil justice. *Mississippi Law Journal, 79,* 317–369.

Barber, J., Shlonsky, A., Black, T., Goodman, D., & Trocmé, N. (2008). Reliability and predictive validity of a risk assessment tool. *Journal of Public Child Welfare*, 2(2) 173–195.

Barrett, K., & George, W. H. (2005). *Race, culture, psychology, and law*. San Francisco: Sage.

Barsky, A. E. (2007a). *Conflict resolution for the helping professions* (2nd ed.). Belmont, CA: Brooks/Cole.

Barsky. A. E. (2007b). Mediative evaluations: The pros and perils of blending roles. *Family Court Review*, 45(4), 560–572.

Barsky, A. E. (2009). Social work research and the law: How LGBT research can be structured and used to affect judicial decisions. In W. Meezan & J. I. Martin (Eds.), *Research methods with gay, lesbian, bisexual, and transgender populations* (pp. 372–401). New York: Routledge.

Barsky, A. E. (2010). *Ethics and values in social work: An integrated approach for a comprehensive curriculum*. New York: Oxford University Press.

Bartol, C., & Bartol, A. M. (2008). *Introduction to forensic psychology: Research and application* (2nd ed.). San Francisco: Sage.

Bernstein, B. E., & Hartsell, T. L. (2008). *The portable ethicist for mental health professionals: An A to Z guide to responsible practice, with HIPAA update* (2nd ed.). Hoboken, NJ: Wiley.

Bernstein, B. E., & Hartsell, T. L. (2004). *The portable lawyer for mental health professionals: An A to Z guide to protecting your clients, your practice, and yourself* (2nd ed.). Hoboken, NJ: Wiley.

Bottoms, B. L., Najdowski, C. J., & Goodman, G. S. (Eds.). (2009). *Children as victims, witnesses, and offenders: Psychological science and the law*. New York: Guilford Press.

Boynton v. Burglass. (1991). 590 So.2d 446 (FL Dist. Ct. App.).

Braaten, E. (2007). *The child clinician's report-writing handbook*. New York: Guilford Press.

Brayne, H., & Carr, H. (2005). *Law for social workers*. New York: Oxford University Press.

Brewer, N., & Williams, K. P. (2005). *Psychology and law: An empirical perspective*. New York: Guilford Press.

Brodsky, S. L. (1991). *Testifying in court: Guidelines and maxims for the expert witness*. Washington, DC: American Psychological Association Books.

Brodsky, S. L. (2004). *Coping with cross-examination*. Washington, DC: American Psychological Association.

Brodsky, S. L. (2009). *Principles and practice of trial consultation*. New York: Guilford Press.

Brodsky, S. L., Griffin, M. P., & Cramer, R. J. (2010). The witness credibility scale: An outcome measure for expert witness research. *Behavioral Sciences and the Law*, 28(6), 892–907.

Brodsky, S. L., & Terrell, J. J. (2011). Testifying about mitigation: When social workers and other mental health professionals face aggressive cross-examination. *Journal of Forensic Social Work*, 1, 73–81.

Bruck, M., & Ceci, S. J. (2009). Reliability of child witnesses' reports. In J. Skeem,

K. S. Douglas, & S. O. Lilienfeld (Eds.), *Psychological science in the court-room* (pp. 149–171). New York: Guilford Press.

Bruck, M., Ceci, S. J., & Francoeur, E. (1999). The accuracy of mother's memories of conversations with their preschool children. *Journal of Experimental Psychology: Applied, 5*(1), 89–106.

Bureau of Justice Assistance. (n.d.). Retrieved from *www.ojp.usdoj.gov/BJA*

Bush, S. S., Connell, M. A., & Denney, R. L. (2006). *Ethical practice in forensic psychology: A systematic model for decision making.* Washington, DC: American Psychiatric Association.

Butters, R. P., & Vaughan-Eden, V. (2011). Forensic social work ethics. *Journal of Forensic Social Work, 1,* 61–72.

Ceci, S. J., & Bruck, M. (2006). Children's suggestibility: Characteristics and mechanisms. *Advances in Child Development and Behavior, 34,* 247–281.

Cheatham v. Rogers. (1992). 824 S.W. 2d 231; 55 Texas Bar J. 1081 (12th Texas Court of Appeals).

Child Welfare Information Gateway. (n.d.). Retrieved from *www.childwelfare. gov*

Church, W. T., Sun, F., & Li, X. (2011). Attitudes toward the treatment of sex offenders: A SEM Analysis. *Journal of Forensic Social Work, 1,* 82–95.

Clark, Eric Michael v. Arizona. (2006)[0]. U.S. Supreme Court No. 05-5966. Retrieved from *www.law.cornell.edu/supct/html/05-5966.ZO.html*

Clark, M. C. (2010). Narrative learning: Its contours and its possibilities. *New Directions for Adult and Continuing Education, 126,* 3–11.

CogniSyst. (2008).Computerized assessment of response bias. Retrieved from www.cognisyst.com/carb-detail.htm

Colarossi, L., & Forgey, M. A. (2006). Evaluation study of an interdisciplinary social work and law curriculum for domestic violence. *Journal of Social Work Education, 42*(2), 307–323.

Committee on Ethical Guidelines for Forensic Psychologists. (CEGFP). (2011). Specialty guidelines for forensic psychologists (SGFP). Retrieved from *www. ap-ls.org/aboutpsychlaw/SGFP_Final_Approved_2011.pdf.* Some professional practice guidelines (CEGFP, 1991) specifically warn against using codes or shorthand that cannot be understood by others reviewing your notes.

Committee on Professional Practice and Standards. (1998). *Guidelines for psychological evaluations in child protection matters.* Washington, DC: American Psychological Association. Retrieved from *www.psychtech.co.il/Articles/ Guidelines_for_Psychological_Evaluations_in_Child_Protection_Matters. htm*

Commons, M. L., Gutheil, T. G., & Hilliard, J. T. (2010). On humanizing the expert witness: A proposed narrative approach to expert qualification. *Journal of the American Academy of Psychiatry and the Law, 38*(3), 302–304.

Comprehensive Crime Control Act (1984). 18 U.S.C. § 17, Insanity Defense, Retrieved from *www.law.cornell.edu/uscode/18/17.shtml*

Corey, G., Corey, M. S., & Callanan, P. (2011). *Issues and ethics in the helping professions* (8th ed.). Belmont, CA: Brooks/Cole.

Corey, G. (2009). *Theory and practice of counseling and psychotherapy* (8th ed.). Belmont, CA: Brooks/Cole.

Cramer, R. J., Adams, D. D., & Brodsky, S. L. (2009). Jury selection in child sex abuse trials: A case analysis. *Journal of Child Sexual Abuse, 18*(2), 190–205.

Cramer, R. J., Neal, T. M. S., DeCoster, J., & Brodsky, D. L. (2010). Witness self-efficacy: Development and validation of the construct. *Behavioral Sciences and the Law, 28*(6), 784–800.

Crawford v. Washington. (2004). 541 U.S. 36. Retrieved from *www.law.cornell. edu/supct/html/02-9410.ZO.html*

Crimes and Criminal Procedure. (2010). Obstruction of Justice, U.S. Code Title 18, Part I, Chapter 73. Retrieved from *www.law.cornell.edu/uscode/18/usc_ sup_01_18_10_I_20_73.html*

Cross, T. P., Jones, L. M., Walsh, W. A., Simone, M., & Kolko, D. (2007). Child forensic interviewing in children's advocacy centers: Empirical data on a practice model. *Child Abuse and Neglect, 31,* 1031–1052.

Crosson-Tower, C. (2009). *Exploring child welfare: A practice perspective.* Upper Saddle River, NJ: Pearson.

Cunningham, A., & Stevens, L. (2011). *Helping a child be a witness in court: 101 things to know, say, and do.* London, ON, Canada: Center for Children and Families in the Justice System (*www.lfcc.on.ca*).

Daicoff, S. (2006). Law as a healing profession: The comprehensive law movement. *Pepperdine Law Review, 6,* 1. Retrieved from *cdn.law.ucla.edu/SiteCollec-tionDocuments/workshops%20and%20colloquia/clinical%20programs/ susan%20daicoff.pdf*

Daubert v. Merell Dow Pharmaceuticals, Inc. (1993). 113 S. Ct. 2786. Retrieved from *www.law.cornell.edu/supct/html/92-102.ZO.html*

Denzin, N. K., & Lincoln, Y. S. (2011). *The SAGE handbook of qualitative research* (4th ed.). New York: Sage.

Dickson, D. T. (1995). *Law in the health and human services.* New York: Free Press.

Dolgoff, R., Loewenberg, F. M., & Harrington, D. (2009). *Ethical decisions for social work practice* (8th ed.). Belmont, CA: Brooks/Cole.

Drug Enforcement Administration. (2011). Controlled substance schedules. Retrieved from *www.deadiversion.usdoj.gov/schedules*

Family Educational Rights and Privacy Act. (2011). 20 U.S.C. § 1232g; 34 CFR Part 99. Retrieved from *www.ed.gov/policy/gen/guid/fpco/ferpa/index.html*

Federal Judicial Center (2000). *Reference guide on scientific evidence* (2nd ed.). Retrieved from *www.fjc.gov/public/pdf.nsf/lookup/sciman00.pdf/$file/sci-man00.pdf*

Federal Psychotherapy-Patient Privilege. (n.d.). Retrieved from *jaffee-redmond. org/index.htm*

Federal Rules of Civil Procedure. (2010). Retrieved from *www.law.cornell.edu/ rules/frcp/index.html#chapter_v*

Federal Rules of Evidence. (2010). Retrieved from *www.law.cornell.edu/rules/fre/ rules.htm*

Fernandez, K., Davis, K. M., Conroy, M. A., & Boccaccini, M. T. (2009). A model for training graduate psychology students to become legally informed clinicians. *Journal of Forensic Psychology Practice, 9*(1), 57–69.

Fitzgerald v. Commonwealth. (2007). Record No. 061361 (Supreme Court of

Virginia). Retrieved from *caselaw.findlaw.com/va-supreme-court/1239065. html*

Florida Department of Children and Families vs. In re: Matter of Adoption of X.X.G. and N.R.G. (2010). Third District Court of Appeal, Florida. Retrieved from *www.3dca.flcourts.org/Opinions/3D08-3044.pdf*

Frye v. United States. (1923). 293 F. 1013 (D.C. Cir.).

Fulghum, R. (1988). *All I really need to know I learned in kindergarten: Uncommon thoughts on common things.* New York: Villard Books.

Good, A. (2009). Cultural evidence in courts of law. In M. Engelke (Ed.), *The objects of evidence: Anthropological approaches to the production of knowledge* (pp. 44–57). San Francisco: Wiley-Blackwell.

Gould, J. W. (2006). *Conducting scientifically crafted child custody evaluations* (2nd ed.). Thousand Oaks, CA: Sage.

Gould, J. W., & Martindale, D. A. (2009). *The art and science of child custody evaluations.* New York: Guilford Press.

Greene v. Camreta. (2009). United States Court of Appeals, 9th District, No. 06-35333. Retrieved from *www.ca9.uscourts.gov/datastore/opinions /2009/12/10/06-35333.pdf*

Greenfield, D. P., & Gottschalk, J. A. (2009). *Writing forensic reports: A guide to mental health professionals.* New York: Springer.

Greenberg, S., & Shuman, D. (1997). Irreconcilable conflict between therapeutic and forensic roles. *Professional Psychology: Research and Practice, 28,* 50–57.

Gutheil, T. G., & Brodsky, A. (2008). *Preventing boundary violations in clinical practice.* New York: Guilford Press.

Hays, J. R., McPherson, R. & Hansen, V. (2010). *Texas law for the social worker: A sourcebook.* Houston, TX: Bayou Publishing.

Happy Hospitalist. (2007). If you didn't document it, it didn't happen. Retrieved from *thehappyhospitalist.blogspot.com/2007/11/if-you-didnt-document-it-it-didnt_27.html*

Health Insurance Portability and Accountability Act (HIPAA). (1996). Retrieved from *www.cms.hhs.gov/hipaaGenInfo*

Health Resources and Services Administration. (n.d.). Health centers. Retrieved from *bphc.hrsa.gov/ftca/healthcenters/index.html*

Heilbronner, R. L. (Ed.) (2005). *Forensic neuropsychology casebook.* New York: Guilford Press.

Heilbrun, K., Matteo, D., Marczyk, G., & Goldstein, A. M. (2008). Standards of practice and care in forensic mental health assessment. *Psychology, Public Policy, and Law, 14*(1), 1–26.

Ho, H. L. (2003/2004). The legitimacy of medieval proof. *Journal of Law and Religion, 19,* 259-298.

Hunt, D. E. (2001). *Beginning with ourselves.* Cambridge, MA: Brookline Books.

Israel, A. B. (2011). *Using the law: Practical decision making in mental health.* Chicago Lyceum.

Ivey, A., Ivey, M. B., & Zalaquett, C. P. (2010). *Intentional interviewing and counseling: Facilitating client development in a multicultural society* (7th ed.). Belmont, CA: Brooks/Cole.

Jacob, S., & Powers, K. E. (2009). Privileged communication in the school psychologist–client relationship. *Psychology in the Schools, 46*(4), 307–318.

Jaffee v. Redmond. (1996). United States Supreme Court. Retrieved from *jaffee-redmond.org/cases/jr-opin.htm*

James, K. (2010). How to present yourself in court to be optimally likeable and persuasive. *The Jury Expert, 22*(6), 1–6. Retrieved from *www.astcweb.org/public/publication/documents/JamesNov2010Vol22Num6.pdf*

Jenkins v. United States. (1962). 307 F.2d 637. Retrieved from *openjurist.org/307/f2d/637*

Kagle, J. D., & Kopels, S. (2008). *Social work records.* Long Grove, IL: Graveland.

Kansas v. Colorado (2009). United States Supreme Court. Retrieved from *www.supremecourt.gov/opinions/08pdf/105orig.pdf*

Kirkland, K., & Kirkland, K. L. (2001). Frequency of child custody evaluation complaints to state psychology licensing boards: A survey of ASPPB member boards. *Professional Psychology: Research and Practice, 41*(2), 71–76.

Kohn, L. S. (2003). Barriers to reliable credibility assessments: Domestic violence victim-witnesses. *Journal of Gender, Social Policy, and the Law, 11*(2), 733–748.

Kolodinsky, J. (2010). So you want to be an expert witness? *Journal of Consumer Affairs, 44*(3), 607–610.

Koocher, G. P., Norcross, J. C., & Hill, S. S. (Eds.). (2004). *Psychologist's desk reference.* New York: Oxford University Press.

Krimsky, S. (2005). The weight of scientific evidence in policy and law. *Journal of Public Health, 95,* 129–136.

Kumho Tire Co. v. Carmichael. (1999) 526 U.S. 137; 131 F.3d 1433. Retrieved from *www.law.cornell.edu/supct/html/97-1709.ZS.html*

Lamb, M. E., Orbach, Y., Sternberg, K. J., Hershkowitz, I., & Horowitz, D. (2000). Accuracy of investigators' verbatim notes of their forensic interviews with alleged child abuse victims. *Law and Human Behavior, 24*(6), 699–708.

Larson, B. A. (2008). *Personally intrusive cross-examination: How expert response styles and gender affect mock juror decisions* (unpublished dissertation). Tuscaloosa: Department of Psychology, University of Alabama.

Lavin, M., & Sales, B. D. (1998). Moral justifications for limits on expert testimony. In S. J. Ceci & H. Hembrooke (Eds.), *Expert witnesses in child abuse cases: What can and should be said in court* (pp. 59–81). Washington, DC: American Psychological Association.

Lawrence v. Texas. (2003). 539 U.S. 558. Retrieved from *www.law.cornell.edu/supct/html/02-102.ZD.html*

Lilienfeld, S. O., Wood, J. M., & Garb, H. N. (2000). The scientific status of projective techniques. *Psychological Science in the Public Interest, 1,* 27–66.

Loftus, E., & Ketcham, K. (1991). *Witness for the defense: The accused, the eyewitness, and the expert who puts memory on trial.* New York: St. Martin's Press.

Lynch, R. S., & Mitchell, J. (1995). Justice system advocacy: A must for NASW and the social work community. *Social Work, 40,* 9–11.

Madden, R. G. (2003). *Essential law for social workers.* New York: Columbia University Press.

Maschi, T., Bradley, C., & Ward, K. (2009). *Forensic social work: Psychosocial and legal issues in diverse practice settings*. New York: Springer.

Maschi, T., & Killian, M. L. (2011). The evolution of forensic social work in the United States: Implications for 21st-century practice. *Journal of Forensic Social Work, 1,* 8–36.

McAuliff, B. D., & Duckworth, T. D. (2010). I spy with my little eye: Jurors' detection of internal validity threats in expert evidence. *Law and Human Behavior, 34*(6), 489–500.

McQuiston-Surrett, D., & Saks, M. J. (2009). The testimony of forensic identification science: What expert witnesses say and what factfinders hear. *Law and Human Behavior, 33*(6), 436–453.

Melton, G. B., Petrila, J., Poythress, N.G., & Slobogin, C. (2007). *Psychological evaluations for the courts: A handbook for mental health professionals and lawyers* (3rd ed.). New York: Guilford Press.

Meyer, R. G., & Weaver, C. M. (2006). *Law and mental health: A case-based approach*. New York: Guilford Press.

Miller, K. (2009). Keeping secrets: Protecting privilege in pretrial research. *The Jury Expert, 21*(2), 26–32. Retrieved from *www.astcweb.org/public/publication/documents/TheJuryExpertMar2009Volume21No23.pdf*

Moser, R. S., & Barbrack, C. (n.d.). An urgent call: Treating psychologists are not expert witnesses. Retrieved from *www.practiceshapers.com/psychologists-are-not-expert-witnesses.htm*

Munson, C. E. (2009). Forensic social work and expert witness testimony in child welfare. In A. R. Roberts (Ed.), *The social worker's desk reference* (2nd ed., pp. 1060–1070). New York: Oxford University Press.

Munson, C. (2011). Forensic social work practice standards: Definition and specification. *Journal of Forensic Social Work, 1,* 37–60.

National Association of Social Workers (NASW). (2008). *Code of ethics.* Retrieved from *www.naswdc.org*

National Association of Social Workers (NASW). (2011). Social workers and record retention requirements. Retrieved from *www.naswdc.org/ldf/legal_issue*

NASW Legal Defense Fund. (2009). Responding to a subpoena. Retrieved from *www.socialworkers.org/ldf/legal_issue*

NASW Legal Defense Fund. (2010). Social workers and confidentiality for court-ordered juvenile treatment. Retrieved from *http://www.socialworkers.org/ldf/legal_issue*

National Center for Critical Incident Analysis. (n.d.). Retrieved from *www.criticalincident.org*

National Center for State Courts. (n.d.). Jury management. Retrieved from *www.ncsc.org/topics/jury/jury-management/resource-guide.aspx*

National Children's Advocacy Center. (n.d.). Retrieved from *nationalcac.org*

National Institute for Trial Advocacy. (2006). *Selecting and preparing expert witnesses* (DVD). Author: Louisville, CO.

National Organization of Forensic Social Work (n.d.). Retrieved from *www.nofsw.org*

National Registry of Evidence-Based Programs and Practices. (n.d.). Retrieved from *www.nrepp.samhsa.gov*

Neal, T. (2009). Expert witness preparation: What does the literature tell us? *The*

Jury Expert, 21(2), 44–52. Retrieved from *www.astcweb.org/public/pub lication/documents/TheJuryExpertMar2009Volume21No23.pdf*

Orbach, Y., & Lamb, M. E. (2001). The relationship between within-interview contradictions and eliciting interviewer utterances. *Child Abuse and Neglect, 25*(3), 323–333.

Pace, P. (2011). Expert witnesses: Social workers take the stand. *NASW News, 56*(1), 4.

Philip Morris USA v. Williams. (2007). 549 U.S. 346 (Supreme Court). Retrieved from *www.law.cornell.edu/supct/pdf/05-1256P.ZO*

Polowy, C. I., Morgan, S., & Gilbertson, J. (2005). *Social workers and subpoenas.* Washington, DC: NASW Legal Defense Fund.

Polowy, C. I., & Morgan, S. (2010). *The juvenile justice system.* Washington, DC: NASW Press.

Poole, D. A., & Lamb, M. E. (1998). *Investigative interviews of children: A guide for helping professionals.* Washington, DC: American Psychological Association.

Quinn, M. J. (2005). *Guardianships of adults: Achieving justice, autonomy, and safety.* New York: Springer.

Reamer, F. G. (2001). *The social work ethics audit: A risk management tool.* Washington, DC: NASW Press. Retrieved from *www.naswdc.org/ldf/law notes/subpoenas.asp*

Reamer, F. G. (2003). *Social work malpractice and liability: Strategies for prevention* (2nd ed.). New York: Columbia University Press.

Reamer, F. G. (2011, March 8). Delivering services to minors: Ethical and risk-management. National Association of Social Work Webinar. Retrieved from *www.naswdc.org/ldf/lawnotes/subpoenas.asp*

Restorative Justice Online (n.d.). Retrieved from *www.restorativejustice.org*

Roberts, A. R., Monferrari, I., & Yeager, K. R. (2009). Avoiding malpractice lawsuits by following standards of care guidelines and preventing suicide. In *Social workers' desk reference* (2nd ed., pp. 128–135). New York: Oxford University Press.

Sales, B. D., & Shuman, D. W. (2008). Reclaiming the integrity of science in expert witnessing. *Ethics and Behavior, 3*, 223–229.

Schetky, D. H., & Colbach, E. M. (1982). Countertransference on the witness stand: A flight from self? *Bulletin of the American Academy of Psychiatry Law, 10*, 115–121.

Schwerha, J. J. (2009). Occupational medicine forum. *Journal of Occupational and Environmental Medicine, 51*(11), 1350–1352.

Schön, D. (1990). *Educating the reflective practitioner* (2nd ed.). San Francisco: Jossey-Bass.

Skeem, J., Douglas, K. S., & Lilienfeld, S. O. (Eds.). (2009). *Psychological science in the courtroom.* New York: Guilford Press.

Tarasoff v. Regents of University of California. (1976). 17 Cal. 3d 425, 551 P.2d 334 (U.S. Sup. Ct.).

Taylor, S. (2006). Educating future practitioners of social work and law: Exploring the origins of interprofessional misunderstanding. *Child and Youth Services Review, 28*, 638–653.

Tindall, L. J. (2003). *Ethics reference guide for expert witnesses. A tool to assist in identifying and resolving moral dilemmas in providing expert witness testimony.* Boca Raton, FL: Dynamic Ingenuity.

United States v. Leeson. (2006). 453 F.3d 631 (U.S. Court of Appeals). Retrieved from *law.justia.com/cases/federal/appellate-courts/F3/453/631/484912*

USA Patriot Act (2001, as amended). Public Law 107–56. Retrieved from *frwebgate.access.gpo.gov/cgi-bin/getdoc.cgi?dbname=107_cong_public_laws&docid=f:publ056.107.pdf*

Vance, S. (2009). *Citizens in action: A guide to lobbying and influencing government.* Bethesda, MD: The Original US Congress Handbook.

Vogelsang, J. (2001). *The witness stand: A guide for clinical social workers in the courtroom.* Binghamton, NY: Haworth.

Wingate, P. H., & Thornton, G. C. (2004). Industrial/organizational psychology and the federal judiciary: Expert witness testimony and the "Daubert" standards. *Law and Human Behavior, 28*(1), 97–114.

Wright, J. K. (2010). *Lawyers as peacemakers: Practicing holistic, problem-solving law.* Washington, DC: American Bar Association.

Zur, O. (n.d.). Forensic dual or multiple relationships: Treating clinician v. forensic expert. Retrieved from *www.zurinstitute.com/forensic_multiple_relationships.html#general*

INDEX

n indicates a note. Page numbers in **bold** indicate definitions in the glossary.

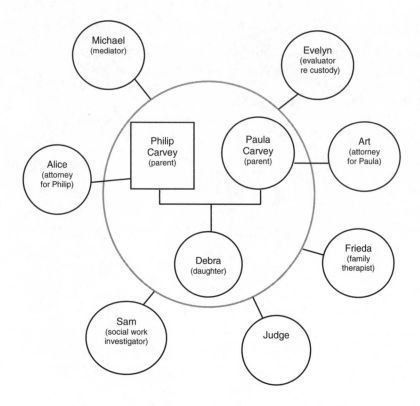

Genogram and ecomap for the Carvey family case scenario.